MY WAY

MY WAY

Essays on Moral Responsibility

John Martin Fischer

OXFORD
UNIVERSITY PRESS

2006

OXFORD
UNIVERSITY PRESS

Oxford University Press, Inc., publishes works that further
Oxford University's objective of excellence
in research, scholarship, and education.

Oxford   New York
Auckland   Cape Town   Dar es Salaam   Hong Kong   Karachi
Kuala Lumpur   Madrid   Melbourne   Mexico City   Nairobi
New Delhi   Shanghai   Taipei   Toronto

With offices in
Argentina   Austria   Brazil   Chile   Czech Republic   France   Greece
Guatemala   Hungary   Italy   Japan   Poland   Portugal   Singapore
South Korea   Switzerland   Thailand   Turkey   Ukraine   Vietnam

Published by Oxford University Press, Inc.
198 Madison Avenue, New York, New York 10016

www.oup.com

Oxford is a registered trademark of Oxford University Press

Library of Congress Cataloging-in-Publication Data

Fischer, John Martin, 1952–
My way: essays on moral responsibility / John Martin Fischer.
    p. cm.
Includes bibliographical references and index.
Contents: Introduction, A framework for moral responsibility—Responsibility and
alternative possibilities—Responsiveness and moral responsibility—Responsibility
for omissions—Responsibility and self-expression—Frankfurt-style compatibilism—
Responsibility and agent-causation—The transfer of nonresponsibility—Transfer
principles and moral responsibility—Free will and moral responsibility—
"Ought-implies-can," causal determinism, and moral responsibility—
Responsibility and manipulation.
ISBN-13 978-0-19-517955-2
ISBN 0-19-517955-2
1. Responsibility.   2. Free will and determinism.   I. Title.
BJ1451.F56 2006
170—dc22   2005048776

9 8 7 6 5 4 3 2 1

Printed in the United States of America
on acid-free paper

To my undergraduate teacher at Stanford University, who first introduced me to these issues and has been a source of inspiration throughout my career: Michael Bratman.

To my dissertation committee at Cornell University, who combined extraordinary conscientiousness (and patience) with great philosophical insight: Carl Ginet, chair; Sydney Shoemaker; and T. H. Irwin.

To three colleagues at Yale University, from whom I learned much about these issues, and whose friendship has sustained me over the years: Harry Frankfurt, Anthony Brueckner, and Phillip Bricker.

And to my colleague at the University of California, Riverside, who is both a tremendous philosopher and a great friend: Gary Watson.

ACKNOWLEDGMENTS

Permission to reprint the following articles is hereby acknowledged:

"Responsibility and Alternative Possibilities," in D. Widerker and M. McKenna (eds), *Moral Responsibility and Alternative Possibilities: Essays on the Importance of Alternative Possibilities* (Ashgate, 2003): 27–52; based on Chapter 7 of John Martin Fischer, *The Metaphysics of Free Will: An Essay on Control* (Blackwell, 1994): 131–159.

"Responsiveness and Moral Responsibility," in Ferdinand Schoeman (ed.), *Responsibility, Character, and the Emotions: New Essays on Moral Psychology* (Cambridge University Press, 1987): 81–106; reprinted in Derk Pereboom (ed.), *Free Will* (Hackett, 1997): 214–241.

"Responsibility for Omissions," Chapter 5 of John Martin Fischer and Mark Ravizza, *Responsibility and Control: A Theory of Moral Responsibility* (Cambridge University Press, 1998): 123–150.

"Responsibility and Self-Expression," *The Journal of Ethics*, Vol. 3, No. 4 (1999): 277–297.

"Frankfurt-Style Compatibilism," in S. Buss and L. Overton, eds., *Contours of Agency: Essays on Themes from Harry Frankfurt* (MIT Press 2002): 1–26; reprinted in Gary Watson, ed., *Oxford Readings on Free Will* (Second Edition), (Oxford University Press, 2003): 190–211.

"Responsibility and Agent-Causation," in D. Widerker and M. McKenna (eds), *Moral Responsibility and Alternative Possibilities: Essays on the Importance of Alternative Possibilities* (Ashgate, 2003): 235–250.

"The Transfer of Non-Responsibility," in J. Campbell, M. O'Rourke, and D. Shier, (eds.), *Freedom and Determinism: Topics in Contemporary Philosophy Series* Vol. 2 (MIT Press, 2004), pp. 189–209.

Eleonore Stump and John Martin Fischer, "Transfer Principles and Moral Responsibility," *Philosophical Perspectives*, Vol. 14 (2000): 47–56.

Chapter 10 is an expanded version of "Free Will and Moral Responsibility," in

David Copp, ed., *Oxford Handbook on Ethical Theory* (Oxford: Oxford University Press, 2006).

"'Ought-Implies-Can,' Causal Determinism, and Moral Responsibility," *Analysis*, Vol. 63, No. 3 (July 2003): 244–250.

"Responsibility and Manipulation," *The Journal of Ethics* Vol. 8, No. 2 (2004): 145–77.

Permission to reprint the following poetry and song lyrics is hereby acknowledged:

Excerpt from "Burnt Norton" in *Four Quartets* by T. S. Eliot, copyright © 1936 by Harcourt, Inc., and renewed in 1964 by T. S. Eliot, reprinted by permission of the publisher.

"My Way," English words by Paul Anka, original French words by Gilles Thibault. Music by Jacques Revaux and Claude François. Copyright © 1967 Chrysalis Standards, Inc. Copyright renewed, all rights reserved. Reprinted by permission.

"When Do I Get to sing 'My Way,'" lyrics by Ron Mael and Russell Mael. Copyright © 1995 Avenue Louise Music (ASCAP). All rights for the world administered on behalf of Avenue Louise Music (ASCAP) by Musik-Edition Discoton GMBH (GEMA). All rights for the U.S. on behalf of Musik-Edition Discoton GMBH (GEMA) administered by BMG Songs, Inc. (ASCAP). Reprinted by permission.

CONTENTS

MY WAY

I

INTRODUCTION
A Framework for Moral Responsibility

Responsibility and Control

The words of Michael Ross, who is described in an article that appeared in *Connecticut Magazine* as "a mild-mannered Cornell graduate who has been sentenced to death for raping and murdering four Connecticut teenagers," are haunting (and not just because I, too, am—arguably—a mild-mannered Cornell graduate):

> Each murder was a fluke—at least that's what I told myself. I knew that I was a "good" person, that I tried to help people, and certainly I didn't want to hurt anybody. . . . Even now, I know that I have done it and know that I could do it again, but I can't imagine myself actually doing it, or even wanting to do it. . . .
>
> For a long time I looked for excuses. . . . But the end result was the same, each murder was a fluke. I made myself believe that there was an excuse and that it would never happen again. And the contradiction that it did happen again, and again, was ignored because it didn't fit in with my perception of myself.
>
> I couldn't acknowledge the monster that was inside. . . . Sometimes I feel that I am slipping away and I'm afraid of losing control. If you are in control you can handle anything but if you lose control you are nothing.[1]

Michael Ross was sentenced to die for his crimes. Coincidentally, as I write this part of the introductory essay (December 2004), Michael Ross is scheduled to be executed on January 26, 2005, in Connecticut. During his years on death row in Connecticut, Ross wrote extensively about his crimes, and he was also the subject of much discussion and analysis. In an essay titled, "It's Time for Me to Die: An Insider's Look at Death Row," published in 1998, Ross writes:

> My name is Michael Ross, and I am a serial killer responsible for the rape and murder of eight women in Connecticut, New York, and Rhode Island. I have never denied

I am extremely grateful to Matt Talbert, Neal A. Tognazzini, Gustavo Llarull, and Manuel Vargas for their very helpful comments on a previous version of this chapter.

what I did, have fully confessed to my crimes, and was sentenced to death in 1987. Now, however, I am awaiting a new sentencing hearing—ordered by the Connecticut State Supreme Court—that will result either in my being re-sentenced to death or in multiple life sentences without the possibility of release. The crucial issue in my case is, as it has been from the beginning, my mental condition at the time of the crimes—the infamous and much maligned "insanity defense." For years I have been trying to prove that I am suffering from a mental illness that drove me to rape and kill, and that this mental illness made me physically unable to control my actions. I have met with little success.

As you might imagine, I have been examined by a multitude of psychiatric experts over the past fourteen years. All of them—even Dr. Miller, the state's own expert psychiatric witness—agree I suffer from a paraphiliac mental disorder called "sexual sadism." This is a mental illness that, according to the testimony of the experts, resulted in my compulsion "to perpetrate violent sexual activity in a repetitive way." The experts also agree that my criminal conduct was a direct result of the uncontrollable aggressive sexual impulses caused by the disorder.

The state's only hope of obtaining a conviction and death sentence was to muddy the waters and inflame the jury members' passions so they would ignore any evidence of psychological impairment. In my case, as you might expect, that was quite easy to do, and the state succeeded in obtaining multiple death sentences.

So why was a new sentencing hearing ordered? An *amicus curiae* ("friend of the court") brief was filed by a group of eminent psychiatrists from Connecticut. They were connected to neither the state nor the defense, but they got involved because—as their brief states—of their concern "that the psychiatric issues were distorted at both the guilt and penalty phase of the trial." They summed up our main point of contention perfectly : "By allowing Dr. Miller to testify in a way that led the jury to believe that Mr. Ross could control his behavior—when in fact he and all the other psychiatric experts were of the view that Mr. Ross could not—the court allowed the jury to be effectively misled." The Connecticut State Supreme Court agreed.

What exactly is a paraphiliac mental disorder? It is very difficult to explain, and even more difficult to understand. I'm not even sure that I myself fully understand this disease, and I've been trying to understand what's been going on in my head for a very long time now. Basically, I am plagued by repetitive thoughts, urges, and fantasies of the degradation, rape, and murder of women. I cannot get those thoughts out of my mind.[2]

Ross seeks further to explain the nature of his disorder as follows:

The best way for the average person to try to understand this is to remember a time when a song played over and over again in your head. Even if you liked the melody, its constant repetition was quite annoying, and the harder you tried to drive it out of your head, the harder it seemed to stick. Now replace that sweet melody with noxious thoughts of degradation, rape, and murder and you will begin—and only just begin—to understand what was running rampant through my mind uncontrollably.

Some people believe that if you think about something day in and day out, you must want to think about it. But that just isn't true when you are discussing mental illness. Most people can't understand because they just can't imagine wanting to commit such horrific acts of unimaginable cruelty. They can't begin to understand this obsession of mine. They think that if you fantasize about something you must want to make the fantasy come true. But it's far more complicated than that. They can't understand how I could fantasize such disgusting imagery, how I could derive such pleasure from that fantasy, and yet be so disgusted later by the exact same thoughts or urges, or at the thought of how much I enjoyed the fantasy just moments before. I could relive the rapes and murders that I committed, and when reliving those despicable acts in my mind I could experience such orgasmic pleasure that it is hard to describe. But afterward I felt such a sense of loathing and self-hatred that I often longed for my execution. I was tired of being tormented by my own sick, demented mind. So unbelievably tired.[3]

In prison Ross was given a medication, Depo-Provera, which caused the obsessive thoughts to diminish. He says:

Having those thoughts and urges is like living with an obnoxious roommate. You cannot get away from him because he is always there. What Depo-Provera did was to move that roommate down the hall to his own apartment. The problem was still there, but it was a whole lot easier to deal with because it wasn't always in the foreground. He didn't control me anymore—I was in control of him. It was an unbelievable sense of freedom. It made me feel as if I were a human being again, instead of some sort of horrible monster. For three years I had a sort of peace of mind.

Then I developed liver problems, a very rare side effect of the hormonal shots, so I was forced to discontinue the medication. Soon thereafter the noxious thoughts, fantasies, and urges returned. It was horrible. I felt like a blind man who had been given the gift of sight only to have it snatched away again. There was an alternative medication, but it lacked FDA approval as a treatment for sex offenders, so the Department of Corrections refused to approve its use. From my past history we knew what the problem was: testosterone. Get it out of my bloodstream so that it can't reach my mind and I am okay. So I asked to be surgically castrated, with the support and approval of my treating psychiatrist. But the department—which I am sure was afraid of headlines such as "Sex Offender Castrated by State"—refused my request. It took more than a year of fighting by a lot of good people here in the Mental Health Department before I was allowed to receive the alternative medication, a monthly shot of a drug called Depo-Lupron, which I have been receiving to date.[4]

Ross exhibits deep ambivalence about his own responsibility in the following passage:

There are times, usually late at night when things finally begin to quiet down around here, that I sit in my cell and wonder, "What the hell am I doing here?" Most people would probably think that this is a pretty silly question; obviously I'm here because I've killed many people and I deserve to be here. And that is okay on one level. But I think of the underlying reasons why I did those terrible things. I believe I am severely mentally ill and that the illness drove me to commit my crimes. I know that I may never be able to prove that in a court of law, but in here, in my cell, I don't have to prove anything to anybody. I know what the truth is. I know that I have an illness and that I'm no more responsible for having that illness than another person is for getting cancer or developing diabetes. But somehow "You're sick, and sometimes people just get sick" doesn't seem to cut it. I feel responsible. I wonder if things in my childhood may have made a difference. My mother was institutionalized twice by our family doctor because of how she was treating, or rather abusing, us kids. Maybe things would have been different if I had run away as my younger brother did. But this is an exercise in futility, because you can't change the past—yet at the same time you can't help but wonder what might have been.[5]

Ross writes that initially he was consumed by a strong desire to prove that he is mentally ill and thus not in control of his behavior at the times of the crimes. He claims that subsequently, however, his desire not to cause more pain to the families of the victims caused him to volunteer for the death penalty. He says:

> One of my doctors once told me that I am, in a sense, also a victim—a victim of an affliction that no one would want. And sometimes I do feel like a victim, but at the same time I feel guilty and get angry for thinking that way. How dare I consider myself a victim when the real victims are dead? How dare I consider myself a victim when the families of my true victims have to live day by day with the pain of the loss I caused?
>
> So what if it is an affliction? So what if I was really sick? Does that really make any difference? Does that absolve me of my responsibility for the deaths of eight totally innocent women? Does it make the women any less dead? Does it ease the pain of their families? No![6]

On death row Michael Ross experienced a religious conversion, and he recorded his thoughts in a journal. He attributed his acceptance of the death penalty, and his peace of mind, to his religious beliefs.[7] (For further developments in the story of Michael Ross, see footnote 70 below.)

It is of course extremely difficult to assess the moral (and legal) responsibility of individuals such as Michael Ross. Psychological abnormality and mental illness are complex and highly contentious subjects, and even Ross himself was obviously ambivalent about his own status as an agent. I do not think that it is in general a good idea to begin one's philosophical analysis by trying to offer an account of a puzzling, difficult case (or set of cases); as they say in jurisprudence, "hard cases make bad law."[8] But it is not necessarily a bad idea *pedagogically* to start with a puzzling, difficult case. Ross's words are gripping. Although they raise highly controversial questions about the conditions for control and moral responsibility, they bring out, in a stark and compelling fashion, the connection between moral responsibility and the crucial notion of *control*. Our distinctive agency, our personhood, our moral responsibility require "free will" or "control." This basic assumption of the association of responsibility and control has not changed in the millennia of thought about these subjects, and it is encoded in our present commonsense and more reflective analysis of our agency, as well as in the criminal law.

In my work I have not sought (as yet) to give a nuanced or refined account of the various forms of pychopathy (unless incompatibilism counts!).[9] Rather, I have chiefly considered certain more abstract, skeptical worries about our commonsense view that, in the ordinary case, we adult human beings are genuine and distinctive agents—we are free and morally responsible for our behavior (and even for central features of our "selves"). For there are very powerful skeptical worries about our status as free agents. I have sought to defend the ordinary view that we (most of us) are (much of the time) free and morally responsible against certain fascinating and potent arguments stemming from religion and science. Additionally, I have attempted to develop some rudiments of a more detailed account of the sort of freedom or control that grounds moral responsibility. Finally, I have sketched an account of the *value* we place on our power to exhibit this characteristic kind of control. Taken together, these can be considered the main elements of a "framework" for moral responsibility.[10]

The Threat from Science

Determinism and Resiliency

I shall here focus primarily on the threat from science, formulated explicitly during the Enlightenment. Consider the doctrine of "causal determinism." It is difficult to give a straightforward account of this doctrine, but for my purposes I take it that the essence of the doctrine is that the total set of facts about the past, together with the natural laws, entail all the facts about what happens in the present and future. (Slightly) more carefully, the doctrine of causal determinism entails (whatever else it entails) that, for any given time, a complete statement of the (temporally genuine or nonrelational) facts about that time, together with a complete statement of the laws of nature, entails every truth as to what happens after that time.[11]

We do not know whether causal determinism is true. Although many physicists would express doubts that it is, others believe that in the end the apparent indeterminacies posited by (say) quantum mechanics will be revealed to have been mere epistemic indeterminacies (gaps in our knowledge). It seems that the truth of causal determinism would call our agency and control into question. Given that we don't know with certainty that causal determinism is false, it would seem to follow that we cannot (legitimately) be confident in our status as free, morally responsible agents. (Similar considerations apply to the existence of a sempiternal, essentially omniscient God.)[12]

I may as well be up front about this: I am motivated in much of my work by the idea that our basic status as distinctively free and morally responsible agents should not depend on the arcane ruminations—and deliverances—of the theoretical physicists and cosmologists. That is, I do not think our status as morally responsible persons should depend on whether or not causal determinism is true (or, for that matter, whether or not a sempiternal, essentially omniscient God exists). Think of it this way. Our fundamental nature as free, morally responsible agents should not depend on whether the pertinent regularities identified by the physicists have associated with them (objective) probabilities of 100 percent (causal determinism) or, say, 98 percent (causal indeterminism). Given that we think of ourselves as morally responsible agents in control of our behavior (in the relevant way), how could the discovery that the laws of nature have 100 percent probabilities associated with them, rather than 98 percent (or 99 percent, or 99.9 percent, and so forth), make us abandon our view of ourselves as persons, as morally responsible agents in control of our behavior? This just seems highly implausible and unattractive to me.[13]

Note that someone could respond by saying that such a discovery (that causal determinism obtains) would in fact necessitate a shift to the view that we are not persons *in just the way we thought we are*, and that we are not *fully* or "robustly" morally responsible. Nevertheless, we could still be "persons" in a somewhat attenuated sense, and we could still be "morally responsible" in a weaker sense. Thus, it might be argued, it is not a good motivation for seeking to defend compatibilism about moral responsibility and causal determinism that, absent compatibilism, our personhood and moral responsibility would "hang on a thread" and be "held hostage to the abstruse ruminations of theoretical physicists."[14]

To reply: I think that our personhood, as we currently conceive it (in its essential form), and our moral responsibility, conceived robustly to include a strong notion of "moral desert" of blame and harsh treatment, should not depend on whether or not causal determinism is true (i.e., upon whether those lawlike regularities are associated with 98 percent probabilities or 100 percent probabilities). How can something so basic, so important, depend on something so fine and so abstruse? Granted, we can discover certain kinds of previously esoteric facts that legitimately call into question our agency and control.[15] But how could *this* sort of difference (the difference between 100 percent and even 99.999 percent) make such a difference (a difference between being robustly responsible and merely responsible in some attenuated sense or not responsible at all)?

The Consequence Argument

Given the motivation of seeking *resiliency* of our fundamental conception of ourselves as possessing control and being morally responsible agents, I have addressed the challenges posed by causal determinism. It is important to distinguish *separate* challenges to our agency, control, and moral responsibility posed by the doctrine of causal determinism. I begin by considering the challenge to our possession of the sort of control that involves genuine metaphysical access to alternative possibilities. In this sense of control, we have control "over" our behavior, and we control which outcome occurs, where there are various outcomes that are available to us. In this sense of control, we *select* from a menu of genuinely available options.

We typically think of ourselves as having this sort of control. But if causal determinism is true, then all of our choices and actions are the "consequences" of the past together with the laws of nature. The argument purporting to show the incompatibility of causal determinism with the sort of control in question, which I shall call "regulative control," is thus dubbed the "Consequence Argument" by Peter van Inwagen.[16] The argument can be formulated in different ways, with varying degrees of precision.[17] For my purposes here, we can present the argument informally.

Suppose that causal determinism obtains and I do X at time t. It follows from the definition of causal determinism that the facts about the past, together with the laws of nature, entail that I do X at t. For me to refrain from doing X at t, either the past (with respect to t) or natural laws (or both) would have to be different. But the past and the natural laws are not up to me or in my control: I am not free so to act that the past or natural laws (or both) are different. Therefore, if causal deter-minism is true, then (despite my sense of my own freedom) I am not able to re-frain from what I actually do—I do not have the sort of control that involves genuine access to alternative possibilities (regulative control).

Some philosophers have found problems with particular ways of formulating the argument, and they have concluded that the argument is unsound. This is hasty, as there are *other* ways of formulating the argument, and these ways seem to render the argument sound. I am inclined to accept the Consequence Argument, although I do not think that it is indisputably sound (in any of its formulations). Given that I am a compatibilist about causal determinism and moral responsibility, I thus need to defend the claim that moral responsibility does *not* require the sort of control that is pertinent to the Consequence Argument—regulative control. In the next section I shall explain my defense of "actual-sequence" compatibilism.

The Consequence Argument crystallizes an important threat to our moral re-sponsibility posed by causal determinism. My brand of compatibilism about causal determinism and moral responsibility is distinctive insofar as I take this threat se-riously, and, indeed, am inclined to accept the conclusion of the Consequence Argument. It is striking that many compatibilists either ignore or dismiss the Con-sequence Argument. Others seek to address it, but (in my view) do so feebly. I have always thought that we need to take seriously and honestly come to terms with an argument that is so firmly rooted in common sense, and also has been around (in one form or other) for centuries (and even millennia, in the case of the structurally similar arguments from God's foreknowledge and fixed truth values).

Sourcehood

But the threat to our possession of regulative control is not the *only* threat to our moral responsibility posed by causal determinism. I recognized this fact many years ago (1981) in one of my first publications on these issues, in which I suggested that there might be some *other* reason why causal determinism threatens our moral responsibility (apart from considerations relevant to regulative control):

> I have not argued *for* incompatibilism about determination and responsibility; I have had the more modest project of showing how the incompatibilist is not forced into inconsistency by Frankfurt-type examples. [I shall discuss such examples below.] Both the compatibilist and incompatibilist alike can unite in conceding that enough information is encoded in the actual sequence to ground our responsibility attribu-tions; as philosophers we need to decode this information and see whether it is con-sistent with deterministic causation.[18]

In subsequent years the view that causal determinism threatens moral responsibil-ity, but not (solely) in virtue of threatening regulative control, has been called "Causal History Incompatibilism" or "Source Incompatibilism." According to this position (in its various versions), causal determination in the actual sequence rules out moral responsibility, quite apart from expunging alternative possibilities. There are various ways of motivating this sort of incompatibilism, and I shall dis-cuss them below.

Although I accept the traditional association of responsibility with control, I am inclined to accept the conclusion of the Consequence Argument—that causal determinism is incompatible with regulative control—and *also* the contention that causal determinism is compatible with moral responsibility. I distinguish two kinds of control: regulative and guidance control. On my view, moral responsibility requires guidance, but not regulative, control. This opens the door to my doctrine of semicompatibilism: that causal determinism would be compatible with moral responsibility, even if it were the case that causal determinism rules out regulative control. Semicompatibilism, thus construed, does not in itself include the view that causal determinism rules out regulative control. As I said above, I do not think that this latter claim is indisputably true, although I am inclined to accept it. Thus, the total package of Fischer views includes semicompatibilism plus the additional view—incompatibilism about causal determinism and regulative control.

Regulative Control and the Frankfurt-Type Examples
The Frankfurt Examples

Moral responsibility is associated with control, and yet the Consequence Argument apparently shows that if causal determinism were true, we would not have regulative control. My contention, however, is that moral responsibility does not require regulative control. To see this, suppose you are at the controls of an airplane, a glider, and you are guiding the plane to the west. Everything is going just as you want, and the plane is making good headway. You consider whether to steer the plane to the east, but you decide to keep guiding it to the west, in part because the scenery is nicer in the west. Unknown to you, the wind currents in the area are such that the plane would continue to go to the west, in just the way it actually goes, even if you had tried to steer it in some other direction. (Alternatively, we could suppose that although the plane's steering apparatus works just fine as you are guiding it to the west, it is defective, and the defect would have "kicked in" and caused the plane to go in precisely the way it actually went if you had tried to steer it in any other direction.) In this example, you steer the plane to the west in the "normal" way. It is not just that you cause it to go to the west (which you would equally have done had you steered the plane in the same way as a result of a sneeze or an epileptic seizure). Rather, you guide the plane in a distinctive way—you exhibit a signature sort of control, which I shall call "guidance control." Here you exhibit guidance control of the plane's movements, but you do not possess regulative control *over* the plane's movements.[19]

This sort of case is similar to John Locke's example of a man who is put in a room while asleep. The man wakes up and thinks about whether to leave the room. He decides for his own reasons to stay in the room, but, unknown to him, the door is locked and he could not have left the room. Locke says he stays in the room voluntarily, although he was not free to leave the room. Similarly, I would say that in the example above you freely guide the plane to the west, although you were not free to guide it in any other direction; you exhibit guidance control of the plane's movements, although you lack regulative control—control *over* the plane's movements.

Do such examples show that one can be morally responsible for some behavior, even though one lacks freedom to choose or do otherwise, that is, lacks regulative control? The problem is that, apart from any special assumptions, such as causal determinism, it is plausible to suppose that you could have chosen to steer the plane in a different direction, tried to do so, pushed the steering apparatus in a different way, and so forth. Similarly, Locke's man could have chosen to leave the room, tried to leave the room, turned the doorknob, pushed on the door, and so forth.

This is where Harry Frankfurt made an innovation in his seminal paper "Alternate Possibilities and Moral Responsibility."[20] It might be said that Frankfurt brought Locke's locked door into the brain (or, alternatively, Frankfurt brought the broken steering apparatus or wind conditions into the brain). Let us suppose, then, as in Frankfurt's examples, that in the example of the plane, a neurosurgeon has secretly implanted a chip in your brain, by which she can monitor your brain activities. If everything goes as she wants, she does not intervene, and let us imagine that she wants you to go to the west, just as you actually guide the plane. But, for her own reasons (which may be nefarious or nice), if you were about to choose to steer the plane in any other direction, she would use a remote-control device to cause the chip to stimulate your brain in such a way as to induce a choice to guide the plan to the west in the exact same way you actually choose to guide the plane (and to ensure that you do in fact act in accordance with that choice, just as you actually do). As things actually play out, you choose to steer the plane to the west, but in virtue of the presence of the chip and the neurosurgeon monitoring your brain, you could not have even chosen to do otherwise (or have done otherwise).

But how can the neurosurgeon tell what you are about to choose to do (and do)? This is a vexed question. But suppose you reliably show some involuntary indication—say, a blush—prior to choosing to go west, and a different indication (say, a furrowed brow) prior to choosing to go in any other direction. Seeing the involuntary blush, the neurosurgeon does not trigger the electronic stimulation of your brain, and you choose and act in the "normal way," just as you would have had there been no neurosurgeon monitoring your brain. But if you were to furrow your brow (involuntarily), the neurosurgeon would trigger an electronic intervention in the brain that would ensure a choice to go west. As things actually play out, it seems that you freely guide the plane west, although you could not have even chosen or tried to cause the plane to go in any other direction. Arguably, you exhibit guidance control (and could legitimately be held morally responsible for your choice and behavior, as well as its reasonably foreseeable consequences), even though you lack regulative control.

What about that residual possibility that you exhibit a different sign—the furrowed brow instead of the blush? Isn't that an alternative possibility? I reply that this sort of possibility is a mere flicker of freedom, and not sufficiently robust to ground attributions of moral responsibility, on the picture according to which regulative control is required for moral responsibility.[21] I myself do not accept this alternative-possibilities picture, but my point is that *if* you do, then you should recognize that mere involuntary blushes (and relevantly similar behaviors) are not sufficiently robust to play the requisite role in your theory: adding them to a scenario in which there is no moral responsibility does not plausibly get you to moral responsibility, and it is *not* in virtue of their existence that an agent actually exhibits the sort of control relevant to moral responsibility.

Consider the classic problem for indeterministic theories of moral responsibility. On these views, it is possible, say just before the choice, for the agent to choose otherwise. But the *mere possibility* of a different choice is notoriously insufficient to ground moral responsibility for the actual choice, given that it is genuinely indeterminate, just prior to the time in question, which choice the agent makes. Put differently, if it is a *random* matter which choice is made, given all the relevant antecedent events, then the mere existence of the possibility of an alternative choice does not add enough to generate moral responsibility for the actual choice. Similarly, the mere possibility of something different occurring does not show that an agent exhibits *control* of his actual behavior or its consequences, given that it was genuinely random whether the actual course of events would unfold as it did. Now I do not here contend that an indeterministic approach to moral responsibility cannot answer these worries. I simply point out that they need to be answered, and that the *mere existence* of flickers of freedom—alternative possibilities without voluntariness or, to use my favorite technical term, "oomph"—is not enough to warrant ascriptions of moral responsibility.[22]

Van Inwagen's Critique

Frankfurt-type examples or "Frankfurt-Style Counterexamples to the Principle of Alternative Possibilities" (the principle that moral responsibility requires alternative possibilities or regulative control) have generated a huge literature, and their analysis can be somewhat complex. Peter van Inwagen has helpfully reminded us to be careful about precisely *what the agent is being held morally responsible for*.[23] Van Inwagen points out that we might hold someone morally responsible for an action, an omission, or a consequence. Further, he claims that we sometimes think of consequences as "particulars," and sometimes as "universals." (For van Inwagen, an event-particular is individuated finely in terms of its causal antecedents, whereas an event-universal is individuated more coarsely, such that various different causal sequences can issue in the *same* event-universal. "Universal" here is used somewhat nonstandardly simply to denote a state of affairs individuated relatively coarsely.)

In an elegant argument, van Inwagen has argued that the surface plausibility of the conclusion drawn above from Frankfurt-type examples (that moral responsibility does not require regulative control) stems from confusion resulting from not being sufficiently careful in specifying what exactly the agent is responsible for and what is unavoidable. His argument is that there is no one item of which it is both true that the agent cannot avoid (or prevent) it and that the agent is morally responsible for it.

More carefully, van Inwagen argues that whenever we are morally responsible for anything, we are morally responsible for either a consequence-particular, a consequence-universal, or an omission. Further, according to van Inwagen, in the typical Frankfurt-type case we are morally responsible for a consequence-particular, but we can prevent this (since in the alternative sequence a *different* event-particular would have been brought about, insofar as it would have had a *different* causal history). In such a case, we are unable to prevent the relevant consequence-universal from obtaining—but then we are *not* morally responsible for it. Finally, van Inwagen contends that it is impossible to produce a Frankfurt-type case for omissions in which it is plausible to say that the agent is morally responsible for failing to do X, where he cannot do X; he may be morally responsible for failing to try to do X, for failing to choose to do X, and so forth, but he is not morally responsible for failing to do X (insofar as he cannot do X).

Van Inwagen says:

> In attempting to construct Frankfurt-style counter-examples [to the principle that moral responsibility for a consequence-universal requires the ability to prevent that universal from obtaining], we have been imagining cases in which an agent "gets to" a certain state of affairs by following a particular "causal road," a road intentionally chosen by him in order to "get to" that state of affairs; but, because this state of affairs is a *universal*, it can be reached by various causal roads, some of them differing radically from the road that is in fact taken; and, in the cases we have imagined, *every* causal road that *any* choice of the agent's might set him upon leads to this same state of affairs. This is why the agent in our attempts at Frankfurt-style counter-examples always turns out not to be responsible for the state of affairs he is unable to prevent.[24]

Van Inwagen makes his point concrete by employing an example that involves roads literally:

> Suppose Ryder's horse, Dobbin, has run away with him. Ryder can't get Dobbin to slow down, but Dobbin will respond to the bridle: whenever Ryder and Dobbin come to a fork in the road or a crossroad, it is up to Ryder which way they go. Ryder and Dobbin are approaching a certain crossroad, and Ryder recognizes one of the roads leading away from it as a road to Rome. Ryder has conceived a dislike for Romans and so, having nothing better to do, he steers Dobbin into the road he knows leads to Rome, motivated by the hope that the passage of a runaway horse through the streets of Rome will result in the injury of some of her detested citizens. Unknown to Ryder, however, all roads lead to Rome: Dobbin's career would have led him and Ryder to Rome by *some* route no matter what Ryder had done. Therefore, Ryder could not have prevented [the obtaining of the consequence-universal, *that Ryder passes through Rome on a runaway horse*]. Is Ryder responsible for this state of affairs? It is obvious that he is not. And it seems obvious that he is not responsible for this state of affairs just because it would have been the outcome of *any* course of action he might have elected.[25]

Similarly, van Inwagen asks us to imagine that an individual witnesses a crime outside her apartment, and she considers calling the police.[26] Having thought about it, she does not want to get involved, and she decides not to call the police. Unknown to her, her telephone line has been cut, and she could not have successfully reached the police. Van Inwagen contends that she may well be morally responsible for her decision and for not trying to call the police (not dialing 911), and so forth. But according to van Inwagen, she is *not* morally responsible for not informing the police by telephone (during the relevant time). On van Inwagen's view, this is an instance of the general principle that in order for an agent to be morally responsible for not doing X, she must have been able to do X.

Reply to van Inwagen

Above I argued that it is plausible that there are Frankfurt-type cases pertaining to actions, that is, there are cases (with the signature structure of preemptive overdetermination) in which an agent chooses and acts freely, and thus is morally responsible for his action, even though he could not have chosen or done otherwise. Although there may exist flickers of freedom in these cases, the mere existence of these possibilities cannot plausibly ground responsibility; thus, in the relevant sense, the agent could not have chosen or done otherwise. (He could not have freely chosen to do another kind of act, and he could not have freely performed another kind of action.) Contrary to van Inwagen, I believe there are Frankfurt-type *omissions* cases in which it is plausible that the agent is morally responsible for not doing X, even though he cannot (in the relevant sense) do X.[27]

Frank is considering whether to raise his hand (to signal to a friend that he is ready to leave the party). He briefly considers various reasons and decides not to, and, as a result of this decision, does not raise his hand. Unknown to Frank, he was suffering from a temporary paralysis due to a bizarre side effect of a medication he had begun earlier in the day (not an illegal drug tried at the party!). So, unknown to Frank, he could not have raised his hand. I am inclined to say that Frank freely refrained from raising his hand and that he is morally responsible for not raising his hand, even though he could not have raised it. I do not see any relevant difference between this sort of case and the sort of action case discussed above. There is no reason to suppose that actions and omissions are asymmetric with respect to the requirement of alternative possibilities (for moral responsibility).[28]

I contend that van Inwagen goes wrong by focusing on a proper subset of the relevant omissions cases. I agree with him about his case of failing to successfully reach the police. But I do not believe that one can extrapolate from such a case to the claim that an agent is legitimately held morally responsible for not doing X (for *any* X) only if he could have done X. Van Inwagen's case is one of not doing X, where doing X would be or involve something more than a simple movement of the body. But in a case (such as that of Frank's not raising his hand) in which doing X would be a simple movement of the body, I believe that the agent can legitimately be held morally responsible for not doing X, even though he could not have done X.[29]

Similarly, I argue that van Inwagen goes wrong in his view about consequence-universals by focusing on a proper subset of the relevant examples. I agree with van Inwagen that Ryder is not morally responsible for the fact that a runaway horse ends up in Rome. But now consider an assassin who freely pulls the trigger and shoots the president of the United States. Suppose that he is part of an elaborate plan, and arrangements have been made to ensure that if he does not shoot the president, someone else will. Since the assassin freely shoots the president as planned, the backup arrangement remains just a backup scheme. Clearly, the assassin who actually pulls the trigger and shoots the president is morally responsible for his action; but I also think he is morally responsible for the fact that the president is shot, even though the president would have been shot had he not pulled the trigger. Supposing that the actual assassin could not prevent the backup scheme from being triggered by his own failure to pull the trigger, I would still say that he is in the actual course of events morally responsible for the fact that the president is shot, even though he could not have prevented the obtaining of the consequence-universal *that the president is shot.* Thus, there are various different contexts in which an agent could not prevent a consequence-universal from obtaining, and van Inwagen does not attend to the *full array* of such cases.[30]

Another source of the view that it is not legitimate to hold an agent morally responsible for bringing about a consequence-universal he could not have prevented from obtaining is the conflation of certain "modalized" and "descriptive" consequence-universals. So I agree that the assassin may not be morally responsible for the fact that, if he weren't to pull the trigger, someone else would shoot the president, or the fact that the president *has* to be shot, one way or the other, and so forth. But I nevertheless believe that the assassin who actually shoots the president is morally responsible for the descriptive consequence-universal *that the president is shot.* He may not be morally responsible for the fact that, given the circumstances, it is *inevitable* that the president is shot (one way or another); but he *is* morally responsible for the fact that the president is shot (which would have obtained, no matter which particular causal process produced it).

So van Inwagen's elegant and powerful response to Frankfurt can be defeated.[31] An agent can be morally responsible for failing to do X, even though he cannot do X; van Inwagen's view to the contrary is attractive only if one focuses on a proper subset of the relevant cases. Similarly, an agent can legitimately be held morally responsible for a consequence-universal he could not have prevented from obtaining; again, van Inwagen's view to the contrary is attractive only if one focuses on a proper subset of the relevant cases. And, finally, an agent can be morally responsible for bringing about a consequence-particular, even though he lacks the power to bring about *the relevant sort of alternative possibility.* Granted, when an agent is morally responsible for a consequence-particular in a Frankfurt-type case, a *different* consequence-particular would have occurred in the alternative sequence (because it would have been produced by a different causal process). But the mere existence of this sort of flicker of freedom is not sufficient to ground moral responsibility ascriptions. At the very least, if one accepts a regulative-control model of moral responsibility, the alternative sequence must contain voluntary or free action—agency with oomph. But the alternative sequences in the Frankfurt-type cases do not contain alternatives with oomph.

Van Inwagen appears to think that the only way one could show the falsity of the contention that moral responsibility for an consequence-particular requires the ability to bring about a different event particular is by displaying a scenario in which the agent is morally responsible for the consequence-particular and in the alternative sequence the very same consequence-particular occurs. Granted, on the fine-grained method of individuating consequence-particular, this is impossible.

But there is another way of refuting the contention: by displaying a scenario in which the agent is morally responsible for the consequence-particular even though he lacks access to an alternative sequence in which he freely brings about a different event-particular. This is precisely the case in the Frankfurt-type scenarios.[32]

To summarize: van Inwagen argues that whenever an agent is morally responsible for *anything*, he is morally responsible for either a consequence-particular, a consequence-universal, or an omission. But (according to van Inwagen) in all of these instances, moral responsibility requires regulative control. In reply, I have argued that, although in all of the above instances (as well as the case of action) moral responsibility is indeed associated with control, it is associated not with regulative control but, rather, with guidance control.

I have concluded from the above sort of argumentation (and supplementary considerations) that we should move away from the regulative control model of moral responsibility.[33] That is, I have concluded that moral responsibility does not require regulative control (or alternative possibilities). Thus, I have concluded that, if causal determinism rules out moral responsibility, it is *not* in virtue of ruling out alternative possibilities and regulative control.[34] Of course, as I said above, there are *other* reasons why it might be thought that causal determinism threatens moral responsibility, and I have sought to explore such worries.

Direct Arguments for Incompatibilism

The indirect argument for the incompatibility of causal determinism and moral responsibility goes via the intermediate claims that causal determinism rules out regulative control and that regulative control is required for moral responsibility. There are various "direct" arguments—arguments that do not go via the claim that moral responsibility requires regulative control.[35]

The Transfer of Nonresponsibility

One such direct argument employs the Principle of Transfer of Nonresponsibility.[36] This is the principle (roughly) that if no one is morally responsible for p, and no one is morally responsible for "if p, then q," then no one is morally responsible for q. If we assume that no one is morally responsible for the remote past, and no one is morally responsible for the laws of nature or anything entailed by the laws of nature (or, more specifically, any instance of the laws of nature), then it appears as if causal determinism implies that no human being is morally responsible for anything.

The appearance is misleading, however, and we can see that the Principle of Transfer of Nonresponsibility is problematic by considering an example that involves simultaneous overdetermination (rather than preemptive overdetermination, as in the Frankfurt-type cases). Suppose the assassin's behavior is exactly as it is in the above example—he shoots the president for his own reasons, freely and intentionally, and brings it about that the president dies. (The president is standing on the shore, perhaps declaiming the virtues of his newly announced Clean Water Act.) Unknown to the assassin and president, an earthquake has occurred at sea, and no one is morally responsible for the earthquake. Additionally, if an earthquake of that magnitude occurs at sea (in the relevant location), then a tsunami will hit the shore and kill anyone standing there, and no one is morally responsible for this fact. Given these suppositions, the Principle of Transfer of Nonresponsibility would entail that no one is morally responsible for the fact that the president is killed. And yet it is manifestly true that the assassin is morally responsible for the fact that the president is killed.

Note that the assassin is not morally responsible for the fact that, given the circumstances, the president *has* to be killed, one way or another, or the fact that it is inevitable that the president will be killed (under the circumstances), or that even if the assassin does not pull his trigger, the president will be killed by the tsunami, and so forth. One might be tempted to think that the assassin is not morally responsible for the descriptive consequence-universal, *that the president is killed*, by conflating this with some sort of *modalized* consequence-universal, such as *that the president must be killed (one way or another)*.

Additionally, one might think that the assassin is not morally responsible for the fact that the president is killed because the assassin is not morally responsible for the earthquake, and he is not morally responsible for the earthquake's leading to the president's being killed. If this inference were sound, then the assassin would not be morally responsible for killing the president in a case where an independent second assassin simultaneously shoots and kills the president (and where the assassin has no moral responsibility for the second assassin, or control of whether the second assassin's bullet will kill the president). If the assassin is not morally responsible for the fact that the president is killed in a case such as this (of simultaneous and independent causal overdetermination), then, since the argument is entirely symmetric, neither is the second assassin. But now we have the absurd result that, in the case of simultaneous independent causal overdetermination, no one is morally responsible for the fact that the president is killed! Since it leads to absurdity, I reject the inference being considered: the inference from the facts that the assassin is not morally responsible for the earthquake, and he is not responsible for the earthquake's leading to the president's being killed, to the conclusion that he is not morally responsible for the (descriptive) fact that the president is killed.

We have, then, a case in which the assassin is not morally responsible for the earthquake, he is not morally responsible for the earthquake's producing a tsunami that kills the president, and yet he is morally responsible for the (descriptive) consequence-universal *that the president is killed*. After all, the assassin intentionally and freely pulls the trigger, intending to kill the president; he exhibits guidance control of his action and also the consequence-universal *that the president is killed*. I conclude that the Principle of Transfer of Nonresponsibility is invalid. In some of the essays in this volume, I explore and reject the possibility of resurrecting a direct argument based on any sort of Transfer of Nonresponsibility Principle— any modified version of the Principle of Nonresponsibility sketched above.[37]

Sourcehood

There are various other direct arguments against the compatibility of causal determinism and moral responsibility.[38] On these views, the flickers of freedom—the exiguous but nevertheless difficult-to-expunge alternative possibilities that seem to exist even in the most sophisticated Frankfurt-type cases—are important because they are signs that causal determinism is false. If there were absolutely no such flickers, and causal determinism were true, and thus human behavior were the product of causally deterministic sequences, this would rule out moral responsibility (according to the proponent of the direct argument) but *not* in virtue of ruling out regulative control. Rather, according to this kind of approach, causal determinism would rule out moral responsibility by threatening such notions as being the originator, initiator, or source of one's behavior, being creative, active, and so forth. In order to explain my strategy of response, I shall fix on one such notion—origination; I contend that the same considerations apply *mutatis mutandis* to the other notions.

Note that there is a perfectly acceptable, ordinary or commonsense notion of origination that is compatibilistic. We say that the boy's striking a match started the fire, or that a lightning bolt started a fire, and we might well persist in those assertions, even if someone were to convince us that we live in a causally deterministic world. Now a proponent of the direct argument may say, "OK, I grant that there is an ordinary notion of origination that is perfectly acceptable in many contexts in everyday life. And when we ascribe responsibility in ordinary contexts, we presuppose that causal determinism is false. But if we were really convinced that causal determinism were true, we could not say that, strictly speaking, the lightning bolt or the boy's striking the match started the fire, and we certainly could not say that, strictly speaking, any human being is the 'origin' or 'source' of his behavior."

To reply: I concede that there is a strict sense in which origination requires the falsity of causal determination. Thus, in a causally deterministic world, nothing would start anything or be the source of anything in this strict sense, and, in particular, no one would initiate or be the source of his behavior in the strict sense. But why exactly should *this* be the sense that is relevant to moral responsibility? I grant that an agent must initiate or be the source of his behavior to be morally responsible for that behavior; but why is it obvious that the relevant notion of origination is the strict notion that presupposes indeterminism? There is, everyone agrees, a perfectly reasonable compatibilistic notion of origination, according to which the lightning bolt could be said to have started the fire even in a causally deterministic world. On what basis is it legitimate to *insist* that the relevant notion of origination, the notion connected to moral responsibility, is the indeterministic notion?

Now if moral responsibility required regulative control, then there would be some motivation for the contention that origination would need to involve causal indeterminism. But the proponent of the direct argument is not entitled to this presupposition, given that good reasons have been offered to call into question the indirect argument. Apart from a reliance on the requirement of regulative control, how could it be argued that the relevant notion of origination must be indeterministic?

Taking stock, I do not claim to have argued that it is obvious that the compatibilistic notion of (say) origination is the one that should be linked to moral responsibility. Rather, I have suggested that there is no reason to prefer the indeterministic notion, apart from a prior (and, in my view, gratuitous) commitment to something like the Principle of Alternative Possibilities. The dialectic terrain has shifted in a way that is felicitous for compatibilism, for the Consequence Argument is considerably more powerful than any of the direct arguments. Given the importance of the resiliency of personhood and responsibility, I opt, all things considered, for compatibilism about moral responsibility and causal determinism.[39]

Guidance Control for Dummies

So far I have sought to explain how I have argued against several of the salient ways of pressing the worry that causal determinism would threaten moral responsibility. Now I wish to sketch my account of guidance control. I have filled in this sketch in a bit more detail (although not as much as I would like!) elsewhere, especially in *Responsibility and Control: A Theory of Moral Responsibility* with Mark Ravizza. As the main development of the account of guidance control is not included in this volume, I shall try to give enough detail to explain the main ideas and to show how the account applies to some of the puzzling cases we have discussed above. I will not develop the account in detail here.

Heeding van Inwagen's advice to be careful about what precisely we are holding someone morally responsible for, I shall begin with actions, and then move on to consequences (construed as particulars and also universals), and then omissions. A virtue of my account of guidance control is that it provides a *unified and systematic* approach to moral responsibility for these items. That is, the same basic ingredients can be employed in constructing structurally similar accounts of moral responsibility for all of the items; thus, seemingly disparate phenomena can be tied together by a unified deep theory.

The Elements of Guidance Control

An insight from the Frankfurt-type cases helps to shape the account: moral responsibility is a matter of the history of an action (or behavior)—of how the actual sequence unfolds—rather than the genuine metaphysical availability of alternative possibilities. (On this view, alternative scenarios or nonactual possible worlds might be relevant to moral responsibility in virtue of helping to specify or analyze modal properties of the actual sequence, but not in virtue of indicating or providing an analysis of genuine access to alternative possibilities.)

Note that, in a Frankfurt-type case, the actual sequence proceeds "in the normal way" or via the "normal" process of practical reasoning. In contrast, in the alternative scenario (which never actually gets triggered and thus never becomes part of the actual sequence of events in our world), there is (say) direct electronic stimulation of the brain—intuitively, a different way or a different kind of mechanism. (By "mechanism" I simply mean "way"—I do not mean to reify anything.) I assume that we have intuitions at least about clear cases of "same mechanism," and "different mechanism." I rely on these intuitive judgments in the absence of a general reductive account of mechanism individuation.[40] The actually operating mechanism (in a Frankfurt-type case)—ordinary human practical reasoning, unimpaired by direct stimulation by neurosurgeons, and so forth—is in a salient sense responsive to reasons. That is, holding fixed that mechanism, the agent would presumably choose and act differently in a range of scenarios in which he is presented with good reasons to do so. For example, holding fixed the operation of normal practical reasoning, the pilot in the example above would presumably choose to steer the plane to the east, if told (reliably) that there is a fierce storm to the west (but not the east). Further, holding fixed the normal, proper functioning of the aircraft (and the lack of a strong wind current), this choice would be translated into action, and the pilot would guide the plane eastward.

The above discussion suggests the rudiments of an account of guidance control of action. On this account, we hold fixed the kind of mechanism that actually issues in the choice and action, and we see whether the agent responds suitably to reasons (some of which are moral reasons). My account presupposes that the agent can recognize reasons, and, in particular, recognize certain reasons as moral reasons. The account distinguishes between reasons-recognition (the ability to recognize the reasons that exist) and reasons-reactivity (choice in accordance with reasons that are recognized as good and sufficient), and it makes different demands on reasons-recognition and reasons-reactivity.[41] The sort of reasons-responsiveness linked to moral responsibility is "moderate reasons-responsiveness."[42]

But one could exhibit the right sort of reasons-responsiveness as a result (say) of clandestine, unconsented-to electronic stimulation of the brain (or hypnosis, brainwashing, and so forth). So moderate reasons-responsiveness of the actual-sequence mechanism is necessary but not sufficient for moral responsibility. I contend that there are two elements of guidance control: reasons-sensitivity of the appropriate sort and mechanism ownership. That is, the mechanism that issues in the behavior must (in an appropriate sense) be the *agent's own mechanism*. (When one is secretly manipulated through clandestine mind control as in *The Manchurian Candidate*, one's practical reasoning is not *one's own*.)

My coauthor, Mark Ravizza, and I argue for a subjective approach to mechanism ownership. On this approach, one's mechanism becomes one's own in virtue of one's having certain beliefs about one's own agency and its effects in the world, that is, in virtue of *seeing oneself in a certain way*. (Of course, it is *not* simply a matter of saying certain things—one actually has to have the relevant constellation of beliefs.) In our view, an individual becomes morally responsible in part at least by taking responsibility; he makes his mechanism his own by taking responsibility for acting from that kind of mechanism. In a sense, then, one acquires control by *taking control*.[43]

In the words of the song by P. Anka, J. Revaux, and C. Francois, made famous by Frank Sinatra:

> And now the end is near and so I face the final curtain;
> My friend, I'll say it clear, I'll state my case, of which I'm certain;
> I've lived a life that's full, I traveled each and every highway,
> And more, much more than this, I did it my way.[44]

The second element of the account of guidance control—the account of mechanism ownership—is an attempt to say what it is to "do it my way" in the sense relevant to "doing it freely." That is, the second element of the account of guidance control specifies what my way consists in, where my way is mechanism ownership.

I care about, and place a certain distinctive value on, acting freely—on doing it my way—and I turn in the next section to an attempt at specifying this character-istic value. (Here "doing it my way" is interpreted more broadly to mean "acting freely.") But prior to addressing the question of the value of acting freely, I shall build on the account of guidance control of actions to sketch an account of guid-ance control of consequences (and omissions). The specific account will help to defend my views about the puzzling cases of moral responsibility for actions, con-sequences, and omissions discussed above.

As I said above (following van Inwagen), we need to distinguish between consequence-particulars and the more abstract states of affairs that van Inwagen calls "consequence-universals." The account of guidance control of consequence-particulars is a reasonably straightforward extension of the account of guidance control of actions. On this approach, an agent S has guidance control of a consequence-particular C just in case S has guidance control of some act A (i.e., A results from the agent's own, moderately reasons-responsive mechanism), and it is reasonable to expect S to believe that C will (or may) result from A.

The account of guidance control of consequence-universals also builds on the account of guidance control of actions, but in a different way. It posits two inter-locked and linked sensitivities. In the first stage, the agent's bodily movements must issue from his own, moderately reasons-responsive mechanism. In the second stage, the relevant event in the external world must be suitably sensitive to the agent's bodily movements. In the first stage, one holds fixed the kind of mecha-nism that actually operates; in the second stage, one holds fixed the kind of pro-cess that actually takes one from the bodily movement to the event in the external world. At this second stage, one distinguishes the background conditions from the events that take place within the context of those conditions; one holds fixed the background conditions, and the nonoccurrence of actually nonoccurring or even simultaneously occurring triggers of the event in question. Put slightly dif-ferently, one holds fixed the background conditions, and one also "brackets" or "subtracts" any simultaneously occurring triggering event; additionally, one as-sumes that any nonoccurring triggering event (some initiating event that occurs only in a range of alternative scenarios, but not in the actual sequence) does *not* occur. Given these presuppositions, and against this background, one evaluates the sensitivity of the event in the external world to one's bodily movements.

Applying the Account

The puzzles introduced above about moral responsibility for consequence-universals can be resolved by employing this sort of account of guidance control. Just as moral responsibility for actions is linked to guidance control, so is moral re-sponsibility for consequences. More specifically, an agent is morally responsible for a consequence-universal insofar as he exhibits guidance control of that universal, even if he lacked regulative control over it (i.e., even if he could not have pre-vented it from obtaining, one way or another). In van Inwagen's case of Ryder and

Dobbin, the runaway horse ends up in Rome, no matter what Ryder does (no matter how he moves his body); thus the second stage does not exhibit the required sensitivity, and Ryder does not have guidance control of the consequence-universal, *that Dobbin ends up in Rome*. In contrast, the assassin who shoots the president in the context of preemptive overdetermination does exhibit guidance-control of the consequence-universal, *that the president is shot*. Holding fixed the background conditions and the *nonoccurrence* of the intervention by the *other* assassin (the assassin who is disposed to shoot but does not shoot), there is no reason to suppose that the second stage does not exhibit the required sensitivity. That is, holding fixed the background conditions and the nonoccurrence of other triggering events, it is plausible to suppose that the president would not have been shot if the actual assassin had not pulled the trigger.

It appeared to van Inwagen that the only way to explain why Ryder is not morally responsible for the consequence-universal, *that Dobbin ends up in Rome*, is that Ryder could not have prevented this consequence-universal from obtaining, one way or another. But the putative explanation yields the intuitively incorrect result in the assassin case (and others). If one accepts the association of moral responsibility with guidance control, and one accepts the sort of account of guidance control of consequence-universals that I have proposed, one can say just the right thing about *both* of the cases.

Recall van Inwagen's explanation of the (alleged) failure of the Frankfurt-type cases to impugn the Principle of Alternative Possibilities (the association of moral responsibility with regulative control):

> In attempting to construct Frankfurt-style counter-examples [to the principle that moral responsibility for a consequence-universal requires the ability to prevent that universal from obtaining], we have been imagining cases in which an agent "gets to" a certain state of affairs by following a particular "causal road," a road intentionally chosen by him in order to "get to" that state of affairs; but, because this state of affairs is a *universal*, it can be reached by various causal roads, some of them differing radically from the road that is in fact taken; and, in the cases we have imagined, *every* causal road that *any* choice of the agent's might set him upon leads to this same state of affairs. This is why the agent in our attempts at Frankfurt-style counter-examples always turns out not to be responsible for the state of affairs he is unable to prevent.[45]

In the examples we have been considering, it is indeed true that every causal road that any choice of the agent's might set him upon leads to the same state of affairs. In a proper subset of the cases this is because some *other* mechanism or process would be triggered by certain nonactual choices (or perhaps some *other*, nonoccurring triggering event would have occurred). But in this proper subset, holding fixed the relevant features of the way things played out (the actual kind of mechanism issuing in the bodily movement and the actual kind of process leading to the event in the external world), different choices of the agent might well set him upon a causal road that leads to a *different* state of affairs. The account of guidance control of consequence-universals requires that we hold fixed the background conditions against which the actual triggering event occurred and had its effects—and that we subtract or bracket other actual or hypothetical triggering events. My claim is that moral responsibility for consequence-universals is linked with guidance control of those universals; this, rather than van Inwagen's view, best tracks our considered judgments about the full array of cases.

Similarly, the solution to the puzzle about omissions—that in some but not all cases where an agent cannot do X, he can be held morally responsible for failing to do X—also involves the link between moral responsibility and guidance control.[46] I pointed out above that there is an intuitive distinction between simple and complex omissions regarding the conditions for moral responsibility. A simple omission is fully constituted by a failure to move one's body in certain ways, and we can take the actual bodily movement, whatever that is—call it B—as fully constituting that failure. Now the account of guidance control of actions can essentially be applied to B. That is, where an agent's not doing X is his moving his body as in B, then he is morally responsible for not doing X insofar as he exhibits guidance control of B.

When the omission is complex (such as the failure to communicate with police in van Inwagen's example above), I analyze the omission as the agent's bringing about a "relatively fine-grained negative consequence-universal," such as *that the police are not reached successfully by me.*[47] Now it is straightforward to apply the account of guidance control of consequence-universals. Since one's not successfully reaching the police is not sensitive to one's bodily movements (dialing the phone and so forth), one cannot fairly be held morally responsible for the omission. Again, as with actions and consequences (particulars and universals), our approach allows us to say exactly the intuitively correct things about *all* of the puzzling cases, and to do this without positing the necessity of regulative control for moral responsibility. Hence, the overall theory is both more in line with our reflective, intuitive judgments about the *full* array of cases, and also is helpful in the project of defending compatibilism about moral responsibility and causal determinism (and thus the resiliency of our basic conception of ourselves as agents, and, indeed, persons).

The Value of Guidance Control

We place value on acting freely, or, in other words, exercising a distinctive kind of control: guidance control. We value being the sort of creatures who can display this sort of control and thereby be held morally accountable for our behavior. As Peter Strawson has famously argued, it is hard to imagine a world without genuine moral responsibility, where this sort of responsibility involves a set of distinctively moral attitudes (which he dubbed the "reactive attitudes").[48] Arguably we would not especially miss certain retributive attitudes, such as indignation, resentment, and hatred.[49] But a world in which we simply seek to change people's behavior through manipulation, conditioning, and therapy (without applying *any* of the reactive attitudes identified by Strawson) would be a world missing something important. Additionally, I believe a world in which we simply mouth the words that typically express genuine attributions of moral responsibility, or engage in the practices of (say) punishment on purely instrumental grounds (and apart from claims of moral desert), would be a cynical, empty world.[50]

The Free Will Defense is offered as a theodicy, an answer to the problem of evil that exhibits the possibility of God's existence in a world with considerable suffering. Part of this theodicy is the claim that in order to create the best of all possible worlds, God must create free creatures. Quite apart from whether one accepts this sort of theodicy, I think the claim is correct: a world in which creatures never acted freely could not possibly be the best of all possible worlds. Much of what we value in life would be missing from such a world.

Making a Difference

But why precisely do we value the possession of this distinctive capacity to act freely? One answer is the value of making a difference. But I have argued that one can act freely and thus exhibit guidance control even in the absence of regulative control. The value of moral responsibility (or guidance control), then, cannot be the value of making a difference; one can act freely even though one cannot make a difference to the world through one's free choice and behavior.

Now it might be objected that, as I noted above, even in the most sophisticated sort of Frankfurt-type example, there may be a residual flicker of freedom— an ineliminable alternative possibility, exiguous as it may be. But, as I argued in reply, these sorts of alternatives are not substantial enough to play a certain role in one's theory of moral responsibility: adding them to a context without alternatives of any sort cannot plausibly transform a case of no responsibility to one where there is moral responsibility. Similarly, the difference one can make in this sort of context is not between *meaningfully different* outcomes, where "outcomes" are understood in terms of end states (rather than the paths to those end states). In a natural way of taking the claim, in a Frankfurt-type case I do *not* make a difference as to what sort of end state is brought about (what sort of consequence-universal obtains).

Imagine that I save a drowning child freely, although my saving the child was preemptively overdetermined in a Frankfurt-type manner. Let's suppose that, had I been about to choose not to jump into the pool, a neuroscientist would electronically stimulate my brain in such a way as to produce a choice to save the child. Why was it valuable that I freely saved the child? On the "make-a-difference" model, it is alleged that I make a certain sort of difference to the world through my free choice and act of saving the child. But what is this difference? The child would have been saved in any case, and saved *by me* in any case. Yes, I make it the case that one event-particular or sequence of event-particulars (constituting saving the child) occurs rather than a different event-particular or sequence of event-particulars (which would also have constituted saving the child); but *this* surely is not the sort of difference typically invoked by the proponent of the make-a-difference model, and it is not plausible that *this* sort of difference is what we value in acting freely. I believe that I could have a Frankfurt-type counterfactual intervener associated with me my entire life, and that it could thus be true that I never have regulative control; nevertheless, I could still act freely, exhibit an important kind of control, and be morally responsible. And my free actions would have a distinctive kind of value, even if I could never make a difference in the relevant sense.

Making a Statement

The distinctive value of free behavior in virtue of which we can be held morally responsible is not the value of making a difference. Rather, it is the value of making a certain kind of statement. It is thus the value of a certain sort of self-expression. This is of course not a value that trumps or outweighs all others, and it is perhaps given a different weight by different people. My contention is that the value of guidance control is a species of the value of self-expression, whatever that value is.[51]

When one acts freely, I claim, one renders it true that one's life has a certain distinctive kind of value: narrative value. Acting freely is the specific ingredient that makes us the sort of creatures that are capable of living lives with a certain signature sort of meaning: narrative meaning. Although one can write the account of a rock's history or a rat's life, only humans have "stories" in the sense that their lives are narratives that can have distinctively narrative meaning and value. Part of what it is to have narrative value is that the function that determines the overall value of one's life does not simply add up all the momentary levels of well-being; rather, it is also sensitive to certain characteristic *relationships* among events. Building on the important work of David Velleman, I have attempted to highlight some of the salient defining features of narrative value.[52]

Here I shall simply suggest that we can think of free action, an agent's exhibiting guidance control, as the agent's writing a sentence in the story or narrative of his life. It is then an act of artistic self-expression. We value creative or artistic self-expression quite apart from the aesthetic value of the piece of art that is the product; we also place value in the artistic self-expression involved in free action—freely writing a sentence in the story, the narrative, of one's life. In this sense, when we act freely we make a certain sort of statement. The value of acting freely, then, is not the value of making a difference, but the value of making a characteristic kind of statement.

My view about the value of acting freely and having moral responsibility has the implication that someone who is thoroughly manipulated to choose and act in just the same sort of way he would have chosen and acted but for the manipulation is *not* morally responsible for his actual choice and behavior. Such an agent is not engaging in *self-expression* through his choice and behavior; that is, his choice and behavior are not acts of self-expression, even if they match or correspond to something deep about the agent—his enduring character, for instance.

Note that my view is an actual-sequence approach to moral responsibility. One implication is that being morally responsible does not require genuine metaphysical access to alternative possibilities. (As I pointed out above, this does not imply that alternative scenarios or nonactual possible worlds are irrelevant to the specification of the pertinent modal or dispositional properties of the actual sequence.) Another implication is that it does not suffice for moral responsibility that the agent would have done the same sort of thing had he not been manipulated (without his consent); what matters here is the actual sequence, not the hypothetical manipulation-free sequence.

Similarly, my view entails that an agent who is manipulated or brainwashed into choosing the right thing for the right reasons (and so acting) is *not* morally responsible for his choice (and subsequent behavior). Again, moral responsibility is a matter of self-expression—of making a statement rather than making a connection with values (or having the possibility of so connecting with values).[53]

Responsibility, Morality, and Deliberation

A Kantian Worry

I have argued that moral responsibility does not require regulative control (and thus genuine metaphysical access to alternative possibilities). Additionally, I have argued that there are no strong reasons to think that causal determinism threatens moral responsibility "directly" (i.e., for some reason other than ruling out regulative control). Additionally, I have presented a systematic approach to moral responsibility, employing the central notion of guidance control, according to which moral responsibility is compatible with causal determinism. On this approach, our fundamental status as morally responsible agents need not be held hostage by the possibility that causal determinism is true.[54]

Some philosophers have agreed with me about the relationship between causal determinism and moral responsibility, but *not* about causal determinism and a range of moral judgments involving the circle of notions "ought," "right," "ought not," and "wrong."[55] Although the argumentation can get intricate, we can think of the basic point this way. Accept the maxim "Ought implies can," associated with Kant, and also accept both that causal determinism obtains and that it rules out regulative control (in accordance with the Consequence Argument). Now imagine that someone does something that appears to be wrong. It follows that the agent ought not to have done what he did. Now it also follows that he ought to have done something else instead, which could include simply not doing anything. But, given the maxim, it now follows that the agent could have done something else instead. But this is inconsistent with the assumptions of causal determinism and the conclusion of the Consequence Argument.

It would render my semicompatibilism considerably less interesting if causal determinism ruled out central moral judgments (even if not other moral judgments or moral responsibility). I reply to the argument by denying the Kantian maxim "Ought implies can." The basis of my argument is again the Frankfurt-style situations involving preemptive overdetermination. Crucial to my argument is the contention that there are Frankfurt-type omissions cases, that is, examples in which it is plausible that an agent is morally responsible for failing to do X, although he could not have done X. Consider a slightly different version of the sort of simple omissions case discussed above. Suppose that by raising her hand, Sally can save a drowning child (by alerting the lifeguard that the child is drowning); Sally cannot swim herself, but she has an arrangement with the lifeguard to signal by raising her hand if someone needs help. Sally sees a child drowning, and there is no good reason why she should not raise her hand, but she simply does not raise her hand. Imagine, further, that this is a Frankfurt-type omissions case, and, unknown to Sally, she is temporarily paralyzed in such a way as to make her unable to raise her hand.

In my view, she is morally responsible (and blameworthy) for not raising her hand, even though she could not have raised her hand. Further, since she is blameworthy for not raising her hand, I would claim that she acted wrongly in failing to raise her hand, and thus that she ought to have raised it. But she could not have raised it. Thus, ought does *not* imply can, and the Kantian maxim is to be rejected.[56]

Deliberation and Openness

Agency has many facets. Oversimplifying a bit, one could distinguish the forward-looking and backward-looking elements of agency. Moral responsibility is backward-looking. I have argued that this dimension of agency does not require genuinely available alternative possibilities. Practical reasoning and deliberation are forward-looking. Whereas some philosophers have argued that this dimension of agency requires alternative possibilities, or at least the supposition by the agent of genuine metaphysical access to alternative possibilities, I disagree. Neither dimension of agency requires regulative control, metaphysically available alternative possibilities, or even the assumption by the relevant agent of the availability of such options.

I argue against various "libertarian" pictures of practical reasoning and deliberation (according to which metaphysically available alternative possibilities are required for practical reasoning, or at least the assumption of such availability is required).[57] The point of practical reasoning is not to select which path to set oneself upon, where one has various options from which to choose. That is, the point of practical reasoning is *not* to make a *difference* (or to make a *selection* from available alternatives). Rather, the point of practical reasoning is to figure out what one has reason to do, all things considered. Further, one wants to conform one's choice to one's all-things-considered judgment about what is best. These aims would still be present even if the agent knew the world in which she lived were causally deterministic and that she thus has only one genuinely available alternative possibility. Even in such a world, there would still be a point to figuring out what one has reason to do, and a point to seeking to act in accord with what is rational.

Note that even if an agent knows that, whatever she ends up choosing and doing are the *only* things she can choose and do, she need *not* thereby know what these are (or will be). She thus may have epistemic alternatives (alternatives that are open to her, for all she knows), even if she lacks genuinely accessible metaphysical alternatives. Whereas causal determinism arguably rules out metaphysical access to alternative possibilities, it need not rule out the existence of a range of epistemic possibilities. Practical reasoning can operate on the domain of epistemic possibilities.[58] Causal determinism, or even an agent's knowledge of the truth of causal determinism, need not threaten the point of the forward-looking dimension of agency.

My Way

I have sought to present an overall "framework" for moral responsibility. The framework includes various ideas in a certain arrangement. It involves the motivational idea of the importance of the *resiliency* of our fundamental view of ourselves as robustly free agents who are genuinely morally responsible. One can distinguish forward-looking and backward-looking facets of free agency, and I contend that there are no good arguments from causal determinism that threaten these elements. Further, I sketch a theory of guidance control and a picture of practical reasoning according to which both moral responsibility and practical reasoning are arguably compatible with causal determinism. Finally, I give the outlines of an account of the value of acting so as to be morally responsible. If the value of acting in this fashion is the value of artistic self-expression, this provides additional reason to suppose that regulative control is not necessary for moral responsibility, insofar as there is no reason to suppose that artistic self-expression requires access to metaphysically available alternative possibilities.

If moral responsibility involves a distinctive kind of self-expression, it is perhaps not surprising that philosophers have found it illuminating to model the practices involved in holding agents morally responsible along the lines of a "conversation."[59] When one expresses oneself in certain ways, it is appropriate for others to respond in ways that are keyed to the initial act of self-expression—all members of the conversation have to speak the same language. I have suggested, roughly speaking (and oversimplifying greatly), that acting freely involves self-expression in a certain language: the language of reasons. A morally responsible agent speaks the language of reasons; an agent who cannot even speak this language is not an appropriate candidate for the characteristic attitudes of moral responsibility.

Is someone such as Michael Ross morally responsible for his behavior? To gain even a lamentably sketchy first approximation of an understanding of the complex and multifaceted phenomena of abnormal psychology and psychopathy, one would have to know whether a particular candidate for moral responsibility can speak the language of reasons. One can sensibly talk with someone who can speak one's language, even if that individual chooses not to speak. But it is pointless to speak to someone in a language he cannot understand. Participants in a conversation require a common language. Moderate reasons-responsiveness, with its twin and interlocked capacities for reasons-recognition and reasons-reactivity, is my preliminary move toward understanding the capacity to speak the language of reasons.

The conversation model of moral responsibility suggests an answer to Martha Klein's provocative idea that individuals who were significantly abused or deprived as children should not be punished later for their crimes, since they have *already* been punished. On this view, the childhood abuse or deprivations are the punishment.[60] One could reply by invoking the fact that conversation has a definite structure. By its nature, punishment is analogous to a *reply* in a conversation, which must come *after* the statement to which it is a reply.

The conversation model may also illuminate certain initially puzzling phenomena pertaining to punishment. We spend considerable resources trying to save the lives of prisoners on death row who try to commit suicide, only to put them to death later. Presumably this is because it is the *state* that must *respond* to the criminal's statement in the appropriate sequence of the conversation; it is as if a suicide is speaking out of turn. As with the Klein suggestion, the natural order of a conversation is reversed. Additionally, a prison suicide would be a soliloquy of sorts, rather than a true conversation. Note also that the state may give elaborate psychiatric treatment to a depressed prisoner on death row, even including the involuntary use of antidepressant and/or antipsychotic medication, prior to executing him. This practice may be less puzzling under the conversation model. A conversation needs to be a two-way street at least insofar as all parties must have the capacity to understand—must be capable of speaking the language and attending to the conversation.

When I started writing about free will and moral responsibility more than two decades ago, I had no idea where I was going. I am reminded of Bob Hope and Bing Crosby in one of the *Road to . . .* movies, perhaps *The Road to Morocco* (or maybe it was *The Road to Zanzibar*). Bob Hope asks Bing Crosby where each of the forks in the road leads, and Crosby says, "I have no idea." Hope replies, "Ok, let's get going, then." I certainly never thought at the beginning, nor do I think now, that all philosophical roads lead to semicompatibilism.

Gerald Dworkin writes, "There are those who know from the start where they are going and those who only realize after the journey where they have been traveling."[61] I know that I have come some distance from the beginning, but I also know that I have much more distance to travel. (I have always thought it prudent to define progress as increased distance from the beginning, rather than diminished distance to the goal.) Along the way I have learned much from my collaborators and critics, for which I am extremely grateful.[62] In addition to helping me in ways that are too numerous and substantial to spell out, they have made the journey enormously enjoyable and rewarding.

My monograph *The Metaphysics of Free Will: An Essay on Control* ends as follows:

> Even if there is just one available path into the future, I may be held accountable for *how I walk down this path*. I can be blamed for taking the path of cruelty, negligence, or cowardice. And I can be praised for walking with sensitivity, attentiveness, and courage. Even if I somehow discovered there is but one path into the future, I would still care deeply how I walk down this path. I would aspire to walk with grace and dignity. I would want to have a sense of humor. Most of all, I would want to do it my way.[63]

To which Gary Watson replied:

> This affirmation, incompatibilists might complain, is a rhetorical flourish to which Fischer is not strictly entitled. Here the path metaphor seems a bit misused. In the abstract sense required by the argument, a "way" is of course a path, a metapath, perhaps, of which there is only one if determinism is true. The aspiration to define one's

own way (expressed so differently by Kant and Sinatra) might be called an ideal of autonomy. Can we understand this ideal without presupposing that very power "to guide [one's actions] in a different *way*" . . . that is, without what Fischer calls regulative control, without alternative possibilities?[64]

Speaking of different ways of taking the one path may seem to reintroduce the problematic alternative possibilities I have sought so assiduously to expunge. But, as with the Frankfurt examples and those irrefragable flickers of freedom, the alternative ways or metapaths are so exiguous as to be irrelevant. Their mere existence does not provide the sort of alternative possibilities that would be required, on any plausible alternative-possibilities or make-a-difference model. As I put it (in a footnote appended to the passage addressed by Watson):

> Suppose I walk down the path of life in a certain way. Notice, as with the contexts in which it was alleged that there are [mere] flickers of freedom, that I may *not* be able to deliberate and then choose some *other way of taking the path* and then freely proceed in this alternative manner. And yet I may still walk freely.[65]

The mere existence of alternative possibilities without voluntariness or oomph does not suffice to ground attributions of regulative control. I can walk down a path where, unknown to me, there is a counterfactual intervener whose presence ensures that I do not have genuine, robust alternative possibilities. And yet this does not in any way change the way I walk down the path. The mere existence of flimsy alternative possibilities—exiguous ways or metapaths—cannot be what grounds my concern for *how I actually walk down the path*. I gladly accept the interpretation of my rather florid prose offered by Michael Zimmerman:

> I think that Fischer's final rendition of his "new paradigm" would be improved if slightly reworded. To say that, even if there is just one path available into the future, I may be held accountable for how I walk down this path, suggests (to me, at least) that I have alternative ways of walking down the path open to me. One wonders, then, whether we should be talking of one path or two; even if we stick to talking of just one path, that there are alternative ways of walking down it is something that the semicompatibilist must declare unnecessary. What I think Fischer should have said is this: even if there is just one available path into the future and just one available way of walking down it, I may be held accountable for walking down it in that way.[66]

That having been settled, please allow me a final flourish, this time from neither Kant nor Sinatra, but Sid Vicious:

> Regrets. I've had a few
> But then again, too few to mention.
> . . . Of that, take care and just
> Be careful along the highway
> And more, much more than this
> I did it my way.
>
> There were times,
> I'm sure you knew

> When there was but
> F—ing else to do.
> But through it all,
> When there was doubt . . .
> I faced the wall . . .
> And did it my way.[67]

Sometimes, when thinking and writing about free will, one feels, as it were, up against the wall. The stakes are so high—people's lives depend on issues of freedom and responsibility.[68] The very meaning of life is at stake.[69] One wants so badly to say something more nuanced and penetrating, not just a rough first approximation to guide further thought. The issues are complex and important, and yet resistant to formulaic solutions. When I have been on the verge of despair, I have taken to heart Franz Kafka's injunction: When you're up against the wall, start describing the wall.[70]

NOTES

1. Karen Clarke, "Life on Death Row," *Connecticut Magazine* 53 (1990), pp. 51–55; 63–67. I began my first monograph, *The Metaphysics of Free Will: An Essay on Control* (Oxford: Blackwell, 1994), with this quotation (p. 1). For further discussion, see John Martin Fischer and Mark Ravizza, *Responsibility and Control: A Theory of Moral Responsibility* (Cambridge: Cambridge University Press, 1998), pp. 219–20.

2. Michael Ross, "It's Time for Me to Die: An Inside Look at Death Row," *Journal of Psychiatry and Law* 26 (winter 1998): 475–91; the quoted remarks are from pp. 476–77 and 481–82.

3. Ross, "It's Time for Me to Die," pp. 482–83.

4. Ibid., pp. 484–85.

5. Ibid., p. 486. In a fascinating discussion of murderer Robert Alton Harris, Gary Watson identifies a similar ambivalence in our reflective attitudes toward Harris. (See Gary Watson, "Responsibility and the Limits of Evil: Variations on a Strawsonian Theme," in *Responsibility, Character, and the Emotions*, ed. Ferdinand D. Schoeman (Cambridge: Cambridge University Press, 1987), pp. 256–86. In the case of Harris, the ambivalence stems (in part) from a recognition of the extreme circumstances of Harris's childhood rather than a belief that Harris has a mental illness (or, perhaps, a mental illness similar to Ross's).

6. Ross, "It's Time for Me to Die," p. 486.

7. In a fascinating, yet (based on the last line) not entirely convincing journal entry, Ross says:

> When I came to death row some thirteen years ago, I could never have imagined the true blessing that it would ultimately turn out to be. And while I never would have chosen this path in retrospect, I wouldn't change places with anyone. I know this is hard to believe—how could anyone find death row to be a blessing? But when I look over the past decade that I have been here and I see the spiritual transformation and growth that I have undergone, I know, without a shadow of a doubt, the love and abundant graces that God has bestowed upon me. And because of this, I can say that even though I do not understand why God chose for me to remain here on death row, I know that with a strong faith that [sic] there is a reason and a purpose for this which will in the end glorify God.

Life may sometimes seem senseless, and people may at times be thoughtless or even vindictive. But God's will for us is good. And God will prevail. So I accept this situation—even though I don't fully understand—and I patiently and humbly await the day that I do understand and see how all of this fits into God's plan for me, and for humanity in general. Still it doesn't seem fair does it? (Journal entry, "Walking with Michael, 2000," available at http://www.ccadp.org/michaelross-walkingmay 2000.html.)

8. Some philosophers object to what they take to be an inordinate emphasis on hypothetical examples in a certain sort of philosophical methodology. Of course, Michael Ross's case is all too real.

9. For some tentative and preliminary thoughts, see Fischer and Ravizza, *Responsibility and Control*, pp. 62–91.

10. It is helpful to distinguish the concept of moral responsibility from its conditions of application. Most of my work has addressed the latter issue, rather than the former. Here I shall focus primarily on the conditions of application of the concept of moral responsibility. For the distinction, and more discussion of the concept of moral responsibility, see Fischer and Ravizza, *Responsibility and Control*, pp. 1–27; and John Martin Fischer and Mark Ravizza, eds., *Perspectives on Moral Responsibility* (Ithaca, N.Y.: Cornell University Press, 1993).

11. For more sophisticated discussion of the different varieties of causal determinism and different attempts at characterizing causal determinism, see John Earman, *A Primer on Determinism* (Dordrecht: D. Reidel, 1986); and Jordan Howard Sobel, *Puzzles for the Will* (Toronto: University of Toronto Press, 1998).

T. S. Eliot wrote:

> Time present and time past
> Are both perhaps present in time future,
> And time future contained in time past.
> (*Four Quartets* 1: "Burnt Norton")

The problem of distinguishing the temporally nonrelational or "hard" facts about a time from the temporally relational (regarding the future) or "soft" facts about a time is vexed. See *God, Foreknowledge, and Freedom*, ed. John Martin Fischer (Stanford, Calif.: Stanford University Press, 1989); and John Martin Fischer, "Recent Work on God and Freedom," *American Philosophical Quarterly* 29 (1992): 91–109.

12. I discussed the structural similarities (and differences) in *The Metaphysics of Free Will*. See also Fischer, *God, Foreknowledge, and Freedom*.

13. Of course, this consideration does not in itself provide a defense of compatibilism, or even a reason for adopting it; rather, it provides a motivation for seeking to defend compatibilism, that is, for attempting to defend it against criticisms and to identify reasons for adopting it.

14. For this point, see, for example, Randolph Clarke, *Libertarian Accounts of Free Will* (Oxford: Oxford University Press, 2003), p. 8.

15. Peter Van Inwagen offers a "fanciful but logically adequate example" in which "when any human being is born, the Martians implant in his brain a tiny device . . . which contains a 'program' for that person's entire life" (*An Essay on Free Will* [Oxford: Clarendon, 1983], p. 109). The device is undetectable by the individual being manipulated by it but is not in principle undetectable. I agree that a discovery that an individual (or all of us) were manipulated in this fashion could reasonably cause us to give up our view of ourselves

as free and morally responsible agents. So my claim is not that there are no possible empirical discoveries that could call our agency and moral responsibility into question.

16. Peter van Inwagen, "The Incompatibility of Free Will and Causal Determinism," *Philosophical Studies* 27 (1975): 185–99, and *Essay on Free Will*. For a precursor in contemporary philosophy, see Carl Ginet, "Might We Have No Choice?" in *Freedom and Determinism*, ed. Keith Lehrer (New York: Random House, 1966), pp. 87–104. For further discussion, see Carl Ginet, *On Action* (Cambridge: Cambridge University Press, 1990). I discuss such arguments in *Metaphysics of Free Will*.

17. For some very rigorous presentations, see Sobel, *Puzzles for the Will*.

18. John Martin Fischer, "Responsibility and Control," *Journal of Philosophy* 79 (1982): 40.

19. I discuss the distinction between regulative and guidance control, and give more such examples, in chapter 2.

20. Harry Frankfurt, "Alternate Possibilities and Moral Responsibilities," *Journal of Philosophy* 66 (1969): 829–39.

21. I first suggested this sort of move in "Responsibility and Control." For further developments and discussions, see chapters 2 and 10.

22. I introduce "oomph" in chapter 7.

23. See Peter van Inwagen, "Ability and Responsibility," *Philosophical Review* 87 (1978): 201–24, and *Essay on Free Will*, pp. 153–189.

24. Van Inwagen, *Essay on Free Will*, p. 176.

25. Ibid., pp. 176–77.

26. Ibid., pp. 165–66.

27. In an early paper, "Responsibility and Failure" (*Proceedings of the Aristotelian Society* 86 [1985/6]: 251–70), I agreed with van Inwagen's position. In subsequent years I changed my view as a result of helpful criticism by various philosophers, including Harry Frankfurt ("An Alleged Asymmetry Between Actions and Omissions," *Ethics* 104, [1994]: 620–23. I discuss these issues in chapter 4.

28. See chapter 4.

29. See chapter 4.

30. For further discussion, see John Martin Fischer and Mark Ravizza, "Responsibility for Consequences," in *In Harm's Way: Essays in Honor of Joel Feinberg*, ed. Jules Coleman and Allen Buchanan (Cambridge University Press, 1994), 183–208; Fischer and Ravizza, "The Inevitable," *Australasian Journal of Philosophy* 70, no. 4 (December 1993): 388–404; and Fischer and Ravizza *Responsibility and Control*, pp. 92–122.

31. For a more detailed and systematic discussion, see John Martin Fischer, "Frankfurt-Type Examples and Semicompatibilism," in *The Oxford Handbook of Free Will*, ed. R. Kane (Oxford: Oxford University Press, 2002).

32. See chapter 7.

33. I certainly do not think that the employment of examples such as the Frankfurt-type cases is the *only* route to this sort of conclusion. Indeed, I welcome and embrace the employment of other sorts of argumentation to get to the same result. For example, R. Jay Wallace argues from "Strawsonian" considerations about our practices of excusing and justifying behavior to this same conclusion in his monograph *Responsibility and the Moral Sentiments* (Cambridge: Harvard University Press, 1994). For yet other considerations for abandoning the idea that moral responsibility requires regulative control (at least as construed in certain natural ways), see Daniel Dennett, *Elbow Room: The Varieties of Free Will Worth Wanting* (Cambridge: MIT Press, 1984) and *Freedom Evolves* (New York: Viking, 2003). Insofar as Frankfurt-style, Strawson-style, and Dennett-style argumentation all "triangulate" upon the same result, and to the extent that these pathways appear to be genuinely distinct, this

should give us more confidence in the result. The argumentation is mutually reinforcing. I wish to emphasize that thought experiments such as the Frankfurt cases should not be the only important consideration in an overall evaluation of semicompatibilism; one's views about a range of hypothetical cases should fit with one's considered judgments about actual cases, as well as one's general principles. Here, as elsewhere in philosophy, I believe that the Rawlsian idea of seeking a "wide reflective equilibrium" is fruitful.

34. The literature on the Frankfurt-style cases is huge, and I seek to crystallize what I take to be the "moral of the stories" in chapter 10. In chapter 6, I discuss a challenging "dilemmatic" argument against the conclusion I draw from the examples.

35. In "Farewell to the Direct Argument" (*Journal of Philosophy* 6 [2002]: 316–24), David Widerker points out that the direct argument's plausibility depends on certain contentious assumptions about the relationship between causal determinism and regulative control. This may be so, but it does not follow that the direct argument depends on the contention that moral responsibility requires regulative control. Since the direct argument does not depend on the Principle of Alternative Possibilities, it is an interestingly distinct argument (or family of arguments).

36. Peter van Inwagen, "The Incompatibility of Responsibility and Determinism," in *Bowling Green Studies in Applied Philosophy*, Vol. 2, ed. M. Bradie and M. Brand (Bowling Green, Ohio: Bowling Green State University Press, 1980), pp. 30–37; and van Inwagen, *Essay on Free Will*, pp. 182–88.

37. See Fischer and Ravizza, *Responsibility and Control*, pp. 151–69; and "Reply to Stump" (part of a book symposium on *Responsibility and Control*), *Philosophy and Phenomenological Research* 61 (2000): 477–80; and chapters 8 and 9 of this book.

38. I discuss these in "Responsibility and Control"; *Metaphysics of Free Will*, esp. pp. 147–54; and chapters 2 and 6 of this book.

39. See chapter 6 for a discussion of the dialectical situation. For further thoughts on the importance of the semicompatibilistic shift to a new dialectical terrain, and, in particular, the distinctive theoretical role of nonactual possible scenarios in semicompatibilism, see "Responsibility and Manipulation," and John Martin Fischer, "The Free Will Revolution," *Philosophical Explorations*, 8 (2005), 145–156.

40. For a discussion, see chapter 12.

41. Fischer and Ravizza, *Responsibility and Control*, pp. 62–91.

42. Ibid.

43. In *Responsibility and Control*, Mark Ravizza and I suggest the following three "main ingredients" of "taking responsibility": (1) the individual must see that his choices and actions are efficacious in the world; (2) the individual must see himself as a "fair" target of a distinctive set of moral attitudes (what Peter Strawson called the "reactive attitudes") and associated activities, such as praise, blame, reward, and punishment, on the basis of how he exercises this agency in certain contexts; and (3) the beliefs specified in the first two conditions must be based, in an appropriate way, on the individual's evidence for them (pp. 210–14).

It is an implication of this approach that an individual who genuinely does not believe he is a fair target of the relevant attitudes and activities cannot legitimately be held morally responsible insofar as he has not taken responsibility for the kinds of mechanisms that issue in his behavior (and thus he does not act from *his own*, appropriately reasons-sensitive mechanisms). Some have thought this a devastating blow to the theory; not surprisingly, neither I nor my coauthor have been quick to come to this conclusion. But note that, even if one eliminated the second condition, the resulting theory would still have the same structure and fundamental characteristics. It would still be a subjective, historical theory of moral responsibility that is consistent with both causal determinism and causal indeterminism.

Thus I do not think in the end that one ought to discard the entire approach based on worries stemming from the second condition. Of course, the resulting theory would perhaps not employ a central, commonsense notion of "taking responsibility," but it was never our goal to capture and invoke this notion, whatever it is. Rather, our goal was to employ a notion with a specific content as part of an overall theory that has intuitively appealing results.

For helpful critical discussions, see Andrew Eshleman, "Being Is Not Believing: Fischer and Ravizza on Taking Responsibility," *Australasian Journal of Philosophy* 79 (2001): 479–90; and Alfred Mele, "Reactive Attitudes, Reactivity, and Omissions" (part of a book symposium on *Responsibility and Control*), *Philosophy and Phenomenological Research* 61 (2000): 447–52.

44. Sid Vicious of the Sex Pistols had his own version of the song. Gary Oldman gives a particularly striking performance as Sid Vicious in the film *Sid and Nancy*; Oldman sings "My Way" as performed by Sid Vicious. Consider also the chorus to the Sparks' song "When Do I Get to Sing 'My Way'":

> So when do I get to sing "My Way"
> When do I get to feel like Sinatra felt
> When do I get to sing "My Way"
> In heaven or hell . . .
> When do I get to do it my way
> When do I get to feel like Sid Vicious felt
> When do I get to sing "My Way"
> In heaven or hell.
> (http:www.oldielyrics.com)

Perhaps this kind of chorus is why Frank Sinatra allegedly said in 1957 (well before punk rock and the Sparks): "It [rock and roll] is the most brutal, ugly, degenerate, vicious form of expression it has been my misfortune to hear. It is played and written for the most part by cretinous goons, and by means of its almost imbecilic reiteration of . . . dirty lyrics, it manages to be the martial music of every side-burned delinquent on the face of the earth" (Quoted in Annzaunt, "The Sex Pistols," *Alt.Music.Press* 1, no. 1 (1999), available at http://www.geocities.com/SunsetStrip/Gala/4092/first_issue/sexpistols.html).

Of the various versions of "My Way," for what it is worth, that of Sid Vicious, as performed by Oldman in *Sid and Nancy*, is my favorite.

In her wonderful short piece, "Ixnay on the My Way, " Sarah Vowell says:

The only way "My Way" has ever worked is if the person singing it is dumber than the song. Which is why the only successful rendition of it was perpetrated by Sid Vicious. Frank, and Elvis for that matter, was always too complicated, too full of rhythmic freedom to settle into the song's simplistic selfishness. "My Way" pretends to speak up for self-possession and personal vision when really, it only calls forth the temper tantrums of a two-year-old—or perhaps the last words spoken by Eva Braun.

Toward the end of 1996, there were rumors from Belgrade that each night when the government-controlled evening news was on, the townspeople blew whistles or banged on pots and pans so they wouldn't hear the state's lies. Keep that beautiful action in mind when Sinatra's dead and the TVs in your more boring democratic world are playing "My Way." Drown it out. Play something else to the montage in your own heart. Or just turn off the TV sound. Have your stereo cued up and ready to go. (Sarah Vowell, *Take the Cannoli* [New York: Simon and Schuster, 2000], p. 61.)

45. Van Inwagen, *Essay on Free Will*, p. 176.

46. See chapter 4.

47. Here I am quickly presenting material more fully developed and discussed in chapter 4.

48. Peter Strawson, "Freedom and Resentment," *Proceedings of the British Academy* 48 (1962): 187–211. For a selection of papers addressing Strawsonian themes, see Fischer and Ravizza, *Perspectives on Moral Responsibility*.

49. See Watson, "Responsibility and the Limits of Evil."

50. See Richard Posner, *The Problems of Jurisprudence* (Cambridge: Harvard University Press, 1900).

51. See chapter 5. Also see John Martin Fischer, "Free Will, Death, and Immortality: The Role of Narrative," in *Philosophical Papers*, 34 (2005), forthcoming.

52. David Velleman, "Well-Being and Time," *Pacific Philosophical Quarterly* 72 (1991): 48–77; "Narrative Explanation," *Philosophical Review* 112 (2003): 1–26; and Fischer, "Free Will, Death."

53. It is puzzling feature of Susan Wolf's view that she appears to think that the capacity to appreciate the True and the Good and to act in accordance with this appreciation is sufficient for moral responsibility. This would appear to entail that thoroughgoing manipulation, brainwashing, or hypnosis is completely compatible with moral responsibility, although she criticizes what she calls "Real Self" theories (such as Frankfurt's) because they do not rule out thoroughgoing manipulation of precisely this kind (Susan Wolf, *Freedom within Reason* [New York: Oxford University Press, 1990]). The view would be consistent if Wolf believed that the problem with manipulation is that it severs the connection (or eliminates the possibility of a connection) between the agent and the True and Good. But surely this is implausible, as manipulation would seem to threaten moral responsibility even when *achieving* this sort of connection insofar as it precludes the possibility of genuine self-expression.

54. Note that the account of guidance control, including the two elements of mechanism ownership and moderate reasons-responsiveness, are also compatible with causal indeterminism. On this view, then, moral responsibility and our fundamental status as persons are resilient with respect to the truth or falsity of causal determinism *per se*.

55. Ishtiyaque Haji, *Moral Appraisability* (New York: Oxford University Press, 1998), and *Deontic Morality and Control* (New York: Cambridge University Press, 2002).

56. For further discussion, see chapters 10 and 11.

57. See chapter 10.

58. Whether the forward-looking aspect of agency *requires* a range of epistemic alternatives is a vexed issue. For helpful discussion of these matters, see Dana Nelkin, "The Sense of Freedom," in *Freedom and Determinism*, ed. J. Campbell, M. O'Rourke, and D. Shier (Cambridge: MIT Press, 2004), pp. 105–34.

59. Watson, "Responsibility and the Limits of Evil."

60. Martha Klein, *Determinism, Deprivation, and Blameworthiness* (Oxford: Oxford University Press, 1990).

61. Gerald Dworkin, *The Theory and Practice of Autonomy* (Cambridge: Cambridge University Press, 1988), p. ix.

62. Gerald Dworkin says, "Newton said that if he saw further than others it was because he stood on the shoulders of giants. If he had stood on the shoulders of midgets he would also have seen further. Any elevation helps" (*Theory and Practice of Autonomy*, p. xiii).

63. Fischer, *Metaphysics of Free Will*, p. 216.

64. Gary Watson, "Some Worries about Semi-Compatibilism," *Journal of Social Philosophy* 29 (1998): 137.

65. Fischer, *Metaphysics of Free Will*, p. 253.

66. Michael Zimmerman, "Book Review of John Martin Fischer's *The Metaphysics of Free Will: An Essay on Control*," *Canadian Philosophical Reviews* 16 (1996): 344. My view is that the mere existence of flimsy and essentially nugatory alternative possibilities—possibilities that do not affect the way I actually walk down the path—are irrelevant to what I care about in walking down the path. Thus, even if it turned out that there were *no* alternative possibilities (in virtue of the truth of causal determinism or God's foreknowledge), this would not change anything—I would still care about how I actually take the path of life, and I could be held accountable for walking down the path in the way I actually do.

67. These are slightly "cleaned up" and significantly truncated. For the original, see http://www.lyricallysquared.com/viewsong/Sid-Vicious/My-Way/140371.

68. The following describes the night before Robert Harris's execution April 21, 1992:

"The answer, my friend, is blowing in the wind . . ." sang 150 suddenly hopeful opponents of the death penalty as the sun set on San Quentin prison and a surprise legal ruling appeared to temporarily spare Robert Alton Harris.

All this was too much for Claudette Baumgardner, who had come to wait for Harris to die, and to celebrate when he did.

"The answer is the gas chamber!" she bellowed over the soft, impassioned singing of the death penalty opponents standing 20 feet away. (*Los Angeles Times*, April 21, 1992, p. A1)

Here is an excerpt from the account of the execution:

Scanning the faces of 48 witnesses peering through windows just steps away, Harris saw Steve Baker—the father of one of the teen-age murder victims. Harris, his voice inaudible through the thick steel walls, slowly mouthed the words, "I'm sorry." Baker, a San Diego police detective, nodded in return.

Shortly after 6 a.m., a mist of cyanide vapors enveloped the pony-tailed convict. Over the next two minutes, Harris twitched, gave five quick gasps that puffed his flushed cheeks, and slumped forward. Prison doctors said it took him 14 minutes to die.

Harris' relatives and friends—five of whom were witnesses—embraced and turned away as he fell unconscious. Sharon Mankins, the mother of one of his victims, smiled broadly and looked up as if to thank God. Her daughter, Linda Herring, wept in relief. (*Los Angeles Times*, April 22, 1992, pp. A1, 10)

69. Fischer, "Free Will, Death."

70. The January 22, 2005, *Newsday* contained an Associated Press article titled, "Ross Execution Nears, Conn. Residents Mourn":

JEWETT CITY, Conn.—Parents kept their children indoors. Principals locked school doors. For two years, as young women disappeared then turned up dead, Michael Ross terrorized the small rural towns of eastern Connecticut.

Residents were shocked in 1984, when police arrested the 24-year-old insurance salesman for murder, then called him a serial killer and linked him to eight victims.

"He lived right up there on North Main Street," recalls Ronald Jodoin, 70, a life-long Jewett City resident. "The night he got caught, people gathered in the street, all along the sidewalk, and there was this buzz: 'Oh my God, they caught him. It was Michael Ross.' "

Now, with Ross scheduled to die by lethal injection before dawn Wednesday, eastern Connecticut is offering little sympathy for the man who had women looking over their shoulders and whose killing spree changed school rules so children could not take buses to their friends' houses after school.

"No way," said retired Killingly bus driver Paul Boire, 77. "They didn't get off until they got to their own homes."

He was the boogieman, but he was real, someone who smiled his way through the old Yankee mill towns by day, then raped and killed its women at night.

"People wanted to believe it was somebody from out of the area, Boire said.

But with each discovery, the towns kept pointing home: Griswold, Brooklyn, Norwich.

"They began to realize it had to be somebody local," said John Denis, of Jewett City.

There was nothing remarkable about Ross, a scrawny businessman who knocked on their doors, sat in their living rooms and talked about insurance. The Ivy Leaguer had a troubled childhood, but he showed no sign of it.

"It could have been anybody. These are small towns," said Kathy Mitchell of Plainfield. "My husband has (Ross's) picture in his high school yearbook. Killingly High School."

Today, people see a different Ross on television, heavier and not so clean cut in a taped interview with a psychiatrist.

"It's just creepy seeing him now, his long curly hair, his big bug-eyed glasses," said Plainfield hairdresser Debra Smith. She shivered. "I can't stand it."

Ross' execution and the controversy swirling around it has aggravated a wound in the region.

"People are still angry about it today. It was so close to home," said Pat Blain, a former school teacher in Plainfield.

An observant Catholic, she found it hard to sit through Mass recently when her priest read a letter from the bishop condemning the death penalty. At other churches, people walked out.

Blain is active in her church. But this, she says, is different.

"We spent thousands of dollars trying to find him, thousands of dollars to prosecute him and now we're spending thousands of dollars trying to keep him alive?" Denis said. "They were our girls. Most locals don't care about him living."
(http://www.nynewsday.com/news/local/manhattan/nyc-ross0123,0,4829115.
story?coll=nyc-topheadlines-left)

Associated Press writer Stephen Singer wrote of the opposition to the execution in a *Newsday* article of January 28, 2005:

SOMERS, Conn.—The scheduled execution of serial killer Michael Ross galvanized opposition to Connecticut's death penalty.

An alliance of Roman Catholic church leaders, civil libertarians, liberal activists and others sprung into action in the last several months to fight the first execution in New England in 45 years.

Hundreds of opponents of Connecticut's capital punishment—many coming from six states—planned a vigil outside Osborn Correctional Institution late Friday in advance of the execution set for 2:01 a.m. Saturday. The group intended to march to the driveway of the prison just after midnight.

Earlier in the evening, about 75 death penalty opponents gathered for meditation and prayer at Somers Congregational United Church of Christ, only a few miles from the execution site.

At an interreligious service, Rabbi Jeffrey Glickman of Temple Beth Hillel in South Windsor told the crowd to take an active role in opposing capital punishment.

"Do not sit idly while others bleed," he said. "Whenever there is a death penalty on the books, there's blood on everyone's hands. As a rabbi, and as one who has studied books, I don't know how to wash off that blood."

Arthur Laffin's brother, Paul, was stabbed to death in Hartford in 1999, but the killing didn't make him support executions.

"I oppose the death penalty because, ultimately, it violates God's command that 'Thou shalt not kill.' The execution of Michael Ross is a cause of great sorrow," said Laffin, who was among the protesters gathered at the church.

Davida Foy Crabtree, president of the United Church of Christ of Connecticut, also addressed the crowd.

"We're full of deep sorrow for our state and its soul," she said. "From this moment forward, let a new hope and a new possibility take up residence in this land of steady habits. We ask forgiveness and mercy for our state."

Before heading to the gates of the prison, protest organizers huddled around a radio at the church waiting to hear news from the U.S. Supreme Court, which allowed the execution to go forward Friday night by lifting a stay of execution.

"We truly wish we didn't have to do this," said the church pastor, Barry Cass.

The anti–death penalty group includes numerous organizations known for promoting nonviolent and human rights causes. The American Friends Service Committee, Amnesty International, the Connecticut Civil Liberties Union, the Connecticut Coalition for Peace and Justice and the New Haven Green Party are among the organizations that have lobbied against capital punishment and protested state efforts to execute Ross.

The Connecticut Catholic Conference has helped organize opposition to Ross' execution, staking its position on the church's stance against all forms of killing.

Opponents to the death penalty, who have organized around the motto, "Do not kill in my name," cite numerous arguments why the state should be stripped of the power to kill. The death penalty denies an individual's civil liberties, fails as a deterrent to crime, is costlier due to legal appeals than life in prison and risks killing innocent people, they say.

For weeks, as Ross's execution neared, opponents staged prayers and vigils and lobbied the General Assembly to repeal Connecticut's death penalty law (http://www.newsday.com/news/local/wire/connecticut/ny-bc-ct—rossexecution-pro0128jan28,0,7733386.story?coll=ny-region-apconnecticut).

Michael Ross was executed in Connecticut on Friday, May 13, 2005. For several years Ross had maintained that he wished to be executed on the grounds that his continued existence in prison and the litigation surrounding him was causing undue suffering to the families and friends of his victims. He thus refrained from personally initiating any legal actions to block his execution; indeed, he wrote to the governor of Connecticut to request that his execution not be delayed. Despite efforts by his father and various others to postpone the application of the death penalty, his wish was finally granted.

2
RESPONSIBILITY AND ALTERNATIVE POSSIBILITIES

There is a set of challenges to the intuitive and natural picture of ourselves as having a certain sort of control. This sort of control implies that we have various genuinely open pathways branching into the future. The basic problem with this picture is that it may require us to have an implausible power over the past or natural laws. Thus, it is not clear that we do in fact have the sort of control that implies alternative possibilities. And if moral responsibility and personhood require this sort of control, it is not clear that we can legitimately hold each other morally responsible for our behavior and indeed conceive of each other as persons. Because of the power and persistence of the skeptical challenges to our having the sort of control that involves alternative possibilities, perhaps it is advisable to ask whether we really *do* require this sort of control, after all.

Frankfurt-Type Examples

Imagine, if you will, that Black is a quite nifty (and even generally nice) neurosurgeon. But in performing an operation on Jones to remove a brain tumor, Black inserts a mechanism into Jones's brain which enables Black to monitor and control Jones's activities. Jones, meanwhile, knows nothing of this. Black exercises this control through a sophisticated computer which he has programmed so that, among other things, it monitors Jones's voting behavior. If Jones were to show any inclination to vote for Bush, then the computer, through the mechanism in Jones's brain, intervenes to assure that he actually decides to vote for Clinton and does so vote. But if Jones decides on his own to vote for Clinton, the computer does nothing but continue to monitor—without affecting—the goings-on in Jones's head.

Suppose that Jones decides to vote for Clinton on his own, just as he would have if Black had not inserted the mechanism into his head. It seems, upon first thinking about this case, that Jones can be held morally responsible for his choice and act of voting for Clinton, although he could not have chosen otherwise and he could not have done otherwise.[1] That is to say, Jones is rationally accessible to—an appropriate candidate for—the reactive attitudes on the basis of his choice and his action. Of course, it need not follow that we ought to praise him (or blame him); rather, he is an *appropriate candidate* for such attitudes—these attitudes are not ruled out (as they would be in the context of direct manipulation of the brain or certain sorts of coercion, and so forth).

Clearly, the Frankfurt-type example just presented is an unusual case. We are fairly certain that "counterfactual interveners" such as Black generally do not exist. And yet an unusual case can point us to something very mundane—but also very important. It can cause us to focus with increased clarity on what makes us morally responsible in quite ordinary cases.

It seems to me that the conclusion tentatively adopted above is correct: moral responsibility does not require the sort of control which involves the existence of genuinely open alternative possibilities. But this is not to say that moral responsibility does *not* require control of *any* sort. Indeed, it is important to distinguish two sorts of control, and it will emerge that moral responsibility for actions is associated with one (but not the other) kind of control.[2]

Let us suppose that I am driving my car. It is functioning well, and I wish to make a right turn. As a result of my intention to turn right, I signal, turn the steering wheel, and carefully guide the car to the right. Further, I here assume that I was able to form the intention not to turn the car to the right but to turn the car to the left instead. Also, I assume that had I formed such an intention, I would have turned the steering wheel to the left and the car would have gone to the left. In this ordinary case, I guide the car to the right, but I could have guided it to the left. I control the car, and also I have a certain sort of control *over* the car's movements. Insofar as I actually guide the car in a certain way, I shall say that I have "guidance control." Further, insofar as I have the power to guide the car in a different way, I shall say that I have "regulative control." (Of course, here I am not making any special assumptions, such as that causal determinism obtains or God exists.)

To develop these notions of control (and their relationship), imagine a second case. In this analogue of the Frankfurt-type case presented above, I again guide my car in the normal way to the right. The car's steering apparatus *works properly* when I steer the car to the right. But unknown to me, the car's steering apparatus is broken in such a way that, if I were to try to turn it in some other direction, the car would veer off to the right in precisely the way it actually goes to the right.[3] Since I actually do not try to do anything but turn to the right, the apparatus functions normally, and the car's movements are precisely as they would have been if there had been no problem with the steering apparatus. Indeed, my guidance of the car to the right is precisely the same in this case and the first car case.

Here, as in the first car case, it appears that I control the movement of the car in the sense of guiding it (in a certain way) to the right. Thus, I have guidance control of the car. But I cannot cause it to go anywhere other than where it actually goes. Thus, I lack regulative control of the car. I control the car, but I do not have control *over* the car (or the car's movements). Generally, we assume that guidance control and regulative control go together. But this Frankfurt-type case shows how they can at least in principle pull apart: one can have guidance control without regulative control. That is, one can have a certain sort of control without having the sort of control that involves alternative possibilities.

The Frankfurt-type cases, unusual as they are, may well point us to something as significant as it is mundane. When we are morally responsible for our actions, we *do* possess a kind of control. So the traditional assumption of the association of moral responsibility (and personhood) with control is quite correct. But it need not be the sort of control that involves alternative possibilities. The suggestion, derived from the Frankfurt-type cases, is that the sort of control necessarily associated with moral responsibility for action is *guidance control*. Whereas we may intuitively suppose that regulative control always comes with guidance control, it is not, at a deep level, regulative control that grounds moral responsibility.

I have not sought to give a precise (or even very informative) account of the two sorts of control. Rather, I have relied on the intuitive idea that there is a sense of control in which I control the car when I guide it (in the normal way) to the right. Further, I have employed the Frankfurt-type example to argue that this sense of control need not involve any alternative possibilities. Then, I have simply contrasted this sort of control with a kind of control which does indeed require alternative possibilities. Below, I shall attempt to say more about the first sort of control—guidance control—but for now it will suffice simply to have in mind a fairly intuitive distinction between the two sorts of control.

Above I pointed out that, because of the power and persistence of the skeptical challenges to the idea that we have the sort of control that involves alternative possibilities, it would be desirable if moral responsibility did *not* require this sort of control. It is the beauty of the Frankfurt-type examples that they suggest precisely that moral responsibility for our actions does not require the sort of control that involves alternative possibilities—regulative control. If this is indeed so, then a line of argument opens that has at least some chance of answering the skeptic's challenges to our moral responsibility and personhood.

The Flicker-of-Freedom Strategy

The Strategy and Its Significance

A lot, then, is at stake in evaluating the Frankfurt-type examples. They suggest that (perhaps in conjunction with the satisfaction of certain epistemic conditions) the presence of guidance control is sufficient for moral responsibility. They thus suggest a way of meeting the skeptic's challenge, because this challenge is based precisely on the assumption that alternative possibilities are required for moral responsibility and personhood.

But exactly because of the beauty and power of the idea that guidance control is the "freedom-relevant" condition sufficient for moral responsibility for action, we should not be too hasty in the analysis of Frankfurt-type cases.[4] The Frankfurt-type cases seem at first to involve no alternative possibilities. But upon closer inspection it can be seen that although they do not involve alternative possibilities of the normal kind, they nevertheless may involve *some* alternative possibilities. That is to say, although the counterfactual interveners eliminate most alternative possibilities, arguably they do not eliminate all such possibilities: even in the Frankfurt-type cases, there seems to be a "flicker of freedom." Thus, there is an opening to argue that these alternative possibilities (the flickers of freedom) *must* be present, even in the Frankfurt-type cases, for there to be moral responsibility.

To motivate the flicker-of-freedom strategy for responding to the Frankfurt-type cases, let us go back to the second car case presented above. I pointed out that, in virtue of the malfunctioning steering apparatus, it is plausible to say that I had guidance control but not regulative control: although I controlled the car, I didn't have control over its movements. But certainly I possessed *some* alternative possibilities: for example, apart from any special assumptions, there is no reason to deny that I could have formed the intention to guide the car in some direction *other* than right, and I could have attempted to steer the car in this other direction, and so forth. Thus, I had *some* alternative possibilities, even if I could not change the path of the car.

Now this sort of worry is part of the motivation for the elaborate setup of the case of Jones and Black. In this case, should Jones show any indication that he is about to choose to vote for Bush, Black will intervene to assure that he does not even *choose* to vote for Bush. Thus, in contrast to the car case, in the case of Jones and Black, regulative control over *choice* and the formation of intention is also absent.

But, still, one might somehow be unsatisfied with the claim that there are *no* alternative possibilities in the case of Jones and Black. After all, consider again part of the description of the case: "If Jones were to show any inclination to vote for Bush, then the computer, through the mechanism in Jones's brain, intervenes to assure that he actually decides to vote for Clinton and does so vote." This suggests that, at the very least, Jones must be taken to have the power to "show an inclination" to vote for Bush (or perhaps to choose to vote for Bush). But then here is the flicker of freedom! Exiguous as it may be, here is the space—the elbow room—that must exist if we are legitimately to be held morally responsible for what we do.

Before developing the flicker strategy in greater detail, I pause to ask why it is so important to isolate the flicker of freedom. Recall that the skeptic about our moral responsibility urges that, for all we know, we do not have *any* alternative possibilities. More specifically, it is evident that, if the incompatibilistic arguments proposed by such philosophers as Wiggins, Ginet, and van Inwagen are sound, then they show that (if causal determinism obtains or a certain sort of God exists) we have *no* alternative possibilities of *any* sort. Now suppose that there are flickers of freedom, even in Frankfurt-type cases. Then, even if these cases show that we can be morally responsible for what we do even in contexts in which we do not have alternative possibilities as they are traditionally conceived, they could *not* be employed straightforwardly to establish that we can be morally responsible for our actions in a causally deterministic world (or a world in which God exists). For in such a world there cannot be even a flicker of freedom (if the skeptical arguments are correct). Of course, causal determinism would extinguish not just a prairie fire of freedom, but also the tiniest flicker.

Four Versions of the Strategy

Having laid out the basic idea behind the flicker-of-freedom strategy and indicated what is at issue, I turn to the specific development of various versions of this strategy. In the above section I began to develop the first version of the strategy. Basically, on this approach we keep tracing backward in the relevant alternative sequences until we find a flicker of freedom.

Return to the case of Jones and Black. In this case, Jones actually deliberates in the normal fashion, chooses to vote for Clinton, and does so on his own. Further, he cannot choose to do otherwise; nor can he do otherwise. But let us think about a possible alternative sequence in which he *begins* to choose to vote for Bush. If this should occur, Black would immediately intervene, but at least Jones *begins* to choose to vote for Bush and thus Jones can be said to have at least this power— the power to initiate (albeit not complete) the choice to do otherwise. Perhaps, then, this is the flicker of freedom.

But now it seems we can imagine another case in which Jones has a propensity to show some *sign* which reliably indicates his voting behavior prior even to his beginning to make a choice or form an intention. Suppose, that is, that Jones would blush red (or show some other sign that is readable by Black—perhaps a furrowed brow or raised eyebrow or even a complex and arcane neurophysiological pattern) prior to initiating any process of decision making if and only if he were about to choose to vote for Bush. If Jones is like this, then Black could (by reading the sign) prevent him from even *beginning* to make the relevant choice or decision.[5]

But again a flicker emerges, for even here Jones has the power to show the relevant sign—to blush red or display the complex neurophysiological pattern, and so forth. And it is hard to see how a Frankfurt-type example could be constructed that would have absolutely no such flicker. For a Frankfurt-type case must have an alternative sequence in which intervention is triggered in some fashion or other, and it is hard to see how to avoid the idea that the triggering event can serve as the flicker of freedom. Thus, it appears that no matter how sophisticated the Frankfurt-type example, if one traces backward (from the event caused by the agent and toward the agent, as it were) far enough, one will find a flicker of freedom.[6]

Another flicker strategy involves tracing precisely the opposite way along the alternative sequence. On this approach, one proceeds forward (from the agent and toward the event caused by the agent) until one gets to the terminal point, and this constitutes the flicker of freedom. Here let us adopt the assumption that when an agent performs an action, he causes some concrete event to occur. I further suppose that when an agent is morally responsible for performing a particular act, he is morally responsible for causing the relevant concrete event to occur.

Crucial to this version of the flicker-of-freedom strategy is the adoption of some sort of essentialist principle of event-individuation.[7] On the strongest version of this principle, all the actual causal antecedents of a particular event are essential to it; thus, if a given event *e* occurs in the actual world, then any possible event with any different causal antecedent would not be identical to *e*. For simplicity's sake, I start with this strong version of the essentialist principle.

Now consider again the original example of Jones and Black. Recall that Jones actually chooses to vote for Clinton and does vote for Clinton as a result of the ordinary sort of sequence. Imagine, however, contrary to fact, that Jones begins to show an inclination not to choose to vote for Clinton and this triggers the intervention by Black (and the subsequent choice to vote for Clinton and the vote for Clinton). Under these hypothetical circumstances, Jones would indeed have voted for Clinton. But, given the essentialist principle of event-individuation, Jones would have caused a *different* particular event of voting for Clinton from the actual voting event. That is, as things actually went, the neurologist Black played no role in the causal background of the voting event, whereas Black does play such a role in the alternative scenario; thus, on the essentialist principle, the actual particular event cannot be identical to the hypothetical event (in the alternative sequence). So it is *not* the case that Jones could not have caused another particular event to occur. This, then, is the flicker of freedom. Although Jones cannot bring it about that he doesn't vote for Clinton, he does possess the power to bring about a different event-particular. And insofar as responsibility for action involves responsibility for bringing about a particular concrete event, responsibility for action involves alternative possibilities, even in the Frankfurt-type cases.

Note that strictly speaking the strong version of the essentialist principle of event-individuation is not required by the argument. A weaker version of the principle that specifies that certain *salient* or *significant* causal antecedents are essential to event-particulars would presumably also yield the same results, since whether or not an agent such as Black intercedes in the way envisaged is, on any plausible view, a salient or significant feature of the causal background of a particular event.

On this version of the flicker strategy, it is crucial to distinguish the notions of bringing about a particular concrete event and bringing about an event of a certain general type. Although Jones cannot avoid bringing about an event of the general type, "voting for Clinton," he can avoid bringing about the particular event he actually causes to occur. This suggests that the claim that the Frankfurt-type examples show that an agent can be held morally responsible for bringing about an event even though he cannot avoid bringing it about gains some illicit support from a failure to distinguish carefully between bringing about a concrete particular event and bringing about an event of a certain general sort.[8]

There is another set of considerations that issues in a distinctive version of the flicker-of-freedom strategy. These considerations are associated with the 'libertarian' picture of agency. Of course, there are various different libertarian accounts of agency, and I cannot go into the details here. But I shall sketch enough of the basic intuitions of the libertarian to motivate this version of the flicker approach.

Here is one (although certainly not the only) libertarian picture of agency. On this model, what distinguishes an action from a mere event is that an action is preceded by a *volition*. But of course this claim in itself need not lead to the libertarian view. What is added is that the volition must be 'agent-caused,' where agent-causation is a special sort of causation *not* reducible to event-causation. It is assumed that when an agent causes a volition via this special sort of causation— agent-causation—nothing causes the agent to cause the volition. That is, the agent's agent-causing the volition is incompatible with the agent's being caused by some external factor to cause the volition.

Suppose, for the sake of argument, that one adopts this picture of agency. Now the Frankfurt-type case of Jones and Black can be analyzed as follows. Insofar as Jones deliberates, chooses and acts in the normal way, we can suppose that Jones agent-causes his volition to vote for Clinton. Now think about the alternative sequence. It is hypothesized that should Jones begin to show any inclination to choose to vote for Bush, Black would intercede and neurologically ensure that he choose to vote for Clinton. Under such a circumstance we can (again, for the sake of argument) grant that Jones would have some sort of mental state consisting in a choice or decision to vote for Clinton, but he clearly would *not* have agent-caused a volition to vote for Clinton (insofar as his volition is caused by some external entity).

Thus, according to this libertarian analysis, Jones possesses the power to refrain from agent-causing his volition to vote for Clinton. Although he does not have the power to agent-cause a volition to vote for Bush, he *does* have a flicker of freedom: although he actually agent-causes a volition to vote for Clinton, he has it in his power not to agent-cause this sort of volition. On this approach, it is not envisaged that Jones must have the power to act otherwise, or even form a different sort of volition, if he is to be deemed morally responsible for what he does. Rather, it is supposed that Jones must at least have the power not to form the sort of volition he actually forms. And it is alleged that Jones has precisely this power, even in the Frankfurt-type case.[9]

I do not believe that one needs to posit volitions or even agent-causation to get the sort of results just sketched. It may be simply that one believes that mental events cannot, as a conceptual matter, be caused in the way envisaged in the alternative scenario of the case of Jones and Black. If one holds this belief, one would simply deny that in the alternative scenario Jones genuinely chooses (or wills) to vote for Clinton. Thus, again, one can say that, although Jones does not have the power to choose otherwise, he does in fact have the power to refrain from choosing (or willing) to vote for Clinton. Here, again, is the flicker of freedom.

All of the above three flicker-of-freedom strategies start by taking a somewhat careful view of the alternative sequence and thereby generate an alternative possibility that might previously have gone unnoticed. The final strategy starts with a more careful look at the actual sequence. More specifically, it invites us to be more careful in our specification of *what* the agent is (putatively) morally responsible for. Seeing exactly what we hold the agent responsible for, it is alleged, will help us to see that there are indeed alternative possibilities, even in the Frankfurt-type cases.

Return to the original case of Jones and Black. Someone might claim that what we "really" hold Jones morally responsible for is *not* "voting for Clinton," or even "choosing or willing to vote for Clinton." Rather, what we hold Jones morally responsible for is something like "voting for Clinton on his own," or "choosing to vote for Clinton on his own," where we mean by "on his own," at least in part, "not as a result of some weird intervention such as that of Black."[10] But clearly if this is indeed what we hold Jones morally responsible for, then there are alternative possibilities. For, obviously, in the alternative sequence Jones would not be choosing or voting "on his own."

These strategies, although different in interesting respects, have something important in common. They all suggest that the Frankfurt-type examples cannot be employed (at least straightforwardly) to argue that moral responsibility need not require alternative possibilities. Indeed, they suggest that whereas the initial impression from considering a Frankfurt-type case is that there are no alternative possibilities, in fact one can see that there *are* such possibilities if one scratches below the surface just a bit. And although they may not be quite the alternatives traditionally envisaged, they are alternative possibilities nevertheless—and just the sort that would be ruled out (if the skeptical arguments are sound) by causal determinism or God's foreknowledge.

Response

Despite the undeniable appeal of the flicker-of-freedom strategy, I believe that ultimately it is not convincing. I do not have a decisive argument against it, but of course such arguments are few and far between in these realms. I wish now to develop a set of considerations which lead me to reject the flicker-of-freedom approach. The kind of argument I shall sketch will apply, *mutatis mutandis*, to all the versions of the flicker strategy presented above, but it will be most convenient to begin with the second version (and then apply the analysis to the other versions).

Recall the second version of the flicker-of-freedom strategy. On this approach, it is argued that (in the original Jones and Black case) Jones does indeed have an alternative possibility insofar as he has the power to bring about a *particular event different from* the actual event he brings about. I am willing to grant to the flicker theorist the claim that there exists an alternative possibility here, but my basic worry is that this alternative possibility is not sufficiently *robust* to ground the relevant attributions of moral responsibility. Put in other words, even if the possible event at the terminus of the alternative sequence (in the case of Jones and Black) is indeed an alternative possibility, it is highly implausible to suppose that it is *in virtue* of the existence of such an alternative possibility that Jones is morally responsible for what he does. I suggest that it is not enough for the flicker theorist to analyze the relevant range of cases in such a way as to identify an alternative possibility. Although this is surely a first step, it is not enough to establish the flicker-of-freedom view, because what needs also to be shown is that these alternative possibilities *play a certain role* in the appropriate understanding of the cases. That is, it needs to be shown that these alternative possibilities *ground* our attributions of moral responsibility. And this is what I find puzzling and implausible.

Briefly think about the basic picture of control that underlies the alternative-possibilities view (and thus the flicker-of-freedom strategy). Here the future is a garden of forking paths. At various points in life, it is envisaged that there are various paths that branch into the future, and one can determine which of these genuinely open pathways becomes the actual path of the future. The existence of *various* genuinely open pathways is alleged to be *crucial* to the idea that one has *control* of the relevant kind. But if this is so, I suggest that it would be very puzzling and unnatural to suppose that it is the existence of various alternative pathways along which one does *not* act freely that shows that one has control of the kind in question. How exactly *could* the existence of various alternative pathways along which the agent does *not* act freely render it true that the agent has the relevant kind of control (regulative control)? And notice that this is precisely the situation in the Frankfurt-type cases. In particular, note that even if it is granted that the terminus of the alternative sequence in the case of Jones and Black is on an event different from the actual event of Jones's voting for Clinton, it also is evident that Jones would not be *freely* voting for Clinton in the alternative sequence.

The point might be put as follows. The proponent of the idea that regulative control is required for moral responsibility insists that there can be no moral responsibility if there is but one path leading into the future: to get the crucial kind of control, we must add various alternative possibilities. Now it seems that the flicker theorist must claim that the addition of the sort of alternative possibility he has identified would transform a case of lack of responsibility into one of responsibility. But this seems mysterious in the extreme: how can adding an alternative scenario (or perhaps even a set of them) in which Jones does not *freely* vote for Clinton make it true that he actually possesses the sort of control required for him to be morally responsible for his voting for Clinton? This might appear to involve a kind of *alchemy*, and it is just as incredible.

Consider, also, an analogy with epistemology. Certain accounts of knowledge imply that an agent knows that *p* only if he can distinguish a class of situations in which *p* obtains from a contrasting class in which *p* does not obtain. On this approach, knowledge requires a certain kind of *discriminatory capacity*; this model is clearly analogous with the view that moral responsibility requires regulative control. More specifically, on this approach to knowledge, an agent knows that *p* only if there exists a set of alternatives to the actual world in which the agent's beliefs line up with states of the world in the right way. What would be highly implausible would be to suppose that what transforms some case of lack of knowledge into a case of knowledge would be the existence of a range of alternative scenarios in which the agent *gets it wrong!*

Suppose, for example, that we are assessing the claim that a certain individual, Schmidtz, knows that there is a barn in front of him. Of course, some epistemologists urge that it is necessary that Schmidtz be able to distinguish the actual situation (in which there is a barn in front of him) from a class of relevant alternative scenarios (in which there is no barn in front of him), in order for Schmidtz to know that there is a barn in front of him. But it would surely be bizarre and unattractive to point to a set of relevant alternative scenarios in which Schmidtz comes to a *false* belief about states of the world and then to claim that it is in virtue of *this* set of alternatives that Schmidtz actually possesses knowledge! And arguably it is not much more plausible to suggest that it is in virtue of a set of alternative possibilities in which Jones does *not* act freely that he actually can be held morally responsible for his behavior. How could adding a set of alternatives in which Jones does *not* act freely make it the case that he *actually* acts freely?

The point can be put somewhat differently. On the traditional alternative-possibilities picture, it is envisaged that an agent has a choice between two (or more) scenarios *of a certain sort*. In one scenario, he deliberates and forms an intention to perform an act of a certain kind and then carries out this intention in an appropriate way. In at least one other possible scenario, he deliberates and forms an intention to perform a different kind of act (or no act at all) and carries out this intention in an appropriate way. This is what is involved in having robust alternative possibilities, and certainly this is the natural way to think about the sort of alternatives that allegedly ground moral responsibility.

But it is evident that in Frankfurt-type examples these conditions do *not* obtain: the alternative scenarios are not of the requisite kind. In the case of Jones and Black, in the alternative scenario Jones does *not* deliberate and then form an intention to vote for Bush (and then act on this intention in an appropriate way). Thus, even if there is a flicker of freedom in these cases, it does not seem to be *robust* enough to ground moral-responsibility ascriptions. The traditional alternative-possibilities model links moral-responsibility with *control* of a certain kind (regulative control); but for this kind of control to exist, surely the alternative possibilities that are invoked to ground the attributions of responsibility must be more robust.[11]

I have begun my critical discussion of the flicker-of-freedom strategy by focusing on the second version of the strategy. But I believe parallel considerations apply to the other versions. Consider now the third version (the "libertarian version"). On this approach, it is required that an agent have the power not to cause the volition he actually causes, in order for him to be morally responsible. And, as pointed out above, it is indeed true that in the case of Jones and Black, Jones has the power not to cause his volition to vote for Clinton (given the libertarian assumptions about agency). But note further that even so, in the alternative sequence Jones does *not* form an intention to refrain from causing the volition in question (the volition to vote for Clinton) and then proceed to carry out this intention in an appropriate way. Again, it may be granted that Jones has the power not to cause a volition to vote for Clinton. But in not causing such a volition he would of course not be acting freely; because of the nature of Black's intervention, it would *not* be true that Jones freely refrains from causing the volition to vote for Clinton. Thus, even if there is some sort of flicker of freedom here, it does not seem capable of playing the requisite role in grounding ascriptions of moral responsibility—it does not seem sufficiently robust.

Consider, also, the flicker strategy that insists that what Jones is "really" morally responsible for is voting for Clinton on his own (or perhaps choosing on his own to vote for Clinton). If this is the appropriate specification of the content of Jones's moral responsibility, then evidently there is an alternative possibility. But note again that this alternative possibility lacks robustness. After all, in the alternative sequence Jones does not freely refrain from voting for Clinton on his own. Indeed, he does *not* freely behave in any fashion, and he certainly does not deliberate about and choose the possibility of not voting for Clinton on his own (but rather as a result of Black's intervention). Thus, again, it seems to me that the alternative possibilities so nicely generated by the strategy of redescription of the content of moral responsibility lack robustness.

I now turn to a response on behalf of the flicker theorist. Thinking about this response will lead us back to the issues raised by the first version of the flicker-of-freedom strategy. Let us think carefully about the alternative sequence in the original Jones and Black case. In discussing the second version of the flicker strategy, I pointed out that in the alternative sequence Jones does *not* freely *vote for Clinton*. Thus, I suggested that the alternative possibility here envisaged is not sufficiently robust. But the flicker theorist may respond that nevertheless there is at least the following thing in the alternative sequence which is freely done: Jones begins to initiate the process of making a choice to vote for Bush. (Of course, this process is then cut off before it can be completed.) So we seem to have isolated at least *something* in the alternative sequence that can plausibly be thought to be freely done and thus may be able to ground the ascriptions of responsibility. This move can be made to help bolster the second, third and fourth versions of the flicker strategy, or it can be taken to indicate that the most "basic" version of the flicker strategy is the first: it does not really matter for my purposes.

The problem with this move—which finds something, let us call it an "initiating action," which can be said to be freely done and which thus grounds the ascription of responsibility—is that it seems that we can systematically reconstruct the Frankfurt-type examples (as discussed above) so that there is some sign or indication that would *precede* the initiating action and could be read by the counterfactual intervener (the analogue of Black). Further, and this is the important point here, the evincing of such a sign is not even an action and is certainly not plausibly thought to be robust enough to ground responsibility ascriptions. Again, the problem seems to be the lack of robustness of the relevant alternative possibilities.

To explain: Suppose we again consider the version of the Jones and Black case in which Black can be alerted to Jones's future inclination to vote for Bush by the presence of some involuntary sign, such as a blush or twitch or even a complex neurophysiological pattern. So if Jones were (say) to blush red, then Black could intervene prior to Jones's doing *anything* freely and ensure that Jones indeed votes for Clinton. Here the triggering event (that is, what would trigger the intervention of Black) is *not* any sort of initiating action, and thus cannot be said to be freely done. Again, precisely as above, this sort of triggering event appears to be not sufficiently robust to ground responsibility ascriptions.

A bit more specifically, here is the problem. On the current version of the flicker theory, the claim, first, is that if there is *no* alternative possibility, there cannot be the sort of control that grounds moral responsibility. Thus, some sort of alternative possibility must be added to what happens in the actual sequence to get the crucial kind of control. And, further, the claim is that precisely this sort of possibility is present in the Frankfurt-type case of Jones and Black: a certain sort of triggering event (a blush, a twitch, and so forth). But now, in response, it is reasonable to ask how the addition of an alternative possibility of *this sort*—a triggering event that is not even an *initiating action*—could possibly transform a case of no control (of the relevant kind) into a case of control. How exactly does the addition of an alternative possibility, which is (say) an involuntary blush or twitch, transform a case of lack of control into a case of control? The thought that the presence of this sort of etiolated alternative can make *this sort of difference* is puzzling.

If, then, the first version of the flicker strategy is the basic version, then the basic response is as follows. In principle, there is no decisive objection to specifying all Frankfurt-type examples so that they are like the second version of the case of Jones and Black (in which there is a sign that would give away the future choices). That is, they are all to involve some involuntary sign that would precede any voluntary initiating action in the alternative sequence. But the alternative possibilities in such examples are mere triggering events that are *not* voluntary initiating actions and thus not sufficiently robust to ground the ascription of moral responsibility.

But even now the flicker-of-freedom theorist has available one final move. The flicker theorist may not dispute the claim that the alternative possibilities in the Frankfurt-type examples are insufficiently robust to *ground* our ascriptions of moral responsibility. That is to say, he may not wish to argue that the existence of such alternatives in themselves supports our intuitive judgments that individuals are morally responsible for what they do. But he nevertheless may insist that alternative possibilities *must be present*, whenever an agent is legitimately held morally responsible for what he does.

To pursue this line of thought, note that a flicker theorist can point out that even the fanciest, most sophisticated Frankfurt-type example contains *some* alternative possibility, no matter how exiguous. And, indeed, it is hard to imagine how to construct any kind of non-question-begging example in which it is clear both that there are absolutely no such possibilities and the agent is morally responsible for his action. Thus, we have as yet no decisive reason to abandon the claim that moral responsibility requires the *presence* of alternative possibilities, even if the presence of these alternatives is not in itself what drives our judgments about moral responsibility. Further, it is important to note that, if the skeptical arguments mentioned above are correct, causal determinism or God's existence rules out the presence of *any* sort of alternative possibility (even one that does not in itself ground the pertinent responsibility ascriptions).

The flicker theorist's move could be formulated as follows. Even if the alternative possibilities are not what explain our intuitions about moral responsibility, nevertheless there may be some *other factor* which *both* grounds our responsibility ascriptions and *also* entails that there be some alternative possibility (thin and weak as it may be). And if this were so, then moral responsibility would require alternative possibilities, even thin and weak ones.

I do not see any decisive way to rebut the current move by the flicker theorist, but, again, I do not find it attractive. Specifically, I do not see why one would think that there is a factor of the sort described. What could it be? I grant that there is "conceptual space" for the claim that there is a factor of the sort in question, that is, one whose presence in itself grounds our ascriptions of moral responsibility and also entails the existence of alternative possibilities, but it is implausible to me that there really is such a factor. Further, rumination about cases (actual and hypothetical) does not issue in any inclination for me to posit such a factor; that is, simply thinking about cases and seeking to understand the relationship between responsibility and alternative possibilities, I find I have no inclination whatsoever to posit such a factor.

Now of course one might say that there indeed must be such a factor: the falsity of causal determinism or the nonexistence of God. And, again, there is certainly conceptual space for this position. But I do not see *why* one would say this, based simply on consideration of the relationship between moral responsibility and alternative possibilities in a wide range of actual and hypothetical cases. Of course, one could wish to invoke the falsity of causal determinism or the nonexistence of God as the crucial factor because one is *independently* (and prior to a neutral consideration of a range of cases pertaining to the relationship between responsibility and alternative possibilities) committed to the notion that causal determinism (or God's existence) rules out moral responsibility. But, apart from this sort of *prior commitment*, I do not see why one would wish to posit the necessity of the sort of factor under consideration here for moral responsibility.

I believe that the arguments developed above against the flicker-of-freedom strategy are extremely plausible, albeit not ineluctable. I maintain that the arguments come very close to establishing that alternative possibilities are not required for moral responsibility. I am convinced, even in the absence of a knockdown argument, that the alternative possibilities posited by the flicker theorist are simply not sufficiently robust to ground our ascriptions of moral responsibility. Further, I do not see any strong reason to suppose that such alternative possibilities must be present whenever there is moral responsibility. Thus, I conclude that moral responsibility does not require regulative control.

Causal Determinism, God's Existence, and Moral Responsibility

It does not however follow straightforwardly that guidance control is the freedom-relevant condition sufficient for moral responsibility. Note, to begin, that guidance control seems entirely compatible with causal determinism: when I guide my properly functioning automobile to the right in the standard case, my exercise of control does not appear to depend on the falsity of causal determinism. But now it emerges that it is one thing to say that regulative control is not necessary for moral responsibility, and quite another to say that guidance control is sufficient for moral responsibility. Indeed, someone could grant that the sort of control that involves alternative possibilities is not required for moral responsibility but still insist that the lack of causal determinism (or perhaps the nonexistence of God) is *also* required.

For certain incompatibilists about causal determinism and moral responsibility, the reason why determinism threatens moral responsibility is that it rules out alternative possibilities. For such an incompatibilist the concession that moral responsibility need not require regulative control is fatal. But another sort of incompatibilist might grant that an agent can be morally responsible for an action although he has no alternative possibility. For this sort of incompatibilist, the reason why determinism threatens responsibility *need not* be that it undermines alternative possibilities.

To see that there is at least dialectical space for this kind of position, consider again the example of Jones and the counterfactual intervener, Black. Suppose that the world actually proceeds via a sequence that is *not* causally deterministic; that is, although there are some causal laws, not all events are causally determined.

Suppose further that the world proceeds in just the sort of way in which a libertarian says it must if agents are to be morally responsible for what they do. Although an agent's desires and purposes explain his choices and acts, they do not causally necessitate them; the agent freely "identifies" with some of his desires, where this identification is not causally necessitated. Perhaps the identification is explained in terms of agent-causation, although this notion need not be invoked. In this sort of world, one in which human choices and actions are not causally necessitated, the libertarian can certainly say that Jones is morally responsible for voting for Clinton, even if Black *would have* brought it about that Jones vote for Clinton, if Jones had shown signs of deciding to vote for Bush. That is, nothing about Frankfurt's example *requires* the actual sequence issuing in the decision and action to proceed in a deterministic way; if it proceeds in a nondeterministic way that satisfies the libertarian, then Jones can be held responsible, even though he could not have done otherwise.

According to this sort of incompatibilist, the kernel of truth in Frankfurt-type examples is that moral-responsibility attributions are based on what happens in the actual sequence. An incompatibilist about responsibility and determinism can agree with this and thus admit that, if determinism is false, an agent who couldn't have done otherwise might be responsible for his action. But of course this does not show that *causal determinism* is compatible with moral responsibility. After all, causal determinism is a doctrine about what happens in the actual sequence.

The point could be put as follows. There are two ways in which it might be true that one could not have done otherwise. In the first way, the actual sequence involves some factor that operates and makes it the case that the agent could not have initiated an alternative sequence. In the second way, there is no such factor in the actual sequence, but the alternative sequence contains some factor which would prevent the agent from doing other than he actually does. Frankfurt's examples involve such alternative-sequence factors. But since causal determinism implies the presence of an actual-sequence factor of the kind in question, the Frankfurt-type examples do not decisively establish that moral responsibility is compatible with causal determinism.

But I do not find this view attractive. I believe that even (as above) in the absence of a knockdown argument that moral responsibility is compatible with causal determinism, the Frankfurt-type examples (conjoined with other considerations) provide very strong reason to accept this conclusion. This is because it is hard for me to see why causal determinism would threaten moral responsibility for some reason apart from its relationship to alternative possibilities. That is, why exactly would causal determinism be thought to pose a threat to moral responsibility if it were *not* in virtue of undermining the notion that we have alternative possibilities?

I do not know of a compelling answer to this question. I can think of various possible answers, but none is very appealing. For example, it might be thought that moral responsibility requires that an agent be "active" or in some sense "creative." But even if this is so, I do not see any reason to deny that an agent whose action is part of a causally deterministic sequence cannot be active and creative in any sense plausibly taken to be required for moral responsibility. Also, someone might insist that moral responsibility for an action requires that the action be the *agent's own*. Again, even if this is so, I do not see any reason to deny that an action that is part of a causally deterministic sequence can be the agent's own action, in any sense plausibly taken to be required for moral responsibility. Of course, there will be compatibilistic and incompatibilistic accounts of the relevant notions of being active (as opposed to passive), creativity and ownership; but I do not see any reason, apart from a *prior commitment* to incompatibilism about determinism and moral responsibility, to opt for the incompatibilistic analyses.

Take, for example, the notion of creativity. First, consider creativity in the arts. Would we say that (for example) Goya or Picasso were *not* creative, if we discovered that causal determinism were true? Clearly not; our ascription of creativity in the arts (and, I believe, quite generally) does *not* depend on the absence of causal determination. (Who could imagine saying that Kant was not original, if it turned out that causal determinism obtains?) Thus, there must be a sense in which an individual can be artistically (or intellectually) creative (or original) that is compatibilistic; why suppose that an indeterministic sense must be preferable or more natural?

Someone might say that in order for an agent to be morally responsible for an action, the agent must be creative in the sense of being a "self-initiator" or "self-originator" of the action. And the claim would be that these ideas require the absence of causal determination. Now I can see why someone might insist that responsibility requires this sort of incompatibilistic creativity *if* one is committed to the idea that moral responsibility requires alternative possibilities, but I do not see any reason to insist on precisely *this* sort of creativity, *apart* from such a prior commitment.

Let us suppose a lightning bolt strikes a barn, thus (apparently) starting a fire. Would we say that in fact the lightning bolt did *not* start the fire, if it turned out that causal determinism were in fact true? For some purposes and in some contexts, perhaps we would withdraw our claim about the lightning bolt if causal determinism were true; but surely there is a perfectly good sense in which it is true that the lightning bolt started the fire, even given the truth of causal determinism. Thus, there is a perfectly reasonable notion of initiation that is compatible with determinism; why suppose that the indeterministic sense is more appealing in the context of ascription of moral responsibility (*apart from considerations relevant to alternative possibilities*)?

Various philosophers have thought that some sort of indeterministic initiating capacity is required for moral responsibility (or at least for one's actions having the greatest amount of value). Robert Nozick argues for the importance of what he calls "originative value." He says:

> A being with originative value, one whose acts have originative value, can make a difference. Due to his actions, different value consequences occur in the world than otherwise would; these were not in the cards already (with the person's action being one of the cards).[12]

About this notion of originative value, Nozick says, somewhat alarmingly, "Puppets and marionettes lack originative value (except in fairy stories), and the way we resemble them, if causal determinism is true, is that we lack originative value too."[13]

But it seems to me that the Frankfurt-type cases are precisely situations in which it is *not* the case that "due to [the agent's] actions, different value consequences occur in the world than otherwise would." Of course, in these cases the relevant agent does not *act* in the alternative scenario, although the same value consequences ensue. And one can imagine similar cases in which there is a different sort of fail-safe mechanism that does not proceed through the agent—perhaps *someone else* would bring about the same result if the agent who actually brings it about were to refrain from acting. It seems that in these sorts of contexts the agent's actions lack originative value in the sense suggested by Nozick; the agent does not make a difference in the way specified. But nevertheless the agents are surely morally responsible for what they do.[14] Thus, "making a difference" (as defined by Nozick) cannot be invoked to help explain why we would want an indeterministic kind of creative capacity.

I see no promising strategy for arguing that causal determinism threatens moral responsibility apart from its allegedly ruling out alternative possibilities. Further, let me explain my general methodological commitment; this will lend further weight to the conclusion that there is no strong reason to suppose that causal determinism is incompatible with moral responsibility. I am seeking to find an account of moral responsibility that *systematizes* our clear intuitive judgments about cases in which an agent is morally responsible. That is, we have some fairly clear considered judgments about actual and hypothetical cases in which we are inclined to hold agents morally responsible for their actions (and in which we are not so inclined). I seek to elaborate a general account that (at least) captures these reflective intuitive judgments about relatively clear cases. Obviously, this methodology is similar to the Rawlsian methodology of seeking a "reflective equilibrium in matters of distributive justice."[15]

I would hope that my general account of moral responsibility would imply that agents who act as a result of certain sorts of coercion, hypnosis, direct manipulation of the brain, neurological disorders, severe mental diseases, and so forth are *not* to be held morally responsible for their actions. This is surely one of the boundary conditions on a successful general analysis of moral responsibility. And note that it is *not* necessary to posit the absence of causal determinism in order to say that such agents would not be morally responsible for their actions. It is quite well known that invoking the absence of causal determinism is overkill here, since what is involved in all of these contexts is some sort (or sorts) of *special* causation. I maintain, then, that it is a goal of theorizing about moral responsibility that it preserve and capture the distinction between these rather *special* contexts and what we take to be the normal or ordinary contexts of deliberation, practical reflection and action. But since there is nothing in the ordinary contexts that rules out the possibility that causal determinism obtains, there is strong *prima facie* reason to suppose that the account of moral responsibility (at which we are ultimately aiming) will allow that causal determinism is compatible with moral responsibility.

I have urged that the method of seeking a reflective equilibrium between our general principles and particular judgments will issue in principles that allow for the compatibility of causal determinism and moral responsibility. In making this argument I have suggested that it is a plausible considered judgment that causal determinism *in itself, and apart from considerations relevant to alternative possibilities*, does not rule out moral responsibility. But someone might object by pointing out that the ordinary person—the "man on the Clapham Omnibus" or the student in philosophy 1—is likely to recoil at the thought that his actions are causally determined. If such a person is asked whether he would be morally responsible, if his actions are causally determined, he might well insist that this would be impossible.

Of course, an individual might be alarmed by the phrase "causally determined." It just really sounds bad! But when the underlying issue is presented slightly differently, it is not at all evident that a reasonable and reflective person would have the sort of reaction just described. To begin, the question could be framed as follows:

> Assume that moral responsibility need not require freedom to choose or do otherwise. Now if it turned out that there were some scientific theory according to which all truths about human actions could in principle be derived from states of the world in the past, would this fact require us to stop thinking of ourselves and others as *persons*, that is, as legitimate candidates for love and hatred, gratitude and resentment, and reward and punishment? If such a scientific theory were true, and apart from any issues pertaining to alternative possibilities, would it follow that we ought to give up the distinction between the way we treat certain creatures (persons) and others (non-persons)? Would it follow from the existence of such a scientific theory that *all* sequences issuing in actions are "relevantly similar"?

And it is certainly not clear that the answers to *these* questions would be affirmative.

I have already canvassed—and rejected—some possible reasons why someone might be tempted to think that causal determinism in itself would rule out moral responsibility (apart from threatening the existence of alternative possibilities). But suppose now that the reflective individual to whom we are posing our questions says:

> Well, I really *do* think that causal determinism would rule out moral responsibility quite apart from threatening my freedom to choose and do otherwise. After all, if causal determinism, as you have presented it, is true, then all my behavior could be *known and predicted in advance*. And if so, how can I be held morally responsible for what I do?

It is, however, unclear why predictability in advance would threaten moral responsibility. Of course, if God knows in advance what someone will do, then (arguably) that person cannot do otherwise; whereas this argument has considerable force, it is not relevant here, since it pertains to alternative possibilities. Why would (human or divine) foreknowledge (and thus the capacity to predict behavior in advance) *in itself and apart from threatening alternative possibilities* vitiate our moral responsibility? After all, in the Frankfurt-type cases the agent's choices and actions are capable of being known and predicted in advance! And yet this does not in any way diminish the idea that the relevant agents in those cases exercise guidance control and are morally responsible for their actions. Thus, upon reflection, I do not see that the possibility of foreknowledge or accurate prediction in itself threatens moral responsibility. And thus this cannot be a reason causal determinism in itself, apart from considerations relevant to alternative possibilities, would rule out moral responsibility.

I am frankly at a loss to see what *other* consideration could be invoked to support the contention that causal determinism would *in itself* rule out moral responsibility. Of course, it does not follow that there are no such reasons! But I think it is at least reasonable to suggest that there is no obvious, strong reason to think that causal determinism threatens moral responsibility apart from calling into question our possession of alternative possibilities. What is relevant to my project is the considered, reflective intuitive judgments of individuals who seek to fit their judgments into a coherent overall picture; no doubt one's first reaction when one hears the phrase "causally determined" is alarm (or at least anxiety), but I would urge that this initial unreflective response not be considered decisive.[16]

I have then argued that a reliance upon considered and reflective commonsense judgments will support the view that causal determinism *in itself* does not rule out moral responsibility. Against this strategy of relying on commonsense judgments, it might be urged that the same sort of methodology would seem to issue in the claim that we ordinarily have freedom to do otherwise, even if causal determinism were to obtain or God were to exist. Surely, we intuitively *think* we have such freedom, and we intuitively distinguish ordinary cases from special cases; common sense has it that we are ordinarily free to do otherwise, and surely we do not need to invoke the absence of causal determination to explain why agents lack such freedom in the *special* cases. But of course I have been at pains to say that we *cannot* legitimately conclude that we have alternative possibilities.

I grant that common sense posits that we normally have alternative possibilities, and that it is only in special circumstances that we lack this sort of freedom. But what is crucial here is that there exists a powerful *skeptical challenge* to this commonsense view. This challenge gains its force from appealing precisely to aspects of common sense (such as the fixity of the past and the fixity of the natural laws, and so forth). Thus, when common sense is properly considered *in its totality*, it is indeed impossible straightforwardly to conclude that we sometimes have alternative possibilities.

In contrast, I do not know of any powerful skeptical challenge that has its foothold in common sense to the effect that causal determinism *directly* threatens moral responsibility (that is, apart from ruling out alternative possibilities).[17] I conclude that the context of the evaluation of the relationship between causal determinism and moral responsibility is crucially different from the context of the evaluation of the relationship between causal determinism and alternative possibilities: in the latter there is a powerful skeptical challenge, whereas in the former there is no such challenge.

Frankfurt-Type Examples and Schizophrenic Situations

Some might worry that I have relied too heavily upon (alleged) insights gained from Frankfurt-type cases. After all, they are somewhat unusual and, frankly, weird. In response, I certainly do not think that the Frankfurt-type cases are weirder than, for example, many Gettier-type examples, or twin-earth thought experiments. And yet many philosophers have thought that these sorts of examples force radical changes in our accounts of knowledge, belief, and meaning. Although these sorts of examples raise complicated and delicate methodological issues, I do not think Frankfurt-type examples are *prima facie* any *less* appropriate than these (and many other) prominent and influential philosophical thought experiments.

Further, I believe Frankfurt-type cases are actually a special case of a rather more general and quite pervasive (at least, in philosophy) set of situations: Schizophrenic Situations. In a Schizophrenic Situation, important features change (in certain characteristic ways) in various relevant alternative scenarios. In general, Schizophrenic Situations pose problems for subjunctive conditional analyses of various notions; indeed, they appear to decisively defeat *simple* conditional analyses.

Consider, for example, a variant on an example suggested by Alvin Goldman.[18] Suppose there is an ordinary grain of salt, with the typical internal structure of salt. As it sits before us (not placed in water), there is nothing unusual about it. But somehow associated with it is a certain sort of counterfactual intervener. This is a magician who would cause an impermeable coating to surround the piece of salt, just before it made contact with water, if the grain of salt were to come near water.

We intuitively believe that, the grain of salt is water-soluble. In part this is because its failure to dissolve in water would issue not from its internal structure but from some external source. And yet it would not dissolve if it were placed in water. Thus, a simple subjunctive conditional analysis of water solubility must be false.

This is what I would call a Schizophrenic Situation. It is in many ways similar to Frankfurt-type contexts. Indeed, it is the analogue of a Frankfurt-type case for a *passive power* such as solubility. (Frankfurt-type cases pertain to the active power of freedom.) Note that similar problems arise for the analysis of such passive powers as malleability, fragility, flexibility, and so forth.

Here is another set of Schizophrenic Situations. Many philosophers have been attracted to moral theories according to which one acts rightly insofar as one acts *because* of one's acceptance of some moral rule. On these approaches, it cannot be that one acts *merely* in accordance with the rule, in order for one to be acting rightly; one's acceptance of the rule must in some way motivate one's action. But a problem emerges for such views (in their Kantian and also consequentialist forms). It is surely implausible to suppose that acting rightly requires one in every instance explicitly to think about the principle in question (the Categorical Imperative or the Principle of Utility or whatever); this is surely too stringent a demand. Thus, certain moral philosophers have been tempted to accept some sort of counterfactual approach according to which an agent need not actually think about the relevant moral principle before each act, but instead must meet some subjunctive conditional test.[19]

For example, suppose you see an individual drowning, and without *any* explicit thought about moral principles, you jump in and save his life. On the approach we are now considering, this action may have moral value—you may be acting rightly. What must be the case is that if it had not been the right thing to do, you would not have jumped in to save the individual's life. So, for example, we must ask what you would do if there had been five people drowning in another part of the lake and only you could save them (with your boat). If under these hypothetical circumstances you would have acted to save the five, then you are acting rightly in actually saving the one. But if under these hypothetical circumstances you still would have jumped in and saved the one, then you are not acting rightly in actually saving the one individual.

But it is evident that this sort of simple subjunctive conditional test cannot be correct. Imagine that you meet this test, and thus you are deemed to act rightly in saving the one. But now imagine someone who does exactly what you do and has all the same values and long-term dispositions. It's just that this other person has a counterfactual intervener associated with him who would cause him to save the one even if the five needed help. Now it would turn out, on the approach that accepts the simple subjunctive conditional, that *you* act rightly, but the *other person* does not. But both of you do the same thing, have the same values, and have the same long-term dispositions to act. It would be very implausible to say that you act rightly whereas the other person does not. It is admittedly too much to ask that agents (who "accept principles" or "act from duty" or "act rightly") think about the relevant principles prior to every action; but it is also evidently too much to ask that they meet some sort of simple, unrefined subjunctive conditional test.

Let me mention one other Schizophrenic Situation. In her intriguing paper "Asymmetrical Freedom," Susan Wolf says:

> Determination, then, is compatible with an agent's responsibility for a good action, but incompatible with an agent's responsibility for a bad action. The metaphysical conditions required for an agent's responsibility will vary according to the value of the action he performs.[20]

Wolf assumes that the sort of determination in question is incompatible with freedom to do otherwise. She then suggests the following as a way of capturing the sort of freedom required for responsibility:

> He could have done otherwise if there had been good and sufficient reason, where the "could have done otherwise" in the analysans is not a conditional at all. For presumably an action is morally praiseworthy only if there are no good and sufficient reasons to do something else. And an action is morally blameworthy only if there are good and sufficient reasons to do something else.[21]

But note that one can easily construct a Schizophrenic Situation that would show that the sort of subjunctive conditional employed by Wolf will not succeed in capturing her point. Imagine, for example, a very ordinary case in which Mary does some good deed: she helps a motorist fix a flat tire. Suppose that this is an entirely ordinary situation, and intuitively Mary could have done otherwise. Here we would want to say that Mary is morally responsible—indeed, praiseworthy—for her action. But imagine that associated with Mary is some sort of counterfactual intervener who would have compelled her to fix the tire anyway under the circumstance that Mary has a good and sufficient reason not to fix the tire. So, if Mary were rushing to the hospital with a sick child, the counterfactual intervener would render her unable to do anything but fix the tire. Here is an example in which Wolf's condition is *not* met: Mary could not have done otherwise if there had been a good and sufficient reason not to fix the tire. And nevertheless her action seems to be a clear case of a praiseworthy action: the counterfactual intervener played no role whatsoever in her choice or action.

Frankfurt-type cases are, then, special cases of a rather more general phenomenon: Schizophrenic Situations. In such a situation, crucial features change (in unusual ways) from the actual context to the hypothetical scenario. In general, these situations appear to show that simple analyses that employ subjunctive conditionals or posit capacities of certain sorts are false. Schizophrenic situations are a kind of swerve in logical space.

Here I can only gesture at the existence of such situations, and say what I think they suggest. First, they suggest that the Frankfurt-type cases are not so special or unique as some have supposed: insofar as they are a special case of a more general phenomenon, a phenomenon that arguably poses problems for a wide variety of philosophical analyses, the worry about relying on them can to some degree be defused. Further, whereas they suggest that simple analyses of certain sorts do not work, they surely should not cause us to think that those analyses are not in some way on the right track. And in seeking more refined accounts, they strongly suggest that we should adopt actual-sequence approaches; that is, we should look to the properties manifested in the actual sequence and make appropriate use of them in our more sophisticated accounts.

So, for example, if one has the intuition that the piece of salt (described above) is water-soluble, one wants to make use of the fact that it would dissolve in water if it were placed in water and had its actual physical constitution when placed in contact with the water. Similarly in the other cases. For example, if Mary had sufficient reason not to fix the tire *and she retained her actual physical capacities*, then she could do otherwise. I claim that all the schizophrenic situations suggest that we somehow need to reach into the actual sequence and employ *actual* features to generate our more refined and sophisticated understandings of the phenomena in question. And this is precisely the sort of approach I take elsewhere in giving an actual-sequence account of guidance control.

Conclusion

Traditionally it has been supposed that moral responsibility requires control. But our possession of the sort of control that involves alternative possibilities (regulative control) can be called into question. In this piece I have argued that we can have a very robust and significant sort of control—guidance control—even if we lack regulative control. What is true about the traditional view is that moral responsibility for actions is associated with control; but it need not be the sort of control that involves alternative possibilities.

The Frankfurt-type examples may seem arcane, bizarre, and unusual. But nevertheless they point us to something both remarkably pedestrian and extraordinarily important: moral responsibility for action depends on what actually happens. That is to say, moral responsibility for actions depends on the actual history of an action and not upon the existence or nature of alternative scenarios. This is a simple, powerful insight. Indeed, it is sometimes necessary to employ complex or unusual examples or theoretical structures to bring out clearly some very plain, simple truth. The abstruse nature of the instruments employed to identify and present the point crisply does not in any way threaten the natural appeal of the truth itself.

In this chapter, I have developed in some detail the most powerful challenge to the conclusion typically drawn from the Frankfurt-type cases (that alternative possibilities are not required for moral responsibility): the flicker-of-freedom strategy. I have argued that this strategy fails, in all its various forms. The basic problem is that the flicker of freedom it posits is too weak to ground our moral-responsibility ascriptions. The alternative possibilities envisaged are essentially irrelevant to the intuitive view that the agents in the Frankfurt-type cases are morally responsible for their actions. This view is driven by what *actually* occurs in the history of the action, *not* by the existence or nature of alternative possibilities.[22]

Finally, I have suggested that guidance control is the freedom-relevant condition sufficient for moral responsibility. That is, guidance control is all the freedom required for moral responsibility. One does *not* have to say that guidance control must be accompanied by (say) the absence of causal determinism. There is simply no good reason to suppose that causal determinism in itself (and apart from considerations pertaining to alternative possibilities) vitiates our moral responsibility.

Notes

1. This sort of example, and the associated philosophical point, is presented in Harry Frankfurt, "Alternate Possibilities and Moral Responsibility," *Journal of Philosophy* 66 (1969): 829–39; and "Freedom of the Will and the Concept of a Person," *Journal of Philosophy* 68 (1971): 5–20; both pieces are reprinted in *Moral Responsibility*, ed. John Martin Fischer (Ithaca, N.Y.: Cornell University Press, 1986).

2. For a parallel distinction between two kinds of control, see Michael J. Zimmerman, *An Essay on Moral Responsibility* (Totowa, N.J.: Rowman and Littlefield, 1988), pp. 32–34.

3. Note that the example would have precisely the same implications if alternative possibilities were ruled out by virtue of the existence of *another agent*. So imagine that the car is a "driver instruction" automobile with dual controls. Although I actually guide the car to the right, we can imagine that the instructor would have intervened and caused the car to go to the right if I had shown any inclination to cause it to go in some other direction.

4. Aristotle argued that there are two conditions that rule out the voluntariness of an action: ignorance and force. Following Aristotle, I shall suppose that there are at least two sorts of conditions relevant to moral responsibility: epistemic conditions and freedom-relevant conditions. In this chapter, I shall focus primarily upon the freedom-relevant condition. In conversation, Gary Watson has convinced me that there are (arguably) other conditions—perhaps pertaining to psychological complexity or "normative competence"—that are not naturally subsumed under the epistemic or freedom-relevant categories. A full theory of moral responsibility would need to say something about these further conditions.

5. David Blumenfeld develops this kind of Frankfurt-type example in "The Principle of Alternate Possibilities," *Journal of Philosophy* 67 (1971): 339–44.

6. It is not absolutely clear to me that this is so: it seems to me at least conceivable that a Frankfurt-type case could be constructed in which the counterfactual intervention would not be triggered by any specific event but would by an extraordinary *cosmic accident* occur at just the right time. I do not know why this sort of example is impossible, but I will not press the point.

7. This strategy is developed by Peter van Inwagen in his *An Essay on Free Will* (Oxford: Clarendon, 1983), pp. 166–71.

8. For a development of this sort of view, see van Inwagen, ibid., pp. 166–80. Van Inwagen's elegant approach is basically as follows. When one thinks about a Frankfurt-type example, it may at first appear that it is a situation in which both of the following are true: the agent cannot avoid bringing an event about, and he is morally responsible for bringing it about. But this appearance is misleading; it is not clear that both claims are true *of the same thing*. More specifically, it can be granted that the agent is morally responsible for *something*, but this is the event-particular (which he *can* in fact avoid bringing about). Also, it can be granted that the agent cannot avoid bringing about *something*. But this is the event-universal, and he is not responsible for bringing *this* about.

9. William Rowe attributes this sort of libertarian view to Thomas Reid in William L. Rowe, *Thomas Reid on Freedom and Morality* (Ithaca, N.Y.: Cornell University Press, 1991). He applies the view in the way suggested to the analysis of the Frankfurt-type cases; see especially pp. 75–93. For a discussion of Rowe's book, see John Martin Fischer, "Review of Rowe's *Thomas Reid on Freedom and Morality*," *Faith and Philosophy* 10 (1993): 266–71.

10. Margery Bedford Naylor suggests this sort of approach in "Frankfurt on the Principle of Alternate Possibilities," *Philosophical Studies* 46 (1984): 249–58.

11. I believe that the argument presented in the text exhibits the flaw in van Inwagen's defense of the second version of the flicker of freedom strategy. Van Inwagen considers

> PPP1 (Principle of Possible Prevention 1): A person is morally responsible for a certain event-particular only if he could have prevented it.

Van Inwagen, *Essay on Free Will* (p. 170), wonders if a Frankfurt-type counterexample to this principle can be constructed. He tries, as follows:

> Gunnar shoots and kills Ridley (intentionally), thereby bringing about Ridley's death, a certain event. But there is some factor, F, which (i) played no causal role in Ridley's death, and (ii) would have caused Ridley's death if Gunnar had not shot him—or, since factor F might have caused Ridley's death by causing Gunnar to shoot him, perhaps we should say, "if Gunnar had decided not to shoot him"—and (iii) is such that Gunnar could not have prevented it from causing Ridley's death except by killing, or by deciding to kill, Ridley himself. So it would seem that Gunnar is responsible for Ridley's death, though he could not have prevented Ridley's death.
>
> It is easy to see that this story is simply inconsistent. What is in fact denoted by "Ridley's death" is not, according to the story, caused by factor F. Therefore, if Gunnar had not shot Ridley, and, as a result, factor F had caused Ridley to die, then there would have been an event denoted by "Ridley's death" which had factor F as (one of) its cause(s). But then this event would have been an event other than the event in fact denoted by "Ridley's death"; the event in fact denoted by "Ridley's death" would not have happened at all. But if this story is inconsistent it is not a counterexample to PPP1. And I am unable to see how to construct a putative Frankfurt-style counter-example to PPP1 that cannot be shown to be inconsistent by an argument of this sort.

In my view, van Inwagen's mistake here is to assume that the *only* way in which a Frankfurt-type example could threaten the principle would be by presenting an alternative sequence in which the same event-particular (as the actual event) occurs. But I have in effect argued that this is false; I have shown how one could concede that the event-particular in the alternative sequence is different from that in the actual sequence and *still* conclude from the Frankfurt-type examples that PPP1 is false.

To drive home the point, note that if one adopts PPP1, one should also adopt

PPP1*: A person is responsible for event *e* only if there exists some property F such that $F(e)$ and an alternative sequence open to the person in which he brings about $\sim F(e')[e \neq e']$ as a result of an intention to do so.

On PPP1*, Jones is not morally responsible for voting for Clinton, and yet we understand intuitively that Jones *is* morally responsible for voting for Clinton. Since one who accepts PPP1 should also accept PPP1*, and Frankfurt-type examples exhibit the unacceptability of PPP1*, they also call PPP1 into question. Thus, it is *false* that the *only* way in which such examples could threaten PPP1 would be by presenting an alternative sequence in which the same event-particular (as the actual event) occurs.

12. Robert Nozick, *Philosophical Explanations* (Cambridge: Harvard University Press, 1981), p. 312.

13. Ibid.

14. I do not deny that if causal determinism were true, we would share a certain feature—the lack of originative value (as defined by Nozick)—with puppets and marionettes. But I still would maintain that it does not follow that the causal histories of our actions are *relevantly similar* (all things considered) to those of puppets and marionettes.

15. John Rawls, A *Theory of Justice* (Cambridge: Harvard University Press, 1973). Also, for an application of this sort of methodology to the realm of freedom, see Christine Swanton, *Freedom: A Coherence Theory* (Indianapolis: Hackett, 1992).

16. In correspondence, Tim O'Connor reminds me that it need not be solely an untutored, unreflective intuition that supports incompatibilism. Consider, for example, Clarence Darrow's masterful use of an environmental determinism thesis in numerous successful legal defenses, or the effect of Freudian psychology on some people's conception of themselves and others. I certainly confess that I have not offered a knockdown argument against the view that causal determinism in itself rules out moral responsibility. But my sense is that the force of Darrow's arguments (and Freud's insights, if they are indeed insights) derives not from causal determinism *per se* but from adverting to *certain special sorts of determination*.

17. I know of only one "direct" argument. It is presented in Peter van Inwagen's "The Incompatibility of Responsibility and Determinism," in *Bowling Green Studies in Applied Philosophy*, ed. M. Brady and M. Brand 2 (1980), pp. 30–37; this essay is reprinted in Fischer, *Moral Responsibility*. See also van Inwagen, *Essay on Free Will*, pp. 182–88. Van Inwagen here employs a principle structurally parallel to the Transfer Principle, but with a slightly different interpretation of the modality. This issues in what might be called the Principle of Transfer of Nonresponsibility: if you are not morally responsible for one thing, and you are not morally responsible for that thing's leading to another, you are not morally responsible for the other. Now, an argument clearly parallel to the arguments discussed above can be generated to show that causal determinism rules out moral responsibility. Given that you are not morally responsible for the past, and you are not morally responsible for the laws of nature, and assuming the Principle of Transfer of Nonresponsibility, causal determinism seems to rule out moral responsibility *directly*.

But it seems to me that this argument *clearly* does not work. And it is the Frankfurt-type cases that show this by exhibiting the invalidity of the Principle of Transfer of

Nonresponsibility. For example, Jones is not morally responsible for the fact that Black is ready to intervene, and he is not responsible for the fact that, if Black is so ready, Jones will indeed vote for Clinton. But Jones is morally responsible for voting for Clinton. Thus, whereas it is not straightforward to provide a counterexample to the Principle of the Transfer of Powerlessness, Frankfurt-type examples do indeed provide counterexamples to the Principle of the Transfer of Nonresponsibility. Powerlessness is in this respect different from nonresponsibility. For an excellent and very careful discussion of these issues, see Mark Ravizza, "Semicompatibilism and the Transfer of Non-responsibility," *Philosophical Studies* 75 (1994): 61–93.

18. Alvin Goldman, A *Theory of Human Action* (Englewood Cliffs, N.J.: Prentice-Hall, 1970), pp. 199–200.

19. For roughly this kind of move (with refinements), see Barbara Herman, "On the Value of Acting from the Motive of Duty," *Philosophical Review* 90 (1981): 359–82; and Peter Railton, "Alienation, Consequentialism, and the Demands of Morality," *Philosophy and Public Affairs* 13 (1984): 134–71.

20. Susan Wolf, "Asymmetrical Freedom," *Journal of Philosophy* 77 (1980): 157–66.

21. Ibid.

22. Some months ago, I was at the local supermarket. When I got to the checkout counter, the checker asked, "Would you like a paper bag or plastic?" I thought for a moment and replied, "Plastic is fine." Then the checker smiled and said, "It's a good thing—I see we only have plastic!" We both laughed. (On the way home, I turned right at the usual place, not even noticing the sign, which reads, "Right lane must turn right . . .")

3
RESPONSIVENESS AND MORAL
RESPONSIBILITY

We distinguish between creatures who can legitimately be held morally responsible for their actions and those who cannot. Among the actions a morally responsible agent performs, we distinguish between those actions for which the agent is morally responsible and those for which he is not.

An agent is morally responsible for an action insofar as he is rationally accessible to certain kinds of attitudes and activities as a result of performing the action. The attitudes include resentment, indignation, respect, and gratitude; and the activities include moral praise and blame, and reward and punishment.[1] With this approach, an agent can be a rational candidate for praise or blame, even though he is neither praiseworthy nor blameworthy. For instance, an agent can be morally responsible for a morally "neutral" act. A theory of moral responsibility sets the conditions under which we believe that an individual is a *rational candidate* for praise or blame on account of his behavior. This theory needs to be supplemented by a further moral theory that specifies which agents, among those who are morally responsible, *ought* to be praised or blamed (and to what extent) for their actions. Whereas both kinds of theory are obviously important, I focus here on the first sort of theory—one that explains rational accessibility to the pertinent attitudes and activities.

What I present here is really just a sketch of a theory. It needs to be elaborated and defended much more carefully and explicitly. But I hope that enough of its content will be presented to see that it is a worthwhile approach to develop. The kind of theory I present is certainly not radically new and entirely different from its predecessors.[2] But I hope to develop the theory in a way that avoids some of the objections to similar approaches, and I will draw out some implications that have so far gone unnoticed.

I have benefited greatly from comments on previous versions of this paper by Sarah Buss, Anthony Brueckner, and Ferdinand Schoeman. I also benefited from reading a version of this paper at Birkbeck College, University of London.

A Sketch of a Theory of Moral Responsibility

A theory of moral responsibility should capture our intuitive judgments about clear cases. That is, I assume there is at least fairly wide agreement about certain cases in which an agent can reasonably be held morally responsible for what he does and certain cases in which an agent cannot be held responsible. Considered opinions about these sorts of situations are important data to be explained by a theory of moral responsibility. In order to generate a principle that might underlie our reactions to relatively clear cases, it is useful to begin by considering examples in which we are inclined to think that an agent cannot legitimately be held morally responsible.

Imagine that an individual has been hypnotized. The hypnotist has induced an urge to punch the nearest person after hearing the telephone ring. Insofar as the individual did not consent to this sort of hypnotic suggestion (perhaps he has undergone hypnosis to help him stop smoking), it seems unreasonable to hold him morally responsible for punching his friend in the nose upon hearing the telephone ring.

Suppose similarly that an evil person has got hold of Smith's television set and has wired it so as to allow him to subject Smith to a sophisticated sort of subliminal advertising. The bad person systematically subjects Smith to subliminal advertising that causes Smith to murder his neighbor. Because of the nature of the causal history of the action, it is apparent that Smith cannot be held morally responsible for the lamentable deed.

We feel similarly about actions produced in a wide variety of ways. Agents who perform actions produced by powerful forms of brainwashing and indoctrination, potent drugs, and certain sorts of direct manipulation of the brain are not reasonably to be held morally responsible for their actions. Imagine, for instance, that neurophysiologists of the future can isolate certain key parts of the brain, which can be manipulated in order to induce decisions and actions. If scientists electronically stimulate those parts of Jones's brain, thus causing him to help a person who is being mugged, Jones himself cannot reasonably be held morally responsible for his behavior. It is not to Jones's credit that he has prevented a mugging.

Also, if we discover that a piece of behavior is attributable to a significant brain lesion or a neurological disorder, we do not hold the agent morally responsible for it. Similarly, certain sorts of mental disorders—extreme phobias, for instance— may issue in behavior for which the agent cannot reasonably be held responsible.

Many people feel there can be genuinely "irresistible" psychological impulses. If so, then these may result in behavior for which the agent cannot be held morally responsible. Drug addicts may (in certain circumstances) act on literally irresistible urges, and we might not hold them morally responsible for acting on these desires (especially if we believe they are not morally responsible for acquiring the addiction in the first place).

Also, certain sorts of coercive threats (and perhaps offers) rule out moral responsibility. The bank teller who is told he will be shot unless he hands over the money may have an overwhelming and irresistible desire to comply with the demand. Insofar as he acts from such an impulse, it is plausible to suppose that the teller is not morally responsible for his action.[3]

Evidently, the causal history of an action matters to us in making moral responsibility attributions. When persons are manipulated in certain ways, they are like marionettes and are not appropriate candidates for praise or blame. Certain factors issuing in behavior are, we understand intuitively, responsibility-undermining factors.

We can contrast such cases—in which some responsibility-undermining factor operates—with cases in which there is the "normal," unimpaired operation of the human deliberative mechanism. When you deliberate about whether to give 5 percent of your salary to the United Way and consider reasons on both sides, and your decision to give the money is not induced by hypnosis, brainwashing, direct manipulation, psychotic impulses, and so on, we think you can legitimately be praised for your charitable action. Insofar as we can identify no responsibility-undermining factor at work in your decision and action, we are inclined to hold you morally responsible.

Now it might be thought that there is a fairly obvious way of distinguishing the clear cases of moral responsibility from the clear cases of lack of it. It seems that, in the cases in which an agent is morally responsible for an action, he is free to do otherwise, and in the cases of lack of moral responsibility, the agent is not free to do otherwise. Thus, it appears that the actual operation of what is intuitively a responsibility-undermining factor rules out moral responsibility because it rules out freedom to do otherwise.

The point could be put as follows. When an agent is (for example) hypnotized, he is not sensitive to reasons in the appropriate way. Given the hypnosis, he would still behave in the same way no matter what the relevant reasons were. Suppose, again, that an individual is hypnotically induced to punch the nearest person after hearing the telephone ring. Now given this sort of hypnosis, he would punch the nearest person after hearing the telephone ring, even if he had extremely strong reasons not to. The agent here is not responsive to reasons—the behavior would be the same no matter what reasons there were.

In contrast, when there is the normal, unimpaired operation of the human deliberative mechanism, we suppose that the agent *is* responsive to reasons. So when you decide to give money to the United Way, we think that you nevertheless would not have contributed had you discovered that there was widespread fraud within the agency. Thus it is very natural and reasonable to think that the difference between morally responsible agents and those who are not consists in the "reasons-responsiveness" of the agents.

But I believe that there are cases in which an agent can be held morally responsible for performing an action, even though that person could not have done otherwise (and is not "reasons-responsive").[4] Here is a graphic example. Imagine that an evil person has installed a device in Brown's brain which allows him to monitor Brown's mental activity and also to intervene in it, if he wishes. He can electronically manipulate Brown's brain by "remote control" to induce decisions, and let us imagine that he can also ensure that Brown acts on the decisions so induced. Now suppose that Brown is about to murder his neighbor, and that this is precisely what the evil person wishes. That is, let us imagine that the device simply monitors Brown's brain activity, but that it plays no role in Brown's actual decision and action. Brown deliberates and behaves just as he would have if no device had been implanted in his brain. But we also imagine that had Brown begun to decide not to murder his neighbor, the device would have been activated and would have caused him to choose to murder the neighbor (and to do so) anyway. Here is a case where an agent can be held morally responsible for performing an action, although he could not have done otherwise.[5] Let us call such a case a "Frankfurt-type" case.

In a Frankfurt-type case, the actual sequence proceeds in a way that grounds moral responsibility attributions, even though the alternative scenario (or perhaps a range of alternative scenarios) proceeds in a way that rules out responsibility. In a Frankfurt-type case, no responsibility-undermining factor occurs in the actual sequence, although such a factor occurs in the alternative scenario. Such cases impel us to adopt a more refined theory of moral responsibility—an "actual-sequence model" of moral responsibility. With such an approach, we distinguish between the kinds of mechanisms that operate in the actual sequence and in the alternative sequence (or sequences).

In a Frankfurt-type case, the kind of mechanism that actually operates is reasons-responsive, although the kind of mechanism that would operate in the alternative scenario is *not*.[6] In the case discussed above, Brown's action issues from the normal faculty of practical reasoning, which we can reasonably take to be reasons-responsive. But in the alternative scenario, a different kind of mechanism would have operated—one involving direct electronic stimulation of Brown's brain. And this mechanism is not reasons-responsive. Thus, the actual-sequence mechanism can be reasons-responsive, even though the *agent* is not reasons-responsive. (*Brown* could not have done otherwise.)

The suggestion, then, for a more refined way of distinguishing the relatively clear cases of moral responsibility from cases of the lack of it is as follows. An agent is morally responsible for performing an action insofar as the mechanism that actually issues in the action is reasons-responsive. When an unresponsive mechanism actually operates, it is true that the agent is not free to do otherwise; but an agent who is unable to do otherwise may act from a responsive mechanism and can thus be held morally responsible for what he does.

So far I have pointed to some cases in which it is intuitively clear that a person cannot be held morally responsible for what he has done and other cases in which it is intuitively clear that an agent can be held responsible. I have suggested a principle that might distinguish the two types of cases. This principle makes use of two ingredients: reasons-responsiveness and the distinction between actual-sequence and alternative-sequence mechanisms. But I have been somewhat vague and breezy about formulating the principle. It is now necessary to explain it more carefully, beginning with the notion of reasons-responsiveness.

Reasons-Responsiveness

I wish to discuss two kinds of reasons-responsiveness: strong and weak. Let's begin with strong reasons-responsiveness. Strong reasons-responsiveness obtains when a

certain kind K of mechanism actually issues in an action and if there were sufficient reason to do otherwise and K were to operate, the agent would recognize the
sufficient reason to do otherwise and thus choose to do otherwise and do otherwise. To test whether a kind of mechanism is strongly reasons-responsive, one asks
what would happen if there were sufficient reason for the agent to do otherwise
and the actual-sequence mechanism were to operate. Under circumstances in
which there are sufficient reasons for the agent to do otherwise and the actual type
of mechanism operates, three conditions must be satisfied: The agent must take the
reasons to be sufficient, choose in accordance with the sufficient reason, and act in
accordance with the choice. Thus, there can be at least three sorts of "alternative-
sequence" failures: failures in the connection between what reasons there are and
what reasons the agent recognizes, in the connection between the agent's reason
and choice, and in the connection between choice and action.

The first kind of failure is a failure to be *receptive* to reasons. It is the kind of inability that afflicts certain delusional psychotics.[7] The second kind of failure is a
failure of *reactivity*—a failure to be appropriately affected by beliefs. Lack of reactivity afflicts certain compulsive or phobic neurotics.[8] Finally, there is the failure
successfully to translate one's choice into action; this failure is a kind of impo-
tence. If none of these failures were to occur in the alternative sequence (and the
actual kind of mechanism were to operate), then the actually operative mechanism would be strongly reasons-responsive. There would be a tight fit between the
reasons there are and the reasons the agent has, the agent's reasons and choice,
and choice and action. The agent's actions would fit the contours of reasons
closely.[9]

I believe that, when an action issues from a strongly reasons-responsive mechanism, this suffices for moral responsibility; but I do not believe that strong reasons-
responsiveness is a necessary condition for moral responsibility. To see this,
imagine that as a result of the unimpaired operation of the normal human faculty
of practical reasoning, I decide to go (and go) to the basketball game tonight, and
that I have sufficient reason to do so; but suppose that I would have been "weak-
willed" had there been sufficient reason *not* to go. That is, imagine that had there
been a sufficient reason not to go, it would have been that I had a strict deadline
for an important manuscript (which I could not meet, if I were to go to the game).
I nevertheless would have chosen to go to the game, even though I would have
recognized that I had sufficient reason to stay home and work. It seems to me that
I actually go to the basketball game freely and can reasonably be held morally responsible for going; and yet the actual-sequence mechanism that results in my
action is not reasons-responsive in the strong sense. The failure of strong reasons-
responsiveness here stems from my disposition toward weakness of the will.

Going to the basketball game is plausibly thought to be a morally neutral act;
in the approach to moral responsibility adopted here, one can be morally responsible for an action, even though the act is neither praiseworthy nor blameworthy.
The phenomenon of weakness of will also poses a problem for intuitively clear
cases of moral responsibility for *commendable* acts. Suppose, for example, that I de-
vote my afternoon to working for the United Way (and my decision and action
proceed via an intuitively responsibility-conferring mechanism). And imagine

that, if I had a sufficient reason to refrain, it would (again) have been my publication deadline. But imagine that I would have devoted my time to charity even if I had such a reason not to. Here it seems that I am both morally responsible and praiseworthy for doing what I do, and yet the actual mechanism is not strongly reasons-responsive.

Further, it is quite clear that strong reasons-responsiveness cannot be a necessary condition for moral responsibility for morally blameworthy and/or imprudent acts. Suppose that I steal a book from a store, knowing full well that it is morally wrong for me to do so and that I will be apprehended and thus that it is not prudent of me to do so. Nevertheless, the actual sequence may be intuitively responsibility-conferring; no factors that intuitively undermine moral responsibility may actually operate. (Of course, I assume that there can be genuine cases of weak-willed actions that are free actions for which the agent can be held responsible.) Here, then, is a case in which I am morally responsible for stealing the book, but my actual-sequence mechanism is not strongly reasons-responsive: There actually is sufficient reason (both moral and prudential) to do otherwise, and yet I steal the book.

All three cases presented above provide problems for the claim that strong reasons-responsiveness is necessary for moral responsibility. Strong reasons-responsiveness may be both sufficient and necessary for a certain kind of praiseworthiness—it is a great virtue to connect one's actions with the contours of value in a strongly reasons-responsive way. Of course, not all agents who are morally responsible are morally commendable (or even maximally prudent). I believe that moral responsibility requires only a looser kind of fit between reasons and action: "weak reasons-responsiveness."

Under the requirement of strong reasons-responsiveness, we ask what would happen if there were a sufficient reason to do otherwise (holding fixed the actual kind of mechanism). Strong reasons responsiveness points us to the alternative scenario in which there is a sufficient reason for the agent to do otherwise (and the actual mechanism operates), which is *most similar* to the actual situation. Put in terms of possible worlds, the nonactual possible worlds that are germane to strong reasons-responsiveness are those in which the agent has a sufficient reason to do otherwise (and in which the actual kind of mechanism operates) that are most similar to the actual world. (Perhaps there is just one such world, or perhaps there is a sphere of many such worlds.) In contrast, under weak reasons-responsiveness, there must exist *some* possible world in which there is a sufficient reason to do otherwise, the agent's actual mechanism operates, and the agent does otherwise. This possible world need not be the one (or ones) in which the agent has a sufficient reason to do otherwise (and the actual mechanism operates), which is (or are) *most similar* to the actual world.[10]

Consider again my decision to go to the basketball game. In this situation, if I were to have a sufficient reason to do otherwise, this would be a publication deadline; and I would under such circumstances be weak-willed and still go to the game. However, there certainly exists *some* scenario in which the actual mechanism operates, I have sufficient reason not to go to the game, and I don't go. Suppose, for instance, that I am told that I will have to pay $1,000 for a ticket to the game. Even though I am disposed to be weak-willed under some circumstances, there are some circumstances in which I would respond appropriately to sufficient reasons. These are circumstances in which the reasons are considerably *stronger* than the reasons which would exist if I were to have sufficient reason to do otherwise.

Consider, similarly, my commendable act of working this afternoon for the United Way. Even though I would do so anyway, even if I had a publication deadline, I certainly would *not* work for the United Way if to do so I would have to sacrifice my job. Thus, the actual mechanism issuing in my action is weakly reasons-responsive. Also, when an agent wrongly (and imprudently) steals a book (i.e., there actually is sufficient reason not to), the actual mechanism might be responsive to at least some logically possible incentive not to steal. To the extent that it is so responsive, he is properly held morally responsible for stealing the book. Even an agent who acts against good reasons can be responsive to *some* reasons.

I believe that the agent's actual-sequence mechanism *must* be weakly reasons-responsive if he is to be held morally responsible. If (given the operation of the actual kind of mechanism) he would persist in stealing the book even knowing that by so acting he would cause himself and his family to be killed, then the actual mechanism would seem to be inconsistent with holding that person morally responsible for an action.

An agent whose act is produced by a strongly reasons-responsive mechanism is commendable; his behavior fits tightly the contours of value. But a weakly responsive mechanism is all that is required for moral responsibility. In my approach, actual irrationality is compatible with moral responsibility (as it should be). Perhaps Dostoyevsky's underground man is an example of an actually irrational and yet morally responsible individual. Similarly, certain kinds of hypothetical irrationality are compatible with moral responsibility; a tendency toward weakness of the will need not point to any defect in the actual mechanism leading to action. Moral responsibility requires *some* connection between reason and action, but the fit can be quite loose.[11]

In this section I have distinguished two kinds of responsiveness. I have argued that an agent is morally responsible for an action insofar as the action is produced by a weakly reasons-responsive mechanism. In the next section, I discuss an analogy between this theory of moral responsibility and a parallel sort of theory of knowledge. This analogy will help to refine our understanding of the actual-sequence nature of moral responsibility. In the following section, I further sharpen the formulation of the theory by rendering more precise the key idea of a "kind of mechanism issuing in action."

Knowledge and Responsibility

I have sketched an actual-sequence model of moral responsibility. In this approach, an agent can be morally responsible for performing an action although he is not free to do otherwise. It is sufficient that the actual-sequence mechanism be responsive to reasons in the appropriate way. There is an analogy between this sort of theory of moral responsibility and an actual-sequence model of knowledge. In this approach to knowledge, an agent may have knowledge of a certain proposition, even though he lacks the pertinent discriminatory capacity. It is sufficient that the actual-sequence mechanism be sensitive to truth in the appropriate way.

In order for a person to know that p, it is clear that the person must believe that p, and that p must be true; but this is surely not enough, and there are various strategies for providing further requirements.[12] One "externalist" approach claims that the person's belief that p must be a "reliable indicator" of p's truth—or perhaps, that it must "track" p's truth. Very roughly, one might say that, in order for an agent to have knowledge that p, it must be the case both that (1) the agent would not believe that p if p were not true, and (2) under various conditions in which p were true, the agent would believe that p. One asks here about the agent's beliefs in a sphere of worlds that are relatively similar to the actual world—both worlds in which p is true and worlds in which p is false.[13]

So suppose that as you are driving along, you see what you take to be a barn in a field, and that you conclude that it is a barn in the field; and it is an ordinary barn in a field. Unknown to you, had it not been a barn, a demonic farmer would have installed a papier-mâché replica of a barn. In this case you truly believe that it is a normal barn in the field, but your belief does not "track truth": had there been no barn in the field, you still would have believed there to be a barn in the field. In this case you lack a discriminatory capacity that might seem required for knowledge.

Let us contrast this case with another in which you see a banana in a supermarket, and you conclude that there is a banana on the shelf. We suppose here that there is no demonic supermarket manager poised to fool you, and that if there were no banana on the shelf, you would not believe that there is a banana on the shelf. Presumably, in this case your belief tracks truth, and you might be said to know that there is a banana on the shelf. Furthermore, this is so even though *there exists* a logically possible scenario in which a demonic supermarket manager has placed a plastic banana on the shelf and you still conclude that it is a banana. In this account, what is pertinent to knowledge are the scenarios in which p is false that are *most similar* to the actual world; that there are more remote possibilities in which the proposition p is false is not taken by the approach to be germane to whether the individual has knowledge.[14]

The cases described above might suggest that an agent has knowledge that p only if he has the ability to discriminate the conditions that would obtain if p were true from those that would obtain if p were false. However, consider the following examples (from Nozick):

> A grandmother sees her grandson is well when he comes to visit; but if he were sick or dead, others would tell her he was well to spare her upset. Yet this does not mean she doesn't know he is well (or at least ambulatory) when she sees him.[15]
>
> S believes a certain building is a theater and concert hall. He has attended plays and concerts there. . . . However, if the building were not a theater, it would have housed a nuclear reactor that would so have altered the air around it (let us suppose) that everyone upon approaching the theater would have become lethargic and nauseous, and given up the attempt to buy a ticket. The government cover story would

have been that the building was a theater, a cover story they knew would be safe since no unmedicated person could approach through the nausea field to discover any differently. Everyone, let us suppose, would have believed the cover story; they would have believed that the building they saw (but only from some distance) was a theater.[16]

These examples are epistemological analogues to Frankfurt-type cases in which an agent is morally responsible for performing an action although he could not have done otherwise. In these cases an agent knows that p, although he lacks the pertinent discriminatory capacity. Just as we switched from demanding agent-responsiveness to demanding mechanism-responsiveness for moral responsibility, it is appropriate to demand only mechanism-sensitivity to truth in order for an agent to have knowledge.

As Nozick points out, it is possible to believe that p via a truth-sensitive mechanism, and thus know that p, even though an insensitive mechanism would have operated in the alternative scenario (or scenarios). Thus, we want an actual-sequence theory of knowledge, just as we want an actual-sequence theory of responsibility. We need to distinguish between actual-sequence and alternative-sequence mechanisms and focus on the properties of the actual-sequence mechanism. But whereas there is a strong analogy between the theories of responsibility and knowledge sketched above, I now want to point to two important differences between responsibility and knowledge.

First, in the theory of responsibility presented above, if an agent acts on a mechanism of type M, there must be *some* possible scenario in which M operates, the agent has sufficient reason to do otherwise, and he does do otherwise, in order for the agent to be morally responsible for his action. The possible scenario need not be the one that would have occurred if M had operated and the agent had sufficient reason to do otherwise. That is, the scenario pertinent to responsibility ascriptions need not be the scenario (or set of them) in which an M-type mechanism operates and the agent has sufficient reason to do otherwise that are *most similar* to the actual scenario. In contrast, in the theory of knowledge presented above, if an agent believes that p via an M-type mechanism, then it must be the case that if an M-type mechanism were to operate and p were false, the agent would believe that p is false if the agent is to know that p.

Roughly speaking, the logical possibilities pertinent to moral responsibility attributions may be more remote than those pertinent to knowledge attributions. I believe, then, that the connection between reasons and action that is necessary for moral responsibility is "looser" than the connection between truth and belief that is necessary for knowledge. Of course, this point is consistent with the claim that both knowledge and moral responsibility are actual-sequence notions; it is just that actual-sequence truth-sensitivity is defined more "strictly" (i.e., in terms of "closer" possibilities) than actual-sequence reasons-responsiveness.

But I believe there is a second difference between moral responsibility and knowledge. I have claimed that, just as moral responsibility does not require freedom to do otherwise, knowledge does not require the capacity to discriminate; what is sufficient in the case of responsibility is reasons-responsiveness, and in the case of knowledge, truth-sensitivity. Thus both notions are actual-sequence notions. But I wish to point out a stronger sense in which moral responsibility (and not knowledge) depends only on the actual sequence.

I claim that an agent's moral responsibility for an action is supervenient on the actual physical causal influences that issue in the action, whereas an agent's knowledge that *p* is *not* supervenient on the actual physical causal influences that issue in the belief that *p*. First, let me explain the supervenience claim for moral responsibility. It seems to me impossible that there be cases in which there are two agents who perform actions of the same type as a result of exactly the same kind of actual causal sequence, but in which one agent is morally responsible for the action and the other is *not*. Differences in responsibility ascriptions must come from differences in the actual physical factors resulting in action; mere differences in alternate scenarios do not translate into differences in responsibility ascriptions. That is, differences in responsibility ascriptions must come from differences in the actual histories of actions, and not mere "possible" histories.

Suppose you and I both heroically jump into the lake to save a drowning swimmer, and everything that actually happens in both cases is relevantly similar—except that whereas you could have done otherwise, I could not have. (I could not have done otherwise by virtue of the existence of a mechanism in my brain that would have stimulated it to produce a decision to save the swimmer had I been inclined not to.) Insofar as the actual physical sequences issuing in our behavior are the same, we are equally morally responsible.

However, here is an epistemological example of Nozick's:

> Consider another case, of a student who, when his philosophy class is cancelled, usually returns to his room and takes hallucinogenic drugs; one hallucination he has sometimes is of being in his philosophy class. When the student actually is in the philosophy class, does he know he is? I think not, for if he weren't in class, he still might believe he was. . . . Two students in the class might be in the same actual situation, having (roughly) the same retinal and aural intake, yet the first knows he is in class while the other does not, because they are situated differently subjunctively—different subjunctives hold true of them.[17]

The two students have exactly the same actual physical factors issue in beliefs that they are in class. However, one student does not know he is in class: if he were not in class (and he were to employ the method of introspection, which was actually employed), then he would (or at least might) still believe that he is in class (as a result of the drug). The other student—who is not disposed to use the drug—does know that he is in class. Thus knowledge is not supervenient on actual physical facts in the way that moral responsibility is.

I have claimed above that there is a certain parallel between moral responsibility and knowledge: The reasons-responsiveness of the actual mechanism leading to action suffices for responsibility, and the truth sensitivity of the actual mechanism leading to belief suffices for knowledge. How exactly is this claim of parallelism compatible with the further claim that moral responsibility attributions are supervenient on actual physical causal factors, whereas knowledge attributions are *not*? I think the answer lies in our intuitive way of individuating "mechanisms."

We tend to individuate mechanisms more finely in action theory than in epistemology.

In the case of the first student, we take the relevant mechanism issuing in belief to be "introspection." Of course, the same sort of mechanism would have operated had the student taken the drug. With this "wide" kind of individuation of mechanisms, it turns out that the mechanism that issues in the one student's belief is *not* truth-sensitive, whereas the mechanism of the other student *is*.

However, in the case in which I save the drowning child ("on my own"), it is natural to suppose that if I had been stimulated by the scientists, this would have been a kind of mechanism *different* from the one that actually operates. Similarly, had I been injected with a drug that issued in an irresistible desire to save the drowning swimmer, this would have constituted a kind of mechanism *different* from the actual one. With this "narrow" kind of individuation of mechanisms, it turns out that the mechanism that issues in my action of saving the child *is* reasons-responsive (just as yours is).

The asymmetry of supervenience is compatible with the symmetrically actual-sequence nature of knowledge and moral responsibility. The asymmetry of supervenience is generated by the intuitively natural tendency to individuate mechanisms issuing in belief more broadly than mechanisms issuing in action.[18]

Mechanisms

I have suggested that an agent is morally responsible for performing an action insofar as the mechanism that actually issues in the action is reasons-responsive; but this suggestion needs to be refined in light of the fact that various different mechanisms may actually operate in a given case. Which mechanism is relevant to responsibility ascriptions?

Suppose that I deliberate (in the normal way) about whether to donate 5 percent of my paycheck to the United Way, and that I decide to make the donation and act on my decision. We might fill in the story so that it is intuitively a paradigmatic case in which I am morally responsible for my action; and yet consider the actually operative mechanism, "deliberation preceding donating 5 percent of one's salary to the United Way." If *this* kind of mechanism were to operate, then I would give 5 percent of my paycheck to the United Way in any logically possible scenario. Thus, this kind of actually operative mechanism is *not* reasons-responsive.

However, a mechanism such as "deliberating prior to giving 5 percent of one's salary to the United Way" is not of the kind that is relevant to moral responsibility ascriptions. This is because it is not a "temporally intrinsic" mechanism. The operation of a temporally extrinsic or "relational" mechanism already includes the occurrence of the action it is supposed to cause.

Note that the operation of a mechanism of the kind "deliberating prior to giving 5 percent of one's paycheck to the United Way" *entails* that one give 5 percent of one's paycheck to the United Way. In this sense, then, the mechanism already includes the action: its operation entails that the action occurs. Thus, it is a necessary condition of a mechanism's relevance to moral responsibility ascriptions (on the theory proposed here) that it be a "temporally intrinsic" or "nonrelational" mechanism in the following sense: if a mechanism M issues in act X, then M is relevant to the agent's moral responsibility for performing X only if M's operating does not entail that X occurs. I believe that the requirement that a mechanism be temporally intrinsic is an intuitively natural and unobjectionable one. Of course, we have so far only a necessary condition for being a relevant mechanism; there may be various different mechanisms that issue in an action, all of which are temporally intrinsic. Which mechanism is "the" mechanism pertinent to moral responsibility ascription?

I do not have a theory that will specify in a general way how to determine which mechanism is "the" mechanism relevant to assessment of responsibility. It is simply a presupposition of this theory as presented above that, for each act, an intuitively natural mechanism is appropriately selected as *the* mechanism that issues in action, for the purposes of assessing moral responsibility.

I do not think this presupposition is problematic. But if there is a worry, it is useful to note that the basic theory can be formulated without such a presupposition. As so far developed, the theory says that an agent is morally responsible for performing an action insofar as the (relevant, temporally intrinsic) mechanism issuing in the action is reasons-responsive. Alternatively, one could say that an agent is morally responsible for an action insofar as there is no actually operative temporally intrinsic mechanism issuing in the action that is not reasons-responsive. This alternative formulation obviates the need to select one mechanism as the "relevant" one. In what follows I continue to employ the first formulation, but the basic points should apply equally to the alternative formulation.

I wish now to apply the theory to a few cases. We think intuitively that irresistible urges can be psychologically compulsive and can rule out moral responsibility. Imagine that Jim has a literally irresistible urge to take a certain drug, and that he does in fact take the drug. What exactly is the relevant mechanism that issues in Jim's taking the drug? Notice that the mechanism "deliberation involving an irresistible urge to take the drug" is not temporally intrinsic and thus not admissible as a mechanism pertinent to moral responsibility ascription: its operation entails that Jim takes the drug. Consider, then, the mechanism "deliberation involving an irresistible desire." Whereas this mechanism *is* temporally intrinsic, it is also reasons-responsive: There is a possible scenario in which Jim acts on this kind of mechanism and refrains from taking the drug. In this scenario, Jim has an irresistible urge to *refrain* from taking the drug. These considerations show that neither "deliberation involving an irresistible desire for the drug" nor "deliberation involving an irresistible desire" is the relevant mechanism (if the theory of responsibility is to achieve an adequate fit with our intuitive judgments).

When Jim acts on an irresistible urge to take the drug, there is some physical process of kind P taking place in his central nervous system. When a person undergoes this kind of physical process, we say that the urge is literally irresistible. I believe that what underlies our intuitive claim that Jim is not morally responsible for taking the drug is that the relevant kind of mechanism issuing in Jim's taking the drug is of physical kind P, and that a mechanism of kind P is not reasons-responsive. When an agent acts from a literally irresistible urge, he is undergoing a kind of physical process that is not reasons-responsive, and it is this lack of reasons-responsiveness of the actual physical process that rules out moral responsibility.[19]

Consider again my claim that certain sorts of "direct manipulation of the brain" rule out moral responsibility. It is clear that not all such manipulations would rule out moral responsibility. Suppose, for instance, that a scientist manipulates just one brain cell at the periphery of my brain. This kind of manipulation need not rule out responsibility insofar as this kind of physical process can be reasons-responsive. It is when the scientists intervene and manipulate the brain in a way which is *not* reasons-responsive that they undermine an agent's moral responsibility for action.[20]

Similarly, not all forms of subliminal advertising, hypnosis, brainwashing, and so on are inconsistent with moral responsibility for an action. It is only when these activities yield physical mechanisms that are not reasons-responsive that they rule out moral responsibility. Thus, the theory that associates moral responsibility with actual-sequence reasons-responsiveness can help to explain our intuitive distinctions between causal influences that are consistent with moral responsibility and those that are not.

Consider also the class of legal defenses that might be dubbed "Twinkie-type" defenses. This kind of defense claims that an agent ought not to be punished because he ate too much junk food (and that this impaired his capacities, etc.). In the approach presented here, the question of whether an agent ought to be punished is broken into two parts: (1) Is the agent morally responsible (i.e., rationally accessible to punishment), and (2) if so, to what degree ought the agent to be punished? The theory of moral responsibility I have presented allows us to respond positively to the first question in the typical "Twinkie-type" case.

Even if an individual has eaten a diet composed only of junk food, it is highly implausible to think that this yields a biological process that is not weakly reasons-responsive. At the very most, such a process might not be strongly reasons-responsive, but strong reasons-responsiveness is *not* necessary for moral responsibility. Our outrage at the suggestion that a junk food eater is not morally responsible may come from two sources. The outrage could be a reaction to the "philosophical" mistake of demanding strong rather than weak reasons-responsiveness; or the outrage could be a reaction to the implausible suggestion that junk food consumption yields a mechanism that is not weakly reasons-responsive.

Thus the theory of responsibility supports the intuitive idea that Twinkie-type defendants are morally responsible for what they do. Of course, the question of the appropriate *degree* of punishment is a separate question; but it is important to notice that it is *not* a consequence of the theory of responsibility that an agent who acts on a mechanism that is weakly but not strongly reasons-responsive is properly punished to a *lesser* degree than an agent who acts on a mechanism that is strongly reasons-responsive. This may, but need not be, a part of one's full theory of punishment.

Temporal Considerations

I wish to consider a problem for the theory of responsibility that I have been developing. This problem will force a refinement in the theory. Suppose Max (who enjoys drinking but is not an alcoholic) goes to a party where he drinks so much that he is almost oblivious to his surroundings. In this state of intoxication he gets into his car and tries to drive home. Unfortunately, he runs over a child who is walking in a crosswalk. Although the actual-sequence mechanism issuing in Max's running over the child is plausibly taken to lack reasons-responsiveness, we may nevertheless feel that Max *is* morally responsible for running over the child.

This is one case in a class of cases in which an agent acts at a time T_1 on a reasons-responsive mechanism that causes him to act at T_2 on a mechanism that is *not* reasons-responsive. Further, Max ought to have known that getting drunk at the party would lead to driving in a condition in which he would be unresponsive. Thus, Max can be held morally responsible for his action at T_2 by virtue of the operation of a suitable sort of reasons-responsive mechanism at a prior time T_1. When one acts on a reasons-responsive mechanism at time T_1 and one ought to know that so acting will lead to acting on an unresponsive mechanism at some later time T_2, one can be held morally responsible for so acting at T_2. Thus, the theory of moral responsibility should be interpreted as claiming that moral responsibility for an act at T requires the actual operation of a reasons-responsive mechanism at T or some suitable earlier time. (For simplicity's sake, I suppress mention of the temporal indexation below.)

An individual might cultivate dispositions to act virtuously in certain circumstances. It might even be the case that when he acts virtuously, the motivation to do so is so strong that the mechanism is not reasons-responsive. But insofar as reasons-responsive mechanisms issued in the person's cultivation of the virtue, that person can be held morally responsible for his action. It is only when it is true that at no suitable point along the path to the action did a reasons-responsive mechanism operate that an agent will not properly be held responsible for an action.

Semicompatibilism

I have presented a very sketchy theory of responsibility. The basic idea would have to be developed and explained much more carefully in order to have a fully adequate theory of responsibility, but enough of the theory has been given to draw out some of its implications. My claim is that the theory sketched here leads to compatibilism about moral responsibility and such doctrines as God's foreknowledge and causal determinism.

Let us first consider the relationship between causal determinism and moral responsibility. The theory of moral responsibility presented here helps us to reconcile causal determinism with moral responsibility, even if causal determinism is inconsistent with freedom to do otherwise. The case for the incompatibility of causal determinism and freedom to do otherwise is different from (and stronger than) the case for the incompatibility of causal determinism and moral responsibility.

Causal determinism can be defined as follows:

> *Causal determinism* is the thesis that, for any given time, a complete statement of the facts about the world at that time, together with a complete statement of the laws of nature, entails every truth as to what happens after that time.

Now the "basic argument" for the incompatibility of causal determinism and freedom to do otherwise can be presented. If causal determinism obtains, then (roughly speaking) the past together with the natural laws entail that I act as I do now. So if I am free to do otherwise, then I must either have power over the past or power over the laws of nature. But since the past and the laws of nature are "fixed"—for instance, I cannot now so act that the past would have been different from what it actually was—it follows that I am not now free to do otherwise.[21]

This is obviously a brief presentation of the argument; a more careful and detailed look at the "basic argument" is beyond the scope of this presentation.[22] It should be evident, however, that a compatibilist about causal determinism and freedom to do otherwise must either deny the fixity of the past or the fixity of the laws. That is, such a compatibilist must say that an agent can have it in his power at a time so to act that the past would have been different from what it actually was, or that an agent can have it in his power so to act that a natural law that actually obtains would not obtain.[23] Even if these compatibilist claims are not obviously false, they are certainly not easy to swallow.

The approach to moral responsibility developed here allows us to separate compatibilism about causal determinism and moral responsibility from compatibilism about causal determinism and freedom to do otherwise. The theory says that an agent can be held morally responsible for performing an action insofar as the mechanism actually issuing in the action is reasons-responsive; the agent need not be free to do otherwise. As I explain below, reasons-responsiveness of the actual-sequence mechanism is consistent with causal determination. Thus a compatibilist about determinism and moral responsibility can *accept* the fixity of the past and the fixity of the natural laws. He need not accept the unappealing claims to which the compatibilist about causal determinism and freedom to do otherwise is committed. If it is the "basic argument" that pushes one to incompatibilism about causal determinism and freedom to do otherwise, this need not also push one toward incompatibilism about causal determinism and moral responsibility.

The theory of responsibility requires reasons-responsive mechanisms. For a mechanism to be reasons-responsive, there must be a possible scenario in which the same kind of mechanism operates and the agent does otherwise; but, of course, sameness of kind of mechanism need not require sameness of all details, even down to the "micro" level. Nothing in our intuitive conception of a kind of mechanism leading to action or in our judgments about clear cases of moral responsibility requires us to say that sameness of kind of mechanism implies sameness of micro details. Thus, the scenarios pertinent to the reasons-responsivenes of an actual-sequence mechanism may differ with respect both to the sort of incentives the agent has to do otherwise and the particular details of the mechanism issuing in action. (Note that if causal determinism obtains and I do X, then one sort of mechanism which actually operates is a "causally determined to do X" type of mechanism. But of course this kind of mechanism is not germane to responsibility ascriptions insofar as it is not temporally intrinsic. And whereas the kind, "causally determined," is temporally intrinsic and thus may be germane, it is reasons-responsive.)

If causal determinism is true, then any possible scenario (with the actual natural laws) in which the agent does otherwise at time T must differ in *some* respect from the actual scenario prior to T. The existence of such possible scenarios is all that is required by the theory of moral responsibility. It is not required that the agent be able to bring about such a scenario (i.e., that the agent have it in his power at T so to act that the past, relative to T, would have been different from what it actually was). Furthermore, the existence of the required kind of scenarios is compatible with causal determinism.

The actual-sequence reasons-responsiveness theory of moral responsibility thus yields "semicompatibilism": moral responsibility is compatible with causal determinism, even if causal determinism is incompatible with freedom to do otherwise. Compatibilism about determinism and responsibility is compatible with *both* compatibilism and incompatibilism (as well as agnosticism) about determinism and freedom to do otherwise.[24]

Often incompatibilists use the example discussed above of the demonic scientists who directly manipulate one's brain. They then pose a challenge to the compatibilist: In what way is this sort of case *different* from the situation under causal determinism? There is clearly the following similarity: in both the cases of manipulation and determination, conditions entirely "external" to the agent causally suffice to produce an action. Thus, it may be that neither agent is free to do otherwise. However, as I argued above, there seems to be a crucial difference between the case of direct manipulation and "mere" causal determination. In a case of direct manipulation of the brain, it is likely that the process issuing in the action is not reasons-responsive, whereas the fact that a process is causally deterministic does not in itself bear on whether it is reasons-responsive. The force of the incompatibilist's challenge can be seen to come from the plausible idea that in neither case does the agent have freedom to do otherwise; but it can be answered by pointing to a difference in the actual-sequence mechanisms.

The same sort of considerations show that moral responsibility is consistent with God's foreknowledge, even if God's foreknowledge is incompatible with freedom to do otherwise. Let us suppose that God exists and thus knew in the past exactly how I would behave today. If I am free to do otherwise, then I must be free so to act that the past would have been different from what it actually was (i.e., so to act that God would have held a different belief about my behavior from the one he actually held). However, the past is fixed, and so it is plausible to think that I am not free to do otherwise, if God exists.

God's existence, however, is surely compatible with the operation of a reasons-responsive mechanism. God's belief is not a part of the mechanism issuing in my action (on a standard view of the nature of God). His belief is not what causes my action; rather, my action explains his belief. Thus there are possible scenarios in which the actual kind of mechanism operates and issues in my doing otherwise. (In these scenarios, God believes correctly that I will do other than what I do in the actual world.) Again, the cases for the two sorts of incompatibilism—about divine foreknowledge and responsibility and about divine foreknowledge and freedom to do otherwise—are *different*, and the actual-sequence reasons-responsiveness theory yields semicompatibilism.[25]

Structure and History

In this section I wish to contrast my approach to moral responsibility with a class of theories that might be called "mesh" theories of responsibility. My approach is a historical theory.

Consider first a "hierarchical" model of moral responsibility. In this model, a person is morally responsible for an action insofar as there is a mesh between a higher order preference and the first-order preference that actually moves him to action. On one version of this theory, which is suggested by some remarks by Harry Frankfurt, an agent is morally responsible for an action if there is conformity between his "second-order volition" and "will" (the first-order desire that moves the person to action).[26]

In another version of the theory, moral responsibility for an action is associated with conformity between "identification" and will.[27] According to Frankfurt's suggestion, one way of identifying with a first-order desire would be to formulate an unopposed second-order volition to act on it, together with a judgment that no further reflection would cause one to change one's mind.

The problem with such hierarchical "mesh" theories, no matter how they are refined, is that the selected mesh can be produced via responsibility-undermining mechanisms. After all, a demonic neurophysiologist can induce the conformity between the various mental elements via a sort of direct electronic stimulation that is not reasons-responsive. I believe that the problem with the hierarchical mesh theories is precisely that they are purely structural and ahistorical. It matters what kind of process issues in an action. Specifically, the mechanism issuing in the action must be reasons-responsive.

The "multiple-source" mesh theories are also purely structural. Rather than positing a hierarchy of preferences, these theories posit different sources of preferences. One such theory is that of Gary Watson, according to which there are "valuational preferences" (which come from reason) and motivational preferences.[28] Employing Watson's theory, one could say that an agent is morally responsible for an action insofar as there is a mesh between the valuational and motivational preference to perform the action.[29]

Again the problem is that such a theory is purely structural. The mesh between elements of different preference systems may be induced by electronic stimulation, hypnosis, brainwashing, and so on. Moral responsibility is a *historical* phenomenon; it is a matter of the kind of mechanism that issues in action.[30]

Conclusion

I have presented a sketch of a theory that purports to identify the class of actions for which persons are rationally accessible to moral praise and blame, and reward and punishment. I have claimed that this theory captures our clear intuitive judgments about moral responsibility, and that it helps to reconcile moral responsibility with causal determinism. I certainly have not *proved* that moral responsibility is compatible with causal determinism. Rather, my strategy has been to argue that the approach presented here allows the compatibilist about moral responsibility and determinism to avoid the commitments of the compatibilist about freedom to do otherwise and determinism. There might be other sorts of challenges to compatibilism about determinism and moral responsibility that my approach does not, in itself, answer.

The theory I have presented builds upon and extends the approaches of others. It avoids some of the most pressing objections to similar types of theories. These objections might seem convincing if one fails to "hold fixed" the actual-sequence mechanism, or if one employs strong rather than weak reasons-responsiveness, or if one does not suitably temporally index the theory.

I wish to end with a few suggestions about the relationship between the theory of moral responsibility presented here and punishment. A theory of moral responsibility needs to explain why certain creatures (and not others) are appropriate candidates for punishment. Punishment, of course, involves treating an individual "harshly" in some manner. It affects the desirability of performing a certain action. That is, punishment involves reacting to persons in ways to which the mechanisms on which they act are sensitive. My suggestion is that punishment is appropriate only for a creature who acts on a mechanism "keyed to" the kind of incentives punishment provides.

My point here is not that the justification of punishment is "consequentialist"—that it alters behavior. (Of course, this kind of justification does not in itself distinguish punishment from aversive conditioning.) Indeed, it is metaphysically possible that an individual's total pattern of choices and actions throughout life be "unalterable" by virtue of a continuous string of Frankfurt-type situations. (It is even possible that no human's behavior is alterable, because it is possible that all human beings are subject to Frankfurt-type counterfactual interventions.) My justification is nonconsequentialist and "direct": punishment is an appropriate reaction to the actual operation of reasons-responsive mechanisms. When it is justified, punishment involves a kind of "match" between the mechanism that produces behavior and the response to that behavior.

The theory of moral responsibility, then, provides some insight into the appropriateness of punishment for certain actions. But it does not in itself provide a full account of the appropriate *degrees* of punishment. For instance, it may be the case that the appropriate degree of severity of punishment for a particular action is less than (or greater than) the magnitude of the incentive to which the actual-sequence mechanism is responsive. This is entirely compatible with saying that punishment—being a "provider of reasons"—is appropriately directed to agents who act on reasons-responsive mechanisms.

NOTES

1. Strawson calls the attitudes involved in moral responsibility the "reactive attitudes": P. F. Strawson, "Freedom and Resentment," *Proceedings of the British Academy* 48 (1962): 1–25.

2. Some contemporary versions of similar theories are found in Alasdair MacIntyre, "Determinism," *Mind* 56 (1957): 28–41; Jonathan Glover, *Responsibility* (New York: Humanities Press, 1970); Herbert Fingarette, *The Meaning of Criminal Insanity* (Berkeley: University of California Press, 1972); Wright Neely, "Freedom and Desire," *Philosophical Review* 83

(1974): 32–54; Timothy Duggan and Bernard Gert, "Free Will as the Ability to Will," *Nous* 13 (1979): 197–217; Lawrence Davis, *A Theory of Action* (Englewood Cliffs, N.J.: Prentice-Hall, 1979); Michael Levin, *Metaphysics and the Mind-Body Problem* (Oxford: Clarendon, 1979); Robert Nozick, *Philosophical Explanations* (Cambridge: Harvard University Press, 1981); and Daniel Dennett, *Elbow Room: The Varieties of Free Will Worth Wanting* (Cambridge: MIT Press, 1984). For an excellent survey of some aspects of these approaches, see David Shatz, "Free Will and the Structure of Motivation," in *Midwest Studies in Philosophy* 10, ed. Peter French, Howard Weittstein, and Theodore Uehling (Minneapolis: University of Minnesota Press, 1985, pp. 444–74.

3. I contrast this kind of bank teller with one who, in exactly the same circumstances, does not have an irresistible impulse to comply with the demand. Such a teller may be morally responsible (though not necessarily *blameworthy*) for handing over the money.

4. John Locke presented an interesting example of a man who voluntarily stays in a room which, unknown to him, is locked: John Locke, *Essay Concerning Human Understanding*, Bk. II, chap. 12 Secs. 8–11. For a number of examples of agents who are morally responsible for actions although they could not have done otherwise, see Harry Frankfurt, "Alternate Possibilities and Moral Responsibility," *Journal of Philosophy* 46, no.23 (1969): 829–39. Also see John Martin Fischer, "Responsibility and Control," *Journal of Philosophy* 79, no. 1 (1982): 24–40.

5. For a vigorous and interesting criticism of this description of the case, see Peter van Inwagen, "Ability and Responsibility," *The Philosophical Review* 87 (1978): 201–24, reprinted in Peter van Inwagen, *An Essay on Free Will* (Oxford: Clarendon, 1983), pp. 161–82. Although it is inappropriate to pursue the details of the debate here, I defend the claim that there are cases in which an agent is morally responsible for performing an action although he couldn't have done otherwise; see Fischer, "Responsibility and Control."

6. I owe this way of describing the Frankfurt-type cases to Sydney Shoemaker.

7. Here I am indebted to Duggan and Gert, "Free Will as the Ability to Will."

8. Ibid.

9. Robert Nozick requires this sort of close contouring of action to value for his notion of "tracking value": see Nozick, *Philosophical Explanations*, pp. 317–62. In this respect, then, Nozick's notion of tracking value corresponds to strong reasons-responsiveness. Nozick claims that an agent who tracks value displays a kind of moral virtue, but he does not claim that tracking value is a necessary condition for moral responsibility.

10. Here I adopt the constraint that the possible worlds pertinent to the weak reasons-responsiveness of the actual-sequence mechanism must have the same *natural laws* as the actual world.

11. Ferdinand Schoeman has brought to my attention a kind of example that threatens my claim that weak reasons-responsiveness is sufficient for moral responsibility. Imagine someone who is apparently insane. This person commits a barbarous act, such as killing a number of persons on the Staten Island Ferry with a saber. And suppose that this individual would have killed the persons under all possible circumstances except one: he would have refrained if he believed that it was Friday and thus a religious holiday. Intuitively, the individual is highly irrational and should not be considered morally responsible, and yet he seems to satisfy the condition of acting from a reasons-responsive mechanism. Weak reasons-responsiveness obtains by virtue of the agent's responsiveness to a bizarre reason, even though the agent is not responsive to a wide array of relevant reasons.

I am aware that this sort of example poses a problem for the theory of responsibility I present here. At this point, I see two possible responses. First, one might claim that in this kind of case there would be a different mechanism operating in the alternate scenario (in which the agent is responsive) than in the actual sequence. Alternatively, one might restrict the reasons that are pertinent to weak reasons-responsiveness. I hope to discuss such examples and to develop an adequate response in future work.

12. Roughly, one might distinguish between "internalist" and "externalist" accounts of knowledge. An internalist proceeds by requiring that the agent have a certain sort of *justification* for his belief. The externalist abandons the search for refined kinds of justification and requires certain kinds of causal connections between the fact known and the agent's belief.

13. I am obviously presenting only a sketch of a theory of knowledge here. Further, I do not here suppose that this is obviously the *correct* account of knowledge. I am merely pointing to an analogy between my approach to moral responsibility and the externalist conception of knowledge. The approach to knowledge presented here follows those of, among others, Dretske and Nozick: F. Dretske, "Conclusive Reasons," *Australasian Journal of Philosophy* 49 (1971): 1–22; and Nozick, *Philosophical Explanations*, pp. 167–98. Nozick also discusses the analogy between moral responsibility and knowledge.

14. Nozick claims that this fact helps to refute a certain kind of epistemological skeptic. See Nozick, *Philosophical Explanations*, pp. 197–247.

15. Nozick, *Philosophical Explanations*, p.179.

16. Ibid., pp. 180–81. Nozick attributes this example to Avishai Margalit.

17. Ibid., p. 191.

18. I have left extremely vague the crucial notion of "same mechanism." There are certainly very disturbing problems with this notion in epistemology. For a discussion of some of these problems, see Robert Shope, "Cognitive Abilities, Conditionals, and Knowledge: A Response to Nozick," *Journal of Philosophy* 81, no.1 (1984): 29–48. And there may well be similar problems in action theory. Here I am simply relying on some intuitive way of individuating kinds of mechanisms issuing in action, for the purposes of moral responsibility ascriptions. A defense of the sketch of a theory that I am presenting would involve saying more about the individuation of mechanisms.

19. The claim, as stated, relies on the intuition that the physical process P is the relevant mechanism. Alternatively, one could simply point out that in Jim's case *there exists* an actually operative mechanism (of kind P) that is temporally intrinsic and not reasons-responsive.

20. Daniel Dennett says: "The possibility of short-circuiting or otherwise tampering with an intentional system gives rise to an interesting group of perplexities about the extent of responsibility in cases where there has been manipulation. We are generally absolved of responsibility where we have been manipulated by others, but there is no one principle of innocence by reason of manipulation." Daniel Dennett, "Mechanism of Responsibility," reprinted in *Brainstorms*, ed. Daniel Dennet (Montgomery, Vt.: Bradford, 1978), pp. 233–55, esp. p. 248. My suggestion provides a way of distinguishing responsibility-undermining manipulation from manipulation that is consistent with responsibility.

21. For some contemporary developments of the "basic argument" for incompatibilism, see Carl Ginet, "Might We Have No Choice?" in *Freedom and Determinism*, ed. K. Lehrer (New York: Random House, 1966); David Wiggins, "Towards a Reasonable Libertarianism," in *Essays on Freedom of Action*, ed. T. Honderich (Boston: Routledge and Kegan Paul, 1973); J. W. Lamb, "On a Proof of Incompatibilism," *Philosophical Review* 86 (1977); and Peter van Inwagen, "The Incompatibility of Free Will and Determinism," *Philosophical Studies* 27 (1975), and *An Essay on Free Will* (Oxford: Clarendon, 1983), esp. pp. 55–105.

22. I have discussed the argument in John Martin Fischer, "Incompatibilism," *Philosophical Studies* 43 (1983): 127–37; "Van Inwagen on Free Will," *Philosophical Quarterly* 36 (1986): 252–60; and "Freedom and Miracles," *Nous* 22 (1988), pp. 235–252. For a classic

discussion of the argument, see David Lewis, "Are We Free to Break the Laws?" *Theoria* 47 (1981): 113–21.

23. For an interesting alternative challenge to certain formulations of the "basic argument," see Michael Slote, "Selective Necessity and the Free-Will Problem," *Journal of Philosophy* 82 (1982): 5–24.

24. I believe that Frankfurt is a compatibilistic semicompatibilist. I am an agnostic semicompatibilist, although I am perhaps a latently incompatibilistic semicompatibilist. In "Responsibility and Control" I pointed out that Frankfurt-type cases do not in themselves establish the consistency of causal determinism and moral responsibility. Thus, Frankfurt-type cases leave open the position of "ultra-incompatibilism": Causal determinism is incompatible with moral responsibility, even if moral responsibility does not require freedom to do otherwise. Here I have preferred agnostic (or perhaps incompatibilistic) semicompatibilism to agnostic (or incompatibilistic) ultra-incompatibilism.

25. I have here sketched an approach that attempts to reconcile moral responsibility *for action* with causal determinism and God's foreknowledge. My approach relies on the claim that moral responsibility for an action does not require freedom to do otherwise. Elsewhere I have argued that, whereas an agent can be morally responsible for performing an action although he could not have done otherwise, an agent cannot be held responsible for *not* performing an action he could not have performed: John Martin Fischer, "Responsibility and Failure," *Proceedings of the Aristotelian Society* 86 (1985–86): 251–70. If this "asymmetry thesis" is true, then I still have not reconciled moral responsibility *for omissions* (or perhaps, for "not-doings") with causal determinism (and divine foreknowledge).

I do not have the space here fully to develop my theory of responsibility for not performing actions. But I can say that, even if an agent is not responsible for failing to do something he could not do, an agent may be held morally responsible for *something* (perhaps, a "positive" action). And so he will be accessible to praise or blame. I believe that such a theory of moral responsibility can be developed so as to reconcile causal determinism (and divine foreknowledge) with the moral attitudes we think are intuitively appropriate.

26. Harry Frankfurt, "Freedom of the Will and the Concept of a Person," *Journal of Philosophy* 68 (1971): 5–20, esp. p. 15.

27. Frankfurt discusses the notion of identification in "Identification and Externality," in *The Identities of Persons*, ed. A. O. Rorty. (Berkeley: University of California Press, 1976); and "Identification and Wholeheartedness," chap. 2 of *Responsibility, Character, and the Emotions*, ed. Ferdinand Schoeman (Cambridge: Cambridge University Press, 1987).

28. Gary Watson, "Free Agency," *Journal of Philosophy* 72 (1975): 205–20.

29. I am not sure whether Watson himself is committed to the sufficiency of the mesh for moral responsibility. He is committed to the claim that an agent is free insofar as he has the power to effect a mesh between the valuational and motivational systems. Ibid., p. 216.

30. Moral responsibility is in this respect like such notions as justice and love for a particular person. Nozick argues in *Anarchy, State, and Utopia* (New York: Basic Books, 1974) that justice and love are historical rather than "current time-slice" notions. Purely structural approaches to moral responsibility are inadequate in a way that is parallel to the inadequacy of current time-slice approaches to justice.

4
RESPONSIBILITY FOR OMISSIONS

John Martin Fischer and Mark Ravizza

We have argued that persons can be morally responsible for actions and conse-quences that are inevitable for them. That is, there are cases in which an agent can legitimately be held morally responsible for performing an action he could not have avoided performing; and there are cases in which an agent can legitimately be held morally responsible for a consequence-universal that he could not have prevented from obtaining. Further, we have argued that a certain sort of associa-tion of moral responsibility with *control* helps to explain these facts. More specifi-cally, the association of moral responsibility with guidance control helps to explain why moral responsibility for actions and consequences does not require alternative possibilities.

We now turn to omissions. We shall begin, as in our discussion of moral re-sponsibility for consequences, with a puzzle. We shall then look to the nature of control—in particular, guidance control—to help to resolve the puzzle.

Some Examples
Omissions and Alternative Possibilities

Performing actions and bringing about consequences are instances of what might be called "positive agency."[1] It will be useful to recall here an example involving positive agency, "Hero."

In "Hero," Matthew is walking along a beach, looking at the water. He sees a child struggling in the water, and he quickly deliberates about the matter, jumps

Some of this chapter is based on material previously presented in John Martin Fischer, "Re-sponsibility and Failure," *Proceedings of the Aristotelian Society* 86 (1985–86): 251–70; John Martin Fischer and Mark Ravizza, "Responsibility and Inevitability," *Ethics* 101 (1991): 258–78; and John Martin Fischer, "Responsibility, Control, and Omissions," *Journal of Ethics* 1 (1997): 45–64.

into the water, and rescues the child. We can imagine that Matthew does not give any thought to not trying to rescue the child, but that if he had considered not trying to save the child, he would have been overwhelmed by literally irresistible guilt feelings that would have caused him to jump into the water and save the child anyway. We simply stipulate that in the alternative sequence the urge to save the child would be genuinely irresistible.

Apparently, Matthew is morally responsible—indeed, praiseworthy—for his action, although he could not have done otherwise. Matthew acts freely in saving the child; he acts exactly as he would have acted if he had lacked the propensity toward strong feelings of guilt. Here is a case in which no responsibility-undermining factor operates in the actual sequence, and thus Matthew is morally responsible for what he does.

"Hero" is of course just one example of many cases of moral responsibility for positive agency in which the agent does not have the sort of control that involves alternative possibilities. Are there cases of negative agency in which the agent does not have alternative possibilities and yet in which he can be held morally responsible for his omission?

Before considering some examples, let us pause to say a few words about the problematic notion of "omissions." One way of classifying them distinguishes wider and narrower conceptions of omissions. On the wider conception (which may not link up closely with ordinary usage), whenever a person does not do something A, he fails in the relevant sense to do it, and he omits to do it. Thus, we are all now failing to stop the Earth's rotation (and omitting to stop the Earth's rotation). Omission to do A (according to the wide conception) need not require explicit deliberation about A, and it need not require the ability to do A. We shall, in part for the sake of simplicity, adopt this wide conception of omissions. Our views, however, are compatible with various ways of narrowing the notion of omissions. And even if one takes a rather narrow view of what an omission is, it is still important to have an account of moral responsibility for failures that *don't* count as omissions (narrowly construed). After all, in ordinary usage we do talk of moral responsibility for not doing A, and the various apparently plausible ways of narrowing the notion of omissions may well turn out to be contentious.[2]

Consider, now, "Sloth," which is similar in some respects to "Hero." In "Sloth," John is walking along a beach, and he sees a child struggling in the water. John believes that he could save the child with very little effort, but he is disinclined to expend any energy to help anyone else. He decides not to try to save the child, and he continues to walk along the beach.

Is John morally responsible for failing to save the child? Unknown to John, the child was about to drown when John glimpsed him, and the child drowned one second after John decided not to jump into the water. The facts of the case exert pressure to say that John is not morally responsible for failing to save the child: after all, the child would have drowned even if John had tried to save it. John could not have saved the child. John may well be morally responsible for deciding not to try to save the child and even for not trying to save the child, but he is *not* morally responsible for not saving the child. "Sloth" is no different in this respect from a case ("Sharks") exactly like it, except that the child would not have drowned immediately; rather, a patrol of sharks that (unknown to John) infested the water between the beach and the struggling child would have eaten John, had he jumped in.[3]

Imagine, similarly, that Sue thinks that she can end a terrible drought by doing a rain dance. Of course, Sue is wrong, and she does not in fact have the power to affect the weather. Suppose, also, that there are no clouds in sight (and no clouds within hundreds of miles); atmospheric conditions imply that it will not in fact rain for weeks. Now Sue happens to hate the local farmers, and she would like to hurt them in any way possible. While falsely believing that she could easily end the drought immediately, she deliberately refrains from doing her rain dance.[4]

Is Sue morally responsible for failing to cause it to rain (i.e., for not ending the drought) in "Rain Dance"? Again, there is pressure to say that whereas Sue might be morally responsible for not doing the rain dance and for not trying to end the drought, she is *not* morally responsible for not ending the drought. After all, Sue could not have ended the drought.

The cases presented here are cases in which an agent omits to do something *good*. We now turn to a similar case in which an agent omits to do something *bad*: "Flat Tire." Imagine that you are a small-time thug strolling along a dimly lit street in a deserted part of town. Suddenly, you spy a shiny, new Mercedes with a flat tire stranded by the side of the road. The driver of the car is a well-dressed, elderly gentleman with a bulging billfold in his breast pocket. You are tempted to hurry over to the car, assault the old man, and steal his money. Fortunately, you decide against this, and you continue along your way.

Are you morally responsible for failing to rob the driver? Well, unknown to you (and the driver of the car), the Mafia has put drugs into the trunk of the car. Five Mafioso thugs are watching the car from five other cars in the neighborhood. They have strict instructions: if anyone threatens the driver of the car, they are to shoot that person with their Uzis. In these circumstances, we can safely imagine that, if you had attempted to rob the driver, you would have been killed.

We believe that you are *not* morally responsible for failing to rob the driver. You might be morally responsible for *deciding* not to rob the driver (an action), for *not deciding* to rob the driver (an omission), and for *not trying* to rob the driver (an omission). But there is strong pressure to say that you are simply *not* morally responsible for *not robbing the driver*, and this pressure comes from the fact that you *could not* rob the driver. In "Flat Tire," you are not morally responsible for failing to do a bad thing that you could not do.

These cases suggest that an agent cannot be held morally responsible for not performing an action he cannot perform. Thus, these cases, in conjunction with "Hero" (and a whole array of cases of positive agency), suggest that actions and omissions are *asymmetrical* with respect to the requirement of alternative possibilities. That is, moral responsibility for an action does not require the freedom to refrain from performing the action, whereas moral responsibility for failure to perform an action requires the freedom to perform the action. A similar asymmetry is suggested for moral responsibility for consequences and moral responsibility for omissions: moral responsibility for a consequence does not require the freedom to prevent the consequence, whereas moral responsibility for failure to perform an action requires the freedom to perform the action.[5] Although the "asymmetry thesis" holds that positive agency in general—actions and their consequences—is relevantly different from omissions with respect to the requirement of alternative possibilities, we will focus primarily on the asymmetry between actions and omissions.

Omissions and Frankfurt-Type Cases

The cases of omissions presented in the previous section suggest that moral responsibility for the failure to do A requires the ability to do A. But there are other cases that suggest precisely the opposite. Consider the following remarks by Harry Frankfurt:

> In ["Sharks"] John decides against saving a drowning child who (because there are sharks nearby) would have drowned even if John had tried to save him. Fischer and Ravizza suggest that it is discordant to insist that in these circumstances John is morally responsible for not saving the child. They are right about this. But what explains the discordance is not, as they suppose, the fact that it was impossible for John to save the child.
>
> This fact might have been due to circumstances of quite a different sort than those that they describe. Thus, imagine that if John had even started to consider saving the child, he would have been overwhelmed by a literally irresistible desire to do something else; and imagine that this would have caused him to discard all thought of saving the child. With this change, the case of John exactly parallels another of Fischer's and Ravizza's examples—that of Matthew ["Hero"].[6]

In virtue of the apparent parallel status of "Hero" and the Frankfurt-style version of "Sloth," Frankfurt holds that John should be considered morally responsible for failing to save the child (in his version of "Sloth"). If so, this is a case in which an individual is morally responsible for failing to do A even though he *cannot do A*.

Other philosophers have presented similar "Frankfurt-type" omissions cases.[7] Clearly, the Frankfurt-type version of "Sloth" could be developed with a counterfactual intervener (a nefarious—or even nifty and nice—neurosurgeon who would manipulate the brain in the alternative scenario), as described in previous chapters. Here is just this sort of case (developed by Randolph Clarke):

> Sam promises to babysit little Freddy. But Sam forgets. No one makes Sam forget; it just slips his mind. Consequently, he fails to show up to babysit little Freddy. Unbeknownst to Sam, a mad scientist is monitoring his thoughts. Had Sam been going to remember his promise, the scientist would have intervened and prevented him from remembering it. The scientist would not have intervened in any other way. As it happened, the scientist did not intervene at all; there was no need to.[8]

Clarke's analysis of this case, call it "Babysitter 1," is as follows:

> Here . . . Sam's not showing up depends on his forgetting; had Sam remembered, nothing would have prevented him from keeping his promise. He would have done so. And Sam is responsible for forgetting. Since his not showing up *depends* in this

way on something for which he is responsible, it seems to me that he is responsible for not showing up.[9]

Clarke goes on to suggest a principle according to which an agent is morally responsible for an omission to perform a certain action only if: had he intended to perform that action, and had he tried to carry out that intention, then he would have performed the omitted action. Of course, an agent may be unable to perform the relevant action because he cannot form the appropriate intention: this is true of Sam in "Babysitter 1." But it is also true of him that *if* he had formed this intention and tried to carry it out, he would have succeeded in performing the omitted action. Thus, Sam can be held morally responsible for not showing up to babysit.

A very similar view about moral responsibility for omissions is defended by Alison McIntyre.[10] She first presents the following case, which appears to confirm the idea (of the previous section) that moral responsibility for omissions requires the ability to do the relevant action:

> You are a forest ranger and a large forest fire is approaching from the north. You believe that you could start a backfire heading north which would burn the timber in the fire's path and thereby prevent the forest fire from continuing southward. More specifically, you believe that you could use the gasoline in your truck's fuel tank and some dry matches in your kitchen to do this. But you decide not to start a backfire, the forest fire sweeps onward, and a large area of forest to the south is destroyed. Unbeknownst to you, the truck's fuel tank has sprung a leak and is now empty, and your matches are sitting in a puddle of water. You couldn't have started a backfire if you had tried. If we suppose that there was no other method of stopping the fire available to you, it follows that you could not have prevented the fire from continuing southward if you had tried.[11]

McIntyre goes on to give two versions of the case. In the first version:

> It is your duty as a forest ranger to start a backfire and you believe that you should do so, but out of laziness rationalized with the vain hope that the fire will burn itself out, you do nothing to stop the fire. When you come to be aware of what you believe to be the full consequences of your omission you feel terrible.[12]

Here, in "Forest Ranger 1," it seems that you are not morally responsible for failing to start a backfire (despite the fact that you "feel terrible"). McIntyre agrees with this view, but she now presents a Frankfurt-type version of her case; in this version of the case, she assumes that the fuel tank has *not* sprung a leak and the matches are *not* wet, and she says:

> You, the forest ranger, decide not to start a backfire to prevent the forest fire from advancing southward. A group of fanatical environmentalists who are zealous opponents of forest fire prevention efforts have hired a super-skilled neurologist to monitor your deliberations. If you had shown any sign of seriously considering the option of starting a backfire, the neurologist would have intervened and caused you to decide not to take any preventive action. As things turned out, you decided "under your own steam" not to act, but because of the neurologist's monitoring, you

could not have decided to start a backfire if you had believed that there was reason to do so, and because of this fact, you could not have started a backfire.[13]

As McIntyre points out, in contrast to her first case, in this case (which we shall call "Forest Ranger 2"), you seem to be morally responsible for failing to start the backfire and thus for failing to stop the forest fire. And this is so, even though you could not have started a backfire and you could not have stopped the forest fire. You are responsible for your failures here, on her view, because in the Frankfurt-type version of the case ("Forest Ranger 2"), "you could have started a backfire [and thus stopped the forest fire] if you had decided to do so and had tried."[14] You cannot start the backfire, because the neurologist is set up to *prevent you from deciding and trying*; but given, hypothetically, that you *do* decide and try, there is nothing to prevent you from succeeding. So, in "Forest Ranger 2," you could not have started the backfire; but you could have started it, if you had decided and tried. This fact highlights the difference between "Forest Ranger 1" and "Forest Ranger 2": in "Forest Ranger 1" you would (and could) not have started a backfire if you had tried (because of the leaking fuel tank and wet matches); but in "Forest Ranger 2," you would have succeeded in starting a backfire, if you had tried.

McIntyre and Clarke thus hold a similar view: they contend that in cases in which one could have performed the relevant action, if one had decided (and/or tried), one can be morally responsible for the omission. That is, McIntyre and Clarke hold that when one's ability to do the act in question is dependent on one's decision (and/or efforts), then one may be morally responsible for failing to do A, even if one cannot do A.

Reflection on the cases of omissions presented in this and the previous section leads to a puzzle. Cases such as "Sloth," "Sharks," "Rain Dance," and "Flat Tire" render it plausible that in order to be morally responsible for failing to do A, one must be able to do A. However, cases such as the Frankfurt-style "Sloth" case, "Babysitter 1," and "Forest Ranger 2" suggest precisely the opposite. If one wants to say what seems plausible about the Frankfurt-style omissions cases, how can one also say what is plausible about the first range of cases (including "Sloth," "Sharks," and "Rain Dance")?

There are cases of positive agency—performing actions and bringing about consequences—in which moral responsibility does not require alternative possibilities. But in the realm of negative agency—omissions—we have a puzzle: in part of the realm it seems that there is a requirement of alternative possibilities for moral responsibility, but in another part of the realm it seems that there is no such requirement.

We believe that the puzzle can be solved by appeal to an association of moral responsibility with guidance control. In the following section, we shall develop a notion of guidance control of omissions that builds on the accounts of guidance control for actions and consequences. Then we shall employ this notion to argue that the conditions for moral responsibility for positive and negative agency are *symmetric*: in the case of neither positive nor negative agency does moral responsibility require alternative possibilities. We shall maintain that there is indeed an interesting difference between the two groups of omissions cases described here;

but we shall show how this difference can be acknowledged compatibly with the view that moral responsibility does not require alternative possibilities.

The Symmetric Approach to Moral Responsibility

The Account of Guidance Control of Omissions

The tools for resolving this puzzle are already at hand. We have argued in *Responsibility and Control* that in cases of positive agency, moral responsibility is associated with control in a certain way. More specifically, we have argued that guidance control is the kind of control associated with moral responsibility in cases of positive agency. We started with actions and developed an account of guidance control of actions. This account employs the notion of moderate reasons-responsiveness. We then built on this model to develop an account of guidance control of consequences. On this account, there may be two steps: a certain kind of mechanism issues in the bodily movement, and then a process takes place that connects the bodily movement to some event in the external world. In order for the sequence (involving both steps) to be appropriately responsive to reason, the mechanism leading to the bodily movement must be moderately reasons-responsive, and the process leading to the event in the external world must be sensitive to the bodily movement.

The key to resolving the puzzle about omissions is to develop an analogous account of guidance control for omissions. If guidance control is all the control required for moral responsibility for omissions, then perhaps we can say just the right thing about the entire array of cases presented in the preceding sections. On this approach, it is *not* the case that alternative possibilities are required for *any part* of the realm of omissions. Whereas it may seem that the only way to explain why an agent is not morally responsible for certain omissions is to cite his inability to perform the relevant actions, *another* explanation is available: the agent may lack guidance control of the omission. Further, on this approach, positive and negative agency are symmetric with respect to the requirement of alternative possibilities: guidance control (and not regulative control) is the kind of control associated with moral responsibility for positive and negative agency. Let us call this the Symmetric Principle of Moral Responsibility. (In the rest of this chapter, we shall be focusing primarily on the negative-agency component of the Symmetric Principle; thus, when we speak of the Symmetric Principle, we shall be speaking about the component of it that claims that guidance control is the sort of control necessary and sufficient for moral responsibility for omissions.)

Like actions (and consequences), omissions may be relatively simple or complex. A simple omission would be the failure to move one's body in a certain way (where this can include failure to keep the body still). Let us call these "bodily omissions." For example, a bodily omission might be the failure to keep one's eyes directed straight ahead, or the failure to raise one's hand, and so forth. In these cases, the way one actually moves one's body (where this can include simply keeping the body still) "fully constitutes" the omission.[15] Here the application of the notion of guidance control is also relatively simple: it is natural to say that one has guidance control of one's failure to do A (in a case of a bodily omission) just in case one's actual bodily movement B (which fully constitutes the omission) issues from one's own, moderately reasons-responsive mechanism. As with the case of actions, one here holds fixed the actual-sequence mechanism that issues in B, and asks what would happen in a relevant range of alternative scenarios. The account is parallel to the account in the case of action.

A bit more specifically, let us suppose that the failure to do A here is the actual movement of one's body in a certain way B, which occurs via a mechanism of kind M. What is it for one's failure to do A to issue from a moderately reasons-responsive mechanism? It must be the case that, holding the operation of M and the natural laws fixed, there is a suitable range of scenarios in which the agent recognizes sufficient reasons (some of which are moral reasons) to move in some alternative way B^*, and in at least one scenario in which the agent has a sufficient reason to move in way B^*, he does so (for that reason), and his doing so would count as his doing A. Thus, there is a sense in which our treatment of moral responsibility for simple or bodily omissions is a special case of our treatment of moral responsibility for actions.

Now let us turn to complex omissions. A complex omission is not fully constituted by a bodily movement. For example, an individual's failure to cause an alarm to go off is a complex omission; intuitively, it involves not just a bodily movement, but also a relationship between the bodily movement and the alarm's not going off. In general, a failure to do A is a complex omission insofar as doing A would require more than simply moving one's body. (So, in the preceding example, failure to cause an alarm to go off is a complex omission insofar as causing an alarm to go off involves more than just a bodily movement.) It is natural to say that an agent has guidance control of his failure to do A (where this is a *complex* omission) just in case: (1) his movement of his body in a certain way is moderately responsive to reason, and (2) the relevant event in the external world is suitably sensitive to his failure to move his body in a different way. Of course, this is the structure of the general account of moral responsibility for consequence-universals, presented in our *Responsibility and Control*. Thus, it will be fruitful to think of complex omissions as the bringing about of certain sorts of consequence-universals.

We contend that, when an agent's omission is a complex omission, he should be construed as bringing about a relatively narrowly specified negative consequence-universal. So, for example, imagine that, in "Good Fortune," John walks along a beach, sees a child struggling in the water, and simply decides to continue walking (and not to bother to try to save the child). Here, it seems (at first blush) that John brings about the negative consequence-universal, *that the child is not saved (from drowning)*. But suppose that the child is saved from drowning by floating to a nearby island within a few seconds of John's decision. John has failed to save the child, but he has not brought about the negative consequence-universal, *that the child is not saved (from drowning)*. What he *does* bring about, however, is *that the child is not saved by him*.[16] And, in general, we contend that it is fruitful to construe complex omissions on this model, that is, as the agent's bringing about relatively finely specified negative consequence-universals.

Having thus construed complex omissions, moral responsibility for such omissions is determined simply by applying the analysis of moral responsibility for consequence-universals. Suppose that in the actual world an agent S moves his body in way B at time T via a type of mechanism M, and S's moving his body in way B at T causes some consequence-universal C to obtain at $T+i$ via a type of process P. Then the sequence leading to the consequence-universal C is responsive if and only if there exists a range of possible scenarios R in which an M-type mechanism operates and a way of moving S's body $B*$ (other than B), such that:

1. S recognizes what can be seen as an understandable pattern of reasons for action (in the scenarios that compose R), some of which are moral; and there is some possible scenario in R in which S has reason to move his body in way $B*$ at T, and S does move his body in $B*$ at T (for that reason). [This, together with the right side of the preceding biconditional, corresponds to MRR in the "first stage."]

2. If S were to move his body in way $B*$ at T, all other triggering events (apart from $B*$) that do *not actually* occur between T and $T+i$ were *not* to occur, and a P-type process were to occur, then C would not occur.[17] [This corresponds to sensitivity to action in the "second stage."]

As we said earlier, complex omissions involve a bodily movement and an individual's being related to a relatively finely specified negative consequence-universal. So, for example, to apply the analysis to "Good Fortune," we first consider whether John's bodily movements are moderately responsive to reasons. The answer seems to be yes. Next, we consider whether the relatively finely specified consequence-universal, *that the child is not saved by John*, is sensitive to John's bodily movements. The answer here is negative: the same consequence-universal would have obtained no matter how John moved his body at the relevant time. That is, even if John had jumped into the water, he would not have saved the child (because the child would have floated to the island). Thus, John is not morally responsible for failing to save the child, in "Good Fortune." And this is as it should be, insofar as "Good Fortune" is not relevantly different from "Sharks," as regards John's moral responsibility.

Of course, in a case just like "Good Fortune" but in which there is no nearby island and the child drowns, the analysis implies (as it should) that John *is* indeed morally responsible for not saving the child. In this case, John's bodily movements are appropriately responsive to reasons, and the negative consequence-universal, *that the child is not saved by John*, is sensitive to John's bodily movements (assuming that there are no sharks nearby, and so forth): if he had jumped into the water, he would have saved the child. In general, then, we can ascertain an agent's moral responsibility for a complex omission by simply applying the analysis of moral responsibility for consequence-universals; moral responsibility for complex omissions can be treated as a *special case* of moral responsibility for consequence-universals, where the consequence-universals in question are relatively finely specified negative consequence-universals.

Some Applications

Let us now apply this account to the range of examples already presented. All of the examples in question involve complex omissions. In the first group, "Sloth," "Sharks," "Rain Dance," and "Flat Tire," the agents all actually move their bodies in certain ways. These bodily movements are, presumably, moderately responsive to reasons. In all of these cases, however, there is a problem at the second stage: the relevant events in the external world are not suitably sensitive to the agents' bodily movements. So, in "Sharks," John's bodily movement that constitutes his failure to jump into the water and head toward the struggling child is moderately responsive to reason. (He is thus morally responsible for his simple, "bodily" omission.) But even if John had moved his body in the relevant alternative way, the child would not have been saved by him—the sharks would have eaten him.[18] (So John is not morally responsible for the complex omission.) Similarly, although Sue's failure to do the rain dance is moderately responsive to reason, the drought would not have been ended by her (presumably) even if she had done it. Whereas Sue is responsible for the simple, "bodily" omission, she is not responsible for the complex omission.[19]

The same sort of analysis applies to *all* the cases in the first group. In all of these cases the agents are not morally responsible for the relevant omissions because they lack guidance control of the complex omissions. And they lack such control in virtue of failure to meet the conditions that pertain to the second stage: sensitivity of the external event to one's bodily movements.

Now consider the second group of cases: Frankfurt-type omissions (the Frankfurt-type "Sloth" case, "Babysitter 1," and "Forest Ranger 2"). In all of these cases the agents lack the ability to do the relevant action, in virtue of the presence of a Frankfurt-style counterfactual intervener. But in all of these cases the agents have guidance control of the relevant omissions, and thus are appropriately considered morally responsible for those omissions.

Take, for example, the Frankfurt-type "Sloth" case. Here, in virtue of John's propensity toward certain irresistible urges, John cannot move his body in any way other than the way he actually does, and thus he cannot save the child. But, nevertheless, his actual bodily movements issue from a moderately reasons-responsive mechanism.[20] After all, the irresistible urges play no role in the actual sequence— they are not part of the mechanism that actually issues in action. Further, the child would have been saved by John, if John had moved his body in certain different ways. Thus, John's actual bodily movements are moderately responsive to reason, and the child's not being saved by John is sensitive to John's failure to move his body in the relevant alternative way. John thus displays the linked and interlocking sensitivities characteristic of guidance control. So John has guidance control of his failure to save the child, and is morally responsible for it. And the same sort of analysis applies to *all* the Frankfurt-type omissions cases.

Consider, finally, an interesting case suggested to us by David Kaplan.[21] We shall call this case "Penned-In Sharks." In "Penned-In Sharks" a bad man wants to make sure that the child (struggling in the water) is not saved. He has penned in a number of hungry sharks, which he will release if and only if John were to jump into the water. As it happens, John does not jump into the water (as in "Sharks"), and thus the bad man keeps the sharks in their pen; but had John jumped in, the bad man would have released the sharks, and they would have eaten John.

Our account implies that we must hold fixed the actually existing pen, when ascertaining whether the event of the child's not being saved by John *is* appropriately sensitive to John's bodily movements. Thus, we must say that John is indeed morally responsible for not saving the child in "Penned-In Sharks." We are, then, committed to a distinction between "Penned-In Sharks" and "Sharks," as regards John's moral responsibility.

We admit that such cases are puzzling and difficult. But we maintain that this distinction is, upon reflection, *justified*. In "Penned-In Sharks," one holds fixed the actualized conditions, and "subtracts" or disregards the conditions that *would have obtained* in the alternative sequence. And note that this is precisely what one is doing in the Frankfurt-type omissions cases. That is, in the Frankfurt-type "Sloth" case, one is holding fixed the *actual* kind of mechanism, and subtracting off or disregarding the irresistible urges (which occur only in the *alternative scenario*). We agree with such philosophers as Frankfurt, Clarke, and McIntyre about the Frankfurt-type omissions cases. And if this way of treating such cases is indeed correct, then we submit that our treatment of "Penned-In Sharks" is *also* correct. That is, it is appropriate to treat counterfactual changes in the *second stage* just like counterfactual changes in the *first stage*. How could one justify treating them differently?

To help motivate our position on "Penned-In Sharks," consider William Rowe's "Case A":

> There is a train approaching a fork in the track controlled by a switch. The left fork (#1) leads on to where a dog has been tied to the track. If the train proceeds on #1 it will hit the dog. Track #2, however, leads to a safe stopping point for the train. The switch is set for #2. You throw the switch to #1 with the result that the train proceeds on #1, hitting the dog.[22]

We have claimed (with Rowe) that you are morally responsible for the consequence-universal, *that the dog is hit*. Further, we contended that you would *also* be morally responsible for this consequence-universal if there had been a counterfactual intervener associated with you who would have "zapped your brain" and thereby ensured that you throw the switch to track #1, if you had shown any inclination not to do so. (We shall here call this case "Case A*.") That is, if there is a Frankfurt-type counterfactual intervener in the first stage, this should not matter to your moral responsibility for the consequence-universal.

It is now useful to consider another example from William Rowe. This example, which we shall dub "Case D," is just like "A" except that "a powerful being is poised to bend track #2 around to the place where the dog is tied if, but only if, you do not switch the train to track #1."[23] Rowe claims—and we agree—that in his "Case D" you are morally responsible for the consequence-universal, *that the dog is hit*, given that, as in "Case A," you do in fact switch the train to track #1. "Case D" is then relevantly similar to "Case A*" as regards your moral responsibility. In "Case A*" the counterfactual intervention is in the first stage, and in "Case D" it is in the second stage; but in both cases you are morally responsible for the relevant consequence-universal. And, insofar as complex omissions are being treated on the model of bringing about consequence-universals, there is good reason to think that one's treatment of "Penned-In Sharks" should be similar to one's approach to Rowe's "Case D." In both "Penned-In Sharks" and Rowe's "D," a counterfactual intervention in the second stage would prevent the agent from bringing about a different sort of event than is actually brought about; but in both cases it is appropriate to hold fixed the *lack* of such intervention, in evaluating the moral responsibility of the agent.

Reply to Clarke and McIntyre

Recall the example of Randolph Clarke's, which we have dubbed "Babysitter 1":

> Sam promises to babysit little Freddy. But Sam forgets. No one makes Sam forget; it just slips his mind. Consequently, he fails to show up to babysit little Freddy. Unbeknownst to Sam, a mad scientist is monitoring his thoughts. Had Sam been going to remember his promise, the scientist would have intervened and prevented him from remembering it. The scientist would not have intervened in any other way. As it happened, the scientist did not intervene at all; there was no need to.

Contrast "Babysitter 1" with another example of Clarke's, which we shall call "Babysitter 2":

> Sam promises to babysit little Freddy. But Sam forgets. No one makes Sam forget; it just slips his mind. Consequently, he fails to show up to babysit little Freddy. Unbeknownst to Sam, a malevolent busybody is monitoring his behavior. Had Sam remembered his promise and started out for Freddy's house, the busybody would have intercepted him and prevented him from going to Freddy's house.[24]

Although Clarke believes Sam can be held morally responsible for not showing up at Freddy's house in "Babysitter 1," he believes this is *not* the case in "Babysitter 2." He says, "After all, even if he had remembered his promise and set out to fulfill it, he would not have done so."[25] On Clarke's approach, in assessing moral responsibility for an omission to do A, it is crucial to determine whether the agent would have done A if he had chosen to do A and tried to do A.

But we believe that it is highly implausible to say that in "Babysitter 1," Sam *is* morally responsible for not showing up at Freddy's house, but in "Babysitter 2" he is *not*. In fact, "Babysitter 2" is relevantly similar to "Penned-In Shark" and Rowe's "Case D," in which, we believe, the agents *are* morally responsible. Clarke's differentiation (between the two "Babysitter" cases) is based on whether the counterfactual intervener would intervene just *prior* to the agent's trying to do A or just *after* it. But we don't see why *this* difference should make a difference to Sam's moral responsibility. On our approach, which embraces the Symmetric Principle, the "Babysitter" cases are treated alike: in both cases Sam has guidance control of his not showing up at Freddy's house, and thus in both cases he is morally responsible for his not showing up at Freddy's.

Alison McIntyre is committed to the same sort of implausible differentiation made by Clarke. After presenting her "Forest Ranger 1," we saw that she develops a Frankfurt-style omissions case, which we called "Forest Ranger 2":

> You, the forest ranger, decide not to start a backfire to prevent the forest fire from advancing southward. A group of fanatical environmentalists who are zealous opponents of forest fire prevention efforts have hired a super-skilled neurologist to

monitor your deliberations. If you had shown any sign of seriously considering the option of starting a backfire, the neurologist would have intervened and caused you to decide not to take any preventive action. As things turned out, you decided "under your own steam" not to act, but because of the neurologist's monitoring, you could not have decided to start a backfire if you had believed that there was reason to do so, and because of this fact, you could not have started a backfire.

She claims—and we agree—that this case is crucially different from "Forest Ranger 1." She claims—and we agree—that in "Forest Ranger 2" you are morally responsible for failing to start the backfire. (Recall that in this case the matches are dry and the gas tank is full.) But now we present a version of the case that McIntyre does *not* consider. In this version, which we shall call "Forest Ranger 3," everything is as in "Forest Ranger 2" except that the neurologist would have "zapped" you just *after* you had decided to start a backfire (rather than just *prior*). That is, had you decided to start a backfire, the neurologist would have intervened in such a way as to prevent you from starting the backfire.

We claim that "Forest Ranger 2" and "Forest Ranger 3" should be treated *similarly*: in *both* cases you can legitimately be held morally responsible for failing to start the backfire. "Forest Ranger 2" and "Forest Ranger 3" are parallel to "Babysitter 1" and "Babysitter 2." And yet McIntyre, like Clarke (in the parallel cases), must distinguish "Forest Ranger 2" and "Forest Ranger 3." This is because she endorses the following account of moral responsibility for omissions:

> An agent is morally responsible for omitting to perform an action A only if
> (a) the agent decided not to do A through a process of ordinary deliberation,
> (b) in *some* situation in which the agent believed that there was reason to do A, the agent would have decided to do A through a process of ordinary deliberation, and
> (c) the agent could have done A if he or she had decided to do so in the actual circumstances.[26]

In part because of condition (c), McIntyre (along with Clarke) must distinguish such cases as "Forest Ranger 2" and "Forest Ranger 3." But this differentiation is intuitively implausible. In contrast, our approach treats "Forest Ranger 2" and "Forest Ranger 3" *alike*. In *both* cases you have guidance control of your failure to start the backfire, and thus in both cases you are morally responsible for not starting the backfire.

An Additional Reply to McIntyre

We shall now turn to another example proposed by Alison McIntyre:

> A meeting of the New York Entomological Society features an international array of dishes prepared using insects. [McIntyre here refers to Maialisa Calta, "Bug Seasoning: When Insect Experts Go in Search of Six-Legged Hors d'oeuvres," *Eating Well* 3 (1992), pp. 22–24.] You, a guest, are invited to sample a tempura dish made of fried crickets. You don't find the prospect of eating insects appealing, though you don't find it disgusting either, and you decline the offer. Suppose that in order to have decided to accept the offer, you would have had to look more closely at the fried crickets. But

if you had looked more closely you would have been overwhelmed with revulsion and would have been incapable of deciding to eat some. Since you never do look more closely at the crickets, you decide not to have any without experiencing any feelings of revulsion, and without even suspecting that you would feel revulsion if you examined the dish more closely.[27]

McIntyre employs this example—call it "Insects"—as part of a critique of the Symmetric Principle. She says:

> This approach, when applied to omissions, would yield too liberal a condition of moral responsibility. It will turn out that you are morally responsible for omitting to eat the crickets even if there is no possible situation in which you, as you actually are disposed and constituted, could have eaten them.[28]

McIntyre's point is that, in the story, you are actually so constituted that you would have been overwhelmed with revulsion if you had looked more closely at the fried crickets. And if we assume that this revulsion is so strong that there is no possible situation in which you would have eaten the crickets (given this revulsion), it seems implausible to say that you are morally responsible for your failing to eat the crickets.

But recall that, as things actually went, the revulsion played absolutely no role in your deliberations and your failure to eat the crickets. And note that McIntyre's "Insects" case, in the version she employs to criticize the Symmetric Principle, seems to be precisely parallel to the Frankfurt-style "Sloth" case. Recall that in the Frankfurt-style "Sloth" case, John fails to save the child and indeed fails even to consider doing so; but if he were to start to consider saving the child, he would have been overwhelmed by a literally irresistible desire to do something else. Here it is Frankfurt's view (and ours) that John is morally responsible for failing to save the child. Because we agree with Frankfurt about his version of "Sloth," we are inclined to disagree with McIntyre about "Insects." That is, just as John is morally responsible for failing to save the child in Frankfurt's version of "Sloth," so you are morally responsible for failing to eat the crickets in "Insects."[29]

Conclusion

We began with a puzzle. It seems that in some cases—such as "Sloth," "Sharks," "Rain Dance," and "Flat Tire"—an agent cannot be held morally responsible for failing to do A precisely because he could not have done A. If this were indeed true, then there would be a rather surprising asymmetry between positive and negative agency: responsibility in the context of positive agency would not require alternative possibilities, whereas responsibility in the context of negative agency would. But there are other cases—Frankfurt-style omissions cases such as Frankfurt's version of "Sloth," "Babysitter 1," and "Forest Ranger 2"—in which it seems that the agents can be morally responsible for their failures to do A, even though they are not able to do A.

We have suggested a resolution of this puzzle. The resolution builds naturally on the approach to moral responsibility for positive agency developed in previous chapters. Just as moral responsibility for positive agency is associated with guidance control, so moral responsibility for negative agency is *also* associated with *guidance control*. The account of guidance control in the context of negative agency is parallel to the account in the context of positive agency: given that the relevant mechanism is "one's own," guidance control consists in a certain sort of reasons-responsiveness.

This symmetric approach to moral responsibility for positive and negative agency allows us to say just the right things about the full spectrum of cases. It is also part of a systematic, unified theory of the full content of moral responsibility, which includes (at least) responsibility for actions, consequences, and omissions. Our approach shows how control of a specific kind plays a pivotal role in the account of moral responsibility for the various sorts of things for which we normally hold agents responsible. Finally, the association of moral responsibility for negative agency with guidance control gives further assistance to the semicompatibilistic project, for it is implausible to think that causal determinism rules out guidance control of omissions.

Appendix: The Asymmetric Principle

Presentation of the Principle

As always, we have sought a reflective equilibrium between intuitive judgments about a wide array of cases and principles. We have defended a symmetric approach to moral responsibility for positive and negative agency, according to which the control pertinent to moral responsibility is guidance control. We now wish to consider (and, ultimately, criticize) an alternative principle. This alternative to the Symmetric Principle implies precisely the asymmetry between positive agency and negative agency which we have here rejected: it implies that, whereas moral responsibility for actions does not require alternative possibilities, moral responsibility for omissions does.[30]

In order to state the Asymmetric Principle, we need various ingredients. The first ingredient is the distinction between guidance control and regulative control, which we have developed at some length already. The second ingredient is a certain sort of account of the nature of omissions. We take it that when a person performs an action—does something—he causes (or brings about) a state of affairs (or consequence-universal). So when (say) a pilot performs an act of turning a plane westward, she causes (in an appropriate way) a certain upshot: *that the plane turns to the west*. And when an individual turns on a light, he causes (in a certain way) the state of affairs, *that the light goes on*, and so forth. In performing an action, an agent stands in the "bringing about" relation to a universal.

In the text we contended that omissions involve an agent's bringing about a relatively finely specified negative consequence-universal. In contrast to this account, the proponent of the asymmetric approach claims that omissions involve an agent's *not causing* the relevant positive state of affairs. So, on this approach, when we seek to analyze acts and omissions, we do not have *one* relation—the causing or bringing about relation—and *two* kinds of states of affairs (positive and negative); rather, we seem to have *two* kinds of relations—bringing about (causing) and not bringing about (not causing)—and *one* kind of state of affairs. When an agent performs an action, he stands in the "bringing about" relation to a certain upshot, and when an agent refrains from performing the same sort of action, he stands in the "not bringing about" relation to the same sort of upshot. For the sake of the argument in the appendix, we shall provisionally adopt this analysis of omissions.

We now have the two ingredients required for the statement of the Asymmetric Principle: the distinction between the two kinds of control, and the analysis of the nature of the relations involved in action and omission. We begin by considering a typical case where an agent can be said to be morally responsible for performing an action. Let us say that, under ordinary circumstances (no manipulative scientists, sharks, and so forth) a lifeguard jumps into the water and saves a drowning child. The lifeguard is rationally accessible to praise for saving the child—he is morally responsible for saving the child. The lifeguard, insofar as he saves the child, stands in the "bringing about" relation to the upshot, *that the child is saved*. And, in this case, the lifeguard has (on plausible assumptions, including no presupposition of causal determinism) both guidance and regulative control over the relevant state of affairs—*that the child is saved*. Obviously, other cases could be presented in which an agent is morally responsible for performing an act and the agent has both guidance control and regulative control over the relevant state of affairs.

What is interesting about the Frankfurt-style action cases is that they show that an agent can be morally responsible for performing some act A even though he lacks regulative control over the pertinent state of affairs universal, A*. (If A is "saving the child," then A* is *that the child is saved*.) It seems that in these examples the agent's responsibility for doing A implies that the agent has guidance control of A*. (How could one have guidance control of one's doing A without having guidance control of A*?) Earlier, we claimed that doing A and failing to do A both involve relations (of different kinds) to the same sort of state of affairs, A*. So it is extremely plausible to suggest the following basic principle: moral responsibility for doing A or for failing to do A requires at least one of the two kinds of control with respect to A*. At a deep level, this principle treats actions and omissions uniformly—responsibility for doing A or for failing to do A both require control with respect to A*. But an asymmetric principle of moral responsibility can be derived from this basic principle.

According to the basic principle, moral responsibility requires at least one of the two kinds of control. And there are cases in which an agent is morally responsible for doing A, although he lacks regulative control over A*. But by the very nature of omissions (on the analysis adopted here, for the sake of the argument), when an agent omits to perform A, he does *not* have guidance control of the relevant state of affairs, A*. That is, if the lifeguard fails to save the child, he does not have guidance control of the state of affairs, *that the child is saved*—he does not cause (in the appropriate way) this state of affairs. Thus, when an agent omits to perform A, he *must* have *regulative* control over A*, if he is to have any sort of control of A*. And hence, by the basic principle of moral responsibility, if an agent is to be morally responsible for omitting to do A, he must have regulative control over A*. The Asymmetric Principle is derived from a *symmetric basic principle*; however, it treats positive and negative agency differently to the extent that it requires guidance control of the relevant state of affairs for moral responsibility for actions, but regulative control of the relevant state of affairs for moral responsibility for omissions.

If the lifeguard is to be morally responsible for failing to save the child, he must have regulative control over the state of affairs, *that the child is saved*. But in order to have regulative control over this state of affairs, he must have the power to cause (in the manner appropriate to control) it to be the case that the child is saved. Thus, he must be able to save the child. In general, then, when an agent omits to do A, he must be able to do A, if he is to have any sort of control with respect to A*. And so, in general, if an agent is to be morally responsible for failing to do A, he must be able to do A. But when an agent does A, he may exhibit guidance control without having regulative control over the upshot. The Asymmetric Principle, then, is as follows: an agent may be morally responsible for doing A even though he cannot refrain from doing A, but in order for an agent to be morally responsible for failing to do A, he must be able to do A.

Critique of the Asymmetric Principle

The Asymmetric Principle implies that moral responsibility for failing to do A requires the ability to do A. Since the Frankfurt-type omissions cases convince us that moral responsibility for failing to do A does *not* require the ability to do A, we are inclined to reject the Asymmetric Principle. But on what theoretical grounds can the principle be questioned?

First, the principle's derivation depends on adopting the contentious claim that omissions involve an agent's not causing the relevant positive state of affairs (universal), rather than an agent's causing a relatively finely specified negative consequence-universal (the analysis adopted in the text of the chapter). Given the latter analysis, the Asymmetric Principle cannot be derived. But we shall let this pass, and we shall point out that the derivation of the Asymmetric Principle is problematic, even on the assumption of the former analysis.

The basic problem is that it is not obvious why the *particular* association of responsibility with control suggested by the basic principle (from which the Asymmetric Principle is derived) is correct. More specifically, the basic principle says that moral responsibility for doing A (say, "saving the child") or failing to do A (say, "not saving the child") requires some sort of control of the relevant sort of state of affairs A* (say, *that the child is saved*). But why pick out A* as the item with respect to which some control must be exhibited (or possessed)? After all, there are other possibilities here—other items (such as the actions and omissions themselves, rather than the related positive states of affairs) that could be selected as the items with respect to which control must be exhibited.

Let us look at the situation more carefully. A particular analysis of omissions is developed by the proponent of the basic principle from which the Asymmetric Principle is derived. That analysis posits that omissions involve, by their very nature, relations to positive states of affairs of a certain sort. (So, for example, not saving the child involves an agent's being in the not-causing relation to the positive state of affairs, *that the child is saved*.) The proponent of the basic principle then selects *that positive state of affairs (that the child is saved)* as the item with respect to which (in the case of both actions and omissions) control must be exhibited. But why select *that* item? Why not instead say what the Symmetric Principle says: that moral responsibility for an action (say, the child's being saved) requires guidance control of the *action*, and moral responsibility for an omission (say, not saving the child) requires guidance control of the *omission*? Here is a symmetric picture; but here the same sort of control is required of *actions and omissions* rather than the *state of affairs allegedly involved in actions and omissions*.

We can see no reason to select the item posited by the proponent of the Asymmetric Principle; that is, we can see no *argument* for the selection made by the proponent of the Asymmetric Principle *as opposed to* the selection made by the proponent of the Symmetric Principle. Note that the particular analysis of the nature of omissions offered by the proponent of the Asymmetric Principle simply offers one analysis, of various available analyses, of omissions. (Of course, we have offered a different analysis in the text of this chapter.) If it is correct, then omissions are "not causings" of positive states of affairs of certain sorts. But it *still* remains unclear why the principle of responsibility should *select the positive states of affairs* as the items with respect to which control must be displayed. It does not *follow* from the analysis of omissions that the positive state of affairs is the item with respect to which control must be exhibited, in order for an agent to be morally responsible. Putting it slightly differently, there are two separate steps: the analysis of omissions and the selection of the "control-relevant items." And the analysis of omissions does not in itself entail a particular selection as to the control-relevant items.

There is, then, *no* theoretical reason to prefer the Asymmetric Principle to the Symmetric Principle. The Symmetric Principle has the virtues of simplicity and systematic elegance. And it fits better with our considered judgments about Frankfurt-type omissions cases.[31]

NOTES

1. We shall say that, even if the "bringing about" of the consequence is via an omission, it is positive agency. Nothing substantial hangs on this point.

2. Let us say that one adopted a narrower conception of omissions, according to which omitting to do A requires the ability to do A. This now seems to entail that, if causal determinism is true together with incompatibilism about causal determinism and alternative possibilities (which, as I have suggested in previous work is very plausible), then no one ever omits to do anything. We wish to adopt a conception of omissions that does not have this implausible result, given that we think incompatibilism about causal determinism and ability to do otherwise is very plausible.

Further, in the examples about to be presented in the text, the agents seem to omit to do certain things they in fact *cannot do*. If this is correct, then it is not appropriate to claim that it is a conceptual requirement on omitting to do A that one have the power to do A.

3. As regards the conceptual issue about omissions mentioned in the previous note, it seems pretty clear that in "Sloth" and "Sharks" John omits to save the child; and yet in

neither case does he have the power to save the child. (It must be conceded, however, that we have not adduced considerations that show that one could not seek to associate omitting to do A with having the *general ability* to do A-type things. Nevertheless, we think it prudent to avoid narrowing the notion of omissions in potentially contentious ways.)

4. This kind of example is from Carl Ginet.

5. Note that the consequences in question here may be brought about by either actions or omissions (depending on the nature of the relevant bodily movement B).

6. Harry Frankfurt, "An Alleged Asymmetry between Actions and Omissions," *Ethics* 104 (1994): 620.

7. For interesting and useful discussions of moral responsibility for omissions, including Frankfurt-type omissions cases, see Ishtiyaque Haji, "A Riddle Regarding Omissions," *Canadian Journal of Philosophy* 22 (1992): 485–502; Randolph Clarke, "Ability and Responsibility for Omissions," *Philosophical Studies* 73 (1994): 195–208; David Zimmerman, "Acts, Omissions, and 'Semi-compatibilism,'" *Philosophical Studies* 73 (1994): 209–23; Alison McIntyre, "Compatibilists Could Have Done Otherwise: Responsibility and Negative Agency," *Philosophical Review* 103 (1994): 453–88; and Walter Glannon, "Responsibility and the Principle of Possible Action," *Journal of Philosophy* 92 (1995): 261–74.

8. Clarke, "Ability and Responsibility," p. 203.

9. Ibid., pp. 203–204.

10. McIntyre, "Compatibilists Could Have Done Otherwise."

11. Ibid., p. 458.

12. Ibid.

13. Ibid., pp. 465–66.

14. Ibid., p. 466.

15. These omissions are like Frankfurt's "personal" failures; see Harry Frankfurt, "What We Are Morally Responsible For," in Leigh S. Cauman, Isaac Levi, Charles Parsons, and Robert Schwartz, eds., *How Many Questions? Essays in Honor of Sidney Morgenbesser* (Indianapolis: Hackett, 1983), pp. 321–35; reprinted in John Martin Fischer and Mark Ravizza, eds., *Perspectives on Moral Responsibility* (Ithaca, N.Y.: Cornell University Press, 1993).

16. Of course, John's bodily movements do not result in the child's not being saved by him in the sort of clear, almost "mechanical" way in which someone's bodily movements result in (say) the car's moving in a certain way, when the person steers the car in that way. But it is a mistake to think of causation narrowly in this "mechanistic" way. We contend that, on a plausible conception of causation, John's bodily movements can be said to cause the child's not being saved by John. Note that John's bodily movements are part of a set of conditions sufficient, in the circumstances, for the child's not being saved by John. Further, John's movements could reasonably be cited as offering an *explanation* of the fact that the child is not saved by John. And if, in making causal ascriptions, we are interested in selecting factors that, in general, can be manipulated fruitfully in order to change the outcome, it certainly makes sense to select John's bodily movements as causally relevant to the child's not being saved by John. For an extremely enlightening development of the sort of picture of causality that is relevant here, see Joel Feinberg, *Doing and Deserving: Essays in the Theory of Responsibility* (Princeton, N.J.: Princeton University Press, 1970). Particularly important are the essays "Action and Responsibility," pp. 119–51, and "Causing Voluntary Actions," pp. 152–86.

17. The interval between T and $T+i$ is here understood inclusively.

18. It might be thought that the sharks' sensing that John has jumped into the water is a nonoccurring triggering event whose nonoccurrence must (according to our analysis) be held fixed. But if so, then the sharks would *not* have eaten John, and John would have saved the child. (We are indebted to Ted Levine for raising this worry.) Note, however,

that, in the alternative sequence, John's jumping into the water would antedate and lead to the shark's sensing that he has done so: thus, the shark's sensing John would *not* "initiate"—in the relevant sense—the sequence leading to the child's not being saved by John (and would thus not be a *triggering* event). Similarly, in "Flat Tire," the Mafioso thugs' pulling their triggers in the alternative scenario would not initiate the sequence leading to the gentleman's not being robbed by you; rather, that sequence would be initiated by your moving toward the gentleman with the apparent intention of robbing him. Thus, these pullings of the trigger would be "triggering events" only via a pun. We concede, however, that the notion of "initiation" is vague and context-dependent, and thus that our notion of a triggering event is similarly vague and context-dependent.

19. John Locke presented a case that might be called the "proto-Frankfurt-type case," in which a man voluntarily stays in a room that, unknown to him, is locked. See John Locke, *An Essay Concerning Human Understanding*, ed. Maurice Cranston (New York: Collier, [1690] 1965), pp. 149–50. Some philosophers have contended that this man can be morally responsible for his failure to leave the room. (For this view, see Michael J. Zimmerman, *An Essay on Moral Responsibility* [Totowa, N.J.: Rowman and Littlefield, 1988], pp. 120–26; and Haji, "A Riddle Regarding Omissions," p. 487.) But we contend that insofar as the man's failure to leave the room is a *complex* omission, he is *not* morally responsible for it. That is, the man's failure to leave the room is not simply a matter of his bodily movements; as with complex omissions in general, his performing the relevant act—leaving the room—requires not just certain bodily movements, but also the cooperation of the external world. The man may well be morally responsible for the simple, bodily omission (his failure to move his body in certain ways); but he is not morally responsible for failing to leave the room.

20. We assume that the actual-sequence mechanism in "Frankfurt-type Sloth" is practical reasoning, as it is in "Sloth." In "Sloth"—and thus in "Frankfurt-type Sloth"—John decides not to try to save the drowning child. If deciding not to try to save the child requires considering saving the child, then the most natural interpretation of Frankfurt's description of the case is as follows: if John were to start *seriously to consider* saving the child, he would be overwhelmed by irresistible desires to do something else. Alternatively, if one interprets Frankfurt's example so that the actual-sequence mechanism is nonreflective, then on this interpretation of the example, our approach would also imply that John is morally responsible for failing to save the child.

21. Kaplan suggested this case in conversation after a version of this chapter was given as a lecture at UCLA in February 1995.

22. William L. Rowe, "Causing and Being Responsible for What Is Inevitable," *American Philosophical Quarterly* 26 (1989): 153; reprinted in Fischer and Ravizza, *Perspectives*.

23. Ibid., p. 155.

24. Clarke, "Ability and Responsibility," p. 202.

25. Ibid., p. 203.

26. McIntyre, "Compatibilists Could Have Done Otherwise," pp. 466–67.

27. Ibid., pp. 485–86.

28. Ibid., pp. 486–87.

29. Further support for our position comes from reflection on the theoretical considerations McIntyre invokes as part of her critique of the Symmetric Principle. "According to that approach [of Fischer and Ravizza], even if *you* could not have decided to eat some crickets because of your propensity to revulsion, *the mechanism* that actually produced your decision could have done so, and, as a result, you can be morally responsible for your omission. Of course, if we can stipulate that you do not have, or are not affected by, your propensity to feel revulsion, then there would be no obstacle to identifying some possible

situation in which you eat some crickets. But what justifies this stipulation? It seems that one could quite reasonably object that this is suspiciously similar to inferring that *you could have done otherwise* from the fact that *you could have done otherwise if what would have prevented you from doing otherwise hadn't existed!*" (ibid., 486).

We believe that McIntyre's criticism misses the mark. On our approach to both actions and omissions, freedom to do otherwise is not required for moral responsibility; rather, what is relevant are features of the actual sequence that leads to the action or the omission. We certainly agree that someone who actually faces some insuperable obstacle to doing otherwise cannot do otherwise, and it would simply be irrelevant, for most purposes, to point out (what might, in any case, be true) that the agent would be able to do otherwise if the obstacle were subtracted. Since our approach to moral responsibility does not require alternative possibilities, we are not here in the business of assessing an agent's freedom to do otherwise.

Rather, we are interested in evaluating the mechanisms and processes that actually lead to actions, consequences, and omissions. Since in "Insects" the propensity toward revulsion played no role in your decision or bodily movements, it is not part of the mechanism that actually issues in that decision and those bodily movements. Thus, it is irrelevant to the issue of whether that actual-sequence mechanism is responsive to reasons, and thus also to the issue of whether you are morally responsible for your omissions. Clearly, it would be inappropriate to subtract the propensity toward revulsion in considering whether you could have done otherwise; but it is not inappropriate to subtract it when considering whether the actual-sequence mechanism that issues in your omission has a certain feature—responsiveness. (Of course, "Insects" is in this respect similar to Frankfurt-type cases of the sort we have been discussing throughout the book.)

In focusing on the properties of the actual mechanisms and processes that lead to actions, consequences, and omissions, we are seeking to develop what we have dubbed an "actual-sequence" approach to moral responsibility. But notice that these actual-sequence properties may indeed be dispositional properties; as such, their proper analysis may involve (for example) other possible worlds. In the context of an actual-sequence approach to moral responsibility, we have argued that it is required that a reasons-responsive sequence actually occur; then, we have analyzed reasons-responsiveness in terms of other possible worlds. We have pointed out that, whereas other possible worlds are relevant to ascertaining whether there is some actually operative dispositional feature (such as responsiveness), such worlds are *not* relevant in virtue of bearing on the question of whether some alternative sequence is genuinely accessible to the agent.

30. The argument in favor of the Asymmetric Principle was first presented in John Martin Fischer, "Responsibility and Failure," *Proceedings of the Aristotelian Society* 86 (1985–86), pp. 251–70, reprinted in *The Spectrum of Responsibility*, ed. Peter A. French (New York: St. Martin's Press, 1991). Also, see John Martin Fischer and Mark Ravizza, "Responsibility and Inevitability," *Ethics* 101 (1991): 258–78. Given the argument in the text of the chapter and the following critique of the Asymmetric Principle, it is evident that we have changed our minds about the appropriate treatment of moral responsibility for omissions. We are very grateful to our various critics for helping us here.

31. At one point in Frankfurt's discussion, he suggests a view quite similar to our "guidance control" model. "But what is supposed to account for the difference in the sorts of control that actions and omissions require? Fischer and Ravizza simply provide no reason for believing that cases of the one type require a different sort of control than cases of the other. In my view, there is every reason to prefer an account that is straightforwardly symmetrical. If what moral responsibility requires in a case of action is just 'actual causal control' [guidance control] of the relevant *movement*, then what it requires in a case of omissions is just the same 'actual causal control' [guidance control] of the *omission* of the

relevant movement" (Frankfurt, "An Alleged Asymmetry between Actions and Omissions," pp. 621–22).

Note that Frankfurt's proposal here only applies explicitly to *bodily* omissions. Also, it is a mystery what the relationship is between this proposal and a quite different one presented by Frankfurt (presumably to cover cases of omissions that are not mere bodily omissions): "In Fischer's and Ravizza's version of the example ['Sharks'], John bears no moral responsibility for failing to save the child. This is not, however, because he cannot save the child. The real reason is that what he does has no bearing at all upon whether the child is saved. The sharks operate both in the actual and in the alternative sequences, and they see to it that the child drowns no matter what John does. In the revised version of the example [the Frankfurt-style version], the child is also bound to drown. But the effect of revising the example is that, in the revised actual sequence, the child drowns *only* because John refrains from acting to save him. . . . *That* is why John is morally responsible for failing to save the child even though he cannot prevent him from drowning" (ibid., pp. 622–23).

But why have two different sorts of explanation for the two kinds of omissions cases? (Our model provides a unified account of moral responsibility for omissions.) Also, it just seems false that "the child drowns only because John refrains from acting to save him." Surely, the child drowns at least in part because he was careless in swimming where he shouldn't have, he wasn't wearing a life vest, and so forth.

5
RESPONSIBILITY AND SELF-EXPRESSION

To be morally responsible for one's behavior is to be an apt target for what Peter Strawson called the "reactive attitudes"—and certain associated practices—on the basis of it.[1] The reactive attitudes include resentment, indignation, hatred, love, gratitude, and respect. The associated practices include moral praise and blame, and reward and punishment.

Moral responsibility requires (among other things) control of one's behavior. But there are different kinds of control. One sort of control entails the existence of genuinely accessible alternative possibilities: I call this sort of control "regulative control." The presence of regulative control is typically signaled by the use of the preposition "over." So, when an individual has control over his behavior, he has more than one path available to him; he (say) performs an action, but he could have done otherwise (in the sense of "could" that expresses the distinctive sort of ability involved in free will).

I believe that an agent can control his behavior, and be in control *of* it, without having control *over* it. In such a circumstance, the agent has what I call "guidance control," but not regulative control. He guides his behavior in the way characteristic of agents who act freely, and yet he does not have alternative possibilities with respect to his decision or action. Of course, an agent may have both sorts of control—regulative control and guidance control. But the fact that an agent can

I have benefited from reading versions of this paper to the philosophy departments at the University of Rochester, the University of California, Santa Barbara, the University of California, Riverside, the University of California, Davis, Cornell University and Utah State University. Additionally, I read a version of this paper at the Southern California Philosophy Conference at the University of California, Irvine. I am especially grateful to the following for their generous and helpful comments: Ted Sider, David Braun, Richard Feldman, Christopher McMahon, Kevin Falvey, Matthew Hanser, Mark Ravizza, Michael Bratman, Paul Hoffman, Eric Schwitzgebel, and Gideon Yaffe.

have guidance control without regulative control shows that they are distinct forms of control.

I contend that moral responsibility requires guidance control, but not regulative control. That is, guidance control exhausts the "freedom-relevant" (as opposed to the epistemic) component of moral responsibility. In this chapter I wish to provide a measure of intuitive support for the claim that guidance control is all the control (or freedom) necessary for moral responsibility. I begin by exploring some recent attempts to defend the view that alternative possibilities are required for moral responsibility (and thus that regulative control is an essential ingredient of moral responsibility). I shall propose what I take to be the intuitive "picture" that drives the view that alternative possibilities are required for moral responsibility. I go on to offer an argument against the view that regulative control is required for moral responsibility; on my view, this argument shows that the picture behind the regulative control view of moral responsibility is not the correct one— it doesn't capture what we value about moral responsibility. Finally, I shall develop an alternative picture which I believe both explains, at an intuitive level, what is going on with behavior for which an agent is morally responsible, and also helps to explain exactly why guidance control is all the control required for moral responsibility.

Responsibility and Regulative Control

Frankfurt-Type Cases

There can be cases in which an agent deliberates, chooses, and acts freely, on whatever your favorite account of such things is, and yet because of the presence of a fail-safe device which does not play any actual role in the agent's deliberation or behavior, the agent has no alternative possibilities with respect to choice or action. The fail-safe device does not actually intervene, but would intervene under certain counterfactual circumstances to produce exactly the same sort of choice and action as actually take place. Following recent tradition, I shall call such cases "Frankfurt-type" cases.

Here is a particular version of a Frankfurt-type case. In this sort of case, a crucial role is played by some kind of involuntary sign or indication of the agent's future choices and behavior.[2] So suppose Jones is in a voting booth deliberating about whether to vote for Gore or Bush. (He has left this decision until the end, much as some restaurant patrons wait until the waiter asks before making a final decision about their meal.) After serious reflection, he chooses to vote for Gore, and does vote for Gore by marking his ballot in the normal way. Unknown to him, Black, a liberal neurosurgeon working with the Democratic Party, has implanted a device in Jones's brain which monitors Jones' brain activities.[3] If he is about to choose to vote Democratic, the device simply continues monitoring and does not intervene in the process in any way. If, however, Jones is about to choose to vote (say) Republican, the device triggers an intervention which involves electronic stimulation of the brain sufficient to produce a choice to vote for the Democrat (and a subsequent Democratic vote).

How can the device tell whether Jones is about to choose to vote Republican or Democratic? This is where the "prior sign" comes in. If Jones is about to choose at t_2 to vote for Gore at t_3, he shows some involuntary sign—say a neurological pattern in his brain—at t_1. Detecting this, Black's device does not intervene. But if Jones is about to choose at t_2 to vote for Bush at t_3, he shows an involuntary sign—a different neurological pattern in his brain—at t_1. This brain pattern would trigger Black's device to intervene and cause Jones to choose at t_2 to vote for Gore, and to vote for Gore at t_3.

Given that the device plays no role in Jones's deliberations and act of voting, it seems to me that Jones acts freely and is morally responsible for voting for Gore. And given the presence of Black's device, it is plausible to think that Jones does not have alternative possibilities with regard to his choice and action. So it appears that Jones is morally responsible for his choice and for voting for Gore, although he lacks regulative control over his choice and action.

At this point it may be objected that, despite the initial appearance, Jones *does* have at least *some* alternative possibility. Although Jones cannot choose or vote differently, he can still exhibit a different neurological pattern in his brain N^* (from the one he actually exhibits, N). I have called such an alternative possibility a "flicker of freedom." The flicker theorist contends that our moral responsibility always can be traced back to some suitably placed flicker of freedom; our responsibility is grounded in and derives from such alternative possibilities.

I concede that one can always find a flicker of freedom in the Frankfurt-type cases insofar as they are developed as prior-sign cases. That is, the agent will always at least have the power to exhibit an alternative sign. But I contend that the mere involuntary display of some sign—such as a neurological pattern in the brain, a blush, or a furrowed brow—is too thin a reed on which to rest moral responsibility. The power involuntarily to exhibit a different sign seems to me to be insufficiently robust to ground our attributions of moral responsibility.

I have argued for this contention at some length elsewhere.[4] The debate here is subtle and complex: there are different versions of the flicker strategy, and various different responses. But for my purposes in this paper perhaps it will be enough to reiterate one line of argument I have developed against the flicker approach. Note that in the alternative sequence (in which Jones shows neurological pattern N^*, which is indicative of an impending decision to vote for Bush), the sign is entirely involuntary, and the subsequent decision and vote are produced electronically. Thus, in the alternative sequence Jones cannot be said to be choosing and acting freely, and similarly, cannot be thought to be morally responsible for his choice and action.

Imagine, just for a moment, that there are absolutely no alternative possibilities, even the flimsy and exiguous flickers of freedom we have recently been entertaining. A regulative control theorist would say that under such circumstances the relevant agent cannot be morally responsible for his choice and action. Now add the flickers of freedom we have been considering—the power to exhibit a different neurological pattern, N^*. I find it very hard to see how adding this power can transform a situation in which there is no moral responsibility into one in which there is moral responsibility. How can adding a pathway along which Jones does *not* freely vote for Gore and is *not* morally responsible for voting for Gore make it the case that Jones actually *is* morally responsible for voting for Gore? This would seem to be alchemy, and it is just as incredible.

Similarly, suppose one had a theory of knowledge according to which some individual S (the individual in question is always called "S"!) knows that p only if S can discriminate p from relevant alternatives. This is structurally analogous to the view that moral responsibility requires regulative control. Whereas such a view is plausible, it would certainly be absurd to suppose that what transforms some case of lack of knowledge into a case of knowledge would be the existence of some alternative scenario in which the agent makes a mistake. How can adding a scenario in which S lacks knowledge (in this way) make it the case that S actually has knowledge?

Now of course it has been suggested that on the "relevant-alternatives" model of knowledge, it might paradoxically turn out that one knows less by knowing more. That is, by having more background knowledge one makes fewer alternatives relevant, and it thus becomes more difficult to rule out these alternatives. The flip side of the coin is that one can know more by knowing less. But this is a matter of having less background information; it is not a matter of adding a scenario in which one makes a mistake to a situation of lack of knowledge to transform it—almost as if by magic—into a situation in which one has knowledge.

The "New Defense" of Regulative Control

Recently a number of philosophers have defended the regulative control model in a way that might seem to be promising, even in light of the sort of argument I have just sketched. Basically the strategy involves identifying some more robust alternative possibility which exists, even in the Frankfurt-type examples (with the prior-sign structure). The proponents of this strategy might concede that the power to exhibit a different involuntary sign is a mere flicker of freedom, but they will insist that there are deeper, more important kinds of powers possessed by agents in the examples.

Consider, for example, the following remarks of Michael McKenna:

> Here I believe that Fischer has not fully addressed what motivates the advocate of [regulative control] . . . what intuitively drives [the proponent of regulative control] is the kind of control needed in order for us to avoid being the author of a *particular* act and thus avoid being responsible for the production of *that* particular action. . . . It is a matter of holding people accountable for what they do only if they can avoid any blame or punishment that might fall upon them for performing those very particular actions which they do perform.[5]

McKenna elaborates as follows:

> The issue . . . here is whether the will . . . places *my* stamp upon the world, and whether *it is up to me . . . to have that particular stamp or some other as my mark upon the world.* In the Frankfurt-type cases the alternatives are, either doing what one does of one's own intention, or being coerced into performing the same kind of action

against one's will. These alternatives do seem to be quite impoverished: however, they mean all the difference between one's doing something of one's own will, and one's not doing that kind of thing of one's own will. . . . What more fundamental kind of control can there be here other than the control for one to either have a particular will or not have it?[6]

McKenna is claiming that even in the Frankfurt-type cases, the relevant agent has a significant and robust power: the power either to be the author of his action or not, and thus the power to be morally responsible for his action or not. A similar point is made in an interesting recent article by Keith Wyma. Wyma begins with an example which suggests that many of us experienced something like a Frankfurt-type example as we were growing up:

> When I was four years old and learning to ride a bicycle, I reached a point where my father decided I no longer needed training wheels. But he still worried that I might fall. So on my first attempt "without a net," he ran alongside as I pedaled. His arms encircled without touching me, his hands resting lightly upon me, but not holding me upright. I rode straight ahead. My father did not push or guide me, but if I had faltered or veered suddenly to the side, he would have tightened his grip, keeping me vertical and on track. After finally braking to a stop. I was jubilant but somewhat hesitant over whether I should be. I wondered, had I really ridden my bike on my own? . . . Was the triumph of riding straight down the street mine or not?[7]

Wyma goes on to argue for an intuition very similar to McKenna's. On Wyma's view, moral responsibility requires a certain kind of "leeway." And this leeway is specified by what Wyma calls the "Principle of Possibly Passing the Buck" (PPPB):

> A person is morally responsible for something she has done, A, only if she has failed to do something she could have done, B, such that doing B would have rendered her morally non-responsible for A.[8]

Of course, in a Frankfurt-type case the relevant agent would not be morally responsible in the alternative sequence; Jones would not be morally responsible for voting for Gore, in the circumstance in which Black's device were triggered. Thus Wyma has apparently identified a significant sort of "leeway," even in the Frankfurt-type examples. At the end of his paper. Wyma returns to the analogy with which he started, saying:

> I believe the bike riding triumph *was* mine, because even though I could not have fallen or crashed while my father hovered protectively over me, I could still have faltered enough that he would have had to steady me; and because I had leeway to falter but did not do so, the success of riding was truly mine. *PPPB* vindicates a similar kind of leeway as being necessary for ascriptions of moral responsibility.[9]

Additionally, Michael Otsuka has recently defended a principle similar to Wyma's Principle of Possibly Passing the Buck. Otsuka calls his principle the "Principle of Avoidable Blame":

> One is blameworthy for performing an act of a given type only if one could instead have behaved in a manner for which one would have been entirely *blameless*.[10]

Thus, all three defenders of regulative control seem to be pointing to the same sort of alternative possibility which they claim is present quite generally, and hence even in the Frankfurt-type examples. This is the freedom to "pass the buck" or "escape" or "avoid" moral responsibility. One might say that these theorists are seeking to fan the flickers of freedom.

In my view there is an intuitive picture that drives all proponents of regulative control, no matter what sort of alternative possibility they identify as grounding ascriptions of moral responsibility. The idea is that moral responsibility requires *making a difference*. Slightly more carefully, an agent is morally responsible for his behavior only if he makes a difference to the world in so behaving. But of course an agent can in some sense make a difference when performing an action under coercion, duress, or (say) direct electronic stimulation of the brain. Given that the agent acts in such cases, the world is different than it would have been had he not so acted. Obviously, this mere counterfactual difference is *not* the sort of difference envisaged by the proponent of the regulative control model of moral responsibility.

Rather, the regulative control theorist believes that moral responsibility requires the ability to make a difference in the sense of selecting one from various paths the world could take, where these various paths are all genuinely available to the agent. The basic idea here is *selection* from among options that are really accessible to the agent. When one selects from a set of feasible options, one makes a difference: the world goes one way rather than another, or takes one path rather than another, among various paths the agent can cause the world to take. This, I believe, is the basic intuitive idea behind the regulative control model. The recent defenses of regulative control help to make the idea more compelling by identifying an *important kind* of difference. On this view, an agent is morally responsible insofar as he makes an important difference to the world: he selects a world in which he is accountable for his behavior, rather than one in which he is not.

A Reply

Despite the manifest appeal of the new defenses of the regulative control model, I remain unconvinced. I believe that problems similar to the problems with the earlier defenses of regulative control also plague the new approaches. Recall that the problem with saying that it is the possibility of exhibiting a different prior sign or indicator of future decision (and action) that grounds moral responsibility is that the envisaged possibility is too exiguous and flimsy. The displaying of such a sign would not even be voluntary behavior. How could moral responsibility rest on such a delicate foundation?

Now it might be thought that the possibility of avoiding authorship or the possibility of avoiding moral responsibility would be a more substantial basis for moral responsibility. But I believe there are similar problems here. Note that in the alternative sequence in a Frankfurt-type case the agent would indeed be avoiding (say) moral responsibility, but he would be doing so "accidentally." The agent would *not* be *voluntarily* avoiding responsibility. The suggestion that avoiding responsibility is a sufficiently robust basis for moral responsibility may get some of its plausibility from the fact that in a typical context in which we would say that someone has avoided (say) blameworthiness, it would be in virtue of some voluntary action. Typically, the relevant facts about the various paths available to the agent would be accessible to him, and he would voluntarily choose a right action (rather than a morally objectionable one). Here we would say that the agent avoided blameworthiness; but this is a very different sort of context from the Frankfurt-type cases. In the Frankfurt-type cases, the agent does not choose to be morally responsible rather than not—these issues play no role in his deliberations. And in the alternative scenario in a Frankfurt-type case (of the prior-sign variety), the agent does not choose to escape responsibility, or voluntarily choose anything that implies his escaping responsibility.

To bring this point out a bit more clearly, note that in the alternative scenario in a Frankfurt-type case, the agent does not deliberate about whether or not to embrace moral responsibility. So issues about whether or not to be morally responsible play no explicit role in his deliberations. Further, they play no "implicit" role either. They might play an implicit role in the sort of context discussed above in which an agent has internalized certain norms on the basis of which he chooses to do what he takes to be the right action. If he successfully avoids blameworthiness here, it is partly in virtue of his having internalized norms the relevant community shares. Given these norms, the agent can reasonably expect to escape blame, if he chooses as he does. But in the alternative scenarios in the Frankfurt-type cases, issues about moral responsibility obviously do not play an implicit role of this sort.

To the extent that issues pertaining to moral responsibility play neither an explicit nor an implicit role, I shall say that moral responsibility is not "internally related" to the agent's behavior in the alternative sequence of a Frankfurt-type case. And my point is that it is very plausible that moral responsibility must be so related to the agent's behavior, in order for the alternative possibility in question to be sufficiently robust to ground ascriptions of moral responsibility.

Of course, I do not accept the "alternative-possibilities" or regulative control model of moral responsibility. But my contention is that, *if* you do buy into this traditional picture, then you should *also* accept that the alternative possibilities must be *of a certain sort*—they must be sufficiently robust. This same point has been highlighted by a philosopher with an orientation very different from mine: Robert Kane.[11] (Kane is a libertarian who believes that alternative possibilities are required for moral responsibility.) Kane emphasizes what he calls the "dual" or "plural" voluntariness (and responsibility) conditions on moral responsibility: the relevant alternative possibilities—that is, alternative possibilities sufficiently robust to ground moral responsibility—must themselves involve voluntary behavior (for which the agent is morally responsible). On Kane's picture, it is not enough that an agent have *just any sort of alternative possibility*; it must be an alternative in which the agent acts voluntarily and is morally responsible. Similarly, I would contend that the relevant alternative possibilities must contain voluntary, responsible behavior in which moral responsibility is internally related to the agent's behavior. My view, then, is that the new defenses of the regulative control model discussed above fall prey to the same sort of problem that afflicted earlier such defenses: the alternatives they postulate are not sufficiently robust.

In Frankfurt-type cases, an agent is morally responsible for his action, although he lacks the relevant kinds of alternative possibilities. He cannot, then, make a relevant difference to the world; he does *not* (in the appropriate way) select one path for the world to take, among various genuinely open paths. But the agent is nevertheless fully and robustly morally responsible for what he does.

Return to Wyma's striking claim about his early bike-riding experience: "I believe the bike riding triumph *was* mine, because even though I could not have fallen or crashed while my father hovered protectively over me, I could still have faltered enough that he would have had to steady me; and because I had leeway to falter but did not do so, the success of riding was truly mine."[12] Whereas we could quibble endlessly about details of these sorts of examples, it seems to me that the *intuitive point* is quite clear: it is *not* the possibility of faltering slightly that makes the young Wyma's bike riding triumph truly his. This has to do *not* with whether he could have faltered slightly, but with how he rode the bike—how he moved the pedals, balanced, and so forth, and by what sort of causal process this all took place.

Wyma says, "[The Principle of Possibly Passing the Buck] begins to map out the negative space around the positive core of moral responsibility, similar to the way one might produce a silhouette by coloring in the space outside a person's profile."[13] But in focusing on the negative space, one can be distracted from what really counts; there is a danger that one will be looking at mere shadows, as with Plato's cave-dwellers. Rather than charting the negative space around moral responsibility, I have a modest suggestion for Wyma: Think positive!

La Rochefoucauld suggested that we can learn about death only by not focusing directly upon it, just as it is prudent to avert one's eyes from the sun. I am not sure that he is correct about death, but in any case I would suggest that even if so, moral responsibility is crucially different from the sun and death: in order to understand why someone is morally responsible for his behavior, we ought not to avert our eyes or focus on the "negative space"; we ought to gaze directly at the properties of the causal process that issues in the behavior in question.

Guidance Control and Self-Expression

Our moral responsibility, then, is not—at least in my view—based on our capacity to make a difference to the world. I grant that reasonable people can disagree with this conclusion (and with the associated claim that regulative control is not required for moral responsibility). That is, I concede that the plausibility arguments I offered above (including the claim that responsibility must be internally related to the agent's behavior in the alternative sequence) are not decisive; they leave room for a defense of the regulative control model. I want now to seek to sketch (in what will no doubt be a preliminary way) a different intuitive picture of moral responsibility. With this alternative picture in hand, I will return to the issue of whether regulative control is necessary for moral responsibility.

Begin with an analogy with artistic creativity. Suppose a sculptor creates a sculpture in the "normal" way—the sculptor is not being manipulated, coerced, and so forth, and is driven by his own creativity. But imagine further that, if he hadn't created this sculpture, some other artist would have created exactly the same sort of sculpture—a different particular sculpture that is nonetheless molecule-for-molecule isomorphic to the sculpture actually produced by the artist. I am not sure why exactly the production of this sort of sculpture is overdetermined in this way, but it really doesn't matter exactly why this is so—only that it is so. It may be, for example, that a friend of the artist has discussed the sculpture with him, and is bent on producing it, if the artist doesn't do so himself.

There is a pretty clear sense in which the artist does not make a difference to the world in creating the sculpture. He does not make a difference defined in terms of end states (individuated in a natural, broad way). The very same kind of sculpture would have been produced had he not created the sculpture himself.[14] And yet there is also a clear sense in which the artist's creative activity has value. I suggest that we value the artist's activity not because he makes a certain sort of difference to the world, but because he expresses himself in a certain way. He does not make a difference; but he *does* make a statement.

My idea is that we can understand the intuitive picture behind moral responsibility in a similar way. When an agent exhibits guidance control and is thus morally responsible for his behavior, he need not be understood to be making a difference to the world; or better, it is unattractive to think that the explanation of his moral responsibility—the intuitive reason why we hold him morally responsible—is that he makes a difference to the world. Rather, the suggestion is that the individual is morally responsible when he exhibits guidance control, insofar as he *expresses himself* in a certain way. To a first approximation, the "value" of morally responsible action is understood as analogous to the value of artistic self-expression.

But if the value of morally responsible action is self-expression, what exactly is expressed? This is a question that deserves an answer, and yet it is perhaps not as easy as one might have supposed to answer it. Consider, for example, the following passage from Sarah Broadie's book *Ethics with Aristotle:*

> In voluntary action we pursue an objective which is before us and which figures as a good to us so far as we pursue it: but on another level we enact by our action, and thereby propound into public space, a conception of the kind of practical being that it is good (or at least all right) to be: a kind typified by pursuit of this kind of goal in this sort of way under such conditions.[15]

The problem with the sort of view suggested by Broadie, in my view, is the very real phenomenon of weakness of will. That is, one sometimes freely does what one does *not* believe is good, or rational, or even all right. So, in voluntarily and freely performing some act, it would *not* in general be accurate to take one to be saying that the relevant goal is good or even all right, or that it is good or all right to be the kind of practical being that typically pursues this kind of goal.[16]

I suppose it could be urged that one is at least saying that the goal in question is *to some degree* good, and so one could be taken to be expressing the idea that it is at least to some degree good or defensible to be the sort of practical being who pursues such a goal. But even this seems implausible, as one can presumably freely do something one does not find to any degree good or morally defensible.

Now perhaps it will be replied that whenever one acts, one must have some sort of pro-attitude toward the behavior in question (or the goal it is taken to promote). I agree, but it is somewhat disappointing to be told that the message conveyed by the agent in acting is something we know, as a conceptual point, from the mere fact that the agent has performed an action. Whereas I do not wish to deny that one can find here part of the message of action, I believe that it will be more illuminating to seek an alternative account of what is expressed by the agent in acting.

To develop such an account, I begin by noting that various philosophers have suggested that our lives have "narrative structures"—that our lives are in some sense stories.[17] This is an intriguing and suggestive idea (even if it is difficult to flesh out precisely), and different philosophers have developed it in different ways (and for different purposes). Here I shall rely on David Velleman's presentation of the idea in his seminal paper "Well-Being and Time."[18]

Velleman is concerned to argue that "well-being is not additive." This claim involves various ideas. One is that we cannot simply add up the welfare values of segments of an individual's life to get a total value that accurately reflects our judgments about the value of the individual's life as a whole. Another idea is that the welfare values of the segments depend crucially on their "narrative" or "dramatic" relationships with other parts of the life.

Velleman says:

> Consider two different lives that you might live. One life begins in the depths but takes an upward trend: a childhood of deprivation, a troubled youth, struggles and setbacks in early adulthood, followed finally by success and satisfaction in middle age and a peaceful retirement. Another life begins at the heights but slides downhill: a blissful childhood and youth, precocious triumphs and rewards in early adulthood, followed by a mid-life strewn with disasters that lead to misery in old age. Surely, we can imagine two such lives as containing equal sums of momentary well-being.
>
> . . . Yet even if we were to map each moment in one life onto a moment of equal well-being in the other, we would not have shown these lives to be equally good. For . . . one is a story of improvement while the other is a story of deterioration. . . . The former story would seem like a better life-story—not, of course, in the sense that it makes for a better story in the telling or the hearing, but rather in the sense that it is the story of a better life.[19]

Now it might be thought that the moral of Velleman's story is that we have a general tendency to weight welfare that occurs *later* in life more heavily. But whereas this would issue in a non-additive conception of welfare, it is not the moral Velleman wishes to draw. Rather, Velleman says:

> The reason why later benefits are thought to have a greater impact on the value of one's life is not that greater weight is attached to what comes later. Rather, it is that later events are thought to alter the meaning of earlier events, thereby altering their contribution to the value of one's life. [Additionally] . . . [t]he meaning of a benefit depends not only on whether it follows or precedes hardships but also on the specific narrative relation between the goods and evils involved.[20]

To illustrate this point, Velleman gives the example of the importance of drawing lessons from one's misfortunes. We typically think it important to learn from life's tragedies; the fact that we have been improved *as a result of going through a tragic experience* adds to the total value of our lives in a distinctive way. As Velleman puts it:

> If a life's value were a sum of momentary well-being, learning from a misfortune would be no more important than learning from other sources, since every lesson learned would add so much value and no more to the sum of one's well-being. On being invited to learn from a personal tragedy, one would therefore be entitled to reply, "No, I think I'll read a book instead." Edification would offset the losses incurred in the tragedy, but its having been derived from the tragedy would not render edification more valuable.[21]

Velleman similarly asks us to consider two lives. In the first life you have ten years of unhappiness and trouble in a marriage followed by divorce, after which you remarry happily. In the second life the ten years of unhappiness in marriage lead to eventual happiness as the relationship matures. About this example. Velleman says:

> Both lives contain ten years of marital strife followed by contentment; but let us suppose that in the former, you regard your first ten years of marriage as a dead loss, whereas in the latter you regard them as the foundation of your happiness. The bad times are just as bad in both lives, but in one they are cast off and in the other they are redeemed. Surely, these two decades can affect the value of your life differently, even if you are equally well off at each moment of their duration.[22]

I shall follow Velleman in contending that life has a narrative structure in the specific sense that the meanings and values of the parts of our lives are affected by their narrative relationships with other parts of our lives, and the welfare value of our lives as a whole are not simple additive functions of the values of the parts. In this sense, then, our lives are stories.[23] And in performing an action at a given time, we can be understood as writing a sentence in the book of our lives.

I suggested above that the distinctive value in acting in such a way as to be held morally responsible lies in a certain sort of self-expression. But the question then arose as to what precisely is expressed by ordinary actions. My answer is that it is not most fruitful to look for a "message" of action of the sort suggested by Broadie—that one believes that the action promotes a defensible goal. Rather, what is expressed by an agent in acting is the meaning of the sentence of the book of his life. And this meaning is fixed in part by relationships to other sentences in this book, that is, by the overall narrative structure of the life. In acting, an individual need not be "propounding into public space" *any* sort of vision of the good or defensible life. Rather, his action writes part of the book of his life and gets its meaning from its place in this story. This suggests a more "holistic" picture of what gets expressed by an agent in acting so as to be morally responsible, and one which is more illuminating than the mere fact that the agent had a pro-attitude toward moving his body in a certain way in the context.

I have sketched an analogy between action for which an agent can be held morally responsible and artistic self-expression. Further, I have claimed that when one exhibits guidance control one can be understood to be engaging in a specific kind of self-expression: one is writing part of the book of one's life. It does not follow however that the self-expression involved in action is a kind of *artistic* self-expression. Obviously one can write narratives that are not most appropriately categorized as works of art: for example, one can simply write a history of a region or family. This sort of narrative can have precisely the characteristics identified by Velleman without being properly considered a work of art.[24] The dimensions of assessment of this kind of narrative are not primarily aesthetic. Similarly, the dimensions of assessment of a human life are not primarily aesthetic, but moral and prudential.

I have tried to give an account of what might be called the value we place on acting so as to be morally responsible. In so doing, I have been seeking to sketch what I have suggested is the "picture" which grounds the guidance-control model of moral responsibility—the view that guidance control, and not regulative control, is the freedom required for moral responsibility. Whereas I believe I have put some of the elements of this picture in place, I still don't think I have fully captured the value of acting so as to be morally responsible.

To explain: Consider someone who is, according to our ordinary intuitions, not morally responsible for what he does because he is to a significant degree subject to coercion, manipulation, and pressures that render his behavior not suitably responsive to reasons. Such an individual may nevertheless express himself in the relevant way: he may write the story of his life, a story to which certain moral and prudential judgments can attach. That is, presumably we can evaluate this individual's behavior in such a way as to judge it as good or bad, prudent or imprudent, and so forth. Now of course we need to *distinguish* these normative judgments from the further normative judgments and attitudes constitutive of *moral responsibility*: the reactive attitudes (such as indignation, resentment, gratitude, respect, and so forth). The sort of individual in question can live a life that is legitimately judged in terms of the first kind of normative considerations, but not the second.

Why not simply specify that the picture that grounds moral responsibility requires that the individual's life be subject to normative judgments of the second kind, those involved in the reactive attitudes? Perhaps one could do this, but I feel uncomfortable doing so because it seems to introduce a troubling circularity. My project is to identify what I have called the "picture" that supports the claim that guidance control, and not regulative control, is required for moral responsibility. Alternatively, I have characterized my project as seeking to identify the value we place on acting so as to be morally responsible. Ideally, it seems to me, we should be able to specify this value without importing the notion of moral responsibility. And yet to require that one's life story be accessible to normative evaluation in the sense of the appropriate application of the reactive attitudes would do precisely this, for moral responsibility just is rational accessibility to the reactive attitudes.

In other words, I am trying to identify what exactly we value in cases in which we behave so as to be morally responsible. (Having done this, I want to employ the result—the value of acting so as to be morally responsible—to suggest that guidance control, and not regulative control, exhausts the freedom-relevant component of moral responsibility.) If I were to say, "Well, what we value is acting responsibly," this would obviously be circular and uninteresting—although no doubt true! I believe that it is similarly circular and unhelpful to say that the value of acting so as to be responsible is cashed out in part in terms of acting so as to be accessible to the reactive attitudes.

A more promising approach is to note that when one is subject to coercive pressures, manipulation, and so forth, one's self-expression is hindered in certain ways. What one wants to say, I believe, is that the value of acting so as to be morally responsible consists in *unhindered* or *unimpaired* self-expression of the relevant sort. Perhaps another way of saying the same thing is to note that when one engages in unhindered or unimpaired self-expression of the relevant kind, one is *freely* expressing oneself. I will then suggest that the value of acting so as to be morally responsible consists in one's freely expressing oneself. We value freely—in the sense of not being hindered or impaired in certain ways—writing the book of our lives.

Now someone will say that I have introduced a problematic and contested notion here—the notion of "freely" expressing oneself. I have avoided the circularity mentioned above only by introducing an essentially contested notion: out of the frying pan and into the fire! After all, the proponent of the regulative control model will insist that when one freely does anything, one must have genuinely accessible alternative possibilities. Now I certainly cannot present any decisive arguments that the ordinary notion of "acting freely" does not require alternative possibilities: indeed, this debate will presumably simply reinscribe the debate about whether moral responsibility requires regulative control.

So I will simply stipulate a special notion of "acting freely," call it "acting freely*." When one "acts freely*" one need not have any alternative possibilities. The intuitive idea of acting freely* is that in the actual sequence that leads to one's behavior, no freedom-undermining factors operate or play a role. So, in the Frankfurt-type cases, one uncontroversially is acting freely*, even if it is controversial whether one is acting freely. Put in other words, in the Frankfurt-type cases a proponent of alternative possibilities as a condition for moral responsibility may say that insofar as acting freely is sufficient for moral responsibility, one of course needs alternative possibilities to act freely. But he should be willing to concede that there is some "actual-sequence" notion of freedom which the agent possesses, acting freely*; the agent possesses this freedom insofar as no freedom-undermining factor operates in the actual sequence that issues in the behavior. Of course, the proponent of alternative possibilities will go on to insist that *such* freedom is not sufficient for moral responsibility. Indeed, he will contend that the agents in the Frankfurt-type cases *also* possess a more robust (from his point of view) kind of freedom—one involving alternative possibilities. For my purposes, I simply want to crystallize out the actual-sequence notion of freedom, acting freely*.

My contention then is that the value of acting in such a way as to be morally responsible consists in freely* expressing oneself. Although this account needs to be filled in various ways, I think that it helps to capture something simple and important: the value of moral responsibility, on the guidance control model, consists in a distinctive kind of self-expression.[25]

With this sketch of an account of the value we place in acting so as to be responsible in hand, let us return, finally, to the issue of whether regulative control is required for moral responsibility. If one is in the grip of the picture according to which an individual must be able to make a difference, in order to be held morally responsible, one will press for the regulative control requirement. And one might not see any other plausible picture. This is part of the reason why I believe it is useful to have sketched the "self-expression" picture, which I have presented as underlying the guidance control model.

I suggest that some of the debates about whether alternative possibilities are required for moral responsibility may at some level be fueled by different intuitive pictures of moral responsibility. It may be that the proponents of the regulative control model are implicitly in the grip of the "making-a-difference" picture, whereas the proponents of the guidance control model are implicitly accepting the self-expression picture. Further, I would like to suggest that presenting the self-expression picture can be helpful for the following reason. The debates about whether alternative possibilities are required for moral responsibility have issued in what some might consider stalemates; above I conceded that I do not know of any *decisive* arguments (employing Frankfurt-type examples) for the conclusion that only guidance control, and not regulative control, is required for moral responsibility. My suggestion is that if one finds the self-expression picture of moral responsibility more compelling than the making-a-difference picture, then this should incline one toward the conclusion that guidance control exhausts the freedom-relevant component of moral responsibility.

Again, I do not suppose that this will be a knockdown argument; specifically, I do not suppose that those strongly inclined toward the regulative control model will find the self-expression picture correct. But this certainly should not be surprising; I do not think anyone should expect knockdown arguments in this realm. My point is that if direct reflection on the Frankfurt-type cases does not in itself issue in a decisive conclusion, one can perhaps be moved a bit closer to accepting the guidance control model of moral responsibility by seeing that it is supported by a natural and compelling intuitive picture—a picture one might not have seen, given the clout of the make-a-difference picture.

An Objection

The practices involved in moral responsibility have sometimes been modeled along the lines of a conversation.[26] On this view, the reactive attitudes—such as resentment, indignation, love, hatred, gratitude, and respect—are responses to "statements" made by the agent in acting. One might have thought that a self-expression account of what we value in behavior for which the agent is morally responsible would fit naturally with a conversation model of moral responsibility. But upon reflection it can seem that if a conversation model of moral responsibility is correct, then the view I have been developing here about the content of the agent's self-expression must be is wrong. This is because the reactive attitudes are reactions to an agent's good or ill will (or indifference), as manifested in his actions. And this is quite a different matter from some sort of sentence in a book of the agent's life, the meaning and value of which is determined holistically (in terms of its dramatic relationships to what has come before and what will come after). The reactive attitudes are, after all, *direct* responses to particular bits of behavior; one obviously cannot wait to show resentment or gratitude until one has allowed the agent's entire life to play itself out (so that the appropriate "meaning" can be attached to the behavior)!

It is important, however, to distinguish different layers of meaning. Morally responsible behavior is a complex phenomenon, with various different features. It is not surprising that it may well have different layers of meaning (and different features that are relevant for different purposes). There is no doubt that the reactive attitudes are keyed to features of behavior that reflect the quality of the agent's will (his good or ill will, or his indifference). When an agent manifests ill will through his behavior, the relevant behavior can be said to have this meaning. But this is entirely consistent with its also having a meaning that is determined by the overall narrative structure of an agent's life. And my contention is that it is this latter meaning that helps to explain the value we find in exhibiting guidance control (and thus acting so as to be morally responsible).

One question we may have is, "To what feature of behavior do we respond when we evince one of the reactive attitudes?" This feature may be the ill or good will of the agent, as manifested in the behavior. This is certainly one layer of meaning. But a different question might be, "Why exactly do we value the agent's behaving in such a way as to be morally responsible?" The answer, I have suggested, is self-expression of a different sort; more specifically, it is self-expression that depends for its meaning on a narrative structure. It is analogous to artistic self-expression, but not a species of artistic self-expression.

Consider, again, a sculptor who has created a particular sculpture. The critics may write reviews of the work in which they respond to particular aesthetic features of the sculpture. Thus the sculpture has a set of features relevant to its aesthetic evaluation. It may be said that these features seem to be relevant to the question of what we value in the sculpture. But it is a quite different question to ask what exactly we value in the artist's creative activity. Here I have suggested that it is not necessarily that the sculptor has made a difference to the world: rather, it is that he has engaged in a certain sort of artistic self-expression. Similarly, the good or ill will of the agent as evinced in the relevant action might be the feature of the action pertinent to one's reactive attitudes: and yet the value of the agent's acting in such a way as to be fairly held morally responsible derives from a different feature of the action—that it is a certain sort of self-expression.

Conclusion

Traditionally, most philosophers have thought that moral responsibility requires alternative possibilities. That is, they have thought that moral responsibility requires a certain kind of control, which I have called "regulative control." In my view, these philosophers are to some extent driven by an intuitive picture. On this picture, being morally responsible involves making a certain sort of difference to the world. If you make a difference, in this sense, you *select* which path the world will take, among various paths that are genuinely available. Your selection determines which way the world goes, and you thereby make a crucial difference.

But I have argued that it is at least very plausible that moral responsibility for one's behavior does *not* require that one make this sort of difference. The Frankfurt-type cases seem to me to show that one can be morally responsible for one's actions, even though one does not select the path the world will take, among various paths that are genuinely available; in these cases, suitably filled in, there is just one path the world will take. And what makes the agent morally responsible is *how he proceeds along this single path*. More specifically, the agent can exhibit a certain sort of control—guidance control—even though he lacks regulative control. Guidance control, in my view, is the freedom-relevant condition sufficient for moral responsibility.

There can be examples in the realm of art which are similar in structure (in certain ways) to the Frankfurt-type examples. In these cases the artist creates a work of art "on his own" and as a result of his own creative energies, and yet the very same kind of work of art would have been produced had the artist not been inclined to do so. Typically it *is* the case that the artist has changed the world in an important way in producing a work of art; but the artistic analogues of the Frankfurt-type cases show that the artist's activity can have value *without* this being the case. I have suggested that this value consists in a certain sort of artistic self-expression.

Similarly, I have suggested that it is natural to think of morally responsible behavior as a kind of self-expression. More carefully, what I have argued is that the self-expression picture is what intuitively drives the proponents of the view that guidance control, and not regulative control, exhausts the freedom-relevant component of moral responsibility.

I do not have a knockdown argument that the self-expression picture is superior to the make-a-difference picture, or that the self-expression picture is indeed the correct account of what we value in acting so as to be morally responsible. I hope that the self-expression picture will seem natural and compelling to many open-minded philosophers who are not sure how exactly to respond to the complicated debates concerning the Frankfurt-type cases. If one finds the self-expression model attractive, this can move one toward acceptance of the claim—suggested by the Frankfurt-type cases—that guidance control is all the freedom required for moral responsibility.

NOTES

1. Peter Strawson, "Freedom and Resentment," *Proceedings of the British Academy* 48 (1962): 187–211.

2. For this kind of Frankfurt-type case, see David Blumenfeld. "The Principle of Alternate Possibilities," *Journal of Philosophy* 67 (1971): 339–44.

3. Of course, this sort of example is a highly implausible science-fiction scenario, since most neurosurgeons are certainly not liberal!

4. See chap. 2 of this book.

5. Michael S. McKenna, "Alternative Possibilities and the Failure of the Counterexample Strategy," *Journal of Social Philosophy* 28 (1997): 71–85: the quotation is from pp. 73–74.

6. McKenna, "Alternative Possibilities and the Failure of the Counterexample Strategy," pp. 74–75.

7. Keith D. Wyma, "Moral Responsibility and Leeway for Action," *American Philosophical Quarterly* 34 (1997): 57.

8. Ibid., p. 59.

9. Ibid., p. 68.

10. Michael Otsuka, "Incompatibilism and the Avoidability of Blame." *Ethics* 108 (1998): 688. Otsuka qualifies the principle to apply to cases in which it is not the case that everything one is capable of doing at a given point in time is blameworthy because of some previous choice for which one is to blame.

11. Robert Kane, *Free Will and Values*, SUNY Series in Philosophy (Albany: State University of New York Press, 1985). esp. p. 60: and *The Significance of Free Will* (New York: Oxford University Press, 1996). esp. pp. 107–15.

12. Wyma, "Moral Responsibility and Leeway for Action," p. 68.

13. Ibid., p. 68.

14. Of course, someone might point out that it must be a different particular sculpture in the alternative sequence, since it would have been created by a different individual from the actual artist. I do not deny that one can say this, or that one can contend that the value of the artist's creative activity then consists in making a difference—in creating the actual sculpture rather than a different particular sculpture. But I do not find this explanation as natural and compelling as the explanation sketched in the text. It seems problematic in the same way as the flicker-of-freedom strategy for explaining the value of acting so as to be morally responsible.

15. Sarah Broadie, *Ethics with Aristotle* (Oxford: Oxford University Press, 1991), p. 159.

16. A similar problem afflicts the view that in voluntarily and freely performing some act, one is "standing for something."

17. See, for example, Alasdair MacIntyre, *After Virtue* (Notre Dame, Ind.: University of Notre Dame Press, 1981); Charles Taylor, *Sources of the Self: The Making of Modern Identity* (Cambridge: Harvard University Press, 1989); and Alexander Nehamas, *Nietzsche: Life as Literature* (Cambridge: Harvard University Press, 1985).

18. J. David Velleman, "Well-Being and Time," *Pacific Philosophical Quarterly* 72 (1991): 48–77; this paper is reprinted in *The Metaphysics of Death*, ed. John Martin Fischer, Stanford Series in Philosophy (Stanford, Calif.: Stanford University Press, 1993), pp. 329–57 (all subsequent pages references will be to the reprinted paper).

19. Ibid., p. 331.

20. Ibid., pp. 334–36.

21. Ibid., p. 336.

22. Ibid., p. 337.

23. As Velleman points out, this view should not be confused with the view sometimes attributed to Nietzsche that literary or aesthetic considerations determine the value of a life (see Nehamas, *Nietzsche: Life as Literature*).

24. For this point I am indebted to Eric Schwitzgebel.

25. I do not have an account of what precisely self-expression consists in, nor do I have a good explanation of *why* we value it. It does seem to me that we *do* in fact value something we conceive of as self-expression—something analogous to artistic self-expression. But a full defense of the view I have sketched in the text would say more about what self-

expression is, and exactly why we value it (I am indebted to Paul Hoffman for pushing me on these points). Some are not inclined to find self-expression particularly valuable; these may, however, be precisely the same people who are not inclined to ascribe much intrinsic value to acting so as to be morally responsible. My contention is that the value, whatever one takes this to be, consists in a certain kind of self-expression.

26. Gary Watson, "Responsibility and the Limits of Evil: Variations on a Strawsonian Theme," in *Responsibility, Character, and the Emotions: New Essays on Moral Psychology*, ed. Ferdinand Schoeman (Cambridge: Cambridge University Press), pp. 256–86.

6

FRANKFURT-STYLE COMPATIBILISM

Many philosophers have worried that God's existence (understood in a certain way) or causal determinism (the doctrine that nonrelational features of the past, together with the laws of nature, are causally sufficient for all truths about the present and future) would rule out moral responsibility. One influential reason for this discomfort, although certainly not the only reason, is that it is plausible to suppose that God's existence (construed in a certain way) or causal determinism would rule out "genuine" alternative possibilities. If moral responsibility requires this sort of alternative possibility (at least at some relevant point along the path to behavior), then it would seem that God's existence or causal determinism would be incompatible with moral responsibility.

The thought that moral responsibility requires genuine alternative possibilities—the freedom to will, choose, or do otherwise—has been and continues to be an important motivation for incompatibilism about such doctrines as God's existence or causal determinism and moral responsibility. It is quite natural to suppose that if we have only one option that is genuinely available to us, then we *have* to do what we actually do, and that if we have to do what we actually do, we are *compelled* so to behave. But if we are compelled to behave as we actually do, then surely we cannot legitimately be held morally responsible for what we do.

Joel Feinberg employs the analogy between an individual making decisions about his life and a train going down the railroad tracks. Having genuine freedom—the sort that grounds our moral responsibility—corresponds, on Feinberg's model, to a train's having more than one track available to it. If our lives correspond to a train chugging down a track which is the only track it can take, then it follows, according to Feinberg, that we "could take no credit or blame for any of [our]

I am indebted to thoughtful questions and comments by Michael Zimmerman, Win-Chiat Lee, and Harry Frankfurt at the conference "Contours of Agency: The Philosophy of Harry Frankfurt," Wake Forest University, November 1999.

achievements, and [we] could no more be responsible for [our] lives than are ro-
bots, or the trains in our . . . metaphor that must run on 'predestined grooves.'"[1]
Feinberg here articulates the powerful and influential idea that in order to be
morally responsible, we must have more than one option. The future must be a
branching, treelike structure; following Borges, the future must be a "garden of
forking paths."

Because of the presupposed link between moral responsibility (and even personhood) and alternative possibilities, an extraordinary amount of attention has
been given to arguments purporting to establish that God's existence or causal determinism do indeed rule out the relevant sorts of alternative possibilities. Much
ingenuity has been displayed on both sides. But today, after literally thousands of
years of debates about these issues, there is still heated disagreement about
whether God's existence (understood in certain ways) or causal determinism rules
out alternative possibilities.

Given this disagreement, and the fact (I believe it to be a fact) that rational
people can disagree about whether the doctrines in question are indeed incompatible with the relevant sort of alternative possibilities (that is, the fact that
there is no *knockdown* argument for incompatibilism), we seem to have arrived at
a certain kind of stalemate. In my view, Harry Frankfurt has helped us to make
considerable progress in this dialectic context. Frankfurt has presented a set of
examples that appear to show that moral responsibility does not after all require
alternative possibilities. If he is correct about this, then we can admit that it is
plausible that God's existence or causal determinism would rule out alternative
possibilities but still maintain that we can reasonably be thought to be morally
responsible (even in a causally determined world or a world in which an essentially omniscient, temporal God exists). Slightly more carefully, Frankfurt has
helped us to shift the debate away from issues pertaining to alternative possibilities to issues related to the actual sequence of events leading to the behavior in
question. In my view, this is an important contribution, even if it does not in itself decisively establish compatibilism about (say) causal determinism and moral
responsibility.

In chapter 5 I sketched a particular "Frankfurt-type example." Frankfurt-type
cases seem to sever the putative connection between moral responsibility and alternative possibilities; they appear to show the falsity of the Principle of Alternate
Possibilities (PAP): a person is morally responsible for what he has done only if he
could have done otherwise. And if moral responsibility does not require alternative possibilities, then if causal determinism threatens moral responsibility, it
would not do so in virtue of ruling out alternative possibilities.

I shall now lay out a disturbing challenge to the claim I have made above
that these examples help us to make significant progress in the debates about the
relationship between moral responsibility and causal determinism. (In the discussion that follows, I focus mainly on causal determinism, although I believe the
points will in most instances apply equally to God's existence.)[2] I then will provide a reply to this challenge, and the reply will point toward a more refined formulation of the important contribution I believe Frankfurt has made to defending
a certain sort of compatibilism.

The Challenge

The idea that Frankfurt-type examples help to pave the way for compatibilism has been challenged by various philosophers.[3] The challenge can usefully be put in terms of a dilemma: the Frankfurt-type stories presuppose either that causal determinism is true or that it is false. If the former, then the claim that the relevant agent is morally responsible is question-begging, and if the latter, then the claim that the agent lacks alternative possibilities is false.

Let us start with the presupposition that causal determinism obtains. It does appear as if the relevant agent—Jones, in the example above—cannot choose or do otherwise (cannot choose at t_2 to vote for Bush or vote for Bush at t_3). This is because the "counterfactual intervener"—the liberal neurosurgeon Black—can know, given the prior sign exhibited by Jones at t_1, that Jones will indeed choose to vote for Gore at t_2. If Jones were to choose at t_2 to vote for Bush, the prior sign would have had to have been different; thus Jones cannot at t_2 choose to vote for Bush. But the problem is that the contention that Jones is morally responsible for choosing to vote for Gore, and actually voting for Gore, is put in doubt, given the assumption of causal determinism.

That is, if causal determinism is assumed, it does not seem that someone could say that Jones is obviously morally responsible for his actual choice and action in a context in which the relationship between causal determinism and moral responsibility is at issue. To do so would appear to beg the question against the incompatibilist.

Laura Ekstrom is a good example of a philosopher who insists that if causal determinism is assumed to be true, then one cannot infer that the agent in question is morally responsible for his behavior. Ekstrom says:

> [Let us] focus our attention on the fact that causal determinism might be true. If it is true, then past events together with the laws of nature are together sufficient for Jones's making the particular decision he makes. . . . So Jones's subjective perception of available options is irrelevant; in fact, the past pushes him into one particular decision state, the only state physically possible at the time, given the past and the laws of nature. . . . In fact, according to the incompatibilist, if determinism is true, Jones should not be judged as morally responsible for his decision and his act, given the pushing feature of determinism . . . so P.A.P. is not defeated.[4]

In further support of her view, Ekstrom says:

> Whether or not determinism is true *ought* to be relevant [to our intuitions concerning Jones's moral responsibility]—this is precisely what incompatibilist arguments are designed to show. According to the incompatibilists, our everyday notions concerning our own and others' freedom and moral responsibility in acting can be shown to be, upon reflection, in need of revision if the thesis of causal determinism is true.[5]

Now consider the other horn of the dilemma: that is, suppose that indeterminism (of a certain relevant sort) obtains. Under this supposition it would not be dialectically inappropriate to claim that Jones is morally responsible for his actual choice at t_2 to vote for Gore and his vote for Gore at t_3. But now the contention that Jones cannot choose at t_2 to vote for Bush at t_3 is called into question. This is because there is no deterministic relationship between the prior sign exhibited by Jones at t_1 and Jones's subsequent choice at t_2. So, if we consider the time just prior to t_2, everything about the past can be just as it is consistently with Jones's choosing at t_2 to vote for Bush. Someone might think that if it takes some time for Jones to make the choice, Black can intervene to prevent the completion of the choice; but then Jones will still have the possibility of "beginning to make the choice."

The proponents of the Frankfurt-type examples contend that they are non-question-begging cases in which an agent is morally responsible for his choice and action and yet has no sufficiently robust alternative possibilities. But the challenge appears to show that the examples in question are either not uncontroversial cases in which the agent is morally responsible for his choice and subsequent behavior, or not cases in which the agent lacks alternative possibilities.

Reply

The Assumption of Indeterminism

In giving my strategy for replying to the challenge, I want to start with the assumption of causal indeterminism. The idea behind the worry here is that although the agent can legitimately be deemed morally responsible, there are ineliminable alternative possibilities (given the assumption of indeterminism). I will only sketch the sort of reply I would be inclined to pursue, because I want to focus here on the assumption of causal determinism.

The first thing to say is that various philosophers, including Eleonore Stump, Alfred Mele and David Robb, and David Hunt, have argued that one can indeed construct versions of the Frankfurt-type examples in which it is both the case that indeterminism obtains and there are *no* alternative possibilities.[6] As I have discussed these versions of the Frankfurt-type examples in some detail elsewhere, I shall here simply say that I find these examples, and similar indeterministic Frankfurt-type examples, intriguing and highly suggestive.[7] They may indeed show that one can construct Frankfurt-type examples that explicitly presuppose indeterminism in which there are *no* alternative possibilities.

It may, however, turn out that even in these examples there emerge alternative possibilities of certain sorts; here I would, however, pursue the argument that the alternative possibilities in question are not sufficiently *robust* to ground attributions of moral responsibility. That is, I would argue that it is not enough for the critic of the Frankfurt-type examples to argue that there exist *some* alternative possibilities in the cases, no matter how flimsy or exiguous; if one grounds moral responsibility in alternative possibilities, I believe they must be *of a certain sort*. Someone who believes in the "garden of forking paths" picture (according to which alternative possibilities are necessary for moral responsibility) should also believe that those alternative possibilities are sufficiently robust. The mere possibility of unintentional or involuntary behavior—behavior for which the agent is not morally responsible—does not seem to me to offer sufficient substance on which to base one's attributions of moral responsibility. As in the debates about the relationship between libertarianism and control, there is a crucial difference between the *ability* to do otherwise and the *mere possibility* of something different happening. The same point applies to the debates about the Frankfurt-type cases.

So my view is that either one can entirely expunge alternative possibilities—even in the context of indeterminism in the actual sequence—or the remaining alternative possibilities will not be sufficiently robust. This is not surprising, because I would suggest that what we *value* in action for which an agent can legitimately be held morally responsible is *not* that he makes a certain sort of difference to the world, but rather that he expresses himself in a certain way. And this sort of self-expression does not require alternative possibilities. I have argued elsewhere that adopting this view about the intuitive picture behind our ascriptions of moral responsibility—that what we value, in behavior for which the agent can fairly be held morally responsible, is a distinctive kind of self-expression—can make it considerably more plausible that moral responsibility does not in fact require alternative possibilities.

The Assumption of Causal Determinism

Let's now suppose that causal determinism is true. Under this assumption, it is unfair and question-begging simply to assert that the relevant agent—say, Jones—is morally responsible for his behavior. But the proponent of Frankfurt-style compatibilism should not—and need not—make such an assertion at this point.[8] Rather, the argument is in two parts. The first step is to argue—based on the Frankfurt-type examples—that intuitively it is plausible that alternative possibilities are irrelevant to ascriptions of moral responsibility. If one agrees with this point, the preliminary conclusion could be stated as follows: if the agent (say, Jones) is not morally responsible for his behavior, this is *not* in virtue of his lacking alternative possibilities. That is, the proponent of Frankfurt-style compatibilism does *not* assert, simply on the basis of Frankfurt-type examples, that the relevant agent is morally responsible for his behavior. Such a compatibilist should not take any stand about the responsibility of the agent simply on the basis of reflection on the Frankfurt-type examples. He should just say, "I don't know at this point whether the agent is morally responsible for his behavior, but *if* he is not, it is *not* because he lacks alternative possibilities."

Thus Frankfurt-type examples have the important function of *shifting the debate* away from considerations pertinent to the relationship between causal determinism and alternative possibilities. What now becomes important is to consider whether causal determinism in the actual sequence can plausibly be thought *directly* to rule out moral responsibility, independently of considerations relating to alternative possibilities. It is important to see that the issues here are different. That is, causal determinism is alleged to rule out alternative possibilities in virtue of deeply plausible principles encapsulating the "fixity of the past" and the "fixity of the natural laws." If causal determinism is true, then the past, together with the natural laws, entails all truths about the present and future. So, if the past is fixed and the natural laws are fixed, it would seem that this leaves room for only one present and one future.[9] But such principles (encapsulating the fixity of the past and natural laws) can be embraced by a "semicompatibilist"—a compatibilist about causal determinism and moral responsibility who separates this claim from the claim of the compatibility of causal determinism and alternative possibilities. The factors that would allegedly show that causal determinism directly rules out moral responsibility are *different* from those that appear to show that causal determinism rules out alternative possibilities.

Some philosophers have evidently thought that Frankfurt-type compatibilism must fail insofar as the Frankfurt-type examples in themselves do not decisively establish the compatibility of causal determinism and moral responsibility. Michael Della Rocca argues that the relevance of alternative possibilities—even if they are mere flickers of freedom—is that they are a *sign* of the existence of actual-sequence indeterminism. If causal determination obtains in the actual sequence, then Della Rocca claims that one cannot conclude that the relevant agent is morally responsible.[10] Similarly, recall that Ekstrom has claimed that if causal determinism is assumed to be true, one cannot assert that the relevant agent is morally responsible, and thus "PAP is not defeated."

But the success of the Frankfurt-type strategy should not be judged on the basis of whether the Frankfurt-type cases in themselves decisively establish that moral responsibility is compatible with causal determinism. That they do not do *all* the work does not show that they do not do *some* important work. For example, I believe that the Frankfurt-type cases *do* show the following principle false: (PAP*): Lacking alternative possibilities is a condition which in itself—and apart from anything that accompanies it (either contingently or necessarily)—makes it the case that an agent is not morally responsible for his behavior. That (PAP*) is shown to be false is real progress: now we should turn to the issue of whether something that (perhaps) accompanies the lack of alternative possibilities—actual-sequence causal determination—rules out moral responsibility *directly*. Of course, if the reasons to think that causal determination in the actual sequence rules out moral responsibility directly are just as strong as the reasons to think that causal determinism rules out alternative possibilities, then the progress would be illusory; but I shall be arguing in the rest of this chapter that the reasons are *not* as strong.

Causal Determination in the Actual Sequence

The question now is this: does causal determination in the actual sequence *directly* rule out moral responsibility (i.e., does causal determinism rule out moral responsibility apart from ruling out alternative possibilities)? In my book *The Metaphysics of Free Will: An Essay on Control*, I considered a number of reasons someone might think that causal determination directly rules out moral responsibility.[11] For example, an incompatibilist might insist that the presence of causal determination in the actual sequence is inconsistent with notions of "initiation," "origination," "being active rather than passive," or "creativity," where some (or all) of these notions are requirements of moral responsibility. On this approach, the incompatibilist does not rest his case on principles encapsulating the fixity of the past and the fixity of the laws (or modal "transfer principles" of any sort); rather, he rests his case on factors whose presence in the actual sequence allegedly directly rules out moral responsibility.

None of these notions, however, provides a compelling reason to opt for incompatibilism about causal determinism and moral responsibility. My argument (in *The Metaphysics of Free Will: An Essay on Control* and in chapter 2 of this volume) was that with respect to each of the notions in question—origination, initiation, activity, creativity, and so forth—there are compatibilist and incompatibilist interpretations, and, further, that there is no strong reason to opt for the incompatibilist interpretation, *apart from considerations pertaining to alternative possibilities*. Thus there is no reason that a fair, reflective, and reasonable person not already committed to incompatibilism should conclude that causal determinism, in itself, and apart from considerations about alternative possibilities, is incompatible with moral responsibility. In the rest of this chapter, I want to consider some other reasons it might be thought that causal determinism directly rules out moral responsibility; basically I will be defending and developing my view that there is no good reason a fair-minded person (not already committed to incompatibilism) should be convinced that causal determination in the actual sequence directly precludes moral responsibility.

Robert Kane's book *The Significance of Free Will*, together with related articles, is perhaps the most comprehensive and thoughtful presentation of the motivation of incompatibilism (and also a positive account of libertarian freedom) of which I am aware.[12] Kane distinguishes two separate motivations for incompatibilism: a worry about alternative possibilities, and a worry about "ultimacy." To have "ultimate responsibility," according to Kane, agents must

> have the power to be the *ultimate* producers of their own ends. . . . They have the *power to make choices which can only and finally be explained in terms of their own wills* (i.e., character, motives, and efforts of will). No one can have this power in a determined world.[13]

Thus Kane contends that quite apart from issues about alternative possibilities, the presence of causal determination in the actual sequence would be inconsistent with an agent's being "ultimately responsible" and so would rule out the agent's being morally responsible.

But why exactly must an agent have this sort of ultimate responsibility in order to be morally responsible? Someone could say that on reflection we have a deep preference not to be intermediate links in a deterministic causal chain that begins in events prior to our births. Perhaps *this* is the reason causal determinism rules out moral responsibility (quite apart from threatening alternative possibilities).

I find this answer puzzling and difficult to assess. One reason is that it seems to me to be dangerously close to, if not identical with, simply asserting that on reflection we have a deep preference that causal determinism (as applied to us) not be true. The question at issue is why exactly causal determinism in the actual sequence rules out moral responsibility *directly*. The answer that is proposed is that we can just see that we do not want it to be the case that our deliberations are simply intermediate links in a causally deterministic chain that begins before our births. But this answer does seem to me to be the assertion that we do not want it to be the case that causal determinism is true and thus that our behavior be causally determined. Perhaps this answer could be deemed "question-begging," or perhaps it is simply dialectically unhelpful. In any case, if the question at issue is why there is some reason to suppose that causal determination in the actual sequence directly rules out moral responsibility, and the dialectical context is one in which it is supposed that it is not *immediately obvious* that mere causal determination in the actual sequence directly rules out moral responsibility, then one must say more than that we object to being intermediate links in a deterministic causal chain.

When it is not the case that a person's choice and action are produced by a deterministic causal chain that starts with factors "external" to the person, Kane points out that it can be said of the person, "The buck stops here." Quite apart from wanting alternative possibilities, Kane suggests that we want it to be the case that the buck stops here. But, obviously, in this context, "The buck stops here" is a metaphor. If it simply stands for not being an intermediate link in a deterministic causal chain, then we are back to the problem that this does not make any dialectic progress.

A similar problem afflicts the view of Derk Pereboom, who claims that "if all of our behavior was 'in the cards' before we were born, in the sense that things happened before we came to exist that, by way of a deterministic causal process, inevitably result in our behavior, then we cannot legitimately be blamed for our wrongdoing."[14] Our behavior's "being in the cards" is obviously a metaphor. Pereboom means by this that conditions prior to our births "inevitably result in our behavior by a deterministic causal process." If the problematic notion of inevitability simply implies the notion of entailment, then Pereboom's claim just comes down to the unargued-for assumption that causal determination in the actual sequence rules out responsibility. Again, this is dialectically unhelpful. If "inevitability" also implies some sort of actual-sequence compulsion, this is question-begging within the dialectic context. *Why* exactly is it the case that one's behavior's being "in the cards," in the relevant sense, involves problematic compulsion and thus directly rules out moral responsibility?

I think it is interesting that, once the debate is shifted away from the relationship between causal determinism and alternative possibilities, it is difficult to present a non-question-begging reason that causal determinism rules out moral responsibility. I can, however, identify various additional resources in Kane's work which could be employed to explain why it is that we would object to the presence of causal determination in the actual sequence (apart from worries about alternative possibilities). The first idea seems to be that if we allow for moral responsibility when there is actual-sequence causal determination, then we will need to say that agents who are covertly manipulated in objectionable ways are also morally responsible.

Kane distinguishes between "constraining" and "nonconstraining" manipulation or "control."[15] Constraining control thwarts preexisting desires, values, ends, and purposes. But nonconstraining manipulation (or, in Kane's term, "control") actually implants the desires, values, ends, and purposes. When the nonconstraining control is covert (CNC), the agent is unaware of it. Kane says:

We are well aware of these two ways to get others to do our bidding in everyday life. We may force them to do what we want by coercing or constraining them against their wills, which is constraining or CC control. Or we may manipulate them into doing what we want while making them feel that they have made up their own minds and are acting "of their own free wills"—which is covert nonconstraining or CNC control. Cases of CNC control in larger settings are provided by examples of behavioral engineering such as we find in utopian works like Aldous Huxley's *Brave New World* or B. F. Skinner's *Walden Two*. Frazier, the fictional founder of Skinner's Walden Two, gives a clear description of CNC control when he says that in his community persons can do whatever they want or choose, but they have been conditioned since childhood to want and choose only what they can have or do.[16]

As Kane points out, the citizens of Walden Two are "satisfied" with themselves; they do not have inner motivational conflicts and they are marvelously "whole-hearted" in their attitudes and engagements.[17] Indeed, Frazier, the founder of Walden Two, describes it as the "freest place on earth."[18]

Kane's point is that someone who allows for moral responsibility in the presence of actual-sequence causal determination will also have to allow for it in contexts like Walden Two. His suggestion is that once one concerns oneself with the *sources* of one's purposes and ends, this will necessarily lead to incompatibilism.[19] But I disagree. A compatibilist will certainly insist that not all causal chains are relevantly similar. The kind of manipulation that takes place in Walden Two does indeed rule out moral responsibility; for a compatibilist, this can be in virtue of the *specific nature* of the causal sequences that issue in behavior, rather than the *mere fact* of causal determination.

For example, on the approach to compatibilism I favor, one looks carefully at the *history* of the behavior in question. If there is unconsented-to covert manipulation of certain sorts, this can be the sort of historical factor that rules out moral responsibility. On my approach, one demands that the behavior issue from the agent's own suitably reasons-sensitive mechanism. That is, the agent must—in a specified sense—have "ownership" of the process that leads to the behavior, and this process must be appropriately sensitive to reasons. These conditions are not met in the objectionable cases of CNC, and yet I would argue that they can be met in a context of mere causal determination.[20]

One might press all sorts of worries about the particular account I have simply gestured at here. But the key point is that a compatibilist can offer a robustly historical theory of moral responsibility. A compatibilist may well offer plausible ways of distinguishing between objectionable sorts of manipulation and mere causal determination. In reply to this sort of point, Kane says that in the cases of CNC and mere causal determination, the agents are *equally* unable to choose or do otherwise; that is, alternative possibilities are expunged as effectively by mere determination as by problematic manipulation.[21] I am willing to grant this, but this point is irrelevant to the issue of whether causal determination in the actual sequence *directly* rules out moral responsibility. It is in no way obvious that a compatibilist cannot usefully distinguish between the *actual sequences* involved in problematic manipulation and those involved in mere causal determination.

It is helpful to see how the sort of compatibilism envisaged here—
semicompatibilism—differs from old-style compatibilism. Both sorts of compatibilism insist on the point that not all causal sequences are relevantly similar. But
old-style compatibilism sought to defend the idea that when the causally deterministic sequence is not "problematic," then the agent has a genuine ability or
freedom to choose and do otherwise. In contrast, semicompatibilism concedes
that the mere fact of causal determination rules out alternative possibilities; nevertheless, it seeks to sort through the actual pathways to the behavior in question,
distinguishing between those pathways that confer responsibility and those that
do not. In doing so, the view can look carefully at the *sources* of an agent's values,
preferences, purposes, and ends; it can attend to how the agent got to be the way
he is.[22]

Kane gives great emphasis to a second point, which is related to his view that
a compatibilist cannot adequately account for contexts of covert nonconstraining
control. He claims that the causal determination of all of an agent's behavior is inconsistent with the agent's having "objective worth."[23] To develop the notion of
objective worth, Kane tells the story of Alan the artist:

> Alan has been so despondent that a rich friend concocts a scheme to lift his spirits.
> The friend arranges to have Alan's paintings bought by confederates at the local art
> gallery under assumed names for $10,000 apiece. Alan mistakenly assumes his paint-
> ings are being recognized for their artistic merit by knowledgeable critics and collec-
> tors, and his spirits are lifted. Now let us imagine two possible worlds involving
> Alan. The first is the one just described, in which Alan thinks he is a great artist,
> and thinks he is being duly recognized as such, but really is not. The other imagined
> world is a similar one in which Alan has many of the same experiences, including
> the belief that he is a great artist. But in this second world he really is a great artist
> and really is being recognized as such; his rich friend is not merely deceiving him to
> lift his spirits. Finally, let us imagine that in both these worlds Alan dies happily, be-
> lieving he is a great artist, though only in the second world was his belief correct.[24]

Kane points out that although Alan would feel equally happy in both worlds, most
of us would say that there is an important difference in value in the two worlds for
Alan. To say this, for Kane, is to accept some notion of objective worth, according
to which value is not simply a function of subjective states or experiences. So far
so good. But Kane goes on to say:

> I want to suggest that the notion of ultimate responsibility is of a piece with this no-
> tion of objective worth. If, like Alan, we think that the objective worth of our acts
> or accomplishments is something valuable over and above the felt satisfaction the
> acts have or bring, then I suggest we will be inclined to think that a freedom requir-
> ing ultimate responsibility is valuable over and above compatibilist freedoms from
> coercion, compulsion, and oppression. . . . [I]f objective worth means little to us, or
> makes no sense—if we believe that the final perspective Alan or anyone should take
> is *inside* the worlds, in which subjective happiness is all that counts (even if it is
> based on deception)—we are likely to see no point or significance as well in ultimate
> responsibility and incompatibilist freedom.[25]

But, again, I disagree with Kane's contention that the compatibilist is saddled with the unattractive view. It is admittedly the case that some compatibilist views focus solely on structural arrangements of mental states.[26] But this is not essential to compatibilism. As I pointed out above, the view I favor is *historical*. I have argued elsewhere that there are two problems with purely structural accounts of moral responsibility (such as the hierarchical model): they are ahistorical, and they do not attend to the *connections* between the agent and the world.[27] My compatibilist account of moral responsibility is sensitive to history and it demands certain connections between the agent and the reasons provided by the world.[28] Just as a compatibilist account of moral responsibility can have these features (in virtue of which it is not purely structural), so a compatibilist can certainly agree with the view that there is "objective" worth in the sense that value is not purely a function of experiences—one must be connected to the world in the right way. (I also do not see why even a purely structural or "internalistic" compatibilist could not have an objective view about value, which is, after all, a *different* notion from moral responsibility.) There is absolutely *nothing* about compatibilism that requires a purely subjective account of value.

The attempts discussed above to argue that causal determination of behavior rules out moral responsibility apart from considerations pertinent to alternative possibilities are unconvincing. I now want to explore what Kane takes to be a related theme—the idea of independence. Kane says:

> When one traces the desires we have for incompatibilist free will to their roots, by way of [the idea of ultimate responsibility], one eventually arrives at two elemental (and I think interrelated) desires—(i) the desire to be independent sources of activity in the world, which is connected, I maintain, from the earliest stages of childhood to the sense we have of our uniqueness and importance as individuals; and (ii) the desire that some of our deeds and accomplishments (such as Alan's paintings in my example) have objective worth.[29]

But what exactly is it to be an "independent" source of activity? At this point in the dialectical context, one cannot say that the relevant notion of independence requires that, given the agent's past and environmental niche, he has alternative possibilities; and as we have seen, one cannot simply argue that the relevant notion of independence is captured by the claim that we prefer not to be an intermediate link in a deterministic causal chain.

Alfred Mele has offered a useful suggestion here.[30] This is the idea: an agent is independent, in the relevant sense, according to the incompatibilist, insofar as he makes an explanatory contribution to his behavior, the making of which cannot be fully explained by the laws of nature and the state of the world at some time prior to his having any sense of the apparent options.[31] If an agent's making a contribution to his behavior is fully explained by reference to prior conditions and the laws of nature, then he is not independent in the relevant sense; and of course if there is causal determination in the actual sequence leading to behavior, then the agent's contributions can in fact be entirely explained by prior conditions and the laws of nature. The desire for this sort of independence can then be offered as a reason that causal determination in the actual sequence would rule out moral responsibility quite apart from issues pertaining to alternative possibilities.

Kane attributes great importance to the requirement of incompatibilistic independence. As we saw above, Kane connects this sort of independence to one's "uniqueness and importance as an individual." Kane says, "What determinism takes away is a certain sense of the importance of oneself as an individual."[32] In a further elaboration of this view, Kane quotes William James, from his essay "The Dilemma of Determinism": "The great point [about the incompatibilist view] is that the possibilities are really *here*. At those soul-trying moments when fate's scales seem to quiver [we acknowledge] that the issue is decided nowhere else than *here* and *now*. *That* is what gives the palpitating reality to our moral life and makes it tingle . . . with so strange and elaborate an excitement."[33] About this passage from James, Kane says, "It may be easy to ridicule James's assertion that a certain passion and excitement would be taken out of present and future choice situations if we believed their outcomes were determined. But many ordinary persons and philosophers, myself included, would say that it is true."[34]

If causal determinism were true, would our importance as individuals be diminished? Would the passion, the thrill of life, be gone? I don't have any inclination to think so. Imagine that a consortium of scientists from Cal Tech, Stanford, and MIT announced that despite the previous scientific views, it turns out that the equations that describe the universe are deterministic. That is, the previous indeterministic views—which posited tiny residual indeterminacies at the macro-level based on quantum indeterminacies at the micro-level—were based on inadequacies in our understanding of nature, and the new view is that the equations are universal generalizations. Would you conclude that your life lacks importance, that its importance is significantly diminished, or that your deliberations are empty and meaningless? I certainly would not.

I grant that those who are strongly predisposed to incompatibilism will cling to the requirement of independence (interpreted as above). They think of us as having what might be called the "importance of independence." But there is another sort of importance, which is, in my view, at least as compelling; let us call this the "importance of indispensability." Note that even if causal determinism obtains, invocation of prior states of the world plus the natural laws cannot explain our behavior and its upshots without *also* explaining that *we make a certain sort of contribution to them*. That is, the prior conditions and laws of nature explain what happens only by also explaining that we make a certain sort of contribution—that our deliberations have a certain character, for example. The very factors that explain what happens cannot explain the way the world actually unfolds without *also* explaining that we make a certain sort of contribution through (for example) our unhindered deliberations.[35]

Thus, in a causally deterministic world, although we would lack the importance of independence (interpreted as above), we could have the importance of indispensability. By "unhindered" deliberations I mean deliberations not impaired by factors *uncontroversially* thought to rule out moral responsibility, such as certain sorts of hypnosis, manipulation, subliminal advertising, coercion, and so forth.[36] I believe that when one engages in unhindered deliberation in a causally deterministic world, one can exercise a certain sort of control; this is a kind of actual-sequence control, which does not require the presence of alternative possibilities. If this view is correct, then in a causally deterministic world, invocation of prior conditions together with the laws of nature cannot explain what happens without also explaining that the agent exercises a certain sort of control in contributing to it. Such an agent can surely be important, and—leaving aside the tingling sensation referred to by James—his deliberations can certainly have all the passion and engagement that it is reasonable to want.

Recall Robert Kane's metaphor, "The buck stops here." With apologies to Harry Truman, the compatibilist can suggest an alternative metaphor. To quote—or perhaps I should concede, paraphrase—the former Green Bay Packer Ray Nitschke (not to be confused with the philosopher, Friedrich Nietzsche!), "To get there from here, you have to go through me, baby."

Now the dialectical situation is as follows. We have discussed two different notions of importance related to the explanatory role of prior conditions, the laws of nature, and the self—the importance of independence and the importance of indispensability. I suppose that certain people who are strongly predisposed to incompatibilism will insist on the requirement of independence (as interpreted above) for moral responsibility. But it seems to me that the importance of indispensability is at least an equally attractive notion. It is not obvious that one should prefer the requirement of independence (as interpreted above) to the requirement of indispensability. Given the compatibilistic notion of the importance of indispensability, I do not think that a fair-minded, reasonable person not already committed to incompatibilism will conclude that incompatibilistic independence is a requirement of moral responsibility. The compatibilist, then, can offer an attractive account of the sort of importance related to the explanatory role of prior conditions. Further, it is clear that the compatibilist can offer his own account of "independence," which would posit a freedom from certain *objectionable* kinds of influences (but not necessarily all prior states of the universe and the laws of nature).

Return now to Laura Ekstrom's contention that, if there is causal determination in the actual sequence, "the past pushes [the agent] into one particular decision state, the only state physically possible at the time, given the past and the laws of nature." It seems to me that Ekstrom's idea faces the same problems as the various suggestions discussed above. There is a commonsense notion of "pushing," according to which there is a difference between (say) being pushed by a strong gust of wind and simply walking normally down a trail. On this notion of "pushing," one would not necessarily be pushed by the past and laws of nature, given causal determinism. Of course, one could adopt a special incompatibilist notion of pushing, but this will be attractive only to those already strongly inclined toward incompatibilism, and not to reasonable and fair-minded persons not already strongly committed to a particular view about the compatibility issue.

I suppose Ekstrom could seek to argue that on the commonsense notion of "pushing," the laws of nature push. But there are various different accounts of what makes a generalization a law of nature. On many of these accounts, which have considerable plausibility, there would be no inclination whatsoever to say that laws of nature must "push." On some views, laws of nature do not "necessitate";[37] on other views, laws of nature necessitate, but this necessitation may be cashed out in ways which should not incline one to say that the laws push. So, for example, some would argue that one feature that makes a generalization a law of nature is that it "supports its counterfactuals" in a certain way; surely, however, this feature in itself does not entail problematic "pushing."

To elaborate: On the Stalnaker/Lewis account of the semantics for counterfactuals, the truth of a counterfactual is determined by the similarity relations among possible worlds.[38] (Very roughly, "If P were the case, then Q would be the case" is true, on this approach, just in case Q is true in the possible world or worlds most similar to the actual world in which P is true.) Employing this approach to the truth conditions for counterfactuals, one could say that what helps to distinguish between mere generalizations and the laws of nature is the similarity relations among various possible worlds. But this in itself does not seem to imply that the laws of nature "push" in any objectionable way, and it is hard to see how this, in combination with other factors, would have this sort of implication. Thus, as far as I can see, there is *no* reason that would compel a person not already committed to incompatibilism to think that causal determination in the actual sequence rules out moral responsibility *directly* (i.e., apart from ruling out alternative possibilities).

Conclusion

I said above that the Frankfurt-type examples have helped to shift the debates about free will and moral responsibility from considerations about alternative possibilities to factors present in the "actual sequence." I now want to return explicitly to the issue of whether this is genuine—or merely illusory—progress. The progress would be merely illusory if the reasons to think that causal determination in the actual sequence rules out moral responsibility are just as strong as the reasons to think that causal determinism rules out alternative possibilities.

But I do *not* think that this is so. I believe that a reasonable person, having fairly considered the arguments, should conclude that causal determinism rules out alternative possibilities. The argument to this conclusion from the principles encapsulating the fixity of the past and the fixity of the natural laws seems to me to be strong. I do not think that the argument here is knockdown, or that any rational person needs to accept it simply in virtue of his rationality. But I believe that the argument that causal determinism rules out alternative possibilities is a valid argument based on premises that any fair-minded and reasonable person really *should* accept: the relevant notions of the fixity of the past and laws are deeply embedded in common sense.

In contrast, I do not think that any reasonable and fair-minded person, not already strongly predisposed to or antecedently committed to incompatibilism, should conclude that causal determination in the actual sequence *directly* rules out moral responsibility. There are various factors one might consider here: initiation, creativity, activity, freedom from objectionable manipulation, objective value, importance, and so forth. But for each notion there is a compatibilist account as well as an incompatibilist account. And it seems to me that there is no good reason to think that a reasonable and fair-minded person, not already committed to incompatibilism, should embrace the incompatibilist notion. Of course, the arguments sketched above will not convince a person who comes to the discussion with strong incompatibilist inclinations or is already firmly committed to incompatibilism; but I don't think any argument could do that, and this is certainly not a fair test of success.

So we should not accept the conclusion of the party-poopers who claim that Frankfurt-style compatibilism is not successful. Frankfurt-style compatibilism does represent a genuine advance; Frankfurt has helped to shift the debates from a context in which incompatibilism has an advantage to one in which incompatibilism has no such advantage.[39] If one believes—as I do—that there is a good "positive" reason to adopt compatibilism insofar as our basic views about ourselves—our views of ourselves as persons and as morally responsible—should not be held hostage to the discoveries of a consortium of scientists about the precise nature of the equations that describe the universe, then the progress made by Frankfurt can at least help to clear the way to embracing compatibilism.[40]

NOTES

1. Joel Feinberg, "The Interest of Liberty on the Scales," in *Rights, Justice, and the Bounds of Liberty: Essays in Social Philosophy* (Princeton, N.J.: Princeton University Press, 1980), pp. 36–40.

2. Whether this is the case will depend on how one understands God's attributes, and, in particular, whether God's providential activities involve causation of the human will.

3. For such skepticism, see (among others) David Widerker, "Libertarian Freedom and the Avoidability of Decisions," *Faith and Philosophy* 12 (1995): 113–18, and "Libertarianism and Frankfurt's Attack on the Principle of Alternative Possibilities," *Philosophical Review* 104 (1995): 247–61; Robert Kane, *Free Will and Values* (Albany: State University of New York Press, 1985), p. 51, and *The Significance of Free Will* (New York: Oxford University Press, 1996), esp. pp. 142–45; Carl Ginet, "In Defense of the Principle of Alternative Possibilities: Why I Don't Find Frankfurt's Argument Convincing," *Philosophical Perspectives* 10 (1996): 403–17; Keith D. Wyma, "Moral Responsibility and Leeway for Action," *American Philosophical Quarterly* 34 (1997): 57–70; and Laura Ekstrom, "Protecting Incompatibilist Freedom," *American Philosophical Quarterly* 35 (1998): 281–91.

4. Ekstrom, "Protecting Incompatibilist Freedom," pp. 284–85.

5. Ibid., p. 284.

6. Hunt employs what might be called a "blockage" case, rather than a "prior-sign" case. This sort of case takes its cue from John Locke's example of a man who is, unknown to him, locked in a room and decides voluntarily to remain in the room. In Hunt's case, although the brain actually works by an indeterministic process, all other neural pathways (all neural pathways not actually taken) are blocked (as in the locked door of John Locke's example). David P. Hunt, "Moral Responsibility and Unavoidable Action," *Philosophical Studies* 97 (2000): 195–227. Mele and Robb present a case in which there are two actually operating sequences—one indeterministic and the other deterministic—which simultaneously result in the agent's decision (in which case the indeterministic sequence preempts the deterministic sequence). Alfred R. Mele and David Robb, "Rescuing Frankfurt-Style Cases," *Philosophical Review* 107 (1998): 97–112. And Stump employs the plausible idea

that one could correlate a certain stream of neural events with mental events such as choices or decisions; in her cases, the "counterfactual interveners" (the analogues to Black) can anticipate an impending mental event (of the relevant sort) by "reading" or detecting the *beginnings* of the neural sequence. Stump argues that they can thereby cut off the *mental event* (as opposed to the correlated neural sequence) before it even begins. Eleonore Stump, "Non-Cartesian Dualism and Materialism with Reductionism," *Faith and Philosophy* 12 (1995): 505–31; "Libertarian Freedom and the Principle of Alternate Possibilities," in *Faith, Freedom, and Rationality: Philosophy of Religion Today*, ed. Daniel Howard-Snyder and Jeff Jordan (Lanham, Md.: Rowman and Littlefield, 1996), pp. 73–88; and "Alternative Possibilities and Responsibility: The Flicker of Freedom," unpublished manuscript delivered at the American Philosophical Association Pacific Division Meetings, March 1998, Los Angeles, California.

7. For a more careful description and evaluation of these sorts of indeterministic Frankfurt-type cases, see John Martin Fischer, "Recent Work on Moral Responsibility," *Ethics* 110 (1999): 93–139, esp. 113–23.

8. I sketch this sort of reply in Fischer, "Recent Work on Moral Responsibility."

9. For a development and discussion of such arguments, and the parallel argument with respect to God's foreknowledge, see John Martin Fischer, *The Metaphysics of Free Will: An Essay on Control* (Oxford: Blackwell, 1994).

10. Michael Della Rocca, "Frankfurt, Fischer, and Flickers," *Nous* 32 (1998): 99–105. Indeed, he begins the article with the statement, "In this paper, I argue that John Martin Fischer's most recent argument for the compatibility of causal determinism and moral responsibility does not succeed."

11. See chapter 2 of this book.

12. Kane, *Significance of Free Will*.

13. Robert Kane, "Two Kinds of Incompatibilism," *Philosophy and Phenomenological Research* 50 (1989): 254.

14. Derk Pereboom, "Alternative Possibilities and Causal Histories," chap. 1 of *Living without Free Will*. Department of Philosophy, University of Vermont, Burlington.

15. Kane, *Significance of Free Will*, pp. 64–71.

16. Ibid., p. 65.

17. Ibid.

18. B. F. Skinner, *Walden Two* (New York: MacMillan, 1962), p. 297; as cited in Kane, *Significance of Free Will*, p. 65.

19. A similar point is made by Ekstrom:

But the model of a person as chugging along on a certain line of straight train tracks, without any forks in the path, is the antithesis of a deep-seated and pervasive image of ourselves as free agents. The idea that we can direct our behavior by our thoughts (desires, beliefs, intentions) is welcome, but it is only superficially comforting. It comforts until we think about the possibility that even our thoughts are driven to be what they are by previous neurophysiological events which themselves stand in a chain of events (between which there are deterministic causal links), a chain going backward through events in our childhood brains and to events prior to our birth. (Ekstrom, "Protecting Incompatibilist Freedom," p. 285)

Also, Kane says:

But, as Martha Klein has pointed out, an interest in ultimacy adds a different set of concerns [from those pertaining to alternative possibilities] about the "sources," "grounds," "reasons," and "explanations" of actions and events—that is, concerns about where they came from, what produced them, and who was responsible for them. It is by focusing on such concerns about origins and responsibility, I would argue, and not merely on alternative possibilities, that one arrives at incompatibilism. (Kane, *Significance of Free Will*, p. 74)

20. For developments of this sort of view, see Fischer, *Metaphysics of Free Will*; and John Martin Fischer and Mark Ravizza, *Responsibility and Control: A Theory of Moral Responsibility* (Cambridge: Cambridge University Press, 1998). The conditions on ownership of the mechanism that issues in behavior are set out in *Responsibility and Control*, pp. 207–39; the sort of reasons-sensitivity required for moral responsibility is developed on pp. 62–150. Throughout the book we argue that the conditions on reasons-sensitivity and mechanism ownership can indeed be met in a causally deterministic world; for a discussion of the relevant sorts of "manipulation" and how they would run afoul especially of the ownership condition, see pp. 230–36.

21. Kane, *Significance of Free Will*, 67–69.

22. In her review of my book *The Metaphysics of Free Will: An Essay on Control*, Sarah Buss says:

I do not see how [Fischer's] semicompatibilism differs in any very important way from good old-fashioned compatibilism. Compatibilists have always readily conceded that if causal determinism is true, then no one has the ability to do-otherwise-even-when-the-past-and-the-laws-are-held-fixed. They have simply insisted that agents do not need *this* ability to be morally responsible for their behavior. According to the familiar compatibilist view, the ability to do otherwise relevant to moral responsibility is the ability to do otherwise *if* certain counterfactual conditions obtain—if, for example one chooses to do otherwise. (Sarah Buss, "Review of *The Metaphysics of Free Will*, by John Martin Fischer," *Philosophical Books* [1997]: 117–21. esp. 120)

I admit that there has been some confusion about the "target" of various compatibilist analyses of "could" or "ability." Some compatibilists have indeed taken the relevant notion to be a *conditional ability*, corresponding to "can, if the agent were to choose differently," or something like this. But this seems to me to open the compatibilist to an obvious and devastating objection; it is simply irrelevant that the agent would have been able to do the thing in question *under different circumstances*. What one is interested in is whether the agent can do the thing in question in the particular circumstances he is in. Most compatibilists have understood their project to be to give an analysis of precisely this notion of "can, in the agent's particular circumstances." They take it that they are giving an account of the intuitive notion of "can"—what Austin called the "all-in sense of 'can'"—that corresponds to the notion of "can" that plays a role in our deliberations as agents (where we take it that we have more than one path into the future genuinely available to us—here and now). Given this project, however, their analyses do not necessarily embrace the fixity of the past or the fixity of the natural laws. It is important to distinguish between taking some sort of conditional ability to be the target of one's compatibilist analysis of an unconditional ability, on the one hand, and denying the fixity of the past or the fixity of the natural laws as part of one's compatibilist analysis, on the other. For good examples of such compatibilist approaches, see Keith Lehrer, "'Can' in Theory and Practice: A Possible Worlds Analysis," in *Action Theory: Proceedings of the Winnipeg Conference on Human Action*, ed. M. Brand and D. Walton (Dordrecht: D. Reidel, 1976), pp. 241–70; and Terence Horgan, "'Could,' Possible Worlds, and Moral Responsibility," *Southern Journal of Philosophy* 17 (1979): 345–58.

23. Kane, *Significance of Free Will*, pp. 97–98.

24. Ibid., p. 97.

25. Ibid., p. 98.

26. Harry Frankfurt's "hierarchical" view of moral responsibility is a salient and important example of such a view. The classic presentation is in Harry Frankfurt, "Freedom of the Will and the Concept of the Person," in *The Importance of What We Care About*.

27. See, for example, Fischer and Ravizza, *Responsibility and Control*, esp. pp. 252–53.

28. I believe that a mechanism becomes the "agent's own" in virtue of the process whereby he "takes responsibility" for it; this renders my approach to moral responsibility a historical theory. See *Responsibility and Control*, pp. 170–239. Further, the reasons-responsiveness requirement ensures the appropriate sort of connection between the agent and the world.

29. Kane, *Significance of Free Will*, p. 98.

30. Alfred R. Mele, "Soft Libertarianism and Frankfurt-Style Scenarios," *Philosophical Topics* 24 (1996): 123–42; "Flickers of Freedom," *Journal of Social Philosophy* 29 (1998): 144–56; "Kane, Luck, and the Significance of Free Will," *Philosophical Explorations* 2 (1999): 96–104; and "Ultimate Responsibility and Dumb Luck," *Social Philosophy and Policy* 16 (1999): 274–93.

31. Mele, "Ultimate Responsibility and Dumb Luck," 285–87.

32. Kane, *Free Will and Values*, p. 178.

33. William James, "The Dilemma of Determinism," in *The Will to Believe and Other Essays* (New York: Dover, 1956), p. 183; as cited in Kane, *Significance of Free Will*, p. 88.

34. Kane, *Significance of Free Will*, p. 88.

35. Michael Zimmerman has pointed out that in a case of actual (as opposed to preemptive) overdetermination, reference to one's (unhindered) deliberations may not be necessary in order to explain the fact that some state of affairs obtains, given that the same state of affairs is caused to obtain by some other route, as well as by one's deliberations. But it is nevertheless true that reference to one's unhindered deliberations is essential to an explanation of *how the actual sequence unfolds*, and thus, *of how it comes about* that the state of affairs obtains. The intended notion of explanation is not simply an explanation *that* a state of affairs obtains; it is an explanation of how it comes about that the state of affairs obtains.

36. Of course, an incompatibilist will contend that causally determined deliberations are not *unhindered*. I cannot here argue against the incompatibilist's contention; I am not here seeking to "prove" that my notion of "unhindered" is somehow the "correct" notion. Rather, I am employing what I admit to be a compatibilist notion. My claim is that this notion can be employed to present something—the importance of indispensability—that is at least as attractive (to the target audience—reasonable and fair-minded people not already committed to incompatibilism) as the incompatibilistically construed importance of independence.

37. For such a view, and its role in rendering compatibilism more appealing, see Bernard Berofsky, *The Metaphysical Basis of Responsibility* (New York: Routledge and Kegan Paul, 1987).

38. Robert Stalnaker, "A Theory of Conditionals," in *Studies in Logical Theory, American Philosophical Quarterly Series*, ed. N. Rescher (Oxford: Blackwell, 1968), pp. 98–112; and David Lewis, *Counterfactuals* (Cambridge: Harvard University Press, 1973).

39. In "Frankfurt, Fischer, and Flickers," Della Rocca says:

> I should like to call attention to a connection between my criticism of Fischer and what is, perhaps, Fischer's guiding insight in his approach to moral responsibility. For Fischer, in accounting for moral responsibility, we should focus not directly on any alternative sequence of events there may be, but on properties of the actual

sequence, including especially facts about the actual causes of the relevant action. In criticizing Fischer, I have, in effect, used this insight or at least an implication of it against Fischer himself. The problem I have raised stems from his focusing on what the flicker of freedom shows about the alternative scenario (viz. that Jones does not do A freely in the alternative scenario), but not on what the flicker shows about the actual situation (viz. that Jones' action is not externally determined in the actual situation). If my objection to Fischer succeeds, it does so in virtue of drawing our attention to a connection between the presence of the flicker and a feature of the actual causal sequence. My procedure here thus reinforces, in a way that is perhaps not entirely welcome to Fischer, his exhortation to focus on the actual sequence. (pp. 103–104)

But Della Rocca's "procedure" is not at all unwelcome to me. If his point is that once one focuses on the actual sequence, there will be no *knockdown* argument (acceptable even to those already strongly inclined toward incompatibilism), I do not disagree. Rather, my point is that the debate will have been shifted to terrain considerably more hospitable to compatibilism. This is why I think it is useful to see that the presence of alternative possibilities does not *in itself* ground ascriptions of moral responsibility, and why I welcome the focus on the actual sequence.

40. I do not believe that our personhood and moral responsibility should be insulated from *every* empirical discovery about the world. Rather, I believe that these central notions should be resilient with respect to this particular issue—whether the equations that describe the macroscopic universe are universal generalizations or probabilistic generalizations with extremely high probabilities attached to them. For discussions, see Fischer and Ravizza, *Responsibility and Control*, 253–54, and Fischer, "Recent Work on Moral Responsibility."

7
RESPONSIBILITY AND AGENT-CAUSATION

Certain libertarians adopt a view called "agent-causation." Although everyone wishes to say that agents cause certain effects, agent-causation, in the relevant sense, is supposed to be a basic, irreducible sort of causation which relates agents and events. In this chapter I wish to explore the question of whether agent-causation has distinctive resources for responding to the Frankfurt-type cases in which it is alleged that an agent is morally responsible although he lacks alternative possibilities.

My main focus will be Timothy O'Connor's provocative defense of incompatibilism about causal determinism and moral responsibility based on his agent-causal approach to freedom and moral responsibility.[1] O'Connor presents various criticisms of the doctrine of semicompatibilism: the thesis that even though causal determinism evidently rules out alternative possibilities, it does not rule out moral responsibility. Here I wish to present O'Connor's criticisms of semicompatibilism and offer a reply. I will be especially interested in articulating the way in which Frankfurt-type cases challenge the notion that moral responsibility requires alternative possibilities. Once one sees this, it becomes evident that the invocation of agent-causation does not provide any reason to doubt the efficacy of the Frankfurt-type cases in challenging the association of moral responsibility with alternative possibilities. To bring out the generality of my critique, I will also apply my analysis to a recent defense of the agent-causal approach to responding to the Frankfurt-type cases developed by William Rowe.

I am very grateful to helpful suggestions by David Widerker. I presented a previous version of this chapter at the American Philosophical Association Pacific Division Meetings in San Francisco, California, in March 2001. On this occasion Timothy O'Connor and Carl Ginet offered thoughtful and probing comments.

O'Connor's Criticisms of Semicompatibilism

The Frankfurt-Type Cases

O'Connor quotes Harry Frankfurt's famous description of a case which Frankfurt gives in order to impugn the "Principle of Alternative Possibilities" (PAP), the doctrine that a person is morally responsible for what he has done only if he could have done otherwise:

> [Black] waits until Jones is about to make up his mind what to do, and he does nothing unless it is clear to him (Black is an excellent judge of such things) that Jones is going to decide to do something *other* than what he wants him to do. If it does become clear that Jones is going to decide to do something else, Black takes effective steps to ensure that Jones decides to do, and that he does do, what he wants him to do.[2]

The signature element of the Frankfurt-style examples is the presence of a fail-safe device (the counterfactual intervener, Black) which ensures the actual result but does not play any causal role in the pathway to that result. It seemed to Frankfurt, and it has appeared to other philosophers, that in such cases the agent is morally responsible for his choice and action, although he could not have chosen or acted differently.

This conclusion issuing from reflection on the Frankfurt-type examples has not proved entirely irresistible. One important set of concerns pertains to the question of how the counterfactual intervener can know what Jones is about to "make up his mind to do." Note that Frankfurt says, "Black is an excellent judge of such things." Perhaps sensing that this remark would not be completely satisfying, he added, in a footnote:

> The assumption that Black can predict what Jones[4] will decide to do does not beg the question of determinism. We can imagine that Jones[4] has often confronted the alternatives—A and B—that he now confronts, and that his face has invariably twitched when he was about to decide to do A and never when he was about to decide to do B. Knowing this, and observing the twitch, Black would have a basis for prediction. This does, to be sure, suppose that there is some sort of causal relation between Jones[4]'s state at the time of the twitch and his subsequent states. But any plausible view of decision or of action will allow that reaching a decision and performing an action both involve earlier and later phases, with causal relations between them, and such that the earlier phases are not themselves part of the decision or of the action. The example does not require that these earlier phases be deterministically related to still earlier events.[3]

Frankfurt thus anticipated a literature criticizing the employment of his examples to defend compatibilism about determinism and moral responsibility.[4] But his attempt to defuse the worry is manifestly unsatisfying. If the relationship between the prior twitch and the subsequent decision is not causally deterministic, then even though Jones has exhibited the twitch at the prior time, there is no obstacle to his beginning to decide to do B (rather than A) at the later time. After all, the relationship between the prior twitch and his subsequent decisions and actions is explicitly assumed to be causally indeterministic, and the mere fact that Jones has always in the past decided to do A after twitching does not preclude his deciding (or, at least, beginning to decide) this time to do B, even though he has twitched.

The problem then is to defend the idea that the agent in the Frankfurt-style examples is morally responsible while lacking alternative possibilities. If one posits causal determinism, one can get the result that the agent lacks alternative possibilities, but (apparently) at the expense of the uncontroversial truth of the contention that the agent is morally responsible. And if one posits something short of causal determinism, one attenuates the contention that the agent lacks alternative possibilities.

My strategy of response (in previous work) has been to divide the dialectical space in two. I first consider whether the assumption of causal determinism does in fact call into question the contention that the agent is morally responsible. My claim is that even the assumption of causal determinism does not render the examples useless in defending semicompatibilism.[5] I then consider what would be the case under the assumption of indeterminism; here I suggest that one should be able to construct versions of the examples in which the agent does not have appropriate access to alternative possibilities, on the libertarian's own view of what such access must consist in. O'Connor's criticism hones in on this latter claim. There are two separate lines of criticism. I shall begin with one that, if it succeeds, shows that an agent-causation approach would have special resources to block the conclusion that Frankfurt-style examples impugn PAP.

O'Connor's First Criticism of Semicompatibilism

O'Connor points out that Peter van Inwagen has usefully distinguished among different sorts of *items* for which we might be held morally responsible: actions, omissions, consequences, and so forth. Here is a principle van Inwagen presents, as applicable to responsibility for consequences, considered as abstract states of affairs (that is, states of affairs individuated so that the same state of affairs could be reached via different causal paths):

> PPP2: A person is morally responsible for a certain state of affairs only if (that state of affairs obtains and) he could have prevented it from obtaining.[6]

Now O'Connor says:

> The basic strategy of van Inwagen's argument exploits the fact that abstract states of affairs can be more or less fine-grained. For example, let us suppose that the desired action in Frankfurt's scenario is that Jones shoots Stewart. Corresponding to the particular event of Stewart's death are these states of affairs: *Stewart's dying at t, Stewart's being killed by someone at t, Stewart's being intentionally shot by someone at t.* Now, from the facts that an agent is responsible for a state of affairs S and that S entails S*, it does not follow that the agent is responsible for S*. . . . *Stewart's being killed by someone at t*, for example, entails *The universe's existing at t.* Before one considers Frankfurt-type scenarios, it is quite natural to say that the point of "cutoff" in terms of responsibility in a sequence of increasingly less specific states of affairs (where

each entails the one subsequent to it) is precisely the point at which a state of affairs is such that the agent could not have prevented it. If we can show that we needn't absolve the agent of moral responsibility in Frankfurt cases to preserve this intuition, we would seem to have sufficient reason to preserve it.[7]

O'Connor goes on to offer the following way of preserving the intuition while not exculpating the agent in the Frankfurt-style scenarios:

> In the preceding scenario Jones can't prevent any of the states of affairs. So, according to PPP2, he is not responsible for the fact that they obtain, as they are inevitable from the standpoint of his "sphere of influence." But there is at least one other, closely related state of affairs for which we may plausibly hold him responsible without abandoning PPP2: *Stewart's being killed by Jones acting on his own.* This indicates a general formula applicable to any Frankfurt-type situation for characterizing a state of affairs for which the agent may be held responsible. For in all such cases, the agent is in no way caused to act or decide as he does, but rather acts or decides "on his own" or freely. In "ordinary" situations, there will be a variety of other, more broadly delineated states of affairs for which the agent is equally responsible.[8]

O'Connor now notes that I would concede that there exists an alternative possibility, understood as O'Connor suggests, but I would nevertheless argue that it is a "mere flicker of freedom" and thus not sufficiently robust to ground ascriptions of moral responsibility, if one accepts (as O'Connor does) an alternative-possibilities view of the sort of freedom that grounds responsibility. After all, in the alternative scenario Stewart does not *voluntarily* bring it about that he does not choose or act on his own. O'Connor says, however, that he is not convinced by my arguments for this view, and he suggests (on the first line of argumentation) that the agent-causal approach he develops has special resources for showing that my contention is problematic.[9]

What are these special resources? It will be useful here just to give a bare-bones sketch of O'Connor's agent-causal approach to agency and freedom. On O'Connor's account, causation is understood in a "realist, non-reductive" fashion. That is, causation is taken to be a real relation in the world that cannot be reduced to (for example) facts about constant conjunction or counterfactuals. In a case of agent-causation, we have a species of the same relation of causation as relates events; the difference is that the first relatum is an agent, rather than an event. Further, agent-causation is a different species of the genus causation, because it cannot be understood (as event-causation can) as a function directly from circumstances to an effect. Rather, having the properties that ground an agent-causal capacity enables the agent freely to determine an effect (within a certain range), given the circumstances. What is directly agent-caused, on O'Connor's account, is an "immediately executive intention," and the agent's act of causing this intention is (by its very nature) an uncaused event. O'Connor thus disagrees with Richard Taylor's agent-causal view, according to which the agent-causal event— the agent's causing the effect in question—*can* be caused.[10]

O'Connor's claim that the agent-causal event cannot itself be caused is important for his first line of argument against semicompatibilism. He first considers a possible description of a Frankfurt case:

> [One might suppose that] it is possible to construct Frankfurt scenarios in which the entire sequence of events that constitutes what one does in the actual, uncoerced scenario is *induced* in the counterfactual scenario in which the controller takes over. We might describe the first case as the agent's doing something on his own and the second case as his being made to do what he does, but these are just two different descriptions for intrinsically identical action sequences. The two identical sequences merit different descriptions because of the different causal antecedents (internal to the agent in the one case, external in the other).[11]

But now O'Connor brings to bear the resources of his agent-causal theory, saying:

> This cannot be right, however, if one's account of free actions involves agent causation because, as I have argued . . . , we cannot make good sense of the idea of a cause that directly produces an agent's causing some further event. And if we cannot make good sense of something that directly brings about an agent's causing, the alternative sequence in any Frankfurt scenario will differ intrinsically, not just relationally, from the actual sequence.[12]

O'Connor's point, then, is that the Frankfurt scenarios are not cases in which the same events occur (or states of affairs obtain) in the actual sequence and the alternative sequences, or even cases in which only marginally different events occur (or states of affairs obtain). I take it that O'Connor is interpreting my flicker-of-freedom gambit as contending that, although the items in the actual and alternative scenarios are—arguably—different, they are not *importantly* different. On O'Connor's view, there is a *significant* difference between what occurs in the two sequences—an intrinsic, rather than a mere extrinsic, difference. Given this, O'Connor wants to say, there are significant alternative possibilities in the Frankfurt scenarios; there is an intrinsic difference between what happens in the actual sequence and the alternative sequence, and thus the alternative possibilities are not mere flickers of freedom.

O'Connor's Second Criticism

O'Connor offers an additional line of criticism of semicompatibilism. Indeed, he describes this second line of argumentation as his "principal reply."[13] O'Connor begins this portion of his critique by pointing out that one who rejects the requirement of alternative possibilities for moral responsibility should not precipitously conclude that causal determinism is compatible with moral responsibility.[14] O'Connor suggests that I am guilty of such impatience:

> One who accepts both these claims [including the claim that alternative possibilities are not required for moral responsibility] may, without further argument, embrace "semicompatibilism" . . . (This is just the position advocated by Fischer.) I suggest, to

the contrary, that even if one concludes from Frankfurt-type cases that alternative possibilities of any sort are not necessary to moral responsibility, one may not plausibly draw the further conclusion of semicompatibilism. Whatever the proper verdict on Frankfurt's examples may be, the compatibility of determinism and moral responsibility must be settled on independent grounds.[15]

I do not know how others would be inclined to proceed, but I have never argued that the mere fact that alternative possibilities are not required for moral responsibility issues in the compatibility of moral responsibility and causal determinism. Indeed, I have been at pains to point out that the claim that alternative possibilities are not required is the *first step* toward compatibilism, but that ancillary argumentation is certainly needed.[16]

O'Connor continues by emphasizing that the alternative-possibilities requirement (AP) [PAP] is deeply entrenched in common sense. He says:

Suppose for the sake of argument that Frankfurt and others have established possible cases that show that this pretheoretical commitment is false. Then the natural conclusion to draw is that ordinary thought has misidentified the freedom-relevant necessary condition on moral responsibility by conflating the AP condition with some distinct condition it closely tracks. For we shouldn't overlook the obvious, that is, that Frankfurt cases are extremely contrived and (unless we are badly mistaken about the world) never instanced. Ordinary thinking about responsibility proceeds by reflecting on familiar cases. And the common conclusion is that for an agent to bear responsibility in such familiar cases, the condition of one or more significant alternatives must obtain.[17]

O'Connor continues as follows:

So, even if we gave up the strict or conceptual necessity of the AP condition on moral responsibility, the fact that we rely on its presence or absence in actual cases strongly suggests that it must be tightly connected to what is a truly necessary condition. That is, the two conditions are coextensive in ordinary contexts, even if they can in principle come apart. As philosophers, we would want to characterize the truly necessary condition. But a constraint on any proposal is that it entails the presence of alternative possibilities, relative to (conditional on) a broad assumption about actual deliberative environments, that is, that it lacks a purely "counterfactual intervener"—one who does nothing that influences the actual flow of events but merely would do so if circumstances were different in some respect.[18]

Finally, O'Connor considers what he calls the "strongly revisionary conclusion" that some philosophers draw from the Gettier counterexamples to the justified true belief (JTB) analysis of knowledge. O'Connor contends that there is an asymmetry between the Gettier examples and the Frankfurt examples:

It [the conclusion that justified true belief is either insufficient for or irrelevant to knowledge] is an option that one may reasonably consider when reflecting further on a range of examples, for the JTB analysis is a theoretical analysis that philosophers have devised in applying the ordinary, somewhat inchoate notion to various cases. But it is implausible to make a similar move in response to Frankfurt examples, for the AP condition on responsibility is present in ordinary thought (and a deep conviction at that). It isn't a claim that has to be teased out of our thinking.[19]

Replies

Reply to O'Connor's First Criticism

I now turn to O'Connor's suggestion that agent-causation provides special resources for replying to the contention that Frankfurt-type examples show that moral responsibility does not require alternative possibilities. Recall that central to O'Connor's strategy here is the claim that the Frankfurt scenarios are not cases in which the same events occur (or states of affairs obtain) in the actual sequence and the alternative sequences, or even cases in which only marginally different events occur (or states of affairs obtain). Thus, there is alleged to be a *significant* difference between what occurs in the two sequences—an intrinsic, rather than a mere extrinsic, difference.

But why exactly is this point a response to my defense of the relevant part of the doctrine of semicompatibilism (the rejection of the alternative-possibilities requirement for moral responsibility [PAP])? In my view, it is important to distinguish two different ways in which one might think that the Frankfurt examples challenge PAP.

In the first way, the idea is that the Frankfurt examples are supposed to be cases in which an agent has sole access to an alternative pathway along which there is exactly the same thing—action, concrete event-particular, or abstract state of affairs—as is contained in the actual pathway. If this is the way in which Frankfurt examples are supposed to call into question PAP, then O'Connor's reply (employing the resources of the agent-causal approach) is a promising one: if the events in the alternative sequence are intrinsically, and not merely extrinsically, different from those in the actual flow of events, then it is not plausible to say that the agent is restricted to access to an alternative pathway which contains *the same thing* as the actual pathway.

But the first way is not the only way in which it might be supposed that Frankfurt-style examples call into question PAP. In the second way, it is not alleged that the agent is restricted to pathways with the same contents, but rather, that the agent *lacks access* to pathways along which there are *relevantly different* contents. The difference, in a nutshell, is between contending that the Frankfurt examples involve access only to the same contents, and contending that they involve lack of access to relevantly different contents.[20]

To explain: Surely, if one believes in the alternative-possibilities model of moral responsibility—the model according to which what grounds ascriptions of moral responsibility is the sort of control that entails the genuine availability of alternative possibilities—then those alternative possibilities cannot just be *any* sort of alternative possibilities. That is, they cannot be, for example, alternatives in which the agent fails to act voluntarily and fails to be morally responsible. To believe that simply adding such alternatives to the actual sequence can get one to moral responsibility is to believe in a kind of *alchemy*.[21] How can adding alternative pathways in which the fact that the contents are different from those of the actual pathway is entirely *accidental* and *flukish* render the agent morally responsible in the actual pathway?

Quite apart from consideration of Frankfurt-type scenarios, a traditional—and deep—problem for libertarian approaches (of all kinds) is to distinguish the mere possibility of something different happening from genuine *control*. Merely positing causal indeterminism, and the concomitant possibility of something different occurring, is notoriously insufficient to establish that an agent has the relevant sort of *control*—the sort of control linked with moral responsibility. Interestingly, this sort of worry is the basis of O'Connor's own critique of Robert Kane's indeterministic model of practical reasoning.[22]

On Kane's picture, an agent's decision is a result of a causally indeterministic process analogous to indeterministic phenomena posited by quantum mechanics (on certain interpretations). So on Kane's model, for example, when one chooses the moral, as opposed to the merely prudential, path, one's choice is the result of an "effort of will," which is taken to be (or to involve) an amplification of indeterministic microprocesses in the brain. Although Kane seeks to explain how this sort of indeterminism is compatible with control, O'Connor is unsatisfied, stating: "There is still the fundamental question of how it is that I may be said to freely control it [the actual course of events], whichever way it goes in a given case. How is it up to me that, on this occasion, this one among two or more causally possible choices was made?"[23] This is an excellent question. But why can't the same—or an analogous—question be put to the defender of PAP in the context of the Frankfurt examples? How is it, in the Frankfurt examples, that the agent *freely* controls his behavior, *whichever way things go*? How is it *up to the agent* which path is taken?

My contention is that the Frankfurt examples work against PAP in the second way—by showing that there can be cases in which an agent is morally responsible but lacks access to pathways with relevantly different contents. I confess that Frankfurt's own presentation of the examples obscures this point. Recall that, in presenting the example in his original paper (quoted above), Frankfurt says, "If it does become clear that Jones is going to decide to do something else, Black takes effective steps to ensure that Jones decides to do, and that he does do, what he wants him to do." But Frankfurt could just as easily have said, "If it does become clear that Jones is going to decide to do something else, Black takes effective steps to ensure that Jones does not."

To drive the point home, notice that we could have a sort of example that I would—very modestly—dub a "Fischer-type example." In this kind of variant on the Frankfurt-type scenario, if it becomes clear to the counterfactual intervener— he is an excellent judge of such things—that the agent is going to decide to do something else, he will use his machine to destroy the agent's brain and thus kill him instantly! This rather ghoulish Fischer-type example is just as potent in calling into question PAP as is the standard sort of Frankfurt-type example. And, if this is so, then it appears that at a deeper level the Frankfurt-type examples work against PAP in the second way identified above—by exhibiting cases in which there is moral responsibility but lack of access to pathways with relevantly different contents. Of course, in the Fischer-type case the agent in some sense has access to another path—the path on which he is instantaneously killed. (Not a very promising path, by the way!) But this path does not contain any voluntary behavior by the agent or anything with sufficient "oomph" to ground moral responsibility. Thus, the agent lacks access to an alternative pathway with the right sort of contents. If I am correct, then O'Connor's point about the intrinsic difference in the contents of the two pathways is irrelevant: it is not intrinsicality that is at stake, but robustness, and robustness is understood in terms of access to alternatives with the right sort of contents.

To be sure, Frankfurt's remarks—and those of some of his defenders—suggest that he has in mind the first way of challenging PAP. Here O'Connor's defense of PAP is interesting and illuminating; here we can see the distinctive resources of agent-causation in action. But if one takes it that the Frankfurt examples challenge PAP in the second way, one can see that the invocation of the resources of agent-causation and the associated intrinsic difference between the contents of the actual and alternative pathways are not damaging to semicompatibilism.

Reply to Rowe

Consider the following Frankfurt-type case given by William Rowe:

> Suppose Jones desires to keep for himself a significant sum of money he finds on the pavement. He knows the money was lost by a poor woman who had withdrawn her life savings to provide an operation to restore her son's vision. He knows that keeping the money is morally wrong. And this troubles him. But, after some soul-searching, he yields to greed, tells himself that God will surely look after the poor woman and her son, and decides to keep the money for himself. Is he responsible for his decision and subsequent act of keeping the money? . . . [Rowe presents three versions of the case, only the third of which will be relevant here.]
>
> Case 3: No outside influence or internal desire or want caused him to decide to keep the money. He was free to cause and free not to cause his decision to keep the money. As it happened, he followed his selfish desire, rather than the advice of his conscience, and caused his decision to keep the money, having it within his power, nevertheless, not to have caused that decision. However, had he been about to agent-cause the decision to return the money, the devil, let us suppose, would have directly caused in him the decision to keep the money, effectively preventing any decision or action on his part to return the money. Here we have a *little alternative* open to him: *not* causing his decision to keep the money. He is not free, however, to decide to return the money. For had he not caused his decision to keep it, the devil would have caused him to decide to keep it. In a way, given the steady resolve of the devil, it is up to our agent whether he himself *or* the devil will be responsible for his decision to keep the money. By exercising his power to cause his decision to keep the money, he makes himself responsible for that decision. Had he not caused that decision, the devil, and not he, would have been responsible for his decision to keep the money. Here, at long last, we would have a case in which someone might *truthfully* say: "The devil made me do it."[24]

Rowe goes on to agree with me that the agent has a "very little alternative" in terms of what he could will and do. That is, Jones could not will to return the money or actually return it ("big alternatives"), given the presence and resolve of the devil. The only alternative possibility available to Jones here is to "not agent-cause" his decision: in virtue of the very nature of agent-causation, if the devil were to induce a decision, Jones would not be agent-causing his own decision. But, although Rowe admits that this is a "minute" alternative, he still contends that I am mistaken to suppose that it is not robust enough to ground Jones's moral responsibility for deciding and acting to keep the money.[25]

As with O'Connor, on Rowe's approach one points to the alternative sequence and finds an allegedly significantly different sequence of events—one which does not involve Jones's agent-causation. (The "little" alternative is nevertheless supposed to be significant.) I agree that in the alternative scenario Jones would not be agent-causing his decision to keep the money, and thus I do not deny that the contents of the actual and alternative scenarios are different. But, as I have argued above, this fact is irrelevant if the Frankfurt-type scenarios challenge PAP in the second way, that is, by being cases in which the agent is morally responsible but lacks access to relevantly different contents. Note that Jones has access to a scenario in which he fails to agent-cause his keeping the money. But note also that this failure would not be intentional or voluntary; he would not be *freely* refraining from agent-causing his keeping the money. And this lack of voluntariness is, in my view, crucial.[26]

Rowe appears to suggest that I conclude from the minuteness of the alternative possibility possessed by Jones that it cannot be sufficiently robust to ground ascriptions of moral responsibility.[27] But I am not tempted to make this sort of inference. With respect to the evaluation of alternative possibilities, it is important to distinguish between the dimensions of size and voluntariness or oomph. It is not a deficiency along the dimension of size that is problematic in the case of Rowe's Jones; it is a deficiency of oomph. Even a tiny alternative possibility may contain oomph. For example, if an agent begins freely to choose to perform an action, or begins freely to perform that action, these possibilities are voluntary and may contain sufficient oomph to help to ground moral responsibility. In contrast, Jones's failure to agent-cause his keeping the money is both minute and involuntary, and its deficiency lies in its lack of voluntariness and thus oomph.

Reply to O'Connor's Second Criticism

I shall now consider O'Connor's second line of attack against semicompatibilism, which appeals in various ways to our common sense acceptance of PAP. O'Connor challenges the semicompatibilist to say how common sense could be so wrong. He suggests that perhaps the semicompatibilist believes that there is some *other* "truly necessary condition" for moral responsibility, which typically accompanies or "tracks" alternative possibilities. This "distinct" condition would be "coextensive" with PAP in ordinary contexts, even if the two conditions can be pulled apart in Frankfurt scenarios. But what could this condition be?

This is precisely the question I have sought to answer in various writings. My view is that there are two distinct kinds of control. They are distinct, but genuine, forms of control. One sort of control entails the genuine availability of alternative possibilities; I call this sort of control "regulative control." But another sort of control can be exhibited in the actual sequence—the actual flow of events—and does not entail that the agent have access to alternative possibilities; I call this sort of control "guidance control."[28] Typically, these two sorts of control may be thought to go together, although in principle they can be prized apart.

One of the kinds of example I have employed in order to draw out the two kinds of control is as follows. Suppose you are driving your car, and everything is functioning properly—it is a normal car, and nothing is broken. You signal and make a left turn, guiding the car by turning the steering wheel in the normal way. Given plausible ways of filling in the example (and not making any assumptions such as that causal determinism obtains or an omniscient God exists), we assume that you had the power to refrain from turning the car to the left and (for example) continuing straight ahead. Thus, not only did you exhibit guidance control of your car, but you had regulative control over its path—you could have brought it about that the car went in a different direction. Typically, then, these two forms of control are coextensive.

But imagine, now, that your car's steering apparatus suddenly (at the relevant time) breaks in a weird way. That is, imagine that it suddenly (and unknown to you) becomes such that it functions normally when you guide the car to the left, but, if you were to try to keep the car going straight ahead (or to guide it in any direction other than the precise direction in which you actually guide it), it would cause the car to go to the left exactly as it actually does. As things actually develop, you simply guide the car to the left in the normal way—just as you do in the first version of the example, and thus the defect in the car's steering apparatus plays no role in the actual flow of events. Nevertheless, because of the defect, you could not have guided the car in any other direction: you exhibit guidance control of the car, but you do not possess regulative control over it.

Although the two sorts of control are typically coextensive, they can be pulled apart in these sorts of scenarios. Thus there is a condition that closely tracks alternative possibilities and is typically present when alternative possibilities are present; this condition states the presence of a distinct sort of freedom or control: guidance control. And it is this sort of control, and not the sort of freedom that involves alternative possibilities—regulative control—that truly grounds ascriptions of moral responsibility. This provides precisely what O'Connor demands of the semicompatibilist.

Having sought to identify this condition, I have also attempted to develop an account of guidance control.[29] On my view, an agent has guidance control of (say) an action insofar as the action issues from the agent's own, suitably reasons-responsive mechanism. I (and my coauthor, Mark Ravizza) have specified accounts of mechanism ownership and the relevant sort of reasons-responsiveness: moderate reasons-responsiveness. On these accounts, guidance control is compatible with causal determinism (as well as the lack of alternative possibilities).

Recall that O'Connor says:

> As philosophers we would want to characterize the truly necessary condition. But a constraint on any proposal is that it entails the presence of alternative possibilities, relative to (conditional on) a broad assumption about actual deliberative environments, that is, that it [sic] lacks a purely "counterfactual intervener."[30]

Note that typically it would be fair to conclude that the relevant agent has genuine alternative possibilities when he exhibits guidance control, given the assumption that there are no counterfactual interveners. Thus, my proposal of guidance control for the "truly necessary condition" would seem promising. I am a bit puzzled, however, by O'Connor's claim that it is fair to require that any proposed account of this condition *entail* that there be alternative possibilities, assuming that there are no counterfactual interveners. For if this constraint is in place, then no account of the truly necessary condition that is compatible with causal determinism would be acceptable (given that causal determinism entails the lack of genuine access to alternative possibilities). But on what basis can O'Connor claim that such a constraint is applicable? Is it his view that it is somehow a constraint, applicable "in advance" and coming from common sense, on any account of the elements of agency that ground moral responsibility that they be incompatible with casual determinism? If so, then of course the incompatibility of causal determinism and moral responsibility follows, but too quickly, I should have thought.

I take it, then, that the appropriate interpretation of O'Connor's constraint is roughly as follows: any plausible proposal for the "truly necessary condition" must entail the presence of alternative possibilities, relative to (conditional on) a broad assumption about actual deliberative environments, that is, that they lack counterfactual interveners, and apart from any special assumptions, such as causal determinism or the existence of an essentially omniscient, temporal God. On this interpretation of the constraint, guidance control, as I have specified it, provides just what is needed: an account of a condition which is typically present when alternative possibilities are present (or plausibly thought to be present), but which truly grounds moral responsibility. Common sense then gets it *almost* right: it fixes on something closely related to, but distinct from, the true basis of responsibility.

I am also somewhat puzzled by O'Connor's additional ruminations on the role of common sense. He contends that "ordinary thinking about responsibility proceeds by reflecting on familiar cases," and he says that "we shouldn't overlook the obvious, that is, that Frankfurt cases are extremely contrived and (unless we are badly mistaken about the world) never instanced."[31] Obviously, such a contention raises large and difficult methodological considerations.[32] But in my view the two (presumably separate) considerations invoked by O'Connor—that the examples are extremely contrived and that they are, given what we know, never (or very infrequently) instanced—are irrelevant. Or at least I do not see their philosophical relevance.

I take it that ordinary thinking about the mind—about the contents of our cognitive states, such as beliefs—proceeds by reflecting on familiar cases, and not "twin-earth" thought experiments and the like. And, similarly, I assume that ordinary thinking about language—about the meanings and referents of our words—proceeds by reflecting on familiar cases, and not twin-earth thought experiments. But does this show that such experiments are philosophically irrelevant? Ordinary reflection about knowledge does not focus on brain-in-a-vat possibilities or evil demons or other skeptical scenarios; but does it follow that such situations are irrelevant to the philosophical analysis of knowledge?

And what, precisely, does the frequency of instantiation of such possibilities have to do with their relevance? I take it that in fact there are no twin earths; how does this establish the irrelevance of such thought experiments? Additionally, it may indeed turn out that conditions actually obtain in our world which are, arguably, relevantly similar to the conditions that characterize the Frankfurt scenarios.[33] That is, suppose that God exists, and that he is sempiternal and essentially omniscient. Suppose, further, that God does not causally intervene in human agents' practical reasoning (typically). Now an argument can be made, which is, admittedly, highly contentious, that the existence of such a God is incompatible with humans' possessing the sort of freedom that involves alternative possibilities. So, on the assumptions above, God would be a condition that plays no role in humans' choices and actions (typically), but whose presence ensures that humans lack alternative possibilities. On these assumptions then, the crucial characteristics of Frankfurt-type examples are *typically* instantiated. If this were indeed so, would this fact change the relevance of the Frankfurt examples for O'Connor?

I want to touch briefly on a related criticism presented by O'Connor, which I find particularly perplexing. He says:

> It has been pointed out by some recent authors that the standard Frankfurt-style examples make a questionable assumption. In all such examples, I act freely while there is a Frankfurtian agent "in the wings" waiting to cause me to do his bidding should I fail to do so of my own free will. Yet it is not enough that the Frankfurtian agent would take control were I to make the "wrong" decision. . . . it is added that had I "shown signs" of inclining away from the desired option, the Frankfurtian agent would have immediately intervened, causing me to decide and act as he wished. But why suppose that there is always some antecedent psychological or behavioral sign that indicates that a certain decision is likely to be made? . . . After all, much of our behavior proceeds with little or no deliberation.[34]

But the reply seems obvious. The Frankfurt-type cases challenge the Principle of Alternative Possibilities, and thus they challenge the claim that moral responsibility in general requires alternative possibilities. If *one* coherent sort of scenario can be constructed in which we are confident that the agent is morally responsible yet lacks alternative possibilities, that would be sufficient for the purpose.[35] If such a scenario can be constructed in which there is deliberation and opportunity for a prior sign, then this would show that moral responsibility does not *in general* require the sort of control that involves alternative possibilities. It would then be odd if such control were indeed required in contexts of "little or no deliberation." Why would alternative possibilities be required in contexts of spontaneous or habitual action, but not in contexts of deliberation? And the condition which closely tracks alternative possibilities, but which can be seen to be distinct and the true ground of moral responsibility—guidance control—can be present in contexts of lack of deliberation just as much as in deliberative contexts.

Finally, as we saw above, O'Connor wants to insist on a distinction between the alternative possibilities condition (PAP), which he claims is "present in ordinary thought," and the justified true belief (JTB) analysis of knowledge, which he claims must be "teased out of our thinking." But I do not see how this distinction can make a difference. When a condition is teased out of our thinking, I take it that it is present in common sense, but just not readily apparent; philosophical analysis of common sense penetrates to something that is in fact present, but is not easily seen at first. Alternatively, I suppose one could say that philosophical analysis may uncover what is deeply present in common sense, rather than what is obviously or superficially present. If this is so, then I cannot see how there could be an asymmetry of the sort envisaged by O'Connor between the appropriate reaction to JTB and PAP.

Conclusion

I have presented O'Connor's two lines of attack on the sort of semicompatibilism, motivated by the Frankfurt-type examples, that I favor. One line of attack argues that agent-causation has special resources to help in showing that the Frankfurt examples cannot in fact dissociate moral responsibility from alternative possibilities. I have argued that O'Connor's criticism does not address the most powerful way in which Frankfurt-type cases challenge the alternative-possibilities requirement. I have suggested that, so understood, the challenge of the Frankfurt-type cases cannot be met by any agent-causal approach; in any case, I showed how Rowe's agent-causal theory fails, once one understands the force of the Frankfurt-type cases.

A second line of attack proceeds from our commonsense ways of looking at human agency and responsibility. A central thrust of O'Connor's attack here is to challenge the semicompatibilist to identify the condition which "truly" grounds moral responsibility, if it is not what common sense tells us it is—the presence of alternative possibilities. I have replied that the truly necessary condition is a distinctive sort of control. Common sense is correct in supposing that moral responsibility is associated with control, but it does not have a sufficiently fine-grained view of the sort of control in question.

O'Connor complains that the Frankfurt examples are contrived, unusual, unfamiliar, and (presumably) infrequent or nonexistent. But, for all we know, we might be living a giant Frankfurt example. For example, for all we know a certain sort of God exists; his presence would ensure that we lack *any* alternative possibilities at *any* point in our lives, and yet he would not play any causal role in our actual deliberations and behavior. In such a circumstance, the fact that we lack alternative possibilities would not entail that we are not morally responsible. And even if the Frankfurt thought experiments (first sketched by John Locke) are rarely instantiated, this is irrelevant to their distinctively philosophical potency.

It is a good thing that moral responsibility does not require alternative possibilities. For all we know, causal determinism might turn out to be true. And if causal determinism is true, then, arguably, none of us *ever* has had *any* alternative possibilities. It is nice to know that this fact, in itself, does not entail that we are not morally responsible for our behavior.

NOTES

1. Timothy O'Connor, *Persons and Causes: The Metaphysics of Free Will* (New York: Oxford University Press, 2000). I discuss various aspects of this striking and provocative book in John Martin Fischer, "Review of *Persons and Causes: The Metaphysics of Free Will*," *Mind* 110 (2001): 526–31.

2. O'Connor, *Persons and Causes*, p. 18; the original quotation is from Harry Frankfurt, "Alternate Possibilities and Moral Responsibility," *Journal of Philosophy* 66 (1969): 835.

3. Ibid., p. 835 n. 3.

4. Robert Kane, *Free Will and Values* (Albany: State University of New York Press, 1985), p. 51, and *The Significance of Free Will* (New York: Oxford University Press, 1996), pp. 142–45; David Widerker, "Libertarian Freedom and the Avoidability of Decisions," *Faith and Philosophy* 12 (1995): 113–18, and "Libertarianism and Frankfurt's Attack on the Principle of Alternative Possibilities," *Philosophical Review* 104 (1995): 247–61; Carl Ginet, "In Defense of the Principle of Alternative Possibilities: Why I Don't Find Frankfurt's Argument Convincing," *Philosophical Perspectives* 10 (1996): 403–17; and Keith D. Wyma, "Moral Responsibility and Leeway for Action," *American Philosophical Quarterly* 34 (1997): 57–70.

5. See John Martin Fischer, "Recent Work on Moral Responsibility," *Ethics* 110 (1999): 93–139, esp. 113; and chap. 6 of this book.

6. O'Connor, *Persons and Causes*, p. 19; van Inwagen presents this sort of principle in "Ability and Responsibility," *Philosophical Review* 87 (April 1978): 201–24; and *An Essay on Free Will* (Oxford: Oxford University Press, 1983), pp. 153–89.

7. O'Connor, *Persons and Causes*, p. 19.

8. Ibid.

9. O'Connor says, "I am unconvinced by Fischer's argument. After elaborating an account of freedom of will later in this book, I make some points, stemming from that account, which call his argument into question" (ibid., p. 20).

10. O'Connor argues against Taylor's view—and in favor of the view that the agent-causal event cannot itself be caused—in ibid., pp. 49–55.

11. Ibid., p. 82.

12. Ibid., pp. 82–83.

13. Ibid., p. 20.

14. Ibid., pp. 20–21.

15. Ibid.

16. I first made this point in "Responsibility and Control," *Journal of Philosophy* 79 (1982): 24–40. Also see chapter 2 of this book.

17. O'Connor, *Persons and Causes*, p. 21.

18. Ibid.

19. Ibid.

20. I am presupposing in the text here (and in what follows) that on the second way of challenging PAP, the examples are cases in which the agent lacks access to pathways along which there are relevantly different contents, but not in virtue of having sole access to pathways with the same contents as the actual contents.

21. For a development of this sort of argument, see chapters 2 and 5 of this book.

22. O'Connor, *Persons and Causes*, pp. 36–42.

23. Ibid., p. 39.

24. William Rowe, "The Metaphysics of Freedom: Reid's Theory of Agent Causation," *American Catholic Philosophical Quarterly* 74 (2000): 433–35.

25. Ibid., p. 435.

26. For this point, see chapter 2 of this book.

27. Rowe, "Metaphysics of Freedom," says on p. 435: "I agree with Fischer that in our third case there is no alternative action or volition open to the agent. But I think he is mistaken to conclude from this that the alternative open to the agent is not robust enough to ground his moral responsibility for his actual decision to keep the money." These alternatives have been previously identified by Rowe as "big" alternatives (p. 434).

28. I have developed and discussed this distinction in various places; perhaps the most sustained treatments are in "Responsiveness and Moral Responsibility," chapter 3 of this book; the first few pages of chapter 2; and John Martin Fischer and Mark Ravizza, *Responsibility and Control: A Theory of Moral Responsibility* (New York: Cambridge University Press, 1998).

29. See, in particular, Fischer and Ravizza, *Responsibility and Control*.

30. O'Connor, *Persons and Causes*, p. 21.

31. Ibid.

32. I discuss some of these issues near the end of chapter 2 in this book.

33. For this sort of argument, see David Hunt, "Moral Responsibility and Unavoidable Action," *Philosophical Studies* 97 (2000): 195–227, and "Freedom, Foreknowledge, and Frankfurt," manuscript, Department of Philosophy, Whittier College.

34. O'Connor, *Persons and Causes*, p. 81.

35. A similar move is made in Daniel James Speak, "Fischer and Avoidability: A Reply to Widerker and Katzoff," *Faith and Philosophy* 16 (1999): 239–47.

8

THE TRANSFER OF NONRESPONSIBILITY

In ancient times—some fifteen years ago—I suggested that Frankfurt-type examples call into question the principle of transfer of nonresponsibility (which I then called, a bit too narrowly, the "principle of transfer of blamelessness," following John Taurek's usage in his fascinating Ph.D. dissertation at UCLA in 1972).[1] In the introductory essay to my anthology, *Moral Responsibility*, I presented a somewhat informal version of Peter van Inwagen's modal principle (which he called principle "B"), and (following van Inwagen) explained how it could be employed as part of a "direct" argument for the incompatibility of causal determinism and moral responsibility (i.e., an argument for the incompatibility claim that does not employ the claim that causal determinism rules out alternative possibilities):

> If you are not morally responsible for one thing, and you are not morally responsible for that thing's leading to another, you are not morally responsible for the other. [This, roughly speaking, is the principle of transfer of nonresponsibility.] Now, an argument . . . can be generated to show that causal determinism rules out moral responsibility. Given that you are not morally responsible for the past, and you are not morally responsible for the laws of nature, and assuming the principle of transfer of blamelessness [the principle of transfer of nonresponsibility], causal determinism seems to rule out moral responsibility.[2]

Also, I told the following story:

> A man [Green] walks along a beach and, noting that there is a child drowning, dives into the water and rescues the child. Though Green has had a device implanted in

I have read versions of this paper at the University of California, Santa Barbara; the Inland Northwest Philosophy Conference at the University of Idaho, Moscow; and the University of Texas, San Antonio. I have especially benefited from helpful comments by Nathan Salmon, David Robb, Anthony Brueckner, Francis Dauer, Richard Glass, Kevin Falvey, Voula Tsouna, and Harry Silverstein.

his brain [by scientists in a research institute in California—one might now say "crazed neurophilosophers in La Jolla"], the device does not play any role in Green's decision to save the child (and his subsequent action). That is, the device monitors Green's brain activity but does not actually intervene in it. Let us suppose that this is because the scientists can see that Green is about to decide to save the child and to act accordingly [they are morally good, albeit crazed, neurophilosophers]. But let's also suppose that the scientists would have intervened to bring about a decision to save the child if Green had shown an inclination to decide to refrain from saving the child. That is, were Green inclined to decide on his own not to save the child, the scientists would ensure electronically that he decide to save the child and also that he act to carry out this decision.[3]

Of course, this case contains the distinctive characteristics of a Frankfurt-type case: a fail-safe arrangement that plays no actual role but the presence of which nevertheless *ensures* the actual result.[4]

I then suggested that the Frankfurt-type examples are plausible counterexamples to the principle of transfer of nonresponsibility, even though they would not be counterexamples to the parallel modal principle employed in the argument for the incompatibility of causal determinism and alternative possibilities (the principle of the transfer of powerlessness):

> Green is not morally responsible for the fact that the scientists are ready to intervene, and he is not responsible for the fact that, if they are so ready, he will save the child. But he *does* seem to be morally responsible for saving the child. . . . So a compatibilist about determinism and moral responsibility *might* accept the fixity of the past . . . , the fixity of the laws . . . , and the principle of transfer of powerlessness but might reject the principle of transfer of blamelessness.[5]

Thus, semicompatibilism was born. Here I wish to defend the basic intuition, which I still believe is correct, that the principle of transfer of blamelessness (or, more broadly, nonresponsibility) is called into question by the Frankfurt-type cases, and that it cannot be employed in an uncontroversial, decisive argument against the compatibility of causal determinism and moral responsibility.

The Principle of Transfer of Nonresponsibility and a Preliminary Critique

It will be helpful to have a slightly more careful formulation of the principle of transfer of nonresponsibility (Transfer NR):

If
(1) p obtains and no one is even partly morally responsible for p; and
(2) if p obtains, then q obtains, and no one is even partly morally responsible for the fact that if p obtains, then q obtains; then
(3) q obtains, and no one is even partly morally responsible for q.[6]

In *Responsibility and Control: A Theory of Moral Responsibility*, Mark Ravizza and I criticize Transfer NR by presenting the following sort of Frankfurt-type scenario:

[In "Erosion"], Betty plants . . . explosives in the crevices of [a] glacier and [intuitively speaking, freely] detonates the charge at *T1* causing an avalanche that crushes the enemy fortress at *T3* [a result intended by Betty]. Unbeknownst to Betty . . . however, the glacier is gradually melting, shifting, and eroding. Had Betty not placed the dynamite in the crevices, some ice and rocks would have broken free at *T2*, starting a natural avalanche that would have crushed the enemy camp at *T3*.[7]

Our contention is that Betty is morally responsible for bringing it about that there is an avalanche that crushes the enemy base at *T3*, despite the fact that no one is even partly responsible for the fact that the glacier is eroding, and no one is even partly responsible for the fact that if the glacier is eroding, then there will be an avalanche that crushes the enemy base at *T3*. Thus, we reject Transfer NR.[8]

Now it might be objected that the potency of "Erosion" as a counterexample to Transfer NR depends on its being a case of preemptive overdetermination. Consider, now, Transfer NR':

If

(1) p obtains and no one is even partly morally responsible for p; and

(2)   (i) p is part of the actual sequence of events e that gives rise to q at *T3*,

    (ii) p is a part of e that is causally sufficient for the obtaining of q at *T3*, and

    (iii) no one is or ever has been even partly responsible for (2i and ii); then

(3) q obtains at *T3*, and no one is or ever has been even partly morally responsible for q.[9]

But a case similar to Erosion, Erosion*, shows Transfer NR' to be problematic. In Erosion*, the conditions of the glacier *do* actually cause the ice and rocks to break free, triggering an avalanche that arrives at the fortress precisely at the same time as the independent avalanche triggered freely by Betty. Each avalanche is sufficient for the destruction of the fortress, and yet Betty seems to be morally responsible for bringing it about that there is an avalanche that destroys the enemy fortress at *T3*, just as in Erosion. Erosion* is analogous to Erosion in every respect, except in Erosion* the overdetermination is simultaneous, rather than preemptive. This difference does not appear to make a difference with respect to Betty's moral responsibility. Thus, we reject Transfer NR'.

Consider the typical sort of example van Inwagen employs to motivate the acceptance of a principle such as Transfer NR or Transfer NR', "Snake Bite."[10] Imagine that John was bitten by a cobra on his thirtieth birthday, and no one was even partly responsible for this. Suppose, also, that if John was bitten by a cobra on his thirtieth birthday, then John died on his thirtieth birthday, and no one was even partly responsible for this fact. It seems to follow that John died on his thirtieth birthday, and no one was even partly responsible for the fact that John died on his thirtieth birthday.

Similarly, suppose that an earthquake takes place in the middle of the Pacific Ocean, and that no one is even partly morally responsible for this. Also suppose that if this earthquake occurs, then a tsunami will hit the coast of California, and no one is even partly responsible for this fact. It appears to follow that a tsunami will hit the coast of California, and no one is even partly morally responsible for this. Call this case "Tsunami." These sorts of examples seem to support a principle of transfer of nonresponsibility.

But Mark Ravizza and I contend that these examples, like the others invoked by van Inwagen (and other proponents of the idea of transfer of nonresponsibility), appear to support a transfer principle only because one pictures there being *only one* path to John's death (or the tsunami's hitting the coast of California), along which no agents act freely.[11] But the one-path cases are only a proper subset of all the cases involving a putative transfer of nonresponsibility. The mistake of the proponents of transfer is to generalize from a mere proper part of the space of relevant possibilities.

McKenna's Critique of the Fischer and Ravizza Attack on Transfer

The Critique

In an interesting recent paper, Michael McKenna has argued that the criticism of the transfer idea developed above is unsuccessful.[12] He says:

> As Fischer and Ravizza observe, *their reply relies exclusively upon examples that involve "two-path" cases*, i.e., cases in which the obtaining of the event is ensured by *two different causal pathways to the same event*. They do not object to Transfer NR as it applies to one-path cases, but hold that Transfer NR restricted to one-path cases cannot be used to show that moral responsibility is incompatible with causal determinism. This is because causal determinism does not rule out cases of overdetermination. They therefore hang their criticism of Transfer NR on counterexamples involving two-path cases of simultaneous overdetermination.[13]

But McKenna is not sanguine about the prospects for our approach; he goes on as follows:

> This is not a convincing strategy. No doubt, Fischer and Ravizza are correct that causal determinism does not rule out overdetermination. But if determinism is true, then the manner in which the facts of the past and the laws of nature entail one unique future is *not* analogous to the manner in which one set of independently existing causally sufficient conditions (for example, an erosion) ensures a subsequent event also ensured by *some distinct set* of independently existing sufficient conditions (i.e., Betty's action). Assuming determinism, the pertinent facts (consisting in the deterministic order of things) are not *independent* of an agent's reasons for action, *they constitute them!* Therefore, at a deterministic world involving a typical case regarding a judgment of moral responsibility, the case is relevantly like a one-path, *not* a two-path case.[14]

Although we had chastised van Inwagen for attending only to a proper subset of the relevant cases, the one-path cases, it is precisely McKenna's point that these are the *only* cases relevant to causal determinism. Thus, he seeks to formulate a version of the modal principle that captures a restriction to one-path cases. Here is a slight reformulation of McKenna's proposal, Transfer NR":

If

(1) p obtains and no one is or ever has been even partly morally responsible for p; and

(2) (i) p is part of the actual sequence of events e that gives rise to q at $T3$;

  (ii) p is causally sufficient for the obtaining of q at $T3$; and any other part of e that is causally sufficient for q either causes or is caused by p; and

  (iii) no one is or ever has been even partly responsible for (2i and ii); then

(3) q obtains, and no one is or ever has been even partly morally responsible for the fact that q obtains at $T3$.[15]

McKenna points out that Transfer NR" does not rule out moral responsibility in cases of causal overdetermination, even in a causally deterministic world. But he says that it would be very implausible for Ravizza and me to hold that an agent can be morally responsible *only* in cases of simultaneous overdetermination. Indeed, McKenna credits both Carl Ginet and Eleonore Stump with pointing out that it would be a significant problem for the Fischer/Ravizza approach if moral responsibility turned out to be incompatible with causal determinism in all one-path cases, which are, presumably, the vast majority of cases.[16]

A Reply to McKenna

McKenna's paper contains many insightful and helpful points. He makes an important observation when he points out that the manner in which determinism ensures a unique future may well be crucially different from the manner in which one set of independent causally sufficient conditions (say, erosion) ensures a subsequent event also ensured by *some distinct set* of independently existing sufficient conditions (for example, Betty's free action). I will return to this point below, and also in my discussion of Eleonore Stump's defense of the transfer of nonresponsibility idea. But here I wish to disentangle different points. One contention of McKenna's is that the validity of Transfer NR" would pose significant problems for a compatibilist about causal determinism and moral responsibility (like me). Granted. But I think a rather different issue is whether Transfer NR" can be employed to establish the incompatibility of causal determinism and moral responsibility.

Mark Ravizza and I contend that it is futile to seek to restrict the modal principle to one-path cases (as in Transfer NR") precisely because this would render the principle unable to generate incompatibilism about causal determinism and moral responsibility (which is, after all, the conclusion of van Inwagen's argument).[17] To point out that Transfer NR" poses problems for developing a plausible compatibilist theory of moral responsibility is one thing; to suppose that it generates a successful argument for incompatibilism is quite another. One possibility is that there are significant problems for *both* compatibilism and incompatibilism, as Saul Smilansky has recently contended.[18]

To see an additional problem with moving from there being a problem with compatibilism to the general thesis of incompatibilism, suppose causal determinism is true in a world, but that in the world in question some (morally significant) behavior is the result of simultaneous overdetermination. Now that behavior, for all Transfer NR″ tells us, is such that the relevant agent can be held morally responsible for it. Thus, we do not (yet) have the incompatibility of causal determinism and moral responsibility—only the incompatibility of causal determinism with moral responsibility for *some* behavior. If there were a world—unusual as this would be—with all of the morally significant behavior occurring as a result of simultaneous overdetermination, then Transfer NR″ would be entirely consistent with moral responsibility coexisting peacefully with causal determinism in this world. I find this somewhat strange.

Note what is happening with Transfer NR″: the principle entails that when behavior is the result of one causally deterministic sequence, there cannot be moral responsibility, but when the behavior is the result of two or more such sequences, there may be moral responsibility. But if one causally deterministic sequence rules out moral responsibility, it would seem that two or more would be even worse. Transfer NR″, however, gives us precisely the opposite result. Indeed, Transfer NR″ seems to entail, for the relevant sorts of normative notions, that two wrongs may well make a right.[19]

I conclude, then, that whatever problems such a principle poses for compatibilism, it cannot be employed as it is—without further resources—to generate a successful argument for the incompatibility of causal determinism and moral responsibility. But someone might reply that Transfer NR″ might be the *first step* in an argument for incompatibilism. On this approach, one would employ Transfer NR″ to rule out moral responsibility in one-path cases, and then supplement it with the contention that merely adding causally deterministic paths (to a context in which there is no responsibility) cannot issue in moral responsibility.

My reply to this sort of more complex argumentative strategy is to insist that I need not grant the first step: the acceptability of Transfer NR″ in the context of one path. But can I produce any convincing counterexamples to Transfer NR″? Let us say that there is just one path to an outcome, and that this path is causally deterministic. Then of course it would be question-begging, in the context in which Transfer NR″ is presumably employed (i.e., in an argument for the incompatibility of causal determinism and moral responsibility), to contend that nevertheless an agent is morally responsible for that outcome. But that would seem to be the only way one could produce a counterexample to Transfer NR″. Thus, if McKenna's Transfer NR″ actually succeeds in capturing a restriction of Transfer NR to one-path cases, then it is so constructed that it is impossible for there to be a non-question-begging counterexample to it.

Now some philosophers might think this a *good* thing. But I believe that it can lead to a certain distinctive kind of stalemate—what I have called a "dialectical stalemate." McKenna is aware of this possibility, but he nevertheless contends that Transfer NR″ can be supported; I will return to this claim below. I shall now turn to a discussion of Eleonore Stump's defense of the transfer of nonresponsibility, which will raise issues similar to those we have just discussed.

Stump's Defense of Transfer NR

Stump's Defense

In two separate places, Eleonore Stump has sought to defend the basic idea of the transfer of nonresponsibility, and thus the direct argument for the incompatibility of causal determinism and moral responsibility, against the attacks mounted by Ravizza and me. In the first piece, "The Direct Argument for Incompatibilism," Stump agrees that cases such as Erosion and Erosion* show the inadequacy of Transfer NR and Transfer NR'.[20] But she, like McKenna, complains that these are two-path cases. She contends that no one-path case can similarly show the inadequacy of a suitably restricted transfer principle—a principle whose application is restricted to one-path cases.

In the new piece, "Control and Causal Determinism," she offers what she characterizes as a "significant revision" of the argument in her first paper. She says: "In their response . . . Fischer and Ravizza concede the general conclusion of my argument but argue that it constitutes only a stalemate between the incompatibilist and their position. Fischer and Ravizza are not right in this view, as I hope to show in the revised version of the argument I give in this essay."[21]

But this is a bit puzzling. I do not know what Stump means in saying that Ravizza and I "concede the general conclusion" of her argument. At the end of that first paper, Stump says, "Consequently, Fischer and Ravizza have not succeeded in showing that the direct argument for incompatibilism fails." I do not think we agreed with *this* conclusion. We *did* agree that we could not *decisively* show that a transfer principle restricted to one-path cases is unacceptable. But we also pointed out that it is *not* our obligation decisively to prove such a principle problematic, in order to show that one need not accept the argument for incompatibilism. Given that there are considerable attractions to compatibilism (for example, a compatibilist need not think that our very basic views of ourselves and others as morally responsible and as persons are held hostage to a possible scientific discovery by a consortium of scientists that causal determinism is indeed true), and given (what we argued) that a restricted transfer principle cannot be uncontroversially established (i.e., that one reaches a dialectical stalemate in seeking to argue for—or against—such a principle), we concluded that the incompatibilist's argument is not persuasive. That is, in light of the fact that its central principle is essentially contested and cannot uncontroversially be supported, we showed that one need not accept the incompatibilist's argument. We *did* think we were showing that the incompatibilist's argument fails, insofar as we thought we were showing that it does not succeed within the relevant dialectic context.

It will be useful to consider Stump's new formulation of her argument, and to consider it in light of the discussion of McKenna's Transfer NR″ in the previous section. She proceeds by considering Erosion* and constructing a dilemma. On the first horn of the dilemma, one is to assume that the world of Erosion* is not causally deterministic and that Betty acts indeterministically (but in a way that supports the judgments that she is acting freely). Now Stump is willing to concede that this sort of example shows that Transfer NR, unqualified or restricted, is invalid; but she thinks that the principle can simply be qualified so as to rule out the counterexample and still get the desired incompatibilistic result. She says:

> Erosion* shows that in cases of overdetermined effects, one of whose causes is an agent acting indeterministically, Transfer NR fails. But this is not enough to show that Transfer NR should be rejected. Because Transfer NR is a highly plausible principle, we can take Erosion* to show just that the principle needs to be restricted, to exclude such unusual cases as that in which an indeterministic agent is one of the causes of an overdetermined effect.[22]

On the other horn of the dilemma, the assumption is that the world of Erosion* is causally deterministic. But now of course it will be question-begging, in the relevant dialectical context (in which Transfer NR is being deployed in order to establish that causal determinism is incompatible with moral responsibility, and thus the compatibility of causal determinism and moral responsibility is in doubt) simply to assert that Betty is morally responsible for her behavior (and its upshots). But, as we saw in our discussion of McKenna's Transfer NR″, only if Betty is morally responsible can there be a counterexample to Transfer NR. Stump contends, then, that on the assumption of causal determinism, it would be question-begging to assert that Erosion* is a counterexample to Transfer NR.[23]

Reply to Stump

I would contend that there is trouble for Stump's incompatibilistic conclusion, on either horn of the dilemma. Consider, first, the assumption of causal indeterminism. Here Stump suggests a restriction of Transfer NR to one-path contexts. She doesn't actually present the principle, but if such a principle can be crafted, it will have exactly the same problems as McKenna's Transfer NR″. As I explained above, it will not be possible to employ this sort of one-path modal principle in a *general* argument for incompatibilism about causal determinism and moral responsibility. And if the single path contains some ensuring factor, as seems required in order to trigger the application of the modal principle, then it would seem that the principle is implicitly presupposing causal determinism. If this is so (and it explicitly is the case on the second horn of Stump's dilemma), then it is admittedly impossible, within the relevant dialectical context (in which the compatibility of causal determinism and moral responsibility is at issue) to produce a non-question-begging counterexample to Transfer NR.

But I contend that it is equally impossible (within the relevant dialectical context) to provide examples that give the necessary sort of *support* to the principle. That is, I believe that the current dialectical context is what I have characterized in previous work as a dialectical stalemate.[24] This is my characterization of a dialectical stalemate:

> Frequently in philosophy we are engaged in considering a certain argument ... for some claim C. The argument employs a principle P. Allegedly, P supports C. Now the proponent of the argument may be called upon to support the principle, and he

may do so by invoking a set of examples (or other considerations). Based on these examples (or other considerations), he argues that the principle and thus also the philosophical claim are to be accepted.

But the opponent of the argument may respond as follows. The examples are not sufficient to establish the principle P. One could embrace all the examples and not adduce P to explain them; rather, it is alleged that a weaker principle, P* is all that is decisively established by the examples (or other considerations). Further, P*, in contrast to P does not support C. Finally, it is very hard to see how one could decisively establish P. One reason it is so difficult is that it at least appears that one cannot invoke a particular example that would *decisively* establish P without begging the question in a straightforward fashion against either the opponent of P or the opponent of C. Further, it *also* seems that one cannot invoke a particular example that would *decisively* refute P without begging the question against the proponent of P or the proponent of C. These conditions mark out a distinctive—and particularly precarious—spot in dialectical space.[25]

But if in our discussion of the principles of the transfer of nonresponsibility we have reached one of these precarious spots—dialectical black holes, as it were—it must be the case that there is some alternative modal principle, an alternative to a suitably restricted Transfer NR, such as Transfer NR″, which explains the relevant examples equally well but does not entail incompatibilism.

What is this competitor modal principle? In order to frame the principle, I will pause to describe what I believe is the basis of our intuitions in the two-path cases (and thus what explains why these cases are counterexamples to Transfer NR). Having done this, I will be in a position to frame an alternative modal principle that explains all of the uncontroversial cases as well as Transfer NR″, but does *not* (together with other uncontroversial ingredients) entail incompatibilism.

A Compatibilistic Transfer Principle

Return to Erosion*. I would say (to a first approximation, at least) that Betty is morally responsible for her behavior, and its upshot (the destruction of the enemy camp at T3), because she engaged in unimpaired practical reasoning—practical reasoning undistorted by factors that uncontroversially threaten moral responsibility, such as significant delusions, psychoses, coercion, compulsion, irresistible impulses, clandestine manipulation, hypnosis, subliminal advertising, and so forth. I am inclined to say that she is morally responsible, in other words, because no uncontroversially responsibility undermining factor impairs (or in any way affects) her deliberations, her formation of an intention, and her action in accordance with it. This is so, even though there is a *second* path to the same upshot that is a no-responsibility path. The fact that the no-responsibility path is entirely separate *insulates* Betty's path from it, and allows all parties to the disagreement about causal determinism and moral responsibility to agree that Betty is morally responsible here (apart from any special assumption, such as that causal determinism is true). Insofar as the no-responsibility path is separate, it is sequestered and cannot (in the economists' term) "crowd out" the factors that intuitively ground moral responsibility. Erosion, which involves mere preemptive overdetermination, is an even clearer example of this sort of sequestration or partitioning.

The problem with a one-path case is that there is a danger posed by the phenomenon of crowding out: one cannot so easily insulate what putatively grounds moral responsibility from alleged responsibility undermining factors. This is what McKenna has in mind when he says that the manner in which the facts of the past and the laws of nature ensure one unique future under causal determinism is not analogous to the way in which one unique future is ensured in a case in which there are two separate pathways (one of which is indeterministic) that overdetermine the behavior and consequences in question. As McKenna puts the point, "Assuming determinism, the pertinent facts (consisting in the deterministic order of things) are not *independent* of an agent's reasons for action, *they constitute them!*"[26]

I concede McKenna's contention about constitution, but I do not thereby accept that moral responsibility is necessarily crowded out. A one-path case could be thought of as two separate paths that are superimposed. Alternatively, I would recommend that we think of the one path as having (at least) two separate sets of features. Suppose Betty deliberates just as she actually does in the Erosion cases, but there is no "second path"—no glacier that will independently cause the upshot (the destruction of the enemy camp at $T3$). But imagine further that causal determinism obtains in the actual path that leads to Betty's decision and action. One set of features entails that there is along this path just the sort of unimpaired deliberation that obtains in Erosion and Erosion*—practical reasoning and subsequent action undistorted by factors that uncontroversially threaten moral responsibility. But of course another set of features renders the actual sequence of events causally deterministic, and causal determinism is alleged by the incompatibilist to rule out moral responsibility.

Note, however, that causal determination is not a factor that *uncontroversially* rules out moral responsibility. The features in virtue of which the actual path is causally deterministic are thus importantly different from a feature such as an avalanche caused by movements of a glacier, which uncontroversially fails to confer responsibility. A proponent of the incompatibility of causal determinism and moral responsibility is not entitled to help himself, at this point in the disagreement, to the claim that causal determinism crowds out moral responsibility. Note that if he were allowed to help himself to this contention, then there would be no point to looking for a modal principle, such as Transfer NR (or some restriction of it), because the incompatibilistic result would already have been achieved (startlingly easily) right from the start.

On my view, then, causal determination and unimpaired deliberation can be superimposed upon each other without distortion of the deliberation. This is analogous to the possibility of superimposing (the precise technology is not important) two audio tapes—perhaps a tape of a woman singing and a tape of a piano accompaniment. When the tapes are put together (and of course this is how much music is actually produced), the piano need not distort, impair, or otherwise etiolate the singing. The same of course is true about the relationship between the singing and the piano. Similarly, a video tape of one character in a film can be superimposed on a video tape of another character; what emerges may in no way obscure or change the original depiction of each of the characters. My claim is that the relationship between causal determination and undistorted human practical reasoning is relevantly similar: we can see the determination as being superimposed on the practical reasoning without thereby distorting it.

Of course, it would also not be fair for me to say that it is obvious and indisputable that Betty is morally responsible for her behavior and its upshot in the one-path case under consideration; that would straightforwardly beg the question against the incompatibilist. Rather, my claim is that it cannot simply be assumed, within the dialectical context we are exploring, that causal determinism crowds out moral responsibility. Granted, the relationship between the causal determination and the practical reasoning is more intimate than (say) the relationship between the singing and the piano; but this difference in itself cannot be assumed to make a decisive difference.

The above considerations suggest an alternative modal principle; call it Transfer NRC: If

(1) p obtains and no one is even partly morally responsible for p; and

(2) if p obtains, then q obtains, and no one is even partly morally responsible for the fact that if p obtains, then q obtains; and

(3) on the actual path that leads from p's obtaining to q's obtaining, either there is no factor that at least prima facie could be thought to ground moral responsibility, or there is some factor that uncontroversially undermines moral responsibility (e.g., a factor that distorts or impairs the distinctive process of human practical reasoning); then

(4) q obtains, and no one is even partly morally responsible for q.

It will sometimes be helpful to refer to a path that meets conditions (1) and (3) as a "no-responsibility" path, just for simplicity's sake. Transfer NRC is a plausible and attractive modal principle that explains why we transfer nonresponsibility in the clear and uncontroversial cases. For example, it explains why no one is even partly morally responsible for the fact that John dies (from a snakebite) on his thirtieth birthday in Snake Bite, and it explains why no one is even partly morally responsible for the tsunami's hitting the coast of California in Tsunami. It has this implication in all of the examples invoked by van Inwagen in an attempt to support Transfer NR. Note that it does *not* entail that Betty is not morally responsible in Erosion or Erosion*. Note, further, that Transfer NRC cannot be employed as part of a direct argument for the incompatibility of causal determinism and moral responsibility that would appeal to those not antecedently committed to incompatibilism. Transfer NRC thus explains all the uncontroversial examples just as well as (say) Transfer NR' (or an otherwise qualified version of Transfer NR that applies only to one-path cases), but does *not* help to yield incompatibilism. It is thus precisely the sort of principle whose availability shows that the attempt to employ some appropriately restricted version of Transfer NR to establish incompatibilism leads to a dialectical stalemate.

McKenna is (to some degree) aware of the dialectical difficulties faced by someone who wishes to employ Transfer NR'' to argue for incompatibilism about causal determinism and moral responsibility. In response, McKenna says that Transfer

NR″ is not merely *ad hoc*, but is independently confirmed by a range of cases: "Notice that cases like Snakebite can be used to confirm the plausibility of Transfer NR″ as readily as they can the leaner Transfer NR′.[27] I grant that these cases support Transfer NR″ as readily as they do Transfer NR. But this is not the issue. The point is that Snake Bite (and Tsunami and *all* the cases invoked by van Inwagen and other incompatibilists) are unable to support Transfer NR′ *over Transfer NRC*. So, as with dialectical stalemates in general, there is a competitor principle— Transfer NRC—which must be considered when we are evaluating Transfer NR″. It is crucial here that the relevant data do not support Transfer NR″ over Transfer NRC, and Transfer NRC does not help to generate incompatibilism.

I claim then that the attempt to employ Transfer NR, restricted so that it applies only to one-path causally deterministic contexts, as part of an argument for the incompatibility of causal determinism and moral responsibility, issues in a dialectical stalemate. This implies that such an attempt does not generate a successful argument for incompatibilism. I believe that there are certain reasons why compatibilism is attractive. Given these, I am inclined toward compatibilism. I would give up compatibilism if I believed there were a successful argument, employing principles that are broadly and strongly appealing (clearly appealing even to those not already committed to incompatibilism), that has as its conclusion incompatibilism. But I have yet to see such an argument. The argument that employs some restriction or qualification of Transfer NR employs a principle that can be established only by begging the question against the compatibilist; it does *not* employ a principle that is broadly appealing.

Now I do not claim to have proved such a principle unacceptable. Indeed, I have admitted that I do not see how this would even be possible, given the dialectical niche in which it is embedded. Thus, I have certainly not *refuted* the direct argument for incompatibilism. But I do not feel any need to do so. It is *not* my obligation to provide a refutation of this sort of argument. Given that there are considerable attractions to compatibilism, and given that I have shown that there is no successful direct argument (of the sort we have been considering) for incompatibilism, I find no reason (as yet) to abandon the compatibility claim.[28] It is van Inwagen and Stump who claim to have a direct argument that purports to *establish* the untenability of compatibilism. If I have shown that their approach issues, at best, in a dialectical stalemate, then I have shown that they are wrong, at least if they are interested in doing something more than simply preaching to the converted.

Conclusion

Certain incompatibilists about causal determinism and moral responsibility—such as van Inwagen and Stump—have argued that one can employ a valid transfer principle to yield the incompatibilistic result. Transfer NR, originally suggested by van Inwagen, can be seen to be invalid by reference to two-path cases. Others, including Stump and McKenna, have suggested that if the modal principle is either reformulated or restricted in its applicability, the incompatibilistic result can still be achieved. In this chapter I have sought to identify some problems with their strategy.

It might be useful explicitly to distinguish between a "reformulation" of Transfer NR and a "restriction" of it. Both McKenna and Stump have commended a *reformulation* of Transfer NR so that it applies only to one-path cases. I have argued that such a principle does not yield the general incompatibilistic result, and that it is implausible insofar as it has the "two-wrongs-make-a-right" problem. Further, I pointed out that insofar as it is also understood so that it requires a causally deterministic context, then it issues in a dialectical stalemate; this provides an *additional* reason why it cannot be employed in an argument for incompatibilism, and also a reason why it need not be accepted as valid. Finally, Stump commends (as one horn of her dilemma) that Transfer NR be *restricted* in its application to contexts of causal determinism; here, again, this restriction issues in a dialectical stalemate. Restriction shares this latter problematic feature with reformulation.

In her more recent paper on this subject, Stump reminds her reader that Ravizza and I criticize van Inwagen for focusing exclusively on one-path cases. We pointed out that among the two-path cases there is a subclass in which one of the paths to the outcome contains the sort of control that grounds moral responsibility. Stump says, "The question for Fischer and Ravizza, then, is whether causally determined decisions can be shown to belong to the relevant subclass of two-path cases."[29] Stump goes on to argue that causally determined decisions cannot be shown to be part of the relevant subclass of cases.

I do not see why causally determined decisions would need to be shown to belong to the subclass of two-path cases to which Stump points. Rather, it would seem that they need to be shown to be *analogous* in relevant ways to these two-path cases. In the two-path cases in question, there is a path to the outcome along which there are no uncontroversially responsibility undermining factors. (For example, perhaps there is Betty's unimpaired practical reasoning.) Similarly, in the one-path causally deterministic case, I have argued that there need not be any factor that is uncontroversially responsibility undermining. For example, Betty's undistorted practical reasoning might issue in the decision in question and the subsequent action. The fact that the actual flow of events here is causally deterministic is not in itself a factor that *uncontroversially* undermines moral responsibility, and it cannot be assumed to crowd out Betty's unimpaired deliberation. If it *is* taken to do so, then (as I argued above), a modal principle such as Transfer NR is rendered entirely supernumerary. Thus, certain causally deterministic cases *are* analogous in the relevant ways to the indicated subclass of two-path cases.

I have contended that in the relevant two-path cases and in certain causally deterministic one-path cases there are no uncontroversially responsibility undermining factors. This is all that I need for my purposes in this chapter. I acknowledge, however, that there is a gap between this point and the further point that present in these cases is a sort of control that grounds moral responsibility. I do wish to say that the sort of control that grounds ascriptions of moral responsibility can be present even in a causally deterministic sequence, but I certainly concede that the considerations invoked in this chapter do not in themselves establish this result. If, however, I am correct about this further point, then this would show why all of the examples typically invoked by incompatibilists seem to establish— but do not really establish—a transfer principle that could yield incompatibilism:

they have carefully selected examples (such as Snake Bite and Tsunami) in which there is no path to the actual result that contains the appropriate sort of control. But even in a causally deterministic world, the actual sequence of events can contain such control, as I have argued elsewhere.[30] In my view, the relevant sort of control consists in behavior that issues from the agent's own, suitably reasons-responsive mechanism.

Consider, finally, Thomas Nagel's well-known skeptical worries about agency and moral responsibility in a causally deterministic world first expressed in his essay "Moral Luck":

> The area of genuine agency, and therefore of legitimate moral judgment, seems to shrink under this scrutiny [from a perspective assuming causal determinism] to an extensionless point. Everything seems to result from the combined influence of factors, antecedent and posterior to action, that are not within the agent's control. Since he cannot be responsible for them, he cannot be responsible for their results—though it may remain possible to take up the aesthetic or other evaluative analogues of the moral attitudes that are thus displaced.[31]

Later, Nagel elaborates, saying, "The effect of concentrating on the influence of what is not under his control is to make this responsible self seem to disappear, swallowed up by the order of mere events."[32]

Part of Nagel's worry—perhaps the basic thrust of it—is that it is unclear how human actions could be mere events, or persons mere things.[33] This is a deep challenge, whether or not causal determinism obtains, and I have nothing particularly helpful to say about it. I simply wish to suggest that the ruminations in this chapter can suggest a way of conceptualizing at least some—even if they are not the deepest—of the issues Nagel raises. Nagel appears to rely upon a transfer of nonresponsibility principle when he says, "Since he cannot be responsible for them [certain factors not within one's control], he cannot be responsible for their results." I agree that it is an effect of concentrating on what is not under one's control that the scope of our moral responsibility seems to disappear. For example, when one focuses on the glacier and the natural forces that start the avalanche, and the way in which they lead to the destruction of the enemy camp, Betty's responsibility is in danger of disappearing. But, as I have argued above, it would be a mistake to concentrate exclusively on those factors out of Betty's control and the way in which they issue in the destruction of the enemy camp; that path is completely consistent with the existence of a path on which Betty's agency and responsibility are robust.

There can be cases—such as Erosion*—in which factors entirely out of an agent's control and thus for which the agent is not even partly responsible result in certain upshots in a manner that is also entirely out of the agent's control; yet, in these same cases, there can be a path to the relevant upshots along which the agent exercises control. If one focuses exclusively on the no-responsibility paths, the responsibility paths can seem to disappear, and nonresponsibility can seem to transfer to the upshots. But it is a mistake—a kind of metaphysical depression—selectively and exclusively to focus on the negative. If there is robust control in the actual sequence leading to an upshot, I cannot see why the agent should not be morally responsible for it. In a two-path case, it clearly is a mistake to focus solely on the nonresponsibility path, giving it hegemony and implicitly assuming that it crowds out the responsibility-conferring features found on a separate path.

If there is just one path leading to the upshot in question, and this path is deterministic, it may nevertheless be the case that on that path the agent displays the distinctively human capacity for practical reasoning in a way that is neither impaired nor distorted by factors uncontroversially thought to rule out moral responsibility. This sort of one-path case is then relevantly similar to the two-path cases discussed above. Even in a casually deterministic context, the agent may act from his own, appropriately reasons-responsive mechanism. Thus, in my view, in such a context the agent may exhibit the characteristic sort of control—guidance control—that grounds moral responsibility, even though he is not morally responsible for conditions prior to his birth, and he is not responsible for the fact that those conditions issue in his behavior. In place of Nagel's metaphysical depression, I have sought to lift our spirits (if offering the possibility of freedom and responsibility could do this). Although it might be supposed that my suggestion pertains more to Pandora than Pangloss, I nevertheless propose that the glass is half full.

NOTES

1. John Martin Fischer, "Introduction: Responsibility and Freedom," in *Moral Responsibility*, ed. John Martin Fischer (Ithaca, N.Y.: Cornell University Press, 1986), pp. 60–61.

2. Ibid., p. 60.

3. Ibid., p. 41.

4. Van Inwagen presented his principle, and the argument for incompatibilism that employs it, in "The Incompatibility of Responsibility and Determinism," in *Bowling Green Studies in Applied Philosophy*, Vol. 2, ed. M. Bradie and M. Brand (Bowling Green, Ohio: Bowling Green State University Press), pp. 30–37.

5. Fischer, "Introduction," pp. 60–61.

6. John Martin Fischer and Mark Ravizza, *Responsibility and Control: A Theory of Moral Responsibility* (Cambridge: Cambridge University Press, 1998), p. 152.

7. Ibid., p. 157.

8. I am indebted to Nathan Salmon for pointing out that, if the connective in (2) is interpreted as a material conditional, then Transfer NR is clearly valid. This is because any counterexample would have to be a case in which someone is at least in part morally responsible for q. It would seem to follow that someone is at least in part morally responsible for "q or not-p." Thus (2) must be false. So any putative counterexample to the principle would be a case in which the second premise would have to be false, and thus it would not be a genuine counterexample to Transfer NR. I accept this point, but it also nicely shows why Transfer NR, so interpreted, cannot be employed in a sound, uncontroversial argument for incompatibilism. This is because in any "ordinary" context in which a compatibilist is inclined to say that an agent is morally responsible for q and causal determinism is assumed to be true, the compatibilist will point out that (2) is false, given that the connective is interpreted as a material conditional. So (given the dialectical situation) the incompatibilist will not be entitled to apply Transfer NR to get to the incompatibilistic conclusion.

9. Ravizza and I consider such a principle in *Responsibility and Control* (161–63); also, for the formulation of the principle, I am indebted to Michael McKenna, "Source Incom-

patibilism, Ultimacy, and the Transfer of Non-Responsibility," *American Philosophical Quarterly* 38 (2001): 37–52.

10. Peter van Inwagen, *An Essay on Free Will* (Oxford: Clarendon, 1983), p. 187.

11. Fischer and Ravizza, *Responsibility and Control*, p. 166.

12. McKenna, "Source Incompatibilism."

13. Ibid., p. 45.

14. Ibid.

15. McKenna credits Al Mele and Ish Haji for help in formulating this principle. I am not certain that this formulation works to secure the desired restriction to one-path cases, but I shall accept it for the purposes of my argument in this chapter.

16. McKenna, "Source Incompatibilism," pp. 46, 51 n. 39.

17. Fischer and Ravizza, *Responsibility and Control*, p. 167.

18. Saul Smilansky, *Free Will and Illusion* (Oxford: Clarendon, 2000).

19. Of course, Transfer NR" does not entail that in a context of causal overdetermination there *is* moral responsibility; rather, it fails to entail that there is no responsibility. This seems to me to be sufficiently problematic.

20. Eleonore Stump, "The Direct Argument for Incompatibilism," *Philosophy and Phenomenological Research* 61 (2000): 459–66.

21. Eleonore Stump, "Control and Causal Determinism," in *Contours of Agency: Essays in Honor of Harry Frankfurt*, ed. S. Buss and L. Overton (Cambridge: MIT Press, 2002), p. 57 n. 16.

22. Ibid., pp. 40–41.

23. Stump goes on to explore whether Ravizza and I have available to us some reason to call the incompatibilist's judgment into question, but she concludes (lamentably for us) that there is no such reason.

24. John Martin Fischer, *The Metaphysics of Free Will: An Essay on Control* (Cambridge: Blackwell, 1994), pp. 83–85.

25. Ibid., p. 83.

26. McKenna, "Source Incompatibilism," p. 45.

27. Ibid., p. 51 n. 45. McKenna also credits Michael Zimmerman for bringing to his attention the dialectical difficulty in question.

28. As Michael Bratman has pointed out, there is an interesting parallel between my methodology here and John Perry's approach to the mind-body problem in Perry's *Knowledge, Possibility, and Consciousness* (Cambridge: MIT Press, 2001). Here Perry defends what he calls "antecedent physicalism." By this he means that he finds physicalism antecedently plausible and sees his job as blocking dualistic challenges.

29. Stump, "Control and Causal Determinism," p. 42.

30. For a defense of this view, see Fischer, *The Metaphysics of Free Will*, and Fischer and Ravizza, *Responsibility and Control*.

31. Thomas Nagel, "Moral Luck," in *Mortal Questions*, ed. Thomas Nagel (Cambridge: Cambridge University Press, 1979), p. 35.

32. Ibid., p. 36.

33. He also articulates this worry in Thomas Nagel, *The View from Nowhere* (New York: Oxford University Press, 1985), p. 126.

9

TRANSFER PRINCIPLES AND MORAL RESPONSIBILITY

Eleonore Stump and John Martin Fischer

It is useful to divide contemporary arguments for the incompatibility of causal determinism and moral responsibility into two types: indirect and direct. The indirect arguments present reasons why causal determinism is incompatible with the possession of the relevant kind of alternative possibilities and conclude from this that causal determinism is incompatible with moral responsibility. It is, of course, a presupposition of the indirect arguments that moral responsibility requires alternative possibilities. The direct arguments contain no such presupposition, although some of their proponents may believe that moral responsibility does indeed require alternative possibilities.

The direct arguments employ what might be called "transfer" principles. These are principles that transfer a certain property; the relevant property here *is lack of moral responsibility*.[1] Let "Np" abbreviate "p and no one is even partly morally responsible for the fact that p." Then this is a transfer principle introduced by Peter van Inwagen:

$$\text{Rule B: Np and N(p > q) implies Nq.}[2]$$

Van Inwagen's Rule B is a transfer principle insofar as it transfers the property of lack of moral responsibility from one fact to another by the medium of lack of responsibility for the pertinent conditional.

Van Inwagen's direct argument for the incompatibility of causal determinism and moral responsibility can be presented simply as follows. For present purposes, we can understand causal determinism as the doctrine that a complete description of the (temporally nonrelational) state of the universe at a time, and a description of the laws of nature, entail every truth about subsequent times. Let P be a proposition describing the state of the universe before there were any human beings, let

We are grateful to David Widerker, Al Mele, Chris Pliatska, and Ted Warfield for helpful comments on an earlier version of this essay.

L be a proposition describing the laws of nature, and let F be a truth about the way the world is today. Then, if causal determinism is true,

$$(1)\ (P \text{ and } L > F).$$

Clearly, no one is even partly morally responsible for this fact, and so this is also true:

$$(2)\ N[(P \text{ and } L) > F].$$

Since $[(P \text{ and } L) > F]$ is equivalent to $[P > (L > F)]$, this is true as well:

$$(3)\ N[P > (L > F)].$$

Now

$$(4)\ NP,$$

and so by Rule B, from (3) and (4) we can conclude

$$(5)\ N(L > F).$$

Since

$$(6)\ NL,$$

by another application of Rule B, from (5) and (6) we reach the conclusion,

$$(7)\ NF.$$

Since F is an arbitrary truth, this conclusion can be generalized. Consequently, the argument appears to show in a direct fashion that if causal determinism is true, no one is even in part morally responsible for any fact.

But Rule B can be called into question. Mark Ravizza offers the following kind of case to impugn Rule B.[3] At T_1, Betty freely detonates explosives as part of a plan to start an avalanche that will destroy an enemy camp; and, in fact, her explosion does succeed in causing an avalanche that is sufficient to destroy the camp at T_3. Unknown to Betty, however, there is another cause of the camp's destruction by avalanche. At T_1, a goat kicks loose a boulder, and it causes an avalanche, which is also sufficient to destroy the camp at T_3 and which contributes to the actual destruction of the camp at T_3. In the story, no one is even partly morally responsible for the goat's kicking the boulder. And no one is even partly morally responsible for the fact that if the goat kicks that boulder at T_1, then the camp is destroyed by avalanche at T_3. Nonetheless, Betty is at least partly responsible for the camp's being destroyed by avalanche at T_3. Thus, Ravizza's case apparently shows that Rule B is invalid. In cases of simultaneous causation, the rule fails.[4]

In a recent paper, Ted Warfield has suggested a reply on behalf of the incompatibilist.[5] He concedes that Ravizza's case presents a challenge to Rule B. Warfield claims, however, that there is a related but nonequivalent rule—he calls it "Rule Beta □"—which can play a similar role in an argument for the incompatibility of causal determinism and moral responsibility. According to Warfield, Rule Beta □ is not subject to Ravizza-style counterexamples.

This is Rule Beta □:

$$[Np \text{ and } \square (p > q)] \text{ implies } Nq.$$

The key difference between Rule B and Rule Beta □ is in the connection between p and q. For Rule B, it must be the case that if p, then q, and no one is responsible for this fact. For Rule Beta □, the connection between p and q is one of logical necessity. Because the connection between p and q in Warfield's Rule Beta □ is so much stronger than the connection between p and q in Rule B, Warfield supposes that it will be much harder to construct scenarios that present a challenge to his rule. For Ravizza's scenario to serve as a counterexample to an inference licensed by Rule Beta □, the connection between the goat's kicking the boulder at T_1 and the camp's being destroyed by avalanche at T_3 would have to be a logical one; and, of course, it is not. As Warfield says, "The conditional premise (if the goat kicks the boulder at T_1, then the avalanche destroys the camp at T_3), though not a proposition anyone is even partly morally responsible for, does not express a relation of logical consequence, and so Ravizza's example fails to apply to my argument [for incompatibilism]."[6]

Contrary to what Warfield claims, his Rule Beta □ *is* subject to Ravizza-style counterexamples, in our view. In what follows, we present two such counterexamples, each of which is sufficient to show that Rule Beta □ is invalid.

Counterexample A. Let it be the case that, necessarily, if the actual laws of nature obtain and the conditions of the world at T_2 (some time just before T_3) are C, then there will be an avalanche that destroys the enemy camp at T_3. Let it also be the case that at T_1 Betty *freely* starts an avalanche, which is sufficient to destroy the camp at T_3 and which contributes to its destruction at T_3. Finally, let it be the case that Betty's freely starting an avalanche is a result of some suitable indeterministic process.

Then let r be the conjunction of

(r1) the actual laws of nature obtain

and

(r2) the condition of the world at T_2 is C.

And let q be

(q) there is an avalanche which destroys the enemy camp at T_3.

In this example, r is true. Nr is also true: nobody is even partly morally responsible for the obtaining of the actual laws of nature and the condition of the world's being C at T_2. By hypothesis, it is also true that $\square (r > q)$. Any world in which (r1) and (r2) are true is a world in which q is true. And yet it seems clear that Nq is false. Insofar as Betty at T_1 freely starts an avalanche, she is at least in part morally responsible for the camp's being destroyed by an avalanche at T_3.

Warfield anticipates such a case. He says:

Can a Frankfurt-type case (or a Ravizza overdetermination case) be constructed that is a counterexample to Rule Beta □? I don't see how. To illustrate notice that making . . . the avalanche a logical consequence of the goat's kicking the boulder requires that we assume that [the avalanche] is a *deterministic* consequence of the arrangement of natural forces. This change would provide a case that is at least of the right form to serve as a counterexample to Rule Beta □. But to be a counterexample to Rule Beta □ the example must be an example in which the Frankfurtian judgment of moral responsibility [Betty's moral responsibility for the camp's being destroyed by an avalanche] holds up. With the additional assumption of determinism that is needed to make the case applicable to Rule Beta □, however, this Frankfurtian judgment is equivalent to the claim that determinism and moral responsibility are compatible. It is hardly of interest to point out that the assumption of the compatibility of determinism and moral responsibility implies that Rule Beta □ is invalid.[7]

But note that we have not assumed causal determinism in our example. Contrary to Warfield's claim, such an assumption is *not* "needed to make the case applicable to [Rule] Beta □." This is because even in an indeterministic world, *some* events and states of affairs can be causally determined. One can suppose that the enemy camp's being destroyed by an avalanche at T_3 is causally determined by the goat's kicking a boulder at T_1 *without* thereby supposing that Betty's deliberations or actions are causally determined. Even in an indeterministic world, there can be "pockets of local determination."[8] To deny this is to suppose that, for any state of affairs p whatever, the laws of nature and the condition C of the world at T_2 is compatible with p at T_3 and also compatible with $not\text{-}p$ at T_3. But this is to suppose that absolutely everything in the world is indeterministic, and presumably even libertarians don't want to make so strong a claim.

Counterexample B. For those still inclined to worry about the issue of causal determinism, however, we can construct a counterexample which doesn't depend on there being even local determinism. This time let r be a conjunction of these propositions

($r1$) the actual laws of nature obtain

and

($r3$) there is an avalanche, which destroys the enemy camp at T_3.

Now, without doubt, there is a logically necessary connection between r and q (since q is identical to [$r3$]), but the question of whether causal determinism of any sort obtains is irrelevant. Here we have

$$(8)\ Nr$$

and

$$(9)\ \Box\,(r > q),$$

but it isn't the case that

$$(10)\ Nq,$$

for the sort of reasons given in connection with Ravizza's story.

Warfield has an objection to this sort of counterexample, too. He maintains that

(W1) if no one is even partly morally responsible for a conjunction, then no one is even partly morally responsible for either conjunct of the conjunction.[9]

This claim calls into question Nr in our counterexample B. It is not the case that no one is even partly responsible for (r_3). On (W1), then, it isn't the case that no one is even partly morally responsible for r. Consequently, Nr is false.

But is Warfield's claim (W1) right? We think it isn't, because of the connection between conjunctions and conditionals.

To see this, consider again Ravizza's story. It is not the case that if the actual laws of nature obtain, there will not be an avalanche that destroys the enemy camp at T_3. So this is true:

$$(11) \text{ not } (L > not\text{-}q).$$

Furthermore, it seems odd to think that anyone is even partly responsible for (11). It is peculiar to suppose that a human being is to blame for (11), is the source of the state of affairs described by (11), could have brought it about that that state of affairs didn't obtain, and so on. So this also seems true:

$$(12) \text{ N[not } (L > not\text{-}q)].$$

Of course, (11) is equivalent to this:

$$(13) \text{ } (L \text{ and } q).$$

So it seems as if this also has to be true:

$$(14) \text{ N}(L \text{ and } q).[10]$$

But now we have a problem, if (W1) is correct. In Ravizza's story, Betty is partly responsible for q. Therefore, it isn't true that no one is even partly responsible for the conjuncts of (13); Betty is at least partly responsible for q. On (W1), however, for it to be the case that no one is even partly responsible for the conjunction, it would also have to be the case that no one was even partly responsible for either of the conjuncts. Consequently, if Warfield's claim (W1) is true, (14) is *false*.

In that case, however, Warfield must also hold that (12) is false. But the claim that (12) is false strikes us as counterintuitive.

Furthermore, as the preceding discussion shows, if (W1) is true, so is this:

(W2) Given a true antecedent of a conditional,[11] a person is partly responsible for the conditional's being false if he is partly responsible for the falsity of the consequent of the conditional.[12]

That's why commitment to (W1) turns out to require rejecting

$$(12) \text{ N[not } (L > not\text{-}q)].$$

But if (W2) is true, it seems that this ought also to be true:

(W3) Given a true antecedent of a conditional, a person is partly responsible for the conditional's being true if he is partly responsible for the truth of the consequent of the conditional.

Why should we accept that a person is partly responsible for the falsity of a conditional with a true antecedent because of his responsibility for the falsity of the consequent, and yet deny that a person is partly responsible for the truth of a conditional with a true antecedent because of his responsibility for the truth of the consequent?

Another way to see the connection between (W1) and (W3) is to consider the reason Warfield gives for accepting (W1). To make (W1) seem plausible, Warfield says, "being at least partly morally responsible for a conjunct is a way of being partly morally responsible for a conjunction."[13] But if that is right, then it seems that a similar point ought to apply to conditionals: being partly responsible for the truth of the consequent of a conditional with a true antecedent is a way of being partly responsible for the truth of the conditional.

And yet (W3) is clearly mistaken. To see this, consider (9) again:

$$(9) \ \Box \ (r > q),$$

where r is
   (r1) the actual laws of nature obtain,
and
   (r3) there is an avalanche which destroys the enemy camp at $T3$,
and q is identical to (r3). Warfield also accepts this rule of inference, taken from Peter van Inwagen:

$$\text{Rule A: } \Box \ p \text{ implies } Np.$$

Rule A seems entirely uncontroversial. In fact, Warfield says,

> van Inwagen's Rule A is (nearly) as trivial and inconsequential as a rule of inference could be. No one has, to my knowledge, challenged this principle nor has anyone challenged any principle closely related to Rule A.[14]

Now, from (9), by Rule A, we get

$$(15) \ N \ (r > q).$$

On (W3), however, a person is partly responsible for the truth of a conditional with a true antecedent if she is partly responsible for the truth of the consequent of the conditional. So, on (W3), we will have to say that (15) is *false*, just as (12) is, because Betty is partly responsible for q. By Rule A, however, it then follows that (9) is false, since by Rule A (9) implies (15). Without doubt, this is absurd. So either Rule A is after all invalid, or (W3) is false. And if (W3) is false, then by parity of reasoning it seems that (W1) is false also.

For these reasons, we think Warfield's claim (W1) should be rejected. The logic of responsibility is more complicated than (W1) implies. Given the relation between conjunctions and conditionals, it is right to hold that someone can be partly responsible for a conjunct of a conjunction without being partly responsible for the conjunction. Consequently, our counterexample B is also effective against Rule Beta □.

Finally, we think it is worth pointing out that one of us believes that causal determinism is incompatible with moral responsibility, and the other does not. But we unite in thinking that causal determinism cannot be proved incompatible with moral responsibility by Warfield's Rule Beta □.

NOTES

1. In the context of the indirect arguments for the incompatibility of causal determinism and moral responsibility, one can have "Transfer of Powerlessness" principles. For a discussion of such principles, see John Martin Fischer, *The Metaphysics of Free Will: An Essay on Control* (Oxford: Blackwell, 1994), pp. 23–66.

2. Peter van Inwagen, *An Essay on Free Will* (Oxford: Clarendon, 1983), p. 184.

3. Mark Ravizza, "Semi-Compatibilism and the Transfer of Nonresponsibility," *Philosophical Studies* 75 (1994): 61–93, esp. p. 78. For similar examples, see also John Martin Fischer and Mark Ravizza, *Responsibility and Control: A Theory of Moral Responsibility* (Cambridge: Cambridge University Press, 1998), pp. 151–69.

4. One of us (Stump), but not the other, thinks it isn't clear that the invalidity of Rule B shown by Ravizza's example renders van Inwagen's argument irremediably invalid. That is because Rule B fails only in certain cases, and it isn't clear to one of us that cases of moral responsibility can be assimilated to those cases of simultaneous causation in which Rule B fails.

5. Ted A. Warfield, "Determinism and Moral Responsibility Are Incompatible," *Philosophical Topics* 24 (1996): 215–26. In addition to the suggestion explored in the text, Warfield also presents other strategies for replying to the compatibilistic strategy of Ravizza; see, especially, pp. 221–22.

6. Ibid., pp. 222–23.

7. Ibid., p. 223.

8. Daniel Dennett introduces the term "local fatalism" to refer to a related but different notion: Daniel C. Dennett, *Elbow Room: The Varieties of Free Will Worth Wanting* (Cambridge: MIT Press, 1984), pp. 104–106.

9. Warfield, "Determinism and Moral Responsibility Are Incompatible," p. 218. One possible reason for thinking that (W1) is true is the supposition that one is at least partly morally responsible for a conjunction if one is morally responsible for a part of a conjunction. But being morally responsible for a part of a conjunction and being partly morally responsible for a conjunction are not the same thing, as our argument in what follows helps to make clear.

10. This inference is licensed by the fact that if p and q are logically equivalent, then Np if and only if Nq.

11. It's possible to interpret (W1) as applying only to true conjunctions; in that case, this qualification in (W2) is needed.

12. Obviously, we can switch the conjuncts in the conjunction from (L and q) to (q and L), which is equivalent to

$$(12^*) \text{ not } (q > \text{not-L}).$$

Since Betty is partly responsible for (q and L), she will also be partly responsible for (12*). Consequently, accepting (W1) requires accepting not only (W2) but also

(W2*) Given a false consequent, a person is partly responsible for a conditional's being false if he is partly responsible for the truth of the antecedent of the conditional.

13. Warfield, "Determinism and Moral Responsibility Are Incompatible," p. 218.

14. Ibid., pp. 218–19. Similarly, van Inwagen says, "The validity of Rule (A) seems to me to be beyond dispute. No one is responsible for the fact that $49 \times 18 = 882$, for the fact that arithmetic is essentially incomplete, or, if Kripke is right about necessary truth, for the fact that the atomic number of gold is 79" (*Essay on Free Will*, p. 184).

10

FREE WILL AND MORAL RESPONSIBILITY

Much has been written recently about free will and moral responsibility. In this chapter I will focus on the relationship between free will, on the one hand, and various notions that fall under the rubric of "morality," broadly construed, on the other: deliberation and practical reasoning, moral responsibility, and ethical notions such as "ought," "right," "wrong," "good," and "bad." I shall begin by laying out a natural understanding of freedom of the will. Next I develop some challenges to the commonsense view that we have this sort of freedom. I will go on to explore the implications of this challenge for deliberation, moral responsibility, and the central ethical notions.

Free Will and the Challenge from Causal Determinism

We naturally think of ourselves—"normal" adult human beings—as "free." That is, we take it that we have a certain distinctive sort of control. I shall use "free will" (or "freedom of the will") as an umbrella term to refer to the sort of freedom or control we presuppose that we human beings possess, and that is connected in important ways to ascriptions of moral responsibility. As I shall be employing the term, "free will" need not entail that we have a special faculty of the will, but only that we have a certain kind of freedom or control. But what is this freedom?

It is extremely natural and plausible to think that the typical adult human being has freedom in the sense that we often (although perhaps not always) have the freedom to choose or refrain from choosing a particular course of action (where "course of action" can refer to an omission as well as an action, narrowly construed), and to undertake or refrain from undertaking this course of action. That is, we take it that we often (although perhaps not invariably) have "alternative

I am grateful to David Copp for his extremely careful and helpful comments, and also for his patience and support.

possibilities": although we actually choose and undertake a particular course of action, we had it in our power (or "could have") chosen and undertaken a different course of action. Of course, we recognize that sometimes we are "coerced" or "compelled" to choose or act as we do; and some individuals never have control over their choices and actions (because of significant mental illness, brain damage, and so forth). But we assume that the typical adult human being at least sometimes has more than one available path. That is, we assume, in Borges's phrase, that the future is a garden of forking paths.

But there are various skeptical worries or challenges to the intuitive notion that we have free will in the sense that involves alternative possibilities. One of the most important such challenges comes from the doctrine of causal determinism. Causal determinism is the thesis that every event (and thus every choice and bit of behavior) is deterministically caused by some event in the past; thus, every choice and bit of behavior is the result of a casual chain, each link in which is deterministically caused by some prior link (until one gets to the beginning, if there is a beginning). More specifically, one can say that causal determinism is the doctrine that a complete statement of the laws of nature and a complete description of the temporally nonrelational or "genuine" facts about the world at some time T *entail* every truth about the world after T. That is, if causal determinism is true, then the past and the natural laws *entail* a unique present and future path for the world. Note further that if someone had available to her the description of the past and the statement of the laws, she could with certainty state what happens in the present and what will happen in the future. But it does not follow from the truth of the metaphysical doctrine of causal determinism that anyone actually has access to the relevant truths about the universe or its laws.

I contend that no human being currently knows whether or not the doctrine of causal determinism obtains. Certain physicists believe that the study of physical phenomena at the micro-level renders it very plausible that causal determinism is false (and thus that "indeterminism" is true). Note, again, that indeterminism is a metaphysical, rather than an epistemic doctrine; that is, causal indeterminism posits indeterminacies in nature, not just incompleteness in our understanding of nature. But other physicists (and philosophers) cling to the view that causal determinism is true, and that what appear currently to be genuine metaphysical indeterminacies reflect mere inadequacies in our knowledge of the world.[1]

Since we cannot be certain at this point that causal determinism is false, it is perhaps worthwhile to think about what would follow if it turned out that causal determinism is true. It is troubling that there is a very potent argument, employing ingredients from common sense, which appears to show that if causal determinism indeed turned out to be true, then no human being would have free will in the sense that involves alternative possibilities. The argument appears to show that the future is not a garden of forking paths on the assumption of causal determinism. The following is an informal and intuitive presentation of the argument.[2]

Suppose I make some ordinary choice C at time $T2$. If causal determinism is true, then the total state of the universe at $T1$ together with the laws of nature entail that I make C at $T2$. Thus, it was a necessary condition of my making a different choice at $T2$ that either the state of the universe at $T1$ would have been different from what it actually was, or some proposition that expressed a natural law would not have expressed a natural law. But it is intuitively plausible that I cannot—do not have it in my power—at any time so to behave that the past would have been different from the way it actually was. And, similarly, I cannot at any time determine which propositions express the natural laws. Intuitively, the past and the natural laws are "fixed" and not "up to me." It seems to follow from the above ingredients that I could not have chosen otherwise than C at T2 if causal determinism turned out to be true.

Here is a slightly different way of presenting basically the same argument.[3] As I suggested above, intuitively the past and the laws of nature are fixed and out of my control. The future is a garden of forking paths: the paths into the future extend from a given past, holding the laws of nature fixed. So, one might say that my freedom is the freedom to extend the actual (or given) past, holding fixed the laws of nature. Assume, again, the truth of causal determinism, and that I make choice C at T2. It follows from the assumption of causal determinism that the state of the world at T1 together with the laws of nature entail that I make choice C at T2. So in all possible worlds with the same laws as the actual world in which the past is just as it actually is, I make choice C at T2, Thus, it is logically impossible that my making some other choice C* at T2 be an extension of the given past, holding fixed the natural laws. It is evident, then, that if causal determinism is true, I cannot make any choice other than the one I actually make.

The above argument, suitably regimented and refined, appears to be generalizable to show that if it turns out that causal determinism is true, then no human being has the sort of free will that involves alternative possibilities—freedom to choose or do otherwise, or the power to select one path the world will take, from among various paths that are "genuinely" or "really" open. This argument for "incompatibilism"—the incompatibility of causal determinism and (in this instance) the sort of free will that involves alternative possibilities—has been the focal point of much discussion. Although the argument is controversial, here I shall not explore the ways in which it can be resisted.[4] Rather, I shall assume that the argument is sound and explore the implications of this assumption. As I proceed, I shall focus on the question of what would follow, in terms of "morality," broadly construed, if we in fact lack the sort of free will that involves alternative possibilities. Also, I shall consider whether there are features of causal determinism that would threaten morality, apart from its ruling out free will (in the sense that involves alternative possibilities).

Deliberation and Practical Reasoning

Taylor and Van Inwagen

One of the most central aspects of human "persons" is that we can engage in significant deliberation and practical reasoning. In deliberating, we consider and weigh reasons for (and against) various courses of action. We seek to "figure out what is best to do," and to act in accordance with this sort of judgment about what is best, all things considered. We of course are fallible in our judgments, and certainly we sometimes fail to act in accordance with our judgment about what is best to do, all things considered. But in any case the process of deliberation (or practical reasoning) involves identifying and weighing reasons with an eye to figuring out what we have sufficient reason to do.

Some philosophers have argued that it is a conceptual truth that I cannot engage in deliberation if I do not believe that I have free will in the sense that involves alternative possibilities. After pointing out that I can deliberate only about my own behavior (and not the behavior of another), that I can deliberate only about future things (rather than present or past things), and that I cannot deliberate about what I already know that I am going to do, Richard Taylor adds, "and, finally, I cannot deliberate about what to do, even though I may not know what I am going to do, unless I believe that it is up to me what I am going to do."[5] He goes on to argue that the relevant notion of "up to me" is incompatible with causal determinism; on this notion, an act's being up to me implies that it is up to me whether or not I do it.

I am not convinced by Taylor that I would not or could not engage in deliberation if I believed that causal determinism were true and thus that I have it in my power only to choose to do (and to do) what I actually choose to do (and do). As long as I do not know what I will in fact choose, it seems that there is a perfectly reasonable point to deliberation; after all, I still need to figure out what I have sufficient reason to do and to seek to act in accordance with this judgment. This purpose of deliberation would not disappear in a world in which I knew that it is not up to me (in the sense that involves alternative possibilities, incompatibilistically construed) what I will choose. Note that it may still be true, even in a causally deterministic world, that in a particular context I would choose a course of action if and only if I were to judge it best. Further, it does not follow simply from causal determinism that there is some special sort of obstacle to my choosing a particular course of action; causal determinism does not entail that I have some kind of phobia or compulsion that would rule out my choosing a certain sort of action. And if one insists that it is a *conceptual truth* that my process of weighing reasons would not count as "deliberation," then so be it: call it "deliberation*" or simply "figuring out what it would be best to do," and there can be a clear point to such activities even in a world in which I know that I have only one path that is genuinely available into the future.

Peter van Inwagen holds a view which is similar to, but slightly different from, Taylor's. On van Inwagen's account, an agent who believes he lacks free will (in the sense of alternative possibilities) can deliberate, but in so doing he would be contradicting himself. Van Inwagen says, "In my view, if someone deliberates about whether to do A or to do B, it follows that his behavior manifests a belief that it is *possible* for him to do A—that he *can* do A, that he has it within his power to do A—and that it is possible for him to do B."[6] Thus, an individual who sincerely believes that he lacks free will (understood as above) would be contradicting himself in deliberating—he would be holding an inconsistent set of beliefs. Whereas this is not impossible, it is certainly undesirable; for example, holding inconsistent beliefs guarantees that at least one of one's beliefs is false.[7]

But I am not convinced that van Inwagen is correct to say that deliberation manifests the belief in free will (understood as above). He says:

> Anyone who doubts that this is indeed the case may find it instructive to imagine that he is in a room with two doors and that he believes one of the doors to be unlocked and the other to be locked and impassable, though he has no idea which is which; let him then attempt to imagine himself deliberating about which door to leave by.[8]

I agree that it would be odd to think that I could deliberate about which door actually (or "successfully") to open. But surely in such a case I could deliberate about which door to *choose* to open. That is, I could weigh reasons and come to a judgment about which door it would be best to seek to open, and I could form an intention—choose—to act in accordance with my judgment. There is not the same intuitive oddness about saying that I could deliberate about which door to choose to push against that there is to saying that I could deliberate about which door "to leave by." It is important to note that van Inwagen does not purport to be offering an *argument* for the contention that anyone who deliberates must believe that he has alternative possibilities, apart from his invocation of the example of the alleged oddness of deliberating about which door to leave by.

But van Inwagen may reply that the apparent lack of oddness in supposing that I could deliberate about which door (say) to choose to open stems precisely from the fact that I suppose that I am able either to choose to open door A or choose to open door B. I am not so sure, however, that this is the explanation of the asymmetry in our intuitions between deliberating about which door *to open* and deliberating about which door *to choose to open*. Suppose I do in fact choose to open door A. Now if causal determinism is true and the argument for the incompatibility of causal determinism and free will (understood as involving alternative possibilities) is sound, then it turns out that, unknown to me, just prior to my choice I did not have it in my power to choose to open door B. Further, it seems to me that I could know that causal determinism is true and that the incompatibilist's argument is sound, and thus that whichever choice I make is the only one I actually can make. This knowledge does not eliminate the point of deliberation (the need to figure out which door it would be best to choose to open); and I do not have any hesitation in supposing that, even with the knowledge that whatever door I choose will be the *only* door I in fact can choose to open, I can deliberate about which door to choose to open. Thus I do not believe that the asymmetry in our intuitions between deliberating about which door to open and deliberating about which door to choose to open stems from an asymmetry in our beliefs about alternative possibilities.

In a causally deterministic world (and given the incompatibilistic argument), *every* choice and action would be such that, if I make it (or perform it), I could not have made another choice (or performed another action.) But it seems to me that there could still be a perfectly reasonable point to deliberation, and that I need not contradict myself in accepting the truth of causal determinism and the soundness of the argument for incompatibilism, but nevertheless deliberating. All that is required is that I have an interest in figuring out what I have sufficient reason to choose, and that I do not know which course of action I will in fact choose to take (and take).[9] Further, van Inwagen has not produced an example in which it is obvious that *this* yields an odd result.

Searle

John Searle has argued for a point related to the claims of Taylor and van Inwagen, but it is slightly different. Searle's contention is that there would be *no point* to practical reasoning or deliberation if I knew that causal determinism were true. Searle says:

> The gap can be given two equivalent descriptions, one forward-looking, one backward. Forward: the gap is that feature of our conscious decision making and acting where we sense alternative future decisions and actions as causally open to us. Backward: the gap is that feature of conscious decision making and acting whereby the reasons preceding the decisions and the actions are not experienced by the agent as setting causally sufficient conditions for the decisions and actions. As far as our conscious experiences are concerned, the gap occurs when the beliefs, desires, and other reasons are not experienced as causally sufficient conditions for a decision (the formation of a prior intention).[10]

Searle goes on to state:

> I am advancing three theses here.
>
>   1. We have experiences of the gap of the sort I have described.
>   2. We have to presuppose the gap. We have to presuppose that the psychological antecedents of many of our decisions and actions do not set causally sufficient conditions for those decisions and actions.
>   3. In normal conscious life one cannot avoid choosing and deciding.
>
>   Here is the argument for 2 and 3: If I really thought that the beliefs and desires were sufficient to cause the action then I could just sit back and watch the action unfold in the same way as I do when I sit back and watch the action unfold on a movie screen. But I cannot do that when I am engaging in rational decision making and acting. I have to presuppose that the antecedent set of psychological conditions was not causally sufficient. Furthermore, here is an additional argument for point 3: even if I became convinced of the falsity of the thesis of the gap, all the same I would still have to engage in actions and thus exercise my own freedom no matter what. . . .
>
>   For example, there is a kind of practical inconsistency in maintaining the following two theses:
>
>   1. I am now trying to make up my mind whom to vote for in the next election.
>   2. I take the existing psychological causes operating on me right now to be causally sufficient to determine whom I am going to vote for.

The inconsistency comes out in the fact that if I really believe 2, then there seems no point in making the effort involved in 1. The situation would be like taking a pill that I am sure will cure my headache by itself, and then trying to add some further psychological effort to the effects of the pill. If I really believe the pill is enough, then the rational thing to do is to sit back and let it take effect.[11]

In discussing Searle's view, I would point out that when Searle first introduces the notion of a "gap," it is a point about our experiences. Recall that he says, for instance, "the gap is that feature of our conscious decision making and acting where we sense alternative future decisions and actions as causally open to us." But he goes on to say, "We have to presuppose the gap. We have to presuppose that the psychological antecedents of many of our decisions and actions do not set causally sufficient conditions for those decisions and actions." If the second sentence of the latter quotation is intended as exegetical, then "the gap" is now thought to be not so much a feature of our phenomenology, but of the objective relationship between our mental states.[12] This is somewhat confusing. From now on, I will take "the gap thesis" to be the claim that both our experience and the objective reality of the relationship between our mental states are indeterministic.

I believe that Searle's view here is incorrect. Note that Leibniz describes what is essentially this view as the "Lazy Sophism":

> This ... demolishes ... what the ancients [the Stoics, perhaps following Cicero] called the "Lazy Sophism," which ended in a decision to do nothing: for (people would say) if what I ask is to happen it will happen even though I should do nothing; and if it is not to happen it will never happen, no matter what trouble I take to achieve it. . . . But the answer is quite ready: the effect being certain, the cause that shall produce it is certain also; and if the effect comes about it will be by virtue of a proportionate cause. Thus your laziness perchance will bring it about that you will obtain naught of what you desire, and that you will fall into those misfortunes which you would by acting with care have avoided. We see, therefore, that the connexion of causes with effects, far from causing an unendurable fatality, provides rather a means of obviating it.[13]

It seems to me that Searle's view about deliberation falls prey to the same objections as the views of Taylor and van Inwagen. I believe that there would be a clear point to deliberation and practical reasoning, even if I were to reject the gap: I would still have an interest in—and deeply care about—figuring out what I have reason to do and seeking to act accordingly. Even if the gap thesis is false, and antecedent psychological states are causally sufficient for my decision, and I know this, it does not follow that I know what decision I will make and what action I will perform. Hence, insofar as I care about acting in accordance with what I have all-things-considered reason to do, there is a clear point to engaging in deliberation.

Recall that Searle says that there is a practical inconsistency in maintaining the following:

1. I am now trying to make up my mind whom to vote for in the next election.
2. I take the existing psychological causes operating on me right now to be causally sufficient to determine whom I am going to vote for.

He says holding these two theses would be like "taking a pill that I am sure will cure my headache by itself, and then trying to add some further psychological effort to the effects of the pill." But in Searle's analogy you *know* that the pill will cure your headache; in contrast, I am *not* assumed to know whom I will vote for in the next election. If I *did* know whom I would vote for, I agree that the point of making up my mind would appear to vanish.[14]

Suppose I know that my decision about the next election is causally determined by my current configuration of mental states (desires, beliefs, and so forth). Still, I can also know that my decision will *depend* on my practical reasoning in the following sense: if I were to judge it best, all things considered, to vote for Candidate A, I would vote for Candidate A; but if were to to judge it best, all things considered, to vote for Candidate B, I would vote for Candidate B. Further, I can know that nothing distorts or impairs my practical reasoning—my ability to recognize the reasons there are and to weigh them with an eye to making an all-things-considered judgment as to what is best. That is, nothing in the doctrine of causal determinism entails that the counterfactuals (that specify the relevant sort of dependency) are false, and nothing in this doctrine entails that I have any special sort of impairment of my capacity to engage in practical reasoning—certain phobias, compulsions, mental illnesses, and so forth. And, finally, nothing in the doctrine of causal determinism entails that I do not care about choosing and acting in accordance with my judgment about what is best to do. So there is a clear point to deliberation, even if I believe that antecedent mental states are causally sufficient for my decision.

Imagine, to make the point dramatically, that there are two doors in front of you, and you must choose which door to open. You know that behind door 1 is a million dollars, and behind door 2 is a den of rattlesnakes. Imagine, further, that you know that causal determinism is true, that causal determinism rules out alternative possibilities, and that causal determinism in itself does not entail that one has any physical paralysis or impairment of the human capacity for practical reasoning (no intense phobias, compulsions, paranoid schizophrenia, and so forth). Would Searle really not deliberate? What would he do—flip a coin, act arbitrarily, or what? Would he simply "sit back and watch the action unfold?" It would seem perfectly reasonable (at the very least) to take into consideration what is behind the doors, and to choose and act accordingly. Having collected the million dollars, you might pause to reflect that it turns out that that was the *only* thing you could have done (as long as this thought would not unduly delay the celebration!).

Consider another argument of Searle's:

Suppose I believe the doctrine that rational actions are caused by beliefs and desires. Suppose, as a science-fiction fantasy, that there are pills that induce beliefs and desires. Now suppose I want someone to do something rationally. I want him to vote for the Democratic candidate for a reason, so I give him the red pills that give him a desire to vote for the candidate whom he thinks would be best for the economy and I give him the blue pills that convince him that the Democratic candidate is best for the economy.

Now can I just sit back and watch the causes work? Is it just like putting dynamite under a bridge, lighting the fuse, and watching the bridge blow up? No. Even in this case it is not like that, for suppose I wish to induce myself to vote for the Democrats, so I take both the red and the blue pills. After a couple of weeks I might think, well the pills have worked. I have come to believe that the Democrat is better for the economy and I have come to want a candidate who will be good for the economy. But this is still not sufficient. I still have to decide whom I am going to vote for, and that presupposes that the causes are not sufficient.[15]

This is a puzzling argument. The example is supposed to be one in which I want someone else or myself "to do something rationally," that is, to vote for the Democrat. Even if the pills induce the relevant desire and belief, Searle notes, "this is still not sufficient. I still have to decide whom I am going to vote for, and that presupposes that the causes are not sufficient." Well, Searle seems to be pointing first to the fact that desires and beliefs, or particular desires and beliefs, produce rational or intentional action only via a decision of some sort. That is, the "pro-attitudes" issue in an action only when an "executive state," such as a choice or decision, mediates between the attitudes and the action. This is relatively uncontroversial, but it does not entail that the desires and beliefs are not sufficient conditions for the subsequent action; all that follows is that they are not such conditions that work *directly* (and without any causal intermediaries) to produce the actions.

But Searle makes a further assertion, namely that deciding whom I am going to vote for "presupposes that the causes are not sufficient." I think that the *most* Searle is entitled to at this point is that deciding presupposes that I *believe* that the *psychological* causes are insufficient. Additionally, there seems to me to be no *argument* at this point in Searle's book that decisions presuppose the belief in psychological indeterminism. I thought that the example was supposed to help make this thesis plausible; but the example only shows, if anything, that one needs an intervening executive state between the pro-attitudes and the action. It does not in any way suggest that making a decision requires believing that the decision is not psychologically determined; rather, Searle simply asserts this.

Now it may be that Searle is making a point about "reduction," rather than a conceptual point related to the futility of deliberating, when one believes that one's prior mental states constitute sufficient conditions for his decision. Perhaps Searle is here relying on a point he goes on to argue for: that agency cannot be reduced to desires and beliefs, but an irreducible activity of the Self is required. But, again, even if this is true, it would *not* entail that the relevant psychological states do not constitute sufficient causal conditions for the decision that operate indirectly (via the intermediation of the Self). The point in defense of nonreductionism is orthogonal to the issue of the alleged presupposition of psychological indeterminism for agency.

It is interesting to note that Searle takes these putative facts about our experience to rule out causal determinism at the neurobiological level. He admits that it is conceivable that our experience of indeterminism does not map onto the reality of the brain (and that the neurobiological events are causally deterministic); but he argues against this as follows:

This result, however, is intellectually very unsatisfying, because, in a word, it is a modified form of epiphenomenalism. It says that the psychological processes of rational decision making do not really matter. The entire system is deterministic at the bottom level, and the idea that the top level has an element of freedom is simply a systematic illusion. It seems to me at $t1$ that I have a choice between the Burgundy and the Bordeaux and that the causes operating on me are not sufficient to determine the choice. But I am mistaken. The total state of my brain at $t1$ is entirely sufficient to determine every bodily movement as well as every thought process from $t1$ to $t2$ to $t3$. If hypothesis 1 is true, then every muscle movement as well as every conscious thought, including the conscious experience of the gap, the experience of "free" decision making, is entirely fixed in advance; and the only thing we can say about psychological indeterminism at the higher level is that it gives us a systematic illusion of free will. The thesis is epiphenomenalistic in this respect: there is a feature of our conscious lives, rational decision making and trying to carry out the decision, where we experience the gap and we experience the processes as making a causal difference to our behavior, but they do not in fact make any difference. The bodily movements were going to be exactly the same regardless of how these processes occurred.

Maybe that is how it will turn out, but if so, the hypothesis seems to me to run against everything we know about evolution. It would have the consequence that the incredibly elaborate, complex, sensitive, and—above all—biologically expensive system of human and animal conscious rational decision making would actually make no difference whatever to the life and survival of the organisms. Epiphenomenalism is a possible thesis, but it is absolutely incredible, and if we seriously accepted it, it would make a change in our worldview, that is, in our conception of our relations to the world, more radical than any previous change, including the Copernican Revolution, Einsteinian relativity theory, and quantum mechanics.

Why would [the hypothesis under consideration] render consciousness any more epiphenomenal than any other higher-level feature of a physical system? After all, the solidity of the piston in the car engine is entirely explained by the behavior of the molecules but that does not render solidity epiphenomenal. The difference is this: the essential characteristics of solidity matter to the performance of the engine, but the essential characteristic of conscious decision making, the experience of the gap, would not matter in the least to the performance of the agent. The bodily movements would have been the same, regardless of the experiences of the gap.[16]

I have argued above that we do not need to presuppose a "gap" of the sort to which Searle is referring in order to engage in practical reasoning. I have suggested that practical reasoning may require an "epistemic gap"—it may be necessary that we not know exactly what we will choose and do, in order for there to be a point to practical reasoning (and deliberation). Searle's gap then is not an "essential characteristic of conscious decision making." And the epistemic gap clearly *would* make a difference: if it didn't exist, it may well not be reasonable to deliberate, and so my bodily movements might be quite different.

Note that, on the view of practical reasoning I am suggesting, psychological processes of rational decision making *do* matter in a straightforward sense: if my deliberations had gone differently (and had thus issued in a different judgment as to what is best, all things considered), then my decisions and bodily movements would have been different. It is *not* the case that the bodily movements are going to be exactly the same, regardless of how my deliberations go. This surely is the important point about the causal efficacy of practical reasoning. So "the incredibly elaborate, complex, sensitive, and—above all—biologically expensive system of human and animal conscious rational decision making" *does* make a difference to the life and survival of organisms. Surely what is evolutionarily important in our capacities for practical reasoning is a certain capacity to recognize and respond to reasons; it seems bizarre to suppose that what is crucial to our survival—and the crowning glory of evolution—is the experience of the causal insufficiency of our mental states! If there is a gap here at all, it is in Searle's argument.

Kantian Approaches

I further contend that I can at the same time (or from the same "perspective") acknowledge both that my choice is causally determined (and thus that I have but one path genuinely available to me) and deliberate about which choice to make. That is, when I am engaged in practical reasoning and deliberation, I can continue to believe, and to acknowledge, that I am causally determined and thus not free. This follows from the fact that the theses I acknowledge are metaphysical contentions the truth of which can leave an epistemic gap and from the distinctive purpose of practical reasoning. I can thus accept that the characteristic purposes of theoretical and practical reasoning diverge, while maintaining that an agent engaged in practical reasoning can in fact continue to hold such deliverances of theoretical reasoning as that he is causally determined and thus not free (in the sense of possessing alternative possibilities, construed incompatibilistically).

My view here is in stark contrast with the "neo-Kantian" two-perspective approach developed by such philosophers as Hilary Bok and Christine Korsgaard. For example, Hilary Bok says:

> If, when we engage in practical reasoning, we must regard ourselves as standing in the order of reasons rather than the order of causes, and if those orders are distinguished from one another by the relations of necessity to which they appeal, when we engage in practical reasoning we will not regard ourselves as subject to the same sort of necessity appealed to by theoretical reason. Theoretical necessity is causal: one object acts on another, thereby rendering some change in the latter necessary. To see oneself as necessitated in this way is to see oneself as passive: acted on rather than acting.[17]

Further, she says:

> Because we regard ourselves as subject not to causal but to rational necessity, when we engage in practical reasoning we regard ourselves not as the passive object of external forces but as determining our own conduct; not as acted on by things outside us but as choosing for reasons that we are free to accept or reject. And we regard these choices not as events that might simply befall us and with which we might or might not identify but as necessarily our own. For these reasons, as Christine Korsgaard writes, "[a]t the moment of decision, you must regard yourself as the author of your action."[18]

But whereas I agree that at the moment of decision, one must in some suitable sense see oneself as the author of one's decision, I do not think that it follows that one must at that moment believe (either occurrently or dispositionally) that one is not causally determined. I certainly do not think that it should be accepted as uncontroversial that it follows from my choice's being causally determined that I am not the author of it or that I am merely passive with respect to it—these claims require argumentation, as there are ways of seeking to explain authorship and the difference between activity and passivity that are consistent with causal determinism.

Additionally, the quotations from Korsgaard and Bok raise the vexing issue of the relationship between their notion of "regarding" and the more ordinary notion of "believing." With respect to this issue, consider the following passage from Bok:

> Insofar as regarding our choices as caused involves regarding them as determined by antecedent events, we cannot regard ourselves as caused to choose as we do when we engage in practical reasoning. [Here Bok inserts a footnote pointing us to Kant, *Grounding for the Metaphysics of Morals*, p. 50 (Ak. 448); and Korsgaard, "Morality as Freedom," pp. 162–63.] This is not because we believe we are not caused to choose as we do, but because when we engage in practical reasoning, we are concerned with another form of determination.[19]

Bok, however, faces the following dilemma. When we engage in practical reasoning, either we do in fact believe that we are not causally determined or we do not so believe. If we do, then it is obvious that a belief we have from the practical perspective can come into direct conflict with a belief we could have from the theoretical perspective. But it is a central feature of Bok's approach that the two perspectives cannot conflict in this way; the claim that the two perspectives cannot conflict is essential for Bok's project of showing freedom to be compatible with causal determinism.

Thus it seems as if Bok must say that, when we engage in practical reasoning, we do not believe (even dispositionally) that we are not causally determined. (I suppose the picture here is that, when one takes up the practical perspective, one does not believe in either causal determinism or its denial—one fails to form either of these beliefs.) But this leaves the notion of "regarding" somewhat mysterious; it seems as if from the practical perspective we *regard* ourselves as not subject to causal necessity but we do not *believe* we are not subject to causal necessity.

But if regarding is prized apart from believing in this way, what exactly is it to regard ourselves as not subject to causal necessity?[20] Further, I find it unattractive to suppose that from the practical perspective I cannot have (even dispositionally) a belief such as that causal determinism is false. Of course, the mere fact that, when engaged in practical reasoning, I am "concerned with" another form of necessitation does not entail that I do not—perhaps dispositionally—believe that I am in fact subject to causal necessitation. After all, when I am "concerned with" the leaking plumbing in my house, it does not follow that I do not believe (perhaps dispositionally) that the house is painted white (or that George Washington was the first president of the United States). If I do in fact have the belief that causal determinism is false, then why should I be precluded from having access (even dispositionally) to this belief when I take up the practical perspective? On this picture, the practical perspective is epistemically partitioned off from the rest of the agent in a puzzling way. The resulting compartmentalization is unattractive and, as I have suggested above, unnecessary.[21]

Moral Responsibility

The Concept of Moral Responsibility

Some philosophers have argued that if we lacked free will (in the sense that involves alternative possibilities), then we could not legitimately be considered morally responsible agents. There are, of course, different accounts of the concept of moral responsibility and of its conditions of application. I will simply sketch three views about the concept (or "nature") of moral responsibility; an elaboration of these accounts is beyond the scope of this chapter.[22]

On the first view about the nature of moral responsibility, an agent's moral responsibility consists in his or her being an appropriate candidate for ascriptions of certain ethical predicates, such as "good," "bad," "courageous," "charitable," "dastardly," "cruel," and so forth. The view is often put in terms of a metaphor; on this approach, an agent is morally responsible insofar as he has a "moral ledger." The ascription of moral predicates corresponds to making marks on the ledger.[23]

A second view contends that when an agent is morally responsible for some behavior, it would not be inappropriate to expect the agent to provide an explanation of the behavior in question. On this view, when the agent is morally responsible in this sense, it *follows* that he has a moral ledger; but it is the expectation that the agent can provide a certain sort of explanation that is the *essence* of moral responsibility.[24]

A third sort of account of the nature of moral responsibility follows Peter Strawson.[25] On this view, roughly speaking, an individual is morally responsible for some behavior in virtue of being an apt target for one of the "reactive attitudes" on the basis of the behavior. According to Strawson, the reactive attitudes include gratitude, indignation, resentment, love, respect, and forgiveness, and they manifest our involvement with other human beings in distinctively interpersonal relationships. There are various versions of the "Strawsonian" approach to the concept of moral responsibility.

In what follows I shall not take a stand on the correct account of the concept of moral responsibility. I shall simply speak of moral responsibility and let the reader fill in her favorite account of its nature. No matter what particular account of the concept of moral responsibility one accepts, it is clear that if it turned out that human beings lacked free will, there would be a deep and disturbing challenge to the idea that we are in fact morally responsible.

The Principle of Alternative Possibilities and the Frankfurt-Type Examples

As I suggested above, we naturally think that the future is a garden of forking paths—that we at least at some important points in our lives have more than one path branching into the future. If this intuitive picture turned out to be false, then it would seem that we could not legitimately be held morally responsible for our behavior. After all, if I don't have free will in a sense that involves alternative possibilities, then I *have* to choose (and do) what I actually choose (and do). And if I have to choose what I do in fact choose, then presumably I am *compelled* so to choose, and cannot fairly be considered morally responsible for my choice. It is very plausible, then, to accept something like the "Principle of Alternative Possibilities" (PAP), according to which an agent is morally responsible for (say) an action only if he could have done otherwise.[26] If PAP is true, then moral responsibility requires free will (in the sense that involves alternative possibilities); and if causal determinism rules out such alternative possibilities, it would thereby rule out moral responsibility.

Peter van Inwagen gives a particularly pointed defense of PAP:

> If we do not have free will, then there is no such thing as moral responsibility. This proposition, one might think, certainly deserves to be a commonplace. If someone charges you with, say, lying, and if you can convince him that it was simply not within your power *not* to lie, then it would seem that you have done all that is necessary to absolve yourself of responsibility for lying.
>
> . . . without free will there is no moral responsibility: if moral responsibility exists, then someone is morally responsible for something he has done or for something he has left undone; to be morally responsible for some act or failure to act is at least to be able to have acted otherwise, whatever else it may involve; to be able to have acted otherwise is to have free will. Therefore, if moral responsibility exists, someone has free will. Therefore, if no one has free will, moral responsibility does not exist.[27]

Whereas PAP might appear to be an obvious truth, it has been questioned by some philosophers. These philosophers contend (in one way or another) that what matters for moral responsibility is how the relevant choice or action is brought about, not whether the agent has alternative possibilities available to him. In contemporary philosophy, Harry Frankfurt has helped to focus the case against (PAP) with a set of examples with a characteristic structure.[28] These examples contain fail-safe mechanisms that (allegedly) both make it the case that the agent has no (relevant) alternative possibilities and also play no role in the agent's actual choice and action. Frankfurt says that if something plays no role in the agent's choice and action, then it cannot be relevant to his moral responsibility; thus, it would follow that the mechanisms in question both make it the case that the agent has no alternative possibilities and do not thereby threaten the agent's moral responsibility.

Here is a version of my favorite "Frankfurt-type case." Jones is in a voting booth deliberating about whether to vote for the Democrat or the Republican. After weighing reasons and deliberating in the "normal" way, he chooses to vote for the Democrat. Unknown to him, Black, a neurosurgeon with Democratic sympathies, has implanted a device in Jones's brain which monitors Jones's brain activities. If he is about to choose to vote Democratic, the device does not intervene. If, however, Jones is about to choose to vote Republican, the device

triggers an intervention which involves electronic stimulation of the brain sufficient to produce a choice to vote for the Democrat and an actual vote for the
Democrat.[29]

Now one might ask how the device can tell whether Jones is about to choose to
vote Republican or Democratic. Frankfurt himself did not say much about this difficult problem, except that "Black is an excellent judge of such things." We, can,
however, add a "prior sign" to the case as follows.[30] If Jones is about to choose at
$T2$ to vote for the Democrat at $T3$, he shows some involuntary sign—say a blush,
a furrowed brow, or a neurological pattern in his brain readable by some sort of
"neuroscope"—at $T1$. If it detects this, Black's device does not intervene. But if
Jones is about to choose at $T2$ to vote Republican at $T3$, he shows a different involuntary sign at $T1$. This would trigger Black's device to intervene and cause
Jones to choose at $T2$ to vote for the Democrat and actually to vote for the Democrat at $T3$.

It seems that Black's device is precisely the kind of fail-safe device described
above: it plays no role in Jones's deliberations, choice, or action, and yet its presence renders it true that Jones could not have done otherwise than choose and
vote Democratic. Indeed, it seems that in this case Jones freely chooses to vote
Democratic, freely votes Democratic, and can be considered morally responsible
for his choice and action, even though he does not have alternative possibilities
(given the presence of Black's device). This suggests that there is a kind of freedom or control—corresponding to choosing and acting freely—that does not require alternative possibilities, and that *this* sort of control (and not the
alternative-possibilities control) is the freedom-relevant condition necessary for
moral responsibility. There seem to be two kinds of freedom or control, and the
Frankfurt-type examples help us to prize them apart.[31] It appears, then, that we
have a counterexample to PAP.

A Dilemma for the Frankfurt-Type Examples

The suggestion (emerging from the Frankfurt-type examples) that moral responsibility does not require free will in the sense that involves alternative possibilities
has not been entirely irresistible. In fact, a huge literature has developed surrounding these examples.[32] Consider the following dilemma in response to the
Frankfurt-type examples.[33] Notice that in the typical presentation of the examples
(as above) it is not made *explicit* whether causal determinism obtains. So suppose
first that causal determinism obtains in the example. Now it would seem question-
begging to conclude straightforwardly from the example that Jones is morally responsible for voting for the Democrat; after all, the issue of whether causal
determinism is compatible with moral responsibility is in dispute. But if it is assumed that causal determinism is false, and specifically that there is no deterministic relationship between the prior sign at $T1$ and Jones's subsequent choice at $T2$,
then Jones would appear to have free will at (or just prior to) $T2$: he can at least
begin to choose to vote for the Democrat. After all, given the prior sign and the
laws of nature, it does *not* follow that Jones will choose at $T2$ to vote for the
Democrat (on the current assumption of causal indeterminism). So, the proponent

of the dilemma says that either Jones is not morally responsible or there are alternative possibilities for Jones: one does not have a single context in which it is *both* true that Jones has no alternative possibilities and is morally responsible for his choice and action.

This is indeed a worrisome challenge to the conclusion that I (and others) draw from the Frankfurt-type examples—that PAP is false. Elsewhere I have presented a strategy of response to the dilemma.[34] Here I wish briefly to sketch this response and then to consider an important objection to it.

A Response to the Dilemma

First consider the possibility that causal determinism is false (in the relevant way). Various philosophers have proposed that one can construct versions of the Frankfurt-type cases in which the agent is morally responsible and yet there are no alternatives at all, or at least no *robust* alternatives.[35] I think it is promising that such an example can be constructed, although I shall not attempt to defend this possibility here.

Suppose that causal determinism is true. That is, suppose that there is indeed a causally deterministic relationship between the sign exhibited at $T1$ and Jones's choice to vote for the Democrat at $T2$. Now it follows, given the argument for the incompatibility of causal determinism and the sort of control that involves alternative possibilities, that Jones does not have the power at $T2$ to refrain from choosing to vote Democratic at $T2$. It is not my strategy, however, simply to claim that Jones is obviously morally responsible for his choice; I agree that this would not be dialectically kosher.

Rather, I begin by suggesting that the fact that Black's device would intervene and ensure that Jones would choose to vote for the Democrat (and indeed vote for the Democrat), if Jones had shown a different sign at $T1$, does not in itself show that Jones is not morally responsible for his actual choice (if he is in fact not morally responsible). That is, I am not supposing at this point that Jones is morally responsible for his actual choice at $T2$ to vote for the Democrat. Rather, I am saying that the fact that he cannot do otherwise does not in itself (and apart from indicating or pointing to some *other* fact) make it the case that Jones is not morally responsible for his choice at $T2$.

It seems evident to me that the fact that Black's device would intervene in the counterfactual scenario and ensure that Jones choose to vote for the Democrat is *irrelevant* to the "grounding" of Jones's actual moral responsibility for choosing to vote for the Democrat (and actually doing so). Something grounds moral responsibility, in the sense in question, insofar as it explains (or helps to explain) why the agent is morally responsible, apart from simply being an indicator of something else that in fact explains the agent's moral responsibility. Black's counterfactual intervention does not make any difference as to Jones's moral responsibility; if Black's device were "subtracted" from the example (to use Frankfurt's phrase), this would not change my assessment of Jones's moral responsibility in any way. Thus, I think that the example renders it plausible (although it does not decisively establish) that Jones's lack of alternative possibilities is *irrelevant* to the *grounding* of Jones's moral responsibility.

It is important to be a bit more careful here. I have claimed that consideration of the example of Jones (a typical Frankfurt-type case) should first elicit the intuition that the fact that there is a fail-safe device present that would intervene in the counterfactual scenario is *irrelevant* to the grounding of Jones's moral responsibility. My contention is that this then *suggests* that even if Jones had *no* alternative possibilities at all, this would be irrelevant to the grounding of his moral responsibility. It would then follow that in a causally deterministic world, in which it is assumed that Jones has no alternative possibilities at all, his lack of alternative possibilities would be irrelevant to the grounding of his moral responsibility. That is, his lack of alternative possibilities cannot in itself and apart from indicating something else explain why Jones is not morally responsible, if Jones is in fact not morally responsible.

In my view, this then is the moral of the Frankfurt-type cases. They suggest that alternative possibilities are irrelevant to the grounding of moral responsibility. Thus they are an important step along the way toward arguing that causal determinism is compatible with moral responsibility. Of course, someone might say that alternative possibilities are a necessary condition for moral responsibility because their presence indicates *some other factor* (perhaps causal indeterminism in the actual sequence) that must be present for there to be moral responsibility.[36] This is a perfectly reasonable position, which can then be addressed; I shall briefly discuss this maneuver below. But it does not diminish the importance of the moral of the Frankfurt-type cases; in my view, once one establishes that alternative possibilities are irrelevant to the *grounding* of moral responsibility, it is considerably *easier* to argue that causal determinism (and the lack of alternative possibilities) is compatible with moral responsibility.

A Recent Objection and a Further Reply

Before I address the contention that alternative possibilities indicate some other factor that grounds moral responsibility, I wish to consider a recent objection to my strategy for dealing with the "deterministic" horn of the dilemmatic attack on the Frankfurt-type examples. My contention is that Black's presence and counterfactual intervention is irrelevant to the grounding of moral responsibility. But someone might grant this, while insisting that it is not pertinent, since it is not Black's counterfactual intervention, but the condition of the world at $T1$ (including the sign Jones exhibits) that makes it true that Jones does not have it in his power at $T2$ to choose to vote for the Democrat. If it is the condition of the world at $T1$ that makes it true that Jones cannot at $T2$ choose to vote for the Democrat, then it is not so obvious that what makes it the case that Jones cannot at $T2$ choose otherwise is irrelevant to the grounding of Jones's moral responsibility. This line of attack has been developed by Stewart Goetz.

Goetz says:

> [The Frankfurt-style example] creates the appearance that it is Black's device, which is in the alternative sequence of events, that makes it the case that Jones is not free to choose otherwise. This appearance is *illusory* because without the obtaining of

causal determinism in the actual sequence of events, the device cannot prevent Jones from making an alternative choice, and with causal determinism in the actual sequence of events it is not the device that prevents Jones from making an alternative choice. In short, if Jones is not free to choose otherwise, it is because of the occurrence of causal determinism in the actual sequence of events and not because of Black's device in the alternative sequence.[37]

Goetz goes on to say:

[Fischer's strategy] requires the truth of causal determinism in order to create the illusion that it is the presence of something in the alternative sequence of events (e.g., Black's device) that makes it the case that Jones is not free to choose otherwise. It is only through this illusion that one is tempted to endorse the conclusion of the first step of Fischer's argument, which is that the lack of alternative possibilities is not sufficient for the lack of moral responsibility, and, thereby, Jones might be morally responsible even though he is not free to choose otherwise. Once this illusion is exposed, one's initial conviction that the lack of an alternative choice is sufficient for the lack of moral responsibility is vindicated.[38]

Goetz's point could be put as follows. What really makes it the case that Jones cannot choose otherwise at T2 is the prior state of the world together with the laws of nature. In other words, what makes it the case that Jones lacks an alternative possibility at T2 is causal determination in the actual sequence. So it is quite beside the point that Black's counterfactual intervention is irrelevant to the grounding of Jones's moral responsibility; after all, it is not Black's counterfactual intervention that makes it the case that Jones cannot choose otherwise at T2. Thus we do not have a case in which the fact that the agent could not have chosen (or done) otherwise is irrelevant to the grounding of his moral responsibility.

Frankfurt-type scenarios are cases in which an action is causally overdetermined. The overdetermination is considered "preemptive," rather than "simultaneous." In simultaneous overdetermination, two causal sequences both operate and actually issue in the overdetermined action (or event). In preemptive overdetermination, some event is actually caused in a certain way, and it would have been caused in a different way had the actual causal sequence not taken place. So, in the Frankfurt-type scenario presented above, Black's device is part of what makes it the case that Jones's choice at T2 is preemptively overdetermined.

What is of note is that in these scenarios Jones's inability to choose (or do) otherwise is also overdetermined. (I would describe the overdetermination here as simultaneous, rather than preemptive; but is it delicate, as the thing in question is a fact—a modal fact—rather than a concrete action or event.) It is not only the act that is overdetermined; it is also the agent's lack of alternative possibilities. So, my response to Goetz is as follows.

In the Frankfurt-type scenario, two causes make it the case that Jones is unable to choose otherwise at T2: the prior condition of the world (together with the laws of nature) and Black's counterfactual intervention. What the examples show is that the mere fact that Jones is unable to choose otherwise does not in itself establish that Jones is not morally responsible for his choice. This is because Black's counterfactual intervention is one of the factors that make it the case that Jones is unable to choose otherwise at $T2$, and yet it is irrelevant to the grounding of Jones's moral responsibility. Considering this factor (the counterfactual intervention), and bracketing any other factor that might make it the case that Jones is unable to choose otherwise at $T2$, it seems to me that Jones may well be morally responsible for his action. The mere fact that he lacks alternative possibilities, then, cannot in itself be the reason that Jones is not morally responsible, if indeed he is not morally responsible.

Now of course it is also true that the prior condition of the world together with the natural laws makes it the case that Jones lacks alternative possibilities. But, given that the mere fact of lacking alternative possibilities does not in itself rule out moral responsibility, why should this way of lacking alternative possibilities rule out moral responsibility? Why exactly should the significance of causal determination be that it rules out alternative possibilities in a particular way?

In an interesting passage, Goetz states:

> The proponent of PAP thinks that the lack of the freedom to choose otherwise does not by itself explain the absence of moral responsibility. This is because he believes that when this lack obtains, its obtaining is itself explained by, and can only be explained by, the occurrence of causal determinism in the actual sequence of events. What the advocate of PAP believes, then, is that when an agent is not morally responsible because he is not free to choose otherwise, he lacks moral responsibility *not* simply because he is not free to choose otherwise but because he is not free to choose otherwise because of causal determinism.[39]

Precisely this move is made by Derk Pereboom:

> Even if it is not a necessary condition on moral responsibility that the agent could have done or chosen otherwise, the incompatibilist can still claim that one is not morally responsible for an action if one could not have done or chosen otherwise due to the choice's resulting from a deterministic causal process that traces back to factors beyond one's control.[40]

But why exactly does it *matter* that causal determination rules out alternative possibilities? If the mere fact of the lack of alternative possibilities does not in itself rule out moral responsibility, why would a particular *way* of expunging alternative possibilities rule out moral responsibility? Granted that causal determination is a certain way of taking away alternative possibilities. Why should it be thought that causal determination threatens moral responsibility in virtue of constituting a way of ruling out alternative possibilities? The Frankfurt-type examples, then, suggest that one needs to look in a different direction if one seeks to argue that causal determination rules out moral responsibility.

The dialectic could be put somewhat differently. There can be two different ways in which some factor renders an agent unable to choose or do otherwise (or eliminates alternative possibilities). In one way, the factor does not play a role in the actual sequence; it does not flow through the actual course of events. In another way, the factor does flow through the actual sequence. The Frankfurt-type scenarios are all cases in which the ability-undermining factor does not play a role in the actual sequence leading to the relevant choice and action. So it seems unfair to extrapolate from the Frankfurt-type cases to the other sort of cases; that is, even if we are inclined to say that the agent is morally responsible in the Frankfurt-type cases, it would not follow that the agent is morally responsible in a causally deterministic world.

To reply: I grant that the Frankfurt-type examples are not *decisive*. That is, they do not provide examples that would absolutely and uncontroversially decide the issue about the relationship between causal determinism and moral responsibility. But I certainly do not believe that it is reasonable to expect such examples here— or in any contentious area of philosophy! And, as I argued above, the Frankfurt-type examples suggest that if causal determination is indeed problematic, it is not so in virtue of flowing through the actual sequence and thereby ruling out alternative possibilities.

Source Incompatibilism

So far I have been primarily concerned with the issue of whether alternative possibilities are relevant to the *grounding* of moral responsibility. As I pointed out above, even if they are irrelevant to the grounding of responsibility, they may nevertheless be relevant to responsibility as a *sign* of something else that in fact grounds moral responsibility. Many years ago I emphasized that the mere fact that the Frankfurt-type examples show that alternative possibilities are not required for moral responsibility does *not* in itself show that causal determinism is compatible with moral responsibility.[41] I pointed out that causal determinism is a thesis about the "actual sequence," and thus that it does not follow from the falsity of PAP that causal determinism is compatible with moral responsibility.[42] As I put it:

> Both the compatibilist and the incompatibilist alike can unite in conceding that enough information is encoded in the actual sequence to ground our responsibility attributions; as philosophers we need to decode this information and see whether it is consistent with deterministic causation.[43]

In my subsequent work, I have explored various ways in which it might be thought that causal determination in the actual sequence rules out moral responsibility.[44] I have in the end concluded that causal determination in the actual sequence does not rule out moral responsibility.

Other philosophers have disagreed, contending that causal determination in the actual sequence rules out moral responsibility "directly" (and not in virtue of expunging alternative possibilities). Robert Kane has argued that in order to be morally responsible, we have to meet a condition of "ultimacy," according to which the "causal buck must stop here"; that is, we cannot be mere intermediate links in a causally deterministic sequence which begins prior to our births.[45] Similarly, Laura Ekstrom argues that the past and laws "push" us into our choices and actions if causal determinism is true. She thus argues that causal determination in the actual sequence is incompatible with moral responsibility.[46] Additionally, although Derk Pereboom believes that versions of the Frankfurt-type examples successfully show that PAP is false, he nevertheless defends the follow-ing principle:

> An action is free in the sense required for moral responsibility only if it is not pro-duced by a deterministic process that traces back to causal factors beyond the agent's control.[47]

I believe that none of the arguments purporting to show that causal determina-tion in the actual sequence rules out moral responsibility is particularly strong, al-though this of course is a highly contentious matter. One of the difficulties is to see how to *argue* for the incompatibility claim; after all, Pereboom's principle seems to be a simple *restatement* of incompatibilism about causal determinism and moral responsibility, not an argument for it. In any case, I would contend that the Frankfurt-type cases at least help us to make progress toward defending the com-patibility of causal determinism and moral responsibility insofar as they help us to take a very important first step: they render it plausible (although they do not de-cisively establish) that the sort of free will that involves alternative possibilities does not ground attributions of moral responsibility, that is, it does not in itself and apart from indicating some other factor explain why we are morally responsi-ble, if we are in fact morally responsible.

Ethical Judgments

Judgments of Deontic Morality

Above I pointed out that there are various accounts of the concept of moral re-sponsibility. On the "ledger view," if an agent is morally responsible, then he has a moral ledger—the marks correspond to various sorts of moral judgments. Some philosophers hold that these judgments include claims about what the agent ought and ought not to do, and what is right or wrong for the individual to do. These philosophers thus connect moral responsibility tightly to the appropriateness of judgments about ought, ought not, right, and wrong. Peter van Inwagen appears to make this sort of connection in the continuation of a passage quoted above:

> If someone charges you with, say, lying, and if you can convince him that it was sim-ply not within your power *not* to lie, then it would seem that you have done all that is necessary to absolve yourself of responsibility for lying. Your accuser cannot say, "I concede it was not within your power not to lie; none the less you ought not to have lied."[48]

On this sort of approach to moral responsibility, if (contrary to van Inwagen) one has successfully defended the compatibility of causal determinism (and the lack of the sort of free will that involves alternative possibilities) with moral re-sponsibility, one has thereby defended the compatibility of causal determinism (and the lack of free will) with judgments employing "ought," "ought not," "right," and "wrong." But one might accept an alternative account of the concept of moral responsibility, or even a ledger view according to which the relevant "marks" correspond to (say) "goodness" and "badness," but not "ought," "ought not," and so forth. If one accepted (say) a Strawsonian account of moral responsibility (or the sort of ledger view just sketched), it might be that causal determinism is compatible with moral responsibility but *not* with judgments employing "ought," "ought not," "right," and "wrong." This is precisely the view held by Ishtiyaque Haji. Haji accepts the conclusion of the Frankfurt-type cases that moral responsibility does not require alternative possibilities and further that it is compatible with causal determinism; but he rejects the contention that causal determinism is compatible with judgments employing "obligation," "ought," "ought not," "right," and "wrong."[49] (Following Haji, let us call the latter "judgments of deontic morality.") On this sort of view, the Strawsonian "reactive attitudes" are prized apart from the judgments of deontic morality, and whereas the former are compatible with causal determinism, the latter are not. (Note that Haji distinguishes judgments pertaining to notions such "goodness" and "badness" from the judgments of deontic morality; he is willing to concede that the former sorts of judgments are entirely compatible with causal determinism.)

Why might one think that the judgments of deontic morality are incompatible with causal determinism? I will treat "ought not" and "wrong" as interchangeable, and "ought" and "obligatory" as interchangeable. I shall lay out the argument with respect to "wrong." It will be easy to see how to construct parallel arguments for the other judgments of deontic morality. Here is a simple version of the argument:

1. Suppose some individual, John, does something morally wrong.
2. If John's Xing was wrong, then he ought to have done something else instead.
3. If John ought to have done something else instead, then he could have done something else instead.
4. So John could have done something else instead.
5. But if causal determinism is true, then John could not have done anything other than he actually did.
6. So, if causal determinism is true, it cannot be the case that John's Xing was wrong.[50]

This is a potent and disturbing argument. I have sought to argue that causal determinism is compatible with moral responsibility. This result would be considerably less interesting if causal determinism were nevertheless incompatible with the central judgments of deontic morality. There are however various ways of seeking to block the conclusion of the argument. I discuss the rejection of premise 2 in the next chapter.[51] Here, however, I shall focus on the rejection of premise 3 (and thus the rejection of the ought-implies-can maxim (henceforth, "the Maxim").

Copp's Defense of the Maxim

I believe that there are Frankfurt-type omissions cases that are relevantly similar to Frankfurt-type cases with respect to actions. That is, there are cases in which an agent is morally responsible for not Xing, although he cannot in fact X.[52] Some of these are cases in which an agent is blameworthy for not Xing and yet he cannot X. In fact, I believe that anyone who accepts the Frankfurt-type action cases must accept that there are such omissions cases.[53] Further, the basic intuitions elicited by the Frankfurt-type cases conflict with the Maxim and cast doubt on its intuitive plausibility. Although this certainly does not decisively refute the Maxim, it does suggest that it is not *ad hoc* for anyone who accepts that the Frankfurt-type cases show that moral responsibility does not require alternative possibilities to reject the Maxim.[54]

But rejection of the Maxim comes at a steep price. In the most detailed, sustained, and penetrating discussion of the motivation for the Maxim of which I am aware, David Copp contends that it is preferable to preserve the Maxim than to reject PAP on the basis of the Frankfurt-type cases (or on any other basis). Copp presents two primary arguments on behalf of the Maxim, and it will be useful to discuss each of them.

Copp contends that there is a conflict between the interpretation of the Frankfurt-type cases according to which they show that moral responsibility does not require alternative possibilities and the Maxim. According to Copp, "[This] is not a conflict between intuition and a recherché theoretical proposition. It is a conflict among intuitions."[55] Copp says:

> The most basic motivation for the Maxim, it seems to me, begins with the thought that it would be unfair to expect a person to do something, or to demand or require that she do it, if she lacked the ability to do it. This thought is about what we might call "agent-requirements," which arise in cases in which an authoritative agent requires someone under her authority or jurisdiction to do something. An example might be a situation in which a boss requires an employee to do something that the employee lacks the ability to do. A supervisor at the post office might demand that a mail carrier cook a soufflé for everyone in the post office in the next five minutes when the mail carrier does not even know what a soufflé is. We can imagine many similar cases, including cases in which a parent expects a child to do something she cannot do, or a teacher requires a student to do something she cannot do, or a sergeant requires a recruit to do something she cannot do. The intuition is that agent-requirements of this kind are morally unfair when the person of whom the demand is made lacks the ability to comply.[56]

Copp goes on to claim that although the intuition elicited above is about "agent-requirements" rather than "moral requirements," he contends that a similar point applies to moral requirements. As Copp puts it, "if there would be unfairness in the latter case [the mere agent-requirement case], then there is surely a kind of unfairness in the moral requirement in the former case even if there is no agent who is being unfair."[57] So the first argument in favor of the Maxim is the intuition that it would be unfair to morally require someone to do something if he cannot do the thing in question.

Copp's second argument in favor of the Maxim is based on metaethical considerations about the "point" of moral requirements. Copp says:

> The heart of the argument is roughly as follows: any moral theory must somehow account for, or make room for, the intuition that there is a *point* to requiring an action, namely, crudely, to get it done. Clearly, moreover, an action will not be done if the prospective actor cannot perform it.

The argument can be summarized as follows. If an agent is morally required to do A in a particular situation, then all other options she faces are morally ruled out. If the agent cannot do A, then doing A is not among her options. Hence, if an agent is morally required to do A but cannot do A, then *all* of her options are morally ruled out. But information that an agent is morally required to do something provides her with guidance among her options by distinguishing between options that are morally ruled out and options that are not morally ruled out. If all of an agent's options are morally ruled out by a moral requirement, then information about the requirement cannot provide her with such guidance. Given then that moral requirements have a characteristic relevance to our decisions, by distinguishing between options that are morally ruled out and options that are not morally ruled out, it follows that if a person cannot do A, it is not the case that she is morally required to do A. That is, the Maxim follows from the intuition about the relevance of moral requirements to decision-making.[58]

Copp thus offers two strategies for motivating the Maxim: the fairness argument and the argument from the relevance of moral requirements to decision making. He thus points out that if one favors one's intuition that the Frankfurt-type examples show (albeit not decisively) that PAP is to be rejected, then one must give up strong intuitions about fairness and the relationship between morality and practical reasoning. Copp thinks that giving up these latter intuitions would be too steep a price to pay. In accepting PAP, however, Copp admits that his view might be open to incompatibilist worries; if causal determinism turned out to be true along with PAP, then there emerges the danger that no one could legitimately be accountable (blameworthy) for what they do. In the end, Copp concludes that "any adequate analysis of the ability to act must be compatibilist. It must be such that the ability to do something other than what one actually does is compatible with determinism."[59]

Let us first consider Copp's argument from fairness. More specifically, the contention is that it would be unfair to hold someone blameworthy for failing to do X, if he could not do X. In order to bolster this judgment, Copp invokes an example in which it does seem unfair to require a mail carrier to cook a soufflé for everyone in the post office in five minutes. But I would reply that it is crucial to distinguish two importantly different sorts of omissions: "simple" and "complex." If one focuses solely on complex omissions, it does indeed seem as if it would be unfair to hold an individual blameworthy for failing to do X if he is unable to do X. But my intuitions about *simple* omissions are quite different.[60]

Consider an example offered by Harry Frankfurt:

Imagine that a person—call him "Stanley"—deliberately keeps himself very still. He refrains, for some reason, from moving his body at all. . . . [S]uppose that here is someone with a powerful interest in having Stanley refrain from making any deliberate movements, who arranges things in such a way that Stanley will be stricken with general paralysis if he shows any inclination to move. Nonetheless, Stanley may keep himself still quite on his own altogether independently of this person's schemes. Why should Stanley not be morally responsible for keeping still, in that case, just as much as if there had been nothing to prevent him from moving had he chosen to do so?[61]

I agree with Frankfurt here. And surely Stanley could be considered blameworthy should something morally important hang on his moving his body rather than keeping still.

Stanley's not moving his body, or refraining from moving, is a "simple omission": the omission is entirely constituted by his failure to move his body. There are many more such omissions, and in these cases it is plausible that the agents are indeed morally responsible—and potentially morally blameworthy—although they could not have refrained from keeping still.[62]

I do not have any "proof" of my contention that in simple omissions, an agent can be blameworthy for failing to do X, even though he could not have done X. It seems to me however that this is a completely reasonable intuition, shared by many philosophers and supported by a range of examples. I agree, however, that it seems upon initial consideration that in cases of complex omissions, an agent cannot be blameworthy for failing to do X unless he can in fact do X.

My purpose here is simply to suggest that *there are* cases in which an agent can legitimately be considered blameworthy for failing to do X although he could not have done X. I would contend that Copp fails to see this because he focuses entirely on a proper subset of cases—the complex omissions. If I am correct, then the argument from fairness is vitiated—there are cases in which it would not be unfair to blame someone for failing to do something he could not do (and never could do).

Now I suppose someone could say that because it is obviously unfair to blame someone for his failure in the complex omissions cases, we should conclude that it would *also* be unfair to blame the agent in the simple omissions cases. But I think that this gets the dialectic wrong: we are supposed to be generating general principles by reference to intuitions about *all* of the relevant cases. It would seem inappropriate to generate such a principle based on a proper subset of the cases and then apply it to *all* of the cases, even when it does not seem to yield the correct results in all of the cases.

What would be ideal is a theory that explains exactly why the agents are indeed morally responsible in the simple omissions cases and not morally responsible in the complex omissions cases. Such an explanation would obviously not invoke the notion of inability to do otherwise, lest it lead to implausible results in the simple omissions cases. I (and my coauthor) have offered just such a theory of moral responsibility for omissions; on this approach, moral responsibility is associated with freedom (or control), but not the sort of freedom (or control) that involves alternative possibilities.[63] Quite apart from whether this theory is adequate, my point here is that Copp has not really motivated the central claim of the argument for fairness: he has relied on only a proper subset of the relevant data.

Copp's second argument in favor of the Maxim pertains to the role of moral requirements in guiding action. I agree that moral requirements play a distinctive and important role in guiding our practical reasoning (and, thus, our behavior). But, as above in our discussion of practical reasoning and deliberation, it is crucial to distinguish between genuine metaphysical possibilities and possibilities that are, for all the agent knows, possibilities. An "epistemic possibility" is not ruled out by the agent's knowledge. Indispensable to the proper analysis of deliberation and also the Frankfurt-type examples is the fact that one's metaphysical possibilities (the paths that are genuinely available to one) may diverge from one's epistemic possibilities (that paths that are, for all one knows, available to one). I would contend that moral requirements rule out certain of the courses of action that are, for all we know, open to us—certain epistemic possibilities.

Recall Copp's argument, which begins as follows:

> If an agent is morally required to do A in a particular situation, then all other options she faces are morally ruled out. If the agent cannot do A, then doing A is not among her options. Hence, if an agent is morally required to do A but cannot do A, then *all* of her options are morally ruled out. But information that an agent is morally required to do something provides her with guidance among her options by distinguishing between options that are morally ruled out and options that are not morally ruled out.

Given the distinction between the two different kinds of possibilities, the argument becomes:

> Given an agent is morally required to do A in a particular situation, then all other epistemic options she faces are morally ruled out. If the agent cannot do A, then doing A is not among her metaphysical options. Hence, if an agent is morally required to do A but cannot do A, then *all* of her options are morally ruled out. But information that an agent is morally required to do something provides her with guidance among her options by distinguishing between options that are morally ruled out and options that are not morally ruled out.

It is evident where the problems lie. The conclusion that if an agent is morally required to do A but cannot do A, then *all* of her options are morally ruled out, infelicitously elides the distinction between epistemic and metaphysical options. From the mere fact that an agent lacks a certain metaphysical option it does *not* follow that she lacks the corresponding epistemic option. So, from the mere fact that an agent in fact *cannot* do A, it does not follow that she knows that she cannot do A. Thus, all that follows from the moral requirement and the metaphysical fact is that all of the agent's epistemic alternatives *except* A are ruled out. But there is nothing problematic about this; and now the moral requirement can have its distinctive role in guiding deliberation and action. Moral requirements insert themselves into the space of epistemic possibilities, not directly into the space of metaphysical possibilities.

I conclude that despite his noteworthy efforts, David Copp has not successfully presented a compelling motivation for the Maxim. If we reject the Maxim, we can reject PAP. And we are thus not pushed toward a compatibilist account of freedom; as I explained above, a compatibilist must say that we are free either to "change" the past or the natural laws. That is, the compatibilist must *deny* that our freedom is the freedom to extend the given past, holding the laws of nature fixed. But this is quite implausible.

Copp believes that there is independent justification for a rejection of incompatibilism:

> Suppose that it is the championship football game and the quarterback throws a pass to Julian. The pass is incomplete, but when Julian returns to the huddle, he says he *could* have caught the pass. This happens several times in the course of the afternoon, let us suppose. I want to consider four plays of this kind. In each, let us suppose, once the football leaves the quarterback's hands, it follows a causally determined trajectory all the way to the ground. In the first, the quarterback throws the ball inaccurately and much too hard and it bounces off the ground a yard behind Julian. In this case, the quarterback and the other players in the huddle agree that Julian could not have caught the pass. It was a bad pass. Julian is mistaken to think he could have caught it. In the second play, Julian is interfered with by an opposing player just as he reaches for the ball. He is thrown off stride and misses the ball by inches. In this case, everyone in the huddle agrees with Julian that he could have caught the ball if only he hadn't been interfered with. It was a good pass and he would have been in a position to catch it if he hadn't been interfered with. But the quarterback insists that, *given* that Julian was interfered with he couldn't have caught the ball, for he was thrown off stride at the last moment and could not have recovered before the ball hit the ground. In the third play, the quarterback throws a good pass and Julian is in position to catch it, but he holds his hands too rigidly and the ball bounces out of his grip. Everyone in the huddle is disappointed. They agree that Julian could have caught the ball. Julian says he lost his concentration. The final case is more complicated. The temperature had been dropping all afternoon. This time, late in the game, when the ball reaches Julian his hands are stiff with the cold. Once again, the ball bounces out of his grip. He fails to hold on to it. Julian says that nevertheless he could have caught the ball because he could have worn his gloves, or he could have rubbed his hands continuously until the play began. His team-mates agree that he could have caught the ball.[64]

Copp here begins with cases that do not involve moral responsibility or blameworthiness, and he wants to extend the point to the latter sorts of cases. He thinks it is clear that the "degree of control that Julian had over what happened differed from play to play despite the fact that a deterministic process led to the incompletion of the pass in each of the four plays."[65] In the first two cases Copp feels that Julian could not have caught the ball, but in the latter two cases he could have (in some intuitive sense). Copp objects to the incompatibilist's conflation of all of these cases (in a causally deterministic world).

I reply that the four cases are importantly different, even in a causally deterministic world. But it does not follow that we must mark that difference by invoking the notion of freedom to do otherwise (or the sort of control that involves alternative possibilities). Again, I would employ the notion of control of one's failures or omissions (where this sort of control does not require alternative possibilities). In the first two cases, Julian does not control his failures in the relevant sense of "control." In the latter two cases, he does control his failures, again, in the sense of control that does not require alternative possibilities. One can have control *of* an upshot, without having control *over* it. It is a mistake to think that the *only* way of invoking the broad notions of freedom or control to distinguish the four sorts of cases is to make use of the sort of control that implies alternative possibilities. On my approach, in contrast to Copp's, one does *not* have to deny that our freedom is the freedom to add to a fixed past, given the natural laws. As argued above, *any* compatibilist analysis of the freedom to do otherwise in a deterministic world is committed to denying that this freedom is the freedom to add to a given past, holding the laws of nature fixed. But our intuitive picture is that the future possibilities branch off a single past, and that we are not so powerful as to be able to alter the laws of nature. Embracing this picture is a rather important theoretical advantage of an "actual-sequence" approach to moral responsibility.

Judgments of Deontic Morality and Moral Responsibility

I suppose that someone might dig in one's heals and simply insist that "ought implies can" is a conceptual truth. It must be admitted that my argument against the Maxim is not decisive. If the Maxim is indeed valid, then I would grant that causal determinism rules out the judgments of deontic morality. Would this be a disastrous result for a "semicompatibilist," that is, someone who believes that causal determinism is compatible with moral responsibility, even though it rules out the sort of free will that involves alternative possibilities? Perhaps (on the assumption that the ought-implies-can maxim is valid) one will have to bite the bullet and accept that the interconnected circle of judgments of deontic morality is inapplicable in a causally deterministic world. Note, however, that this still leaves room for robust moral responsibility, where this may include reactive attitudes such as resentment, indignation, respect, and so forth.

More important, it seems to me that it leaves room for significant moral judgments, even if they are not the special "judgments of deontic morality." For example, as I said above, the goal of practical reasoning is to figure out what we have sufficient reason to do. We can make the judgment in a particular context (even in a causally deterministic world) that an individual has sufficient reason to do X. It does not seem to me that this judgment entails that he *can* do X. Whereas it is plausible (apart from argumentation of the sort sketched above) that ought implies can, I do not think it is similarly plausible that "having a sufficient" reason implies "can."[66] Thus, even in a world in which causal determinism is true, presumably we can make judgments about what agents have a sufficient reason to do, and we can criticize them for failing to do what they have sufficient reason to do. Presumably individuals are morally blameworthy when they fail to do what they have sufficient reason to do, where they can reasonably be expected to recognize the sufficiency of the reason and they do not know that they will not do the thing in question (i.e., it is epistemically open to the agent to do it). All of the above is completely compatible with the truth of causal determinism.[67]

The W-Defense

David Widerker has argued on behalf of both PAP and the Maxim. One of Widerker's recurring themes is the "W-defense."[68] According to the W-defense, if an agent is blameworthy for some behavior (a choice, act, omission, and so forth), it must be the case that there is an answer (apart from "nothing") to the question, "What should he have done instead?" If there is no positive answer to this question, then it cannot be the case (according to the proponent of the W-defense) that the agent is blameworthy for the behavior in question. Of course, if the Maxim is true, and causal determinism obtains, then one is never free to do otherwise; it would follow that if causal determinism is true, no one is blameworthy, on Widerker's view.

In reply, I would say that Widerker is employing an element of the alternative-possibilities framework; but if one accepts the actual-sequence approach to moral responsibility, one will want to resist all elements of this framework. First, an actual-sequence theorist may reject the Maxim (as suggested above). This completely disarms the W-defense. Second, the actual-sequence theorist may accept the Maxim and say that an agent is blameworthy based on facts about the actual sequence rather than claims about what he ought to have done instead. So, an actual-sequence theorist might say that an agent is blameworthy insofar as his practical reasoning fails to meet some standard (that it is reasonable to expect people to meet). Perhaps the agent was insufficiently attentive to reasons that exist in the relevant situation, or perhaps the agent failed to weigh some reasons appropriately. We can make these judgments quite apart from supposing that an agent should have (and thus could have, given the Maxim) done otherwise. An agent would be blameworthy, on this view, in virtue of a defective exercise of (unimpaired) practical reasoning (or perhaps even a failure to engage in practical reasoning where we would expect someone to do so). On this view, the actual-sequence theorist gives up the circle of "deontic judgments" but keeps a robust sort of moral responsibility.

Now Widerker might protest. He might ask what it is to be "insufficiently attentive to reasons." He might claim that to be insufficiently attentive to reasons implies that one should have been more attentive, and so forth. But this is precisely where the actual-sequence theorist disagrees; the actual-sequence theorist contends that there is a perfectly good sense in which someone can be criticized for being insufficiently attentive to reasons, without its being the case that he could have been more attentive. On this sort of view, one is criticizable for failing to meet a certain standard. This is precisely the intuition elicited by the Frankfurt-type examples.

Conclusion

Causal determinism threatens our intuitive and natural view of ourselves as having free will in the sense that involves genuinely available alternative possibilities. It threatens the commonsense view that the future is a garden of forking paths. For all we know, causal determinism might turn out to be true. In this paper I have explored the question of what would be lost in a world without free will of this sort. Would there still be a point to deliberation and practical reasoning? Could there be moral responsibility and ethical judgments?

The discovery that causal determinism is true would significantly alter our picture of ourselves: in my view, giving up the view that the future is a garden of forking paths is a major change, with important resonances in the way we understand and couch our deliberation, moral responsibility, and ethical judgments. But I do not believe that we would need entirely to jettison any of these aspects of our moral lives. I believe that deliberation, moral responsibility, and judgments of deontic morality are compatible with causal determinism and the lack of free will (in the sense involving alternative possibilities, understood as above).

Other philosophers are not so sanguine, and there is a bewildering distribution of views on these issues. As we have seen, Peter van Inwagen is a philosopher who believes that causal determinism and the lack of free will would rule out both moral responsibility and judgments of deontic morality, as well as render us inconsistent every time we deliberate. Thus, van Inwagen and I represent, as it were, "corner positions." There are various "in-between" views. Ishtiyaque Haji contends that causal determinism and the lack of alternative possibilities are completely compatible with robust moral responsibility, but *not* with judgments of deontic morality. In contrast, Derk Pereboom is willing to concede that robust moral responsibility does not require free will in the sense that involves alternative possibilities, but he insists that causal determinism rules out moral responsibility.[69] Nevertheless, he believes that causal determinism is compatible with judgments of deontic morality. Similarly, Saul Smilansky holds that causal determinism rules out robust moral responsibility, but not the judgments of deontic morality. Both Pereboom and Smilansky argue that although causal determinism would rule out robust moral responsibility, it still leaves room for something akin to moral responsibility—something significant and valuable. It also leaves room for various ethical judgments. So whereas Haji thinks that the more significant threat from causal determinism is to the judgments of deontic morality, Pereboom and Smilansky argue quite the opposite. In contrast, both van Inwagen and I view the threats from causal determinism as equal in strength (although we come to opposite conclusions).

A recurrent theme has been the difference between an agent's epistemic possibilities and metaphysical possibilities, given the truth of causal determinism. This disparity is crucial to understanding practical reasoning and deliberation in a causally deterministic world. It is also an indispensable ingredient in the description of the Frankfurt-type examples. Additionally, the non-identity of these two sets of possibilities explains how moral requirements can play their signature role of guiding action, even in a causally deterministic world. On my view, the collapse of these two sets into one—the set of metaphysical possibilities—would be as dramatic as the collapse of the wave pocket in quantum mechanics. My view is the opposite of the famous biblical contention that the truth shall make us free. But this is really not surprising: if I genuinely knew all my future choices and behavior, then it would seem to me that I *could* just sit back and let the future unroll.

John Searle writes:

> Suppose you go into a restaurant, and the waiter brings you the menu. You have a choice between, let's say, veal chops and spaghetti; you cannot say: "Look, I am a determinist, che sara, sara. I will just wait and see what I order! I will wait to see what my beliefs and desires cause."[70]

Given the fact that the sets of metaphysical and epistemic possibilities are not identical, no determinist need reason in the indicated way. But if we collapse the sets into one, "che sarà, sarà" would not be inappropriate, or out of tune.[71]

NOTES

1. For a philosophical defense of the notion that causal determinism is true, see Ted Honderich, *A Theory of Determinism*, 2 vols. (Oxford: Oxford University Press, 1988).

2. I here closely follow the presentation in John Martin Fischer, "Recent Work on Moral Responsibility," *Ethics* 110 (1999): 93–139, esp. 100. The argument is presented more carefully and critically evaluated in, for example, Peter van Inwagen, *An Essay on Free Will* (Oxford: Clarendon, 1983); Carl Ginet, *On Action* (Cambridge: Cambridge University Press, 1990); and John Martin Fischer, *The Metaphysics of Free Will: An Essay on Control* (Oxford: Blackwell, 1994). There is a discussion of this argument, with bibliographic references, in Fischer, "Recent Work on Moral Responsibility."

3. I present this version in Fischer, *Metaphysics of Free Will*, pp. 88–94.

4. For extensive discussion, see Fischer, *Metaphysics of Free Will*, and "Recent Work on Moral Responsibility."

5. Richard Taylor, *Metaphysics*, 3rd ed. (Englewood Cliffs, N.J.: Prentice-Hall, 1983), 38–9, esp. 39.

6. Van Inwagen, *Essay on Free Will*, p. 155.

7. Ibid., p. 158.

8. Ibid., p. 154.

9. For a helpful and illuminating discussion, see Hilary Bok, *Freedom and Responsibility* (Princeton, N.J.: Princeton University Press, 1998), pp. 109–14.

10. John R. Searle, *Rationality in Action* (Cambridge: MIT Press, 2001), p. 62.

11. Ibid., 71–72.

12. I am indebted to David Copp for this point.

13. G. W. Leibniz, *Theodicy*, trans. E. M. Huggard and C. J. Gerhardt (La Salle, Ill.: Open Court, 1985).

14. As David Copp has pointed out in correspondence, even if I knew whom I would vote for, I might care to know why I would vote for this person and whether I have good reasons. This might give me a reason to make up my mind even if I know whom I will vote for.

15. Searle, *Rationality in Action*, pp. 72–73.

16. Ibid., pp. 285–86.

17. Bok, *Freedom and Responsibility*, p. 160.

18. Ibid. 161. The Korsgaard quotation is from Christine Korsgaard, "Creating the Kingdom of Ends," in *Creating the Kingdom of Ends*, ed. Christine Korsgaard (Cambridge: Cambridge University Press, 1996). For more on Korsgaard's two-perspective approach, see "Morality as Freedom" in the same volume.

19. Bok, *Freedom and Responsibility*, p. 161.

20. Various philosophers wish to distinguish some sort of "proto-belief" state, such as "taking," or "accepting," that falls short of being a genuine belief; but if this is what regarding consists in, it is still unclear why it cannot conflict with the deliverances of theoretical reason.

21. John Martin Fischer, "Book Review of Hilary Bok, *Freedom and Responsibility*," *Mind* 110 (2001): 432–38, esp. 438; and R. Jay Wallace, "Book Review of Hilary Bok, *Freedom and Responsibility*," *Philosophical Review* 109 (2000): 592–95.

22. The concept of moral responsibility is discussed at greater length in John Martin Fischer and Mark Ravizza, *Responsibility and Control: A Theory of Moral Responsibility* (Cambridge: Cambridge University Press, 1998), and Fischer, "Recent Work on Moral Responsibility."

23. For a helpful discussion of such views, see Michael J. Zimmerman, *An Essay on Moral Responsibility* (Totowa, N.J.: Rowman and Littlefield, 1988), p. 38.

24. Marina Oshana, "Ascriptions of Responsibility," *American Philosophical Quarterly*, 34 (1997): 71–83.

25. Peter Strawson, "Freedom and Resentment," *Proceedings of the British Academy* 48, (1962): 187–211. There are particularly detailed and helpful discussions of Strawson's approach in Paul Russell, *Freedom and Moral Sentiment: Hume's Way of Naturalizing Responsibility* (New York: Oxford University Press, 1995); and R. Jay Wallace, *Responsibility and the Moral Sentiments* (Cambridge: Harvard University Press, 1994).

26. A classic discussion of this principle is in Harry Frankfurt, "Alternate Possibilities and Moral Responsibility," *Journal of Philosophy* 66 (1969): 829–39.

27. Van Inwagen, *Essay on Free Will*, pp. 161–62. Van Inwagen goes on to say, "It would be hard to find a more powerful and persuasive argument than this little argument" (162).

28. Frankfurt, "Alternate Possibilities and Moral Responsibility."

29. Robert Allen has brought to my attention the following amusing newspaper story: "*Correction of Sorts:* Last week I quoted an anonymous editor of one of the Detroit-area papers taken over last summer by the New Jersey–based Journal Register Co. as saying he was told 'every editor would endorse Bush or nobody.' Garry Gilbert, executive editor of the Oakland Press, another JRC paper, told me 'our endorsement of Bush was made by the editorial board with no interference from outside the paper.' I believe him—but had his board gone the other way, I still do not believe he would have been allowed to endorse the Democrat." (Jack Lessenberry, *Metro Times* (Detroit), November 11, 2004).

I take it, then, that those who worry about the employment of hypothetical examples will not object to the Frankfurt examples!

30. This is David Blumenfeld's innovation. See David Blumenfeld, "The Principle of Alternate Possibilities," *Journal of Philosophy* 67 (1971): 339–44.

31. Frankfurt distinguishes between freedom of choice and freedom of action, on the one hand, and choosing freely and acting freely, on the other. The former notions imply alternative possibilities (freedom to choose otherwise and freedom to do otherwise), whereas the latter do not. I (and Mark Ravizza) distinguish between "regulative control," which implies alternative possibilities, and "guidance control," which does not, in Fischer and Ravizza, *Responsibility and Control*. We seek to give detailed accounts of guidance control of actions, omissions, and consequences.

32. For a compendious (but nevertheless incomplete) discussion, see Fischer, "Recent Work on Moral Responsibility"; also see the essays in *Moral Responsibility and Alternative Possibilities*, ed. David Widerker and Michael McKenna (Aldershot, England: Ashgate, 2003).

33. Roughly this sort of argument is in Robert Kane, *Free Will and Values* (Albany: State University of New York Press, 1985) and *The Significance of Free Will* (New York: Oxford University Press, 1996), esp. pp. 142–45; David Widerker, "Libertarianism and Frankfurt's Attack on the Principle of Alternative Possibilities," *Faith and Philosophy*, 12 (1995): 113–18, and "Libertarianism and Frankfurt's Attack on the Principle of Alternative Possibilities," *Philosophical Review* 104 (1995): 247–61; Carl Ginet, "In Defense of the Principle of Alternative Possibilities: Why I Don't Find Frankfurt's Argument Convincing," *Philosophical Perspectives* 10 (1996): 403–17; and Keith Wyma, "Moral Responsibility and Leeway for Action," *American Philosophical Quarterly* 34 (1997): 57–70.

34. See, especially, Fischer, "Recent Work on Moral Responsibility," pp. 112–17, and John Martin Fischer, "Frankfurt-Style Compatibilism," in *Contours of Agency: Essays on Themes from Harry Frankfurt*, ed. Sarah Buss and Lee Overton (Cambridge: MIT Press, 2002), pp. 1–26 (chapter 6 in this volume).

35. For some recent attempts, see the essays in Widerker and McKenna, *Moral Responsibility and Alternative Possibilities*. Also see Fischer, "Recent Work on Moral Responsibility," for a survey.

36. See, for example, Michael Della Rocca, "Frankfurt, Fischer and Flickers," *Nous* 32 (1998): 99–105; and Laura Ekstrom, "Protecting Incompatibilist Freedom," *American Philosophical Quarterly* 35 (1998): 281–91, and *Free Will: A Philosophical Study* (Boulder, Colo.: Westview Press, 2000), esp. pp. 181–214.

37. Stewart Goetz, "Frankfurt-Style Counterexamples and Begging the Question," *Midwest Studies in Philosophy* 29 (forthcoming 2005), p. 4.

38. Ibid., pp. 6–7.

39. Ibid., p. 7.

40. Derk Pereboom, *Living without Free Will* (Cambridge: Cambridge University Press, 2001), p. 3.

41. John Martin Fischer, "Responsibility and Control," *Journal of Philosophy* 89 (1982): 24–40.

42. Subsequently, such philosophers as Robert Kane and Derk Pereboom have emphasized this point. See Robert Kane, *Significance of Free Will*, and Derk Pereboom, *Living without Free Will*.

43. Fischer, "Responsibility and Control," p. 40.

44. See chapter 2 of this book, and Fischer, "Frankfurt-Style Compatibilism."

45. Kane, *Significance of Free Will*.

46. Ekstrom, "Protecting Incompatibilist Freedom," and *Free Will: A Philosophical Study*.

47. Pereboom, *Living Without Free Will*, p. 3.

48. Van Inwagen, *Essay on Free Will*, p. 161.

49. Ishtiyaque Haji, *Moral Appraisability* (New York: Oxford University Press, 1998), and *Deontic Morality and Control* (New York: Cambridge University Press, 2002).

50. For helpful and illuminating discussions of essentially this basic argument, see Haji, *Moral Appraisability* and *Deontic Morality and Control*; David Widerker, "Frankfurt on 'Ought Implies Can' and Alternative Possibilities," *Analysis* 51 (1991): 222–24; David Copp, "Defending the Principle of Alternate Possibilities: Blameworthiness and Moral Responsibility," *Nous* 31 (1997): 441–56; and Pereboom, *Living without Free Will*, 141–48.

51. The paper from which chapter 11 of this book was taken was written as a reply to Gideon Yaffe, "'Ought-Implies-Can' and the Principle of Alternative Possibilities," *Analysis* 59 (1999): 218–22.

52. See Fischer and Ravizza, *Responsibility and Control*, pp. 123–50.

53. Ibid.; and Harry Frankfurt, "An Alleged Asymmetry between Actions and Omissions," *Ethics* 104 (1994): 620–23.

54. For critical discussion of my argument, see Haji, *Deontic Morality and Control*, pp. 43–47.

55. David Copp, "'Ought' Implies 'Can,' Blameworthiness, and the Principle of Alternative Possibilities," in Widerker and McKenna, *Moral Responsibility and Alternative Possibilities*, pp. 265–300, esp. p. 271.

56. Copp, "'Ought' Implies 'Can,'" p. 271.

57. Ibid., p. 272.

58. Ibid., pp. 272, 274.

59. Ibid., p. 295.

60. I and Ravizza distinguish between simple and complex omissions, and develop accounts of moral responsibility for both types of omissions, in Fischer and Ravizza, *Responsibility and Control*, esp. pp. 123–50.

61. Frankfurt, 'An Alleged Asymmetry," esp. pp. 620–21.

62. Some such examples are presented in Alison McIntyre, "Compatibilists Could Have Done Otherwise: Responsibility and Negative Agency," *Philosophical Review* 103 (1994): 453–88; Walter Glannon, "Responsibility and the Principle of Possible Action," *Journal of Philosophy* 92 (1995): 261–74; and Randolph Clarke, "Ability and Responsibility for Omissions," *Philosophical Studies* 73 (1994): 195–208; they are discussed in Fischer and Ravizza, *Responsibility and Control*, pp. 123–50.

63. Fischer and Ravizza, *Responsibility and Control*, pp. 123–50 (chapter 4 in this volume). The theory offers a systematic approach to responsibility for actions, omissions, and consequences; it employs the notion of "guidance control" rather than "regulative control." (The latter sort of control requires alternative possibilities, whereas the former does not.) The theory is systematic in the sense that the accounts of guidance control of consequences and omissions build on and extend the account of guidance control of actions.

64. Copp, " 'Ought' Implies 'Can,' " p. 293.

65. Ibid.

66. I owe this suggestion to a conversation with Randolph Clarke.

67. I want to note a puzzling feature of the above analysis. I contend that whereas it is at least plausible that ought implies can, there is no similar plausibility to the claim that having a sufficient reason to X implies the power to X. The puzzle comes form observing that it is sometimes thought that "ought" can be analyzed in terms of having a sufficient reason. That is, it is sometimes suggested that "S ought to X" is true just in case S has a sufficient reason (or perhaps a sufficient reason of a certain sort) to X. But if this analysis is correct, there should not be an asymmetry in the entailments of the sort I have described. I am not sure what to make of this. It seems to suggest either that the asymmetry in the entailments is illusory, or that the proposed analysis of "ought" is incorrect.

68. See, for example, David Widerker, "Blameworthiness and Frankfurt's Argument against the Principle of Alternative Possibilities," in *Moral Responsibility and Alternative Possibilities*, ed. David Widerker and Michael McKenna (Aldershot, England: Ashgate, 2003).

69. For similar views, see David Hunt, "Moral Responsibility and Avoidable Action," *Philosophical Studies* 97 (2000): 195–227; and Eleonore Stump, "Sanctification, Hardening of the Heart, and Frankfurt's Concept of the Will," in John Martin Fischer and Mark Ravizza, eds., *Perspectives on Moral Responsibility* (Ithaca, N.Y.: Cornell University Press, 1993), pp. 211–34. "Intellect, Will, and the Principle of Alternate Possibilities," in *Christian Theism and the Problems of Philosophy*, ed. Michael D. Beaty (Notre Dame, Ind. University of Notre Dame Press, 1990), pp. 354–85, and "Alternative Possibilities and Moral Responsibility: The Flicker of Freedom," *Journal of Ethics* 3 (1999): 299–324.

70. Searle, *Rationality in Action*, p. 14. Searle goes on to argue that the very refusal to exercise one's freedom here would itself be an exercise of freedom.

71. There may be cases in which an agent knows in advance what he or she will choose (and do), because choosing otherwise would be "unthinkable." Various authors believe that such "volitional necessity" is compatible with moral responsibility. See Harry Frankfurt, "Rationality and the Unthinkable," in *The Importance of What We Care About*, ed. Harry Frankfurt (Cambridge: Cambridge University Press, 1988), pp. 177–90; and Susan Wolf,

Freedom within Reason (Oxford: Oxford University Press, 1990). For a helpful discussion, see Gary Watson, "Volitional Necessities," in *Contours of Agency: Essays on Themes from Harry Frankfurt*, ed. Sarah Buss and Lee Overton (Cambridge: MIT Press), pp. 129–59. If such volitional necessity exists, and if it makes literally true that one can know what one will choose in the future, and if it is indeed true that the relevant agents are morally responsible for their choices (and *not* in virtue of past choices, of which it was true that it was epistemically possible for the agent to choose otherwise), then perhaps there is an asymmetry between moral responsibility and deliberation as regards the collapse of epistemic and metaphysical possibilities. The collapse would not entail the lack of moral responsibility, even if it entailed there being no point to deliberation. (But see footnote 14 in regard to this last point [about deliberation]).

11

"Ought-Implies-Can," causal
determinism, and moral responsibility

Ishtiyaque Haji believes that moral responsibility does not require alternative possibilities and further that it is compatible with causal determinism; but he rejects the contention that causal determinism is compatible with judgements employing "obligation," "ought," "ought not," "right," and "wrong."[1] Following Haji, let us call the latter "judgments of deontic morality." Why might one think that the judgments of deontic morality are incompatible with causal determinism? I will treat "ought not" and "wrong" as interchangeable, and "ought" and "obligatory" as interchangeable. I shall lay out the argument with respect to "wrong." It will be easy to see how to construct parallel arguments for the other judgments of deontic morality. Here is a simple version of the argument:

1. Suppose some individual, John, does something morally wrong.
2. If John's Xing was wrong, then he ought to have done something else instead.
3. If John ought to have done something else instead, then he could have done something else instead.
4. So John could have done something else instead.
5. But if causal determinism is true, then John could not have done anything other than he actually did.
6. So, if causal determinism is true, it cannot be the case that John's Xing was wrong.[2]

This is a potent and disturbing argument. I have sought to argue that causal determinism is compatible with moral responsibility (even on the assumption of Premise 5). This result would be considerably less interesting if causal determinism were nevertheless incompatible with the central judgments of deontic morality. There are, however, various ways of seeking to block the conclusion of the

I am indebted to Gideon Yaffe and Randolph Clarke.

argument. I shall first discuss the rejection of Premise 2, and then I shall turn to the rejection of Premise 3—the "ought-implies-can" premise.

Gideon Yaffe has presented an interesting strategy for rejecting the argument; the problematic premise, according to Yaffe, is 2.[3] Yaffe's point is that one can discharge an obligation not to do something without *deliberately refraining* from doing the thing in question. As Yaffe puts it:

> I think one makes a mistake when one equates "ought not to X" with "ought to refrain from Xing." If these two things were the same (or if the first implied the second), then the only way to discharge an obligation not to do something would be by *doing* something else. But this isn't true. A person who gives no thought whatsoever to the fact that she is obligated not to X at *t*, and, in fact, is doing nothing at all at *t*, has managed to fulfill her obligation not to X at *t*. Obligations not to do things are very easy to fulfill; you fulfill them when you're dead, for instance. You fulfill them any time you don't do what you ought not to do.[4]

I am inclined to agree with Yaffe about the above point. Consider, again

2. If John's Xing was wrong, then he ought to have done something else instead.

Yaffe's analysis suggests that we need to make it explicit that "done something else" must be understood broadly to include not-doings generally; the not-doings in question need not be "refrainings" or "deliberate not-doings." So perhaps 2 should be revised to

2*. If John's Xing was wrong, then he ought to have not-Xed instead.

Here "not-Xing" is to be understood to include not-doings in general. Now it seems to me that the argument can be adjusted as follows:

1. Suppose some individual, John, does something morally wrong.
2*. If John's Xing was wrong, then he ought to have not-Xed instead.
3*. If John ought to have not-Xed, then he could have not-Xed.
4*. John could have not-Xed.
5*. But if causal determinism is true, then if John actually Xed, then John could not have not-Xed.
6. So, if causal determinism is true, it cannot be the case that John's Xing was wrong.

Thus, it seems that Yaffe's ploy cannot block the conclusion of the argument. This is because the argument for the incompatibility of causal determinism and free will in the sense that involves alternative possibilities applies to not-Xings (which may be unintentional and nondeliberate) as well as to intentional, deliberate undertakings (or refrainings). It seems to me that the incompatibilist's argument from the fixity of the past and the laws should apply to not-Xings as well as deliberate refrainings from X; thus Premise 5* seems to me to be true. If it is really true that John can not-X, then John's not-Xing must be an extension of the actual past, holding the natural laws fixed.

Consider, however, Yaffe's reply:

Once you grant that the obligation not to X can be discharged through the occurrence of a state of affairs over which the agent has no control, you lose the motivation for thinking that that state of affairs must be an extension of the actual past/laws. . . . if you are admitting that the agent has no control over whether or not the not-X state of affairs comes about, why should you think that, for these purposes, the relevant possible worlds must share the past and laws with the actual world?

Imagine that both agents A and B ought not to X at T. And imagine that there is a possible world sharing the past and laws with the actual world in which A is knocked unconscious at T and does nothing at all. And imagine that there is a possible world in which B is knocked unconscious at T and does nothing at all, but this possible world has a slightly different past, or slightly different laws, or both, from the actual world. We are agreed that A and B both discharge an obligation not to X in the possible worlds under discussion (if they face such obligations). But Fischer says that were "ought-implies-can" true, then A is actually obligated not to X and B is not actually obligated not to X. But I don't think this last inference follows since it matters not one bit what it is which makes it the case that the agent is knocked unconscious at T, it matters only that he is, and thereby doesn't do the thing that he was obligated not to do.[5]

Yaffe's point is that once one allows that one can discharge an obligation to not-X by some unintentional behavior (or no behavior at all), the constraints on the relevance of possible worlds that are pertinent to "control" (and thus the argument for the incompatibility of causal determinism and free will in the sense that involves alternative possibilities) change.

But I disagree. It seems to me that it is crucial here to distinguish something like "deliberate control" from a weaker but still important notion of control—call it "access control." I grant that deliberate control is not required in the path to the not-Xing, in a context in which an obligation to not-X is discharged. But it does *not* follow that control is irrelevant or that the agent need not have genuine access to the possible world in which he does not X.

Note that Yaffe says, "Imagine that there is a possible world in which B is knocked unconscious at T and does nothing at all, but this possible world has a slightly different past, or slightly different laws, or both, from the actual world." What he must additionally hold, in order for his point to be pertinent, is that there *no* possible world in which B is knocked unconscious and does nothing at all and which shares the past and natural laws with the actual world. But this is where the problem comes; under such circumstances, I contend that B is not actually obligated to not-X. And this is completely compatible with Yaffe's intuition that it does not matter at all what makes it the case that B is knocked unconscious at T.

I believe that *if* one accepts "ought implies can," then one *eo ipso* has motivation for accepting that the access in question must be "genuine," as defined by the argument for incompatibilism. (On this view, one has genuine access only to those possible worlds with the same past and natural laws as the actual world.) If one accepts "ought implies can," it seems to me that one should say that "ought to not-X" requires more than simply that one not-X in some (possibly remote) possible world; it requires that one have genuine access to a possible world in which one does not X, where the not-Xing may be unintentional. I do not see why the move from requiring that the not-Xing be intentional to allowing it to be unintentional entails any change in the conditions of accessibility. After all, the *motivation* behind "ought implies can" seems to entail that if one ought not to X, then one not-X's in some possible world one can "get to from here." If one is willing to accept this in the context of actions and intentional not-Xings, one should, it seems, accept it in the context of unintentional not-Xings.

To summarize: I claim that the motivation behind accepting the ought-implies-can maxim should lead one to accept that an agent must have genuine access to the world which renders the "can" claim true. Even if the relevant agent does not need deliberate control, he does need access control. Of course, one could accept some sort of compatibilist analysis of "can," according to which its being true that one can do something does not require that one do that thing in a world which is an extension of the actual past, holding the laws of nature fixed. This would amount to giving a compatibilist analysis of "genuine access." It would then allow one to deny Premise 5. But this is not Yaffe's strategy. Yaffe is willing to accept an incompatibilist analysis of "can" and "genuine access" for deliberate, intentional undertakings, but not for unintentional, nondeliberate behavior. This is what I find puzzling.

Despite its considerable ingenuity, I do not think that Yaffe's move can successfully block the conclusion of the argument. I think we need to reject "ought implies can" and thus Premise 3*. Of course, various philosophers have come to the conclusion that "ought implies can" should be rejected for reasons quite independent of the issues on which we are focusing here; they have based their rejection of the maxim on considerations pertinent to moral dilemmas.[6] My motivation for rejecting the ought-implies-can maxim comes from the Frankfurt-type cases.

To explain: What motivation could be given for the ought-implies-can maxim? I think the most natural justification for acceptance of the maxim is that, if it were not valid, then there could be cases in which an agent ought to do X but cannot do X (and never could do X). Thus, given that if an agent ought to do X, then he would be blameworthy for not doing X, there could be cases in which an agent is blameworthy for not Xing and yet he cannot X. And this seems objectionable—even unfair.[7]

I believe that there are Frankfurt-type omissions cases that are relevantly similar to Frankfurt-type cases with respect to actions. That is, there are cases in which an agent is morally responsible for not Xing, although he cannot in fact X. Some of these are cases in which an agent is blameworthy for not Xing and yet he cannot X. In fact, I believe that anyone who accepts the Frankfurt-type action cases must accept that there are such omissions cases.[8] It is then precisely the basic intuitions elicited by the Frankfurt-type cases which show that the most natural justification of the ought-implies-can maxim is faulty. Although this certainly does not decisively refute the maxim, it does suggest that it is not ad hoc for anyone who accepts the intended interpretation of the Frankfurt-type cases to reject the ought-implies-can maxim.

I suppose that someone might insist that "ought implies can" is a conceptual truth. It must be admitted that my argument against this maxim is not decisive. If the maxim is indeed valid, then I would grant that causal determinism rules out the judgments of deontic morality. Would this be a disastrous result for a semicompatibilist, that is, someone who believes that causal determinism is compatible with moral responsibility, even if it rules out the sort of free will that involves alternative possibilities? Perhaps (on the assumption that the ought-implies-can maxim is valid) one will have to bite the bullet and accept that the interconnected circle of judgments of deontic morality is inapplicable in a causally deterministic world. Note, however, that this still leaves room for robust moral responsibility, where this may include reactive attitudes such as resentment, indignation, respect, and so forth.

More important, it seems to me that it leaves room for significant moral judgments, even if they are not the special "judgments of deontic morality." For example, I would contend the goal of practical reasoning is to figure out what we have sufficient reason to do. We can make the judgment in a particular context (even in a causally deterministic world) that an individual has sufficient reason to do X. It does not seem to me that this judgment entails that he *can* do X. Whereas it is plausible (apart from argumentation of the sort sketched above) that ought implies can, I do not think it is similarly plausible that "having a sufficient reason" implies "can."[9] Thus, even in a world in which causal determinism is true, presumably we can make judgments about what agents have a sufficient reason to do, and we can criticize them for failing to do what they have sufficient reason to do. It would seem that individuals are morally blameworthy when they fail to do what they have sufficient reason to do, where they can reasonably be expected to recognize the sufficiency of the reason and they do not know that they will not do the thing in question (i.e., it is epistemically open to the agent to do it). All of the above is completely compatible with the truth of causal determinism.

I want to end by noting a puzzling feature of the above analysis. I contend that whereas it is at least plausible that ought implies can, there is no similar plausibility to the claim that having a sufficient reason to X implies the power to X. The puzzle comes from observing that it is sometimes thought that "ought" can be analyzed in terms of having a sufficient reason. That is, it is sometimes suggested that "S ought to X" is true just in case S has a sufficient reason (or perhaps a sufficient reason of a certain sort) to X. But if this analysis is correct, there should not be an asymmetry in the entailments of the sort I have described. I am not sure what to make of this. It seems to suggest either that the asymmetry in the entailments is illusory, or that the proposed analysis of "ought" is incorrect.

Notes

1. See Ishtiyaque Haji, *Moral Appraisability* (New York: Oxford University Press, 1998), and *Deontic Morality and Control* (New York: Cambridge University Press, 2002).

2. For helpful and illuminating discussions of essentially this basic argument, see Haji, ibid.; David Widerker, "Frankfurt on 'Ought Implies Can,'" *Analysis* 51 (1991): 222–24; David Copp, "Defending the Principle of Alternate Possibilities: Blameworthiness and Moral Responsibility," *Nous* 31: 441–56, and Derk Pereboom, *Living without Free Will* (Cambridge: Cambridge University Press, 2001): 141–48.

3. Gideon Yaffe, "'Ought Implies Can' and the Principle of Alternate Possibilities," *Analysis* 59 (1999): 218–22.

4. Personal Communication to the author, January, 2003.

5. Ibid.

6. See W. Sinnott-Armstrong, *Moral Dilemmas* (Oxford: Blackwell, 1988).

7. I first presented this argument in "Recent Work on Moral Responsibility," *Ethics* 110: 93–139.

8. See chapter 4 of this book; and Harry Frankfurt, "An Alleged Asymmetry between Actions and Omissions," *Ethics* 104: 620–23.

9. I owe this suggestion to a conversation with Randolph Clarke.

12

RESPONSIBILITY AND MANIPULATION

A compatibilist about causal determinism and moral responsibility wishes to say that the mere fact that the behavior in question is the product of a causally deterministic sequence does not imply that the agent cannot legitimately be held morally responsible for it. At the same time, the compatibilist typically is willing to concede that certain sorts of causal sequences undermine moral responsibility. Certain kinds of "manipulation" that bypass or somehow supersede or fundamentally distort the human capacity for practical reasoning are salient examples of responsibility-undermining factors. Now the challenge is to explain the difference between those sequences that undermine responsibility and those that are consistent with it (and, indeed, confer it). If it is not true that all causal sequences are created equal, how do we distinguish them?

This is a challenge I have sought to address head-on.[1] It is not an easy task, and my preliminary attempts have not elicited unanimous agreement. Below I shall discuss some of the most powerful critical discussions. I wish to begin by thanking my critics for their patient and sympathetic reading of my views, and for their penetrating critiques, from which I have learned much.

A Theory of Moral Responsibility

I shall offer a brief sketch of my approach to moral responsibility in order better to understand the various critiques.[2] The theory has various major components. First, I argue that moral responsibility does not require genuine access to metaphysically open alternative possibilities; thus, causal determinism does not threaten moral responsibility (simply) in virtue of eliminating such access to alternative possibilities. In the course of elaborating this argument, I distinguish between two kinds of control. Regulative control involves genuine access to alternative possibilities, whereas guidance control does not. I thus contend that moral responsibility implies guidance control, but not regulative control. Guidance control is the "freedom-relevant" (as opposed, say, to "epistemic") condition that is both necessary and sufficient for moral responsibility.

I go on to argue that an agent exhibits guidance control of his behavior insofar as it issues from his own, moderately reasons-responsive mechanism. I presuppose a distinction between the kind of mechanism that actually results in the behavior and other sorts of mechanisms. Given that the actual mechanism is identified, it must be the agent's own, and it must be appropriately sensitive to reasons (including moral reasons).

Mark Ravizza and I elaborate the various components of guidance control at some length in *Responsibility and Control: A Theory of Moral Responsibility*. I offer only the briefest of sketches here. One has control of one's behavior at least in part in virtue of having *taken control* of the mechanisms that produce it. One takes control by *taking responsibility*. Taking responsibility involves three elements. First, the agent must see that his choices have certain effects in the world—that is, he must see himself as the source of consequences in the world (in certain circumstances). Second, the individual must see that he is a fair target for the reactive attitudes as a result of how he affects the world. Third, the views specified in the first two conditions—that the individual can affect the external world in certain characteristic ways through his choices, and that he can be fairly praised and/or blamed for so exercising his agency—must be based on his evidence in an appropriate way.[3]

In an earlier work, *The Metaphysics of Free Will: An Essay on Control*, I presented a preliminary sketch of the account of guidance control.[4] In the early presentation, I included only the reasons-sensitivity component, and I explicitly pointed out that this was a mere adumbration of a fuller account to be presented later. Specifically, I noted that the relevant sort of reasons-responsiveness could be induced by manipulation (or other responsibility-undermining factors), and that I would address this problem in future work. The added component of mechanism ownership is an innovation in the account of guidance control presented in *Responsibility and Control: A Theory of Moral Responsibility*, and I (and my coauthor) suggest there that it can help with the problems of manipulation.

The intuition is simple. The mechanism that issues in behavior (or, more broadly, the way the behavior is produced) can be reasons-responsive, but this sensitivity, or significant features of it, could have been induced externally (by clandestine manipulation, hypnosis, subliminal advertising, brainwashing, and so forth). So reasons-sensitivity is not enough for moral responsibility. The reasons-responsiveness itself cannot have been put in place in ways that bypass or supersede the agent—the mechanisms that issue in one's behavior must be *one's own*.

Stump's Critique

Stump's First Critique

In various papers, Eleonore Stump has offered vigorous criticisms of elements of the overall account of moral responsibility I (and my coauthor) have presented.[5] In her recent paper "Control and Causal Determinism," she offers two criticisms I wish to discuss here.[6] She first points out that my coauthor and I simply assume that there can be reasons (and agents can have reasons) in a causally deterministic world.

Actually, Stump frames her critique here in terms of "tracking reasons." That is, she contends that Ravizza and I simply assume that agents can track reasons even in a causally deterministic world, but that we offer no argument for our claim. I suppose that the best way to interpret Stump is as follows: although we offer an account of the specific sort of tracking reasons that is involved in moral responsibility—moderate reasons-responsiveness—and we argue that this sort of tracking is entirely consistent with moral responsibility if *any* kind is, we do not offer any sort of answer to the more fundamental question of whether *any* kind of tracking of reasons is consistent with casual determinism. Stump points out that the more fundamental idea is "crucial to our case" for compatibilism, and she goes on to say, "Without some way of supporting it, Fischer and Ravizza do not have an *argument* for their compatibilism."[7]

In supporting her criticism, Stump invokes the authority of such eminent philosophers as Patricia Churchland and Richard Rorty. She cites Churchland as follows:

> Boiled down to essentials, a nervous system enables the organism to succeed in the four F's: feeding, fleeing, fighting, and reproducing. The principal chore of the nervous system is to get the body parts where they should be in order that the organism may survive. . . . Truth, whatever that is, definitely takes the hindmost.[8]

And Rorty says:

> The idea that one species of organism is, unlike all the others, oriented not just toward its own increased prosperity but toward Truth, is as un-Darwinian as the idea that every human being has a built-in moral compass.[9]

I find this criticism perplexing. Yes, my coauthor and I did simply assume that there is nothing in the very nature of causal determinism or reasons that would preclude agents in a causally deterministic world from having reasons or tracking reasons (quite apart from any particular account of reasons-tracking). But this is not an implausible position, and it has been argued for (convincingly, we should have thought) by various philosophers.[10]

Further, our overall theory has various parts; we offer arguments seeking to establish (or render plausible) various of these elements. Does one not have an *argument* for a contentious philosophical position unless one offers explicit justifications for *every* element of it? For all of its background assumptions and presuppositions? For the methodology one employs in seeking to support it? I would suggest that the methodological views suggested by Stump's critique are impossibly demanding.

Turning to the views of the luminaries, I simply do not see how they are relevant. In developing our account of moral responsibility, we do employ the notion of "reason." But we do not present a specific account of reasons—their ontological status or logic. Our goal was to present at least the rudiments of a systematic theory of moral responsibility—one that could be employed (perhaps *mutatis mutandis*) by proponents of a broad range of particular accounts of reasons. We would hope that the acceptability of a general theory of moral responsibility would not hinge on the viability of any particular (contentious) account of reasons.

So we were rather vague about reasons. We certainly did not say, nor, as far as I can tell, are we committed to the idea that reasons presuppose that there is anything like "Truth" with a capital "T," or that human beings are uniquely "oriented" to "It" (whatever "It" is). An organism—any organism—can have reasons insofar as he or she can have interests or a stake in something. But there are various particular ways of unpacking the concept of reasons (or perhaps their nature or essence), as well as their logic. Nothing in our theory requires us to say that there is some objectionably or problematically objective notion of truth, nor does it require that we bestow hegemony on human beings. Perhaps (for all we have said or are committed to, simply in virtue of offering a theory of moral responsibility) reasons are factors that make (or are taken to make) success in the four F's more likely, or they are the mental states that constitute awareness of such factors, or . . . A theory of moral responsibility is, after all, more abstract than a theory of reasons; and certainly it is more abstract than a first-order theory in ethics (such as utilitarianism or Kantianism, and so forth). So I conclude that Stump's critique here is, if I may put it this way, a bit "reproduced-up."[11]

Stump's Second Critique

Stump's second critique is more probing. She argues that our new account of moral responsibility cannot adequately handle various manipulation cases, even in spite of the new element of mechanism ownership. Indeed, Stump suggests that it is precisely this element that yields unintuitive results in a range of manipulation cases.

It will be helpful to have before us the details of Stump's presentation. She begins:

> A person who is being manipulated by someone else can meet [Fischer and Ravizza's] conditions for acting on a mechanism that is his own and also suitably reasons-responsive. Consequently, a manipulated person can count as morally responsible on their account of moral responsibility.
>
> To see that this is so, consider Robert Heinlein's The Puppetmasters. In the story, an alien race of intelligent creatures wants to conquer the Earth. Part of the alien plan for invasion includes a covert operation in which individual aliens take over particular human beings without being detected. When an alien "master" takes over a human being, the human being (say, Sam) has within himself not only his own consciousness but the master's as well. The master can control Sam's consciousness; he can make Sam's mind blank, he can suppress or even eradicate some affect of Sam's, or he can introduce thoughts and desires into Sam's consciousness. Most of the time, however, the master leaves Sam's consciousness alone but simply takes it off-line. That is, Sam's consciousness runs pretty much as always, but it has no effect on Sam's behavior; the master's consciousness causes Sam to do whatever he does. The master controls Sam indirectly, by controlling Sam's thoughts and desires and then letting Sam's consciousness produce Sam's behavior.

Since it is crucial to the alien plan that their taking over human beings be undetected in the early stages of the invasion, they are careful to make the behavior of
people like Sam correspond to the behavior Sam would normally have engaged in
had he not been infected with the alien. So when, under the control of the alien,
Sam does A, it is also true that if there had been reason sufficient for Sam in his uninfected state to do not-A, the alien would have brought it about that Sam in his infected state did not-A. In this case, then, Sam acts on a mechanism that meets
Fischer and Ravizza's condition for being strongly reason-responsive: "if [a certain
kind of mechanism] K were to operate and there were sufficient reason to do otherwise, the agent would recognize the sufficient reason to do otherwise and thus choose
to do otherwise and do otherwise."[12]

Stump continues:

Suppose that we now rewrite Heinlein's story a little, in order to take account of
Fischer and Ravizza's conditions for a mechanism's being an agent's own. Let it be
the case that, after the alien has infected Sam and before he starts to manipulate
Sam's reason, the alien has what is, in effect, a conversation with Sam. The alien
may have no purpose for this conversation other than to amuse himself. But suppose that, for amusement or some other purpose, the alien wants to convince Sam
that when Sam acts under the control of the alien, Sam is as much an agent and as
suitable a candidate for the reactive attitudes of others as he ever was in his uninfected state.

The alien might, for example, put forward arguments for determinism and compatibilism that Sam finds extremely plausible. In consequence, Sam might come to
believe that all the states of his mind and will are causally determined by factors outside himself and that, nonetheless, when he acts, determined in this way, he is in-
controvertibly an agent and that it is perfectly appropriate for others to maintain the
reactive attitudes toward him. Next, the alien might argue to this effect: It can make
no difference to our assessment of a person S whether the external factors determining the states of S's mind and will are animate or inanimate, intelligent or blind. Our
assessment of S himself should remain the same regardless of whether or not the
causes determining S include something sentient among them. Suppose that Sam
finds this argument, too, very plausible. By this means, Sam, in the revised story, is
brought to believe that, in acting on his mind and will as they are controlled by the
alien, he *is* an agent and a suitable target for the reactive attitudes of others, just as
he was in his uninfected state. These beliefs of Sam's will be false, but, of course, it is
possible for human beings to reason themselves into very peculiar false belief. . . .
Furthermore, these beliefs of Sam's will be founded on the evidence available to
Sam, namely, what Sam knows and believes and the arguments of the alien which
Sam accepts. . . . In this way, then, Sam takes responsibility for the mechanism on
which he acts when he is controlled by the alien, and so this mechanism counts as
his own, on Fischer and Ravizza's account. Since this mechanism is also reasons-
responsive in the way I described, Sam meets the Fischer and Ravizza conditions for
moral responsibility when he is controlled by the alien. . . . I think that the case of
Sam and the puppetmaster is enough to show that Fischer and Ravizza's account has
a serious problem in attempting to deal with manipulation.[13]

Stump goes on to discuss two examples that Ravizza and I presented. She contends that her analysis further elaborates the problem suggested by the Puppetmasters case:

> Here is the first case [Fischer and Ravizza's Judith I]:
>
> A scientist secretly implanted a mechanism in Judith's brain (let us say, a few days ago). Employing this mechanism, the scientist electronically stimulates Judith's brain in such a way as to create what will be a literally irresistible urge to punch her best friend, Jane, the next time she sees Jane. When Judith meets Jane at a local coffeehouse, Judith experiences this sort of urge, and does indeed punch Jane.[14]
>
> Our intuitive response to this case is to think that Judith is not responsible for punching Jane. Fischer and Ravizza think that their account can support this intuition. . . . But it is not difficult to flesh out *Judith I* in such a way that our intuition about the case remains the same, and yet Fischer and Ravizza's account on longer supports that intuition. We can easily assimilate *Judith I* to the sort of story in the revised version of Heinlein's *Puppetmasters*. In that case, the mechanism on which Judith acts in *Judith I* is the mind of the manipulator operating on her brain. As in the case of *Puppetmasters*, we can also suppose that the mechanism is suitably responsive to reasons that both Judith and the manipulator recognize as reasons for Judith, so that the mechanism is even strongly reasons-responsive. Finally, we can imagine that Judith comes to believe that she is an agent and the appropriate target of the reactive attitudes when she is controlled in this way by the manipulator.
>
> Consequently, contrary to what Fischer and Ravizza suppose, a person such as Judith who acts on an irresistible desire produced in her by a manipulator can still meet the Fischer and Ravizza conditions for moral responsibility. She can act on a mechanism that is her own, in virtue of the fact that she has taken responsibility for it, and that mechanism can be suitably reasons-responsive, because the manipulator manipulates his victim in a way that tracks reasons for the victim.[15]

Stump goes on to consider another case, *Judith II,* but we shall focus on her analysis of *Judith I* and her Sam and the *Puppetmasters* case. I pause to note that no less an authority than Harry Frankfurt is in agreement with Stump's criticism:

> Fischer and Ravizza seek to insulate their account of moral responsibility against the possibility that someone who is manipulated by another person might be wrongly held to be morally responsible for what he does. It seems to me that Stump is correct in her claim that their attempt to accomplish this insulation is unsuccessful. Her discussions of the examples involving Sam and Judith show effectively that even an agent who is being manipulated in ways that undermine moral responsibility can, according to the criteria Fischer and Ravizza provide, act on a mechanism that is both suitably reasons-responsive and the agent's own. Thus she shows that their criteria do not satisfactorily identify the conditions upon which moral responsibility depends.[16]

Of course, I hate to spoil the party. But I do not think that Stump's criticism is on target. Note that Stump contends, "The mechanism on which Judith acts in *Judith I* is the mind of the manipulator operating on her brain." She goes on to write, "As in the case of *Puppetmasters*, we can also suppose that that mechanism is suitably responsive to reasons." Why does Stump suggest that in the case of *Puppetmasters*, Sam's mechanism is reasons-responsive? Recall that Stump argues:

> Sam acts on a mechanism that meets Fischer and Ravizza's conditions for being strongly reasons-responsive: "if [a certain kind of mechanism] K were to operate and there were sufficient reason to do otherwise, the agent would recognize the sufficient reason to do otherwise and thus choose to do otherwise and do otherwise."[17]

And this is because:

> When, under the control of the alien, Sam does A, it is also true that if there had been reason sufficient for Sam in his uninfected state to do not-A, the alien would have brought it about that Sam in his infected state did not-A.[18]

Well, if you take the relevant mechanism (on which the agents in question act) to be individuated as broadly as "the mind of the manipulator acting on her brain," then of course it will turn out that the mechanism in question is in the specified way reasons-responsive. Similarly in the case of Sam, and in *any* manipulation case, if the mechanism is individuated as broadly as "manipulation by an external source," then, of course, the mechanism will turn out to be reasons-responsive. This is because, no matter how thoroughly and effectively the external source actually manipulates the agent to do X, under other circumstances the source could have manipulated the agent in a different way to cause the agent to do *not-X*.

I should have thought that this very basic point could be seen to apply even to the simplest cases of manipulation. That is, it should be evident that, in order to render the Fischer-Ravizza account of manipulation cases even minimally plausible, we are not thinking of the relevant mechanisms as individuated so broadly as, for example, "manipulation by an external source." Rather, the mechanism is something like "manipulation of this specific sort," where the sort in question is specified at least in part in terms of neurophysiology.

It is hard to see how there could be any confusion about how my coauthor and I intend the account to work in this specific respect. For example, we say about Judith I:

> Here it is evident that Judith should *not* be held morally responsible for punching Jane. On our approach to moral responsibility, there are two distinct reasons why this is so. First, the mechanism leading to the action is not moderately reasons-responsive; by hypothesis, given the kind of stimulation of the brain that actually takes place, Judith as an irresistible urge to strike Jane. Thus, Judith would strike Jane, no matter what kinds of reasons to refrain were present.[19]

The account of manipulation only works, if it works at all, if one holds fixed the actual kind of brain manipulation, when one holds fixed the kind of mechanism that actually operates. This point is simple and straightforward; if it is not accepted, then one can criticize the Fischer-Ravizza account of moral responsibility right from the start, employing the examples we originally employed; the point does not pertain at all to the account of "one's own mechanism" or "taking responsibility," and no complicated examples such as Sam and the Puppetmasters need be invoked.

Consider, also, the Fischer-Ravizza discussion of "irresistible desires" or "compulsions." Obviously, there need be no external manipulation or induction for an agent to experience an irresistible urge; we might call this sort of urge a "compulsion." Now if the mechanism in question is individuated as broadly as "practical reasoning" or "deliberation," then (say) practical reasoning that involves a compulsive desire will be perfectly reasons-responsive. In order for our account even to get off the ground here, we must be considering the relevant mechanisms as individuated more narrowly. And we say, when first discussing such examples:

> Consider, then, the mechanism, "deliberation involving an irresistible desire." Whereas this mechanism is temporally intrinsic, it is also reasons-responsive: there is a possible scenario in which Jim acts on this kind of mechanism and refrains from taking the drug. In this scenario, Jim has an irresistible urge to refrain from taking the drug. This shows that neither "deliberation involving an irresistible desire for the drug" [because it is not temporally intrinsic] nor "deliberation involving an irresistible desire" is the relevant mechanism (if the theory of responsibility is to achieve an adequate "fit" with our intuitive judgments).
>
> When Jim acts on an irresistible urge to take the drug, there is some physical process of kind P taking place in his central nervous system. When a person undergoes this kind of physical process, we say that his urge is literally irresistible. And we believe that what underlies our intuitive claim that Jim is not morally responsible for taking the drug is that the relevant kind of mechanism issuing in Jim's taking the drug is of physical kind P, and that a mechanism of kind P is not reasons-responsive.[20]

Stump's critique, then, is off the mark because it employs an overly broad notion of mechanism-individuation, contrary to the explicit development of the theory. Further, despite Stump's suggestion that the problems come from the new component of the theory that specifies how agents make the springs of their action their own by taking responsibility for them, the alleged problems come entirely from the original component of guidance control—reasons-responsiveness.

Now it might be noted that so far I have simply pointed out that the Fischer-Ravizza view depends on a certain notion of mechanism-individuation—one quite different from the one adopted, for the sake of her criticism, by Stump. But this is not yet to say that our notion of mechanism-individuation is the "correct" one. Perhaps the problem is not quite the one identified by Stump, but a problem nevertheless. I fully admit that this element of the overall account of moral responsibility is left to some degree vague, and that it is therefore at least to some degree problematic. It is thus entirely fair to point to problems that arise out of this vagueness. Stump's critique helpfully points to some of the commitments of our theory, and challenges us to say more about them. I shall return to these issues later in this chapter.

Pereboom's Critique

In his book *Living without Free Will*, Derk Pereboom presents what he takes to be a problem for *any* compatibilist account of moral responsibility.[21] Pereboom starts with a case in which he believes that anyone would say that the agent is not morally responsible. He then transforms that case, step by step, into a context of causal determinism. Pereboom's position is that the compatibilist cannot distinguish, in a principled way, between cases in which we would all agree that there is not moral responsibility and the context of causal determinism.

Here is the first case:

> Case 1. Professor Plum was created by neuroscientists, who can manipulate him directly through the use of radio-like technology, but he is as much like an ordinary human being as is possible, given this history. Suppose these neuroscientists "locally" manipulate him to undertake the process of reasoning by which his desires are brought about and modified—directly producing his every state from moment to moment. The neuroscientists manipulate him by, among other things, pushing a series of buttons just before he begins to reason about his situation, thereby causing his reasoning process to be rationally egoistic. Plum is not constrained to act in the sense that he does not act because of an irresistible desire—the neuroscientists do not provide him with an irresistible desire—and he does not think and act contrary to character since he is often manipulated to be rationally egoistic. His effective first-order desire to kill Ms. White conforms to his second-order desires. Plum's reasoning process exemplifies the various components of moderate reasons-responsiveness. He is receptive to the relevant pattern of reasons, and his reasoning process would have resulted in different choices in some situations in which the egoistic reasons were otherwise. At the same time, he is not exclusively rationally egoistic since he will typically regulate his behavior by moral reasons when the egoistic reasons are relatively weak—weaker than they are in the current situation.[22]

Pereboom's intuition is that Professor Plum is clearly not morally responsible in this case. He goes on to construct a case in which there is no local manipulation, but in which he believes that we will also agree that there is no moral responsibility:

> Case 2. Plum is like an ordinary human being, except that he was created by neuroscientists, who, although they cannot control him directly, have programmed him to weigh reasons for action so that he is often but not exclusively rationally egoistic, with the result that in the circumstances in which he now finds himself, he is causally determined to undertake the moderately reasons-responsive process and to possess the set of first- and second-order desires that results in his killing Ms. White. He has the general ability to regulate his behavior by moral reasons, but in these circumstances, the egoistic reasons are very powerful, and accordingly he is causally determined to kill for these reasons. Nevertheless, he does not act because of an irresistible desire.[23]

Now Pereboom constructs a case in which the neuroscientists are replaced by parents, community, and so forth. I suppose that one can look at parents as neuroscientists with crude, old-fashioned tools! Pereboom continues:

> Case 3. Plum is an ordinary human being, except that he was determined by the rigorous training practices of his home and community so that he is often but not exclusively rationally egoistic (exactly as egoistic as in Cases 1 and 2). His training

took place at too early an age for him to have had the ability to prevent or alter the practices that determined his character. In his current circumstances, Plum is thereby caused to undertake the moderately reasons-responsive process and to possess the first- and second-order desires that result in his killing White. He has the general ability to grasp, apply, and regulate his behavior by moral reasons, but in these circumstances, the egoistic reasons are very powerful, and hence the rigorous training practices of his upbringing deterministically result in his act of murder. Nevertheless, he does not act because of an irresistible desire.[24]

Finally:

Case 4. Physicalist determinism is true, and Plum is an ordinary human being, generated and raised under normal circumstances, who is often but not exclusively rationally egoistic (exactly as egoistic as in Cases 1–3). Plum's killing of White comes about as a result of his undertaking the moderately reasons-responsive process of deliberation, he exhibits the specified organization of first- and second-order desires, and he does not act because of an irresistible desire. He has the general ability to grasp, apply, and regulate his behavior by moral reasons, but in these circumstances the egoistic reasons are very powerful, and together with background circumstances they deterministically result in his act of murder.[25]

Pereboom basically asks the compatibilist to point to the place (after Case 1) along the slippery slope where responsibility emerges. My answer: there is no such place, as Pereboom suggests. Rather, on a plausible understanding of the case, Professor Plum is morally responsible in Case 1. Thus, there is no impediment to saying that Plum is responsible in Case 4 (and, in general, in the context of causal determinism).

As Pereboom points out, Ravizza and I expressed the concern that in certain cases of significant manipulation that occurs literally from birth (or, in this case, from the very beginning of the existence of Professor Plum), there is no opportunity for a self to develop.[26] But let us allow this point to pass, and I shall concede (for the sake of this discussion) that Professor Plum is a genuine self even in Case 1, although created and directly manipulated by others from the beginning. As Pereboom points out, on my view it turns out that Plum has taken responsibility for the manipulation-mechanism; after all, this is the mechanism on which he always acts, and when an individual develops into a morally responsible agent, he takes responsibility for his actual-sequence mechanisms, even if he does not know their details. Further, Pereboom is at pains to point out that the desires on which Plum acts are not irresistible; I take it that Pereboom wants to say that there is no psychological (or other) *compulsion* here, but mere causal determination. It follows that Plum acts from his own, moderately reasons-responsive mechanism; holding fixed the actual kind of mechanism, there is a suitable range of possible scenarios in which Plum recognizes reasons to do otherwise and does indeed behave in accordance with those reasons.

In this case there is direct manipulation of the brain, but it does not issue in desires so strong as to count as compulsions. Thus, Professor Plum's actual-sequence mechanism has the general power or capacity to respond differently to the very reasons that actually obtain in the case.[27] Although Plum is manipulated by others (without his knowledge or consent), he is not forced or compelled to act as he does; thus, he is not a robot—he has a certain minimal measure of control, and moral responsibility is associated with control (of precisely this sort).[28]

It is crucial here to keep in mind the distinction between moral responsibility and (say) moral blameworthiness (or praiseworthiness).[29] Moral responsibility, as Ravizza and I understand the notion, is more abstract than praiseworthiness or blameworthiness: moral responsibility is, as it were, the "gateway" to moral praiseworthiness, blameworthiness, resentment, indignation, respect, gratitude, and so forth.[30] Someone who is morally responsible is an *apt candidate* for moral judgments and ascriptions of moral properties; similarly, a morally responsible agent is an *apt target* for such attitudes as resentment, indignation, respect, gratitude, and so forth. Someone becomes an apt candidate or target—someone is "in the ballpark" for such ascriptions and attitudes—in virtue of exercising a distinctive kind of control ("guidance control"). But it does not follow from someone's being an apt target or candidate for moral ascriptions and attitudes that any such ascription or attitude is justifiable in any given context. After all, an agent may be morally responsible for morally neutral behavior. Further, an agent can be morally responsible, but circumstances may be such as to render praise or blame unjustifiable.

Once the distinction between moral responsibility and (say) blameworthiness is made, it is natural to suppose that Professor Plum is morally responsible for killing Ms. White, even if he is not blameworthy (or not fully blameworthy) for doing so. After all, Plum is *not* a mere robot—he is *not* compelled or forced to act the way he does. He *does* exercise control, minimal as it may be. It is important to capture this notion of moral responsibility and the associated notion of control, in part because it is important to *mark the difference* between a genuine agent such as Plum (who exercises at least a minimal degree of control) and a robot or individual acting on literally irresistible urges—compulsions. This is the notion of moral responsibility that Ravizza and I aimed to capture.

But it is of course also very important to mark the difference between being morally responsible (in virtue of exercising guidance control) and actually being blameworthy (or praiseworthy). In my view, further conditions need to be added to mere guidance control to get to blameworthiness; these conditions may have to do with the circumstances under which one's values, beliefs, desires, and dispositions were created and are sustained, one's physical and economic status, and so forth. Professor Plum, it seems to me, is not blameworthy, even though he is morally responsible. That he is not blameworthy is a function of the circumstances of the creation of his values, character, desires, and so forth. But there is no reason to suppose that anything like such unusual circumstances obtain *merely* in virtue of the truth of causal determinism. Thus, I see no impediment to saying that Plum can be blameworthy for killing Ms. White in Case 4. Note that there is no difference with respect to the minimal control conditions for moral responsibility in Cases 1 through 4—the threshold is achieved in all the cases. But there are (or may be, for all that has been said in Pereboom's descriptions) wide disparities in the conditions for blameworthiness.

The ingredients for providing an adequate response to Pereboom's challenge involve the distinction between moral responsibility and (say) blameworthiness, and the distinction between mere causal determination and action from a compulsive or irresistible urge. One might wonder how to characterize the latter distinction, or whether it exists at all, since (arguably) no desire on which an agent acts can be resisted in a causally deterministic world. I might try to explain the difference, in a rough and ready way, as follows: An irresistible urge is one whose intensity or intrinsic motivational force (whether experienced or not) explains why the action takes place; there is no possible scenario (including those whose pasts differ in their details from the actual past) in which the agent fails to act on the desire, given its intrinsic motivation force. On the other hand, when an agent actually acts on a desire in a causally deterministic world, he may fail to act from a desire with a similar intrinsic motivational force, given differences in the past (or even the laws).

Black and Tweedale

To further illustrate this important distinction, let us consider an argument of Sam Black and Jon Tweedale.[31] Black and Tweedale suggest that certain information that we could conceivably receive would make us believe that causal determinism obtains and *thereby* expunge our intuitive sense of our moral responsibility:

> Start by identifying a decision from your past of which you are especially proud or alternatively, especially ashamed. For purposes of illustration, suppose you are an alcoholic and have been a pretty tough nut in all of your fractured personal relationships. Next imagine that you receive a letter informing you that an identical twin separated from you at birth is on their way over to make your acquaintance. As the evening's conversation turns intimate you can't resist asking your twin whether he too has succumbed to those vices for which you are most ashamed (it does not matter whether we focus on your accomplishments instead). You discover that your identical sibling has indeed surrendered to identical vices.[32]

Black and Tweedale contend that you might have mixed feelings about such a discovery. On the one hand, you may feel that you may begin to view your "vices" as no different from "warts or boils—although infinitely more shameful."[33] On the other hand, you might still hold onto the view that you are morally responsible. Black and Tweedale argue, "The second reaction to the example depends for its survival, we suspect, on the tacit assumption that although you and your sibling possess identical vices, your conditions are not causally determined."[34] They elaborate:

> As your conversation progresses into the night even more idiosyncratic shared vices come to light. (These we leave to the reader's imagination.) Once these have been catalogued there comes an insistent knocking, and two (the number is not important) additional identical siblings—reared in similarly independent circumstances—appear at the door. Picking up on the conversation's theme, they too confess to having identical vices. There are now four of you who have made identical messes of your lives—with the possibility of more on the way.[35]

They continue:

> When the peculiarities of our personality are viewed in this light they seem no different from the oddities of our physical appearance, such as our height, hair or eye color; that is to say, as natural facts about us for which we take neither credit nor blame. . . . If these reflections are on the right track they support incompatibilism. For the incompatibilist claims that discovering the existence of an identical twin is like discovering the causal determinants of our behavior. The appearances of successive siblings simply render the causal determinants of our behavior increasingly transparent. But in principle we should reach the same conclusion about moral responsibility any time we fully appreciate how the course of someone's deliberations is uniquely determined.[36]

Now it seems to me that this sort of evidence would be in favor of the conclusion that our behavior generally (or always) issues from irresistible desires. What would make such evidence so surprising—indeed, startling—is that it would point to the conclusion that all our behavior is the result of irresistible urges or *compulsions*. Such evidence would *not* be evidence for *mere* causal determination of behavior; it would be evidence that our genes somehow *compel* us to act, even if we are unaware of such compulsion. *This* is why we would find such hypothetical and wildly implausible evidence so startling. It is not the *mere* thought that our choices and behavior is causally determined that is shocking, but rather the thought that all our choices and behavior are *compelled*. At the very least, thought experiments involving hypothetical evidence about identical twins cannot *in itself* show that we would be startled to find that our behavior is causally determined (and that we would thus give up our view of ourselves as morally responsible persons).

Return, now, to Pereboom's Professor Plum of Case 1, whom we discussed above. Let us suppose that as a young man, as he was developing into a morally responsible agent, he took responsibility for his "ordinary" mechanism of practical reasoning (which involves the covert manipulation by the neuroscientists). Many years later (say three decades), he acts from this mechanism, which is, by hypothesis, moderately reasons-responsive. As I said above, I am inclined to say that Plum is morally responsible for killing Ms. White, although most likely not blameworthy (or significantly blameworthy). I would distinguish Plum from Professor Glum, who is *not* manipulated as a young man, and takes responsibility (when a young man) for the exercise of the ordinary human capacity for practical reasoning. Later in his life (say three decades later) the neuroscientists begin to manipulate him in a clandestine fashion. A week later, he acts on this mechanism (that involves covert, undetected manipulation by the scientists) in just the same fashion as Plum: he kills Ms. White, and the operations of his brain and body are isomorphic to those of Plum. We can even assume that Glum's configuration of character traits and motivational states are such that it is plausible to suppose that he would have killed Ms. White in just the same way in which he actually kills her, if he had not been manipulated by the neuroscientists. I believe that, whereas Plum is morally responsible for killing Ms. White, Glum is not. Plum acts from his own, moderately reasons-responsive mechanism, but Glum does not.

Glum's actual-sequence mechanism is not his own—he has not taken responsibility for the manipulation-mechanism.

I concede that it may not be obvious that my intuitions about these cases are correct. Perhaps it will be thought that my theory is driving my intuitions here, rather than the other way around. I do not know how to establish that my intuition is correct, or that it is largely independent of my theory. I can simply display the results of my theory in these cases, and profess my agreement. What may, however, be helpful is that the asymmetry between Plum and Glum (on my approach) shows that the Fischer-Ravizza theory of moral responsibility is "historical" in a strong way.

Zimmerman

To explain. Some years ago my coauthor and I suggested that the notion of moral responsibility is (like justice, love, and other notions) an *essentially historical* notion.[37] We contrasted historical notions with those that are "current-time-slice" notions, such as shape, color, weight, and so forth. You can tell an object's color by looking at it and noticing its current-time-slice characteristics. You cannot tell whether an agent is morally responsible by simply considering the agent's current-time-slice properties, such as his configuration of mental states. Various philosophers have pointed out that this dilemma is not exhaustive; there can be "process notions" that are neither current-time-slice nor deeply historical notions.[38] Perhaps it takes awhile to "identify" with a particular first-order desire; perhaps, for example, this process of identification involves (at least) the formation of a higher order desire to act in accordance with that first-order desire. Roughly this sort of account, suitably filled in and elaborated, is not exactly a current-time-slice model; nor is it historical in a particularly interesting or deep way.[39] One simply has to focus on a suitable *interval*, rather than an instantaneous time slice.

This is a good and helpful point. Of course, such "process accounts" remain problematic, because manipulation can occur *over the relevant interval*. So, although they are not, strictly speaking, current-time-slice models of moral responsibility, they are equally open to the manipulation objection. More to my purpose here, it should be evident from the asymmetric treatment of Professors Plum and Glum that my account of moral responsibility is not merely a process notion, but it is historical in a deeper way. Plum and Glum choose and act in exactly the same way; on the Fischer-Ravizza account of moral responsibility, the difference in their responsibility status comes entirely from events that occurred decades earlier—events that are not plausibly thought to be parts of an extended responsibility-conferring process. Additionally, those events (the taking-responsibility events) are not themselves exercises of guidance control that are related to future behavior in the way that (say) freely getting drunk is related to future out-of-control driving. My theory of moral responsibility, then, is genuinely and deeply historical.[40]

Moral responsibility is in this respect like love. The notion of love is quite mysterious, as is love itself.[41] In understanding the notion of love, and its distinctive "particularity," it is helpful to begin with two features: its essential historicity and non-fungibility (I will add a third dimension below). The historicity of love entails that there cannot be love at first sight. A certain sort of history must be shared in order to have genuine love. Thus, there cannot be literal "love potions," just as there cannot be "virtue pills." The non-fungibility of love entails that if one loves a beloved, and the particular beloved changes (i.e., the object of the attitudes constitutive of love is a different particular person), then one does not any more have *love* toward that new individual. This is of course compatible with there being changes, even radical changes, in the *properties* of the beloved (consistent with the continuation of love).

Imagine that your spouse (I will say, "wife") and three children are all hit by lightning bolts as you are driving home from work. By some inexplicable cosmic accident, there emerge molecule-for-molecule doppelgangers of them—with all of the same properties (mental states, dispositions, memories, and so forth) of the originals. The new individuals—and they are new, for there is no connection at all between the original persons and the replacements—await you at home. If you knew what has happened, what should your reaction be, and how should this be characterized?[42]

Ravizza and I have argued that, since love is essentially historical, it would be inappropriate to characterize your attitudes to the new individuals as love (at first). A period of time during which you interact with the new individuals is necessary. This also follows from the non-fungibility of love. But it seemed to us that it would be unbearably harsh and cold to suppose that you should not have attitudes and feelings toward the new individuals not unlike those toward the originals. After a suitable period, these attitudes could properly be described as love (rather than something like "proto-love"), and one can properly be said to love the new individuals.

David Zimmerman criticizes the above treatment of the notion of love. He believes that it indicates an inappropriate understanding of the deeply historical nature of love (parallel to our alleged misunderstanding of the deeply historical nature of moral responsibility):

> I doubt that Fischer and Ravizza's . . . position is plausible (even if coherent), for the essential historicity of *adult love at time t* seems (to me, anyway) inextricable from the fact that the lover has shared a history with *this particular non-fungible* beloved. To be sure, there is room (just barely) in our lives for a relational emotion which involves a shared history only with a bundle of properties *however instantiated* by particular persons at various stages of the particular lover's history. Call this "Love *de dicto.*" A vivid example would be the James Stewart character's obsessive efforts in *Vertigo* to "recreate" his "Madeleine" (the first Kim Novak character). But a lover who is *aware* of the replacement of the original instantiating particular person and who continues to have all the same old feelings toward the new instantiation of the same set of type-identical properties as he did toward the original, like the husband for his "replacement wife" in Fischer and Ravizza's doppelganger example, is surely suffering from a kind of pathology beyond mere fickleness.
>
> . . . [Fischer and Ravizza's position] brings out yet again the importance of distinguishing between the mere *process* and the deep *source* dimensions of conceptually

historical properties. For the reply makes it sound as though the enduring instantiation of the former beloved properties, *never mind how*, is what does the trick. But surely if contemporary interaction can transform mere proto-love into the genuine article, it does so not simply by virtue of the lover's becoming accustomed to the idea that the beloved set of properties is instantiated anew in a doppelganger replacement, but rather by virtue of the fact that he shares enough time with *this particular* "proto-beloved" so that this very interaction can be the source of *new* lovable properties in both of them.

Amelie Rorty suggests that "love is not love that alters *not* when it alteration finds" because the genuine article has to be open to the possibility that the lovers will so change as a result of dynamic interactions which occur during their shared history (both between them and between each lover and the rest of the world) that one or the other might fall out of love. I offer a (less poetic) corollary: "love is not love for would-be lovers who in the fullness of time do not alter when they replacement find." But this is a *source*-historicist condition, for it requires not only that the husband who is made newly aware of the replacement be afforded some time to get used to the idea that this instantiation of the beloved properties now interacting with him is a doppelganger, but also that the new phase of his historical interaction with his proto-beloved replacement be a potential source of at least some new relational properties of both of them. In other words, emotional *stasis* after the husband becomes aware of the replacement entails that he does not really love the doppelganger wife but just a bundle of properties, however instantiated.[43]

But there is absolutely nothing in the Fischer-Ravizza approach to the puzzle about replacements that entails (or, as far as I can see, even suggests) the sort of "emotional stasis" described by Zimmerman. On our view, you should still have the sorts of general attitudes characteristic of love toward the new individuals; the attitudes simply cannot be described (yet) as love (or part of love). Love is historical, and its object is non-fungible.

In the replacement case, as you interact (say) with your replacement spouse and have many of the general attitudes characteristic of love, the relationship may mature and develop into genuine love. Of course, as with love of one's original spouse, this may include an openness to changes in the interests and personality of the spouse. Nothing in our view precludes this sort of openness, and an associated appreciation for change and development in your beloved.

I have tried to defend a certain view of love as historical in a deep sense. This is not unlike the Fischer-Ravizza view of moral responsibility as deeply historical. I have suggested that the historicist nature of love is a component of the more general *particularity* of love. Love's particularity consists at least in its essential historicity and the non-fungibility of its object. I want finally to suggest that there is a third dimension, perhaps difficult to articulate, of love's particularity; this dimension pertains to its individuation, as it were. Having interacted suitably with the replacement spouse, one can actually be said to love her. But this is not the *same love*—it is a different love because it has a different object.

One can speak of "the great loves of one's life." It may be that one is simply pointing to different beloveds. Or it may be that one is indicating different *instances* of love (where the "instances" are not instantaneous, but take place over durations). Love is particular in the sense that it is defined in terms of general attitudes and also a particular beloved; when the particular beloved changes, even apart from any changes in general properties (interests, character traits, and so forth), there is a different *instance* of love. In the replacement puzzle, your love for your family constitutes a *regulative ideal:* it impels you to have the same general attitudes, including an appreciation of and openness to change in the individuals who are the targets of the attitudes, and it ultimately points to new love.[44]

I began the discussion of love by remarking on its mysteries. The ruminations above remind me of that great, old country and western song, "I Don't Know Why I Love You, But I Do."

Mechanism Individuation: McKenna

The overall theory of moral responsibility that Mark Ravizza and I presented has various components: the contention that moral responsibility does not require the sort of control (regulative control) that involves metaphysically open alternative possibilities, the claim that guidance control is the freedom-relevant condition necessary and sufficient for moral responsibility, the idea that guidance control can be analyzed in terms of mechanism-ownership and moderate reasons-responsiveness, and the claim that guidance control, so construed, is compatible with causal determinism. Of course, these elements can be further broken down into their parts; for example, moderate reasons-responsiveness is analyzed in terms of "sameness of mechanism," regular reasons-receptivity, and weak reasons-reactivity.[45] A part of the overall theory that we conceded to be vague, and which has been fixed on by various commentators, is the notion of "sameness of kind of mechanism."[46]

The theory, as presented by Ravizza and me, does not contain an explicit account of mechanism individuation. We acknowledged this fact, and conceded that it is a potential problem.[47] I want to say a bit more here about the role that this fact plays in the theory—and the assessment of the theory. I shall begin by laying out the critique developed by Michael McKenna. In doing so, I want to address (at least in a preliminary way) McKenna's challenge:

> Fischer and Ravizza's appeal to sameness of mechanism is the lynchpin in their defense of an actual-sequence, reasons-responsive analysis of guidance control. Regrettably, their exclusive reliance on intuition as a basis for mechanism individuation renders their defense of their overall theory unconvincing. There are too many pressure points at which differing intuitions regarding sameness of mechanism yield troubling results for their defense of guidance control. Thus, to defend their compatibilist account of moral responsibility fully they must address this source of trouble.[48]

McKenna elaborates the worry as follows:

> Because they [Fischer and Ravizza] offer no *principled* basis for mechanism individuation, they must rest their thesis purely on *intuitive* reactions to different cases. But, it might be objected, *which* elements from the entire complex (of proximal events and

states antecedent to an action) should figure intuitively into the relevant mechanism will vary relative to explanatory perspective. The neurophysiologist's basis of parsimony will be different than that employed in everyday folk-psychological discourse. What reason have we to assume that Fischer and Ravizza's basis for individuation is the correct one?

The situation worsens if one pushes for a hyper-restricted notion of sameness of mechanism. On the hyper-restricted construal, the entire complex of proximal antecedent events and states function as the pertinent mechanism. If this were the relevant mechanism, an agent could not act from a reasons-responsive mechanism at a deterministic world.[49]

I agree that a *full defense* of our compatibilistic approach might well involve a "principled" account of mechanism individuation. Without such a defense, I fully concede that the overall theory, and its "defense," is *incomplete* (I prefer that word to "unconvincing"). But I also would suggest that it is unreasonable to expect that anyone could present a defense of a highly contentious thesis about free will, *all* of whose elements are decisively and uncontroversially defended (via appeal to "principles" rather than intuitions). I am not sure exactly how one could produce a purely "principled" account of mechanism individuation—an account that did not at some level appeal to intuitions. It is obvious that the notion of "mechanism leading to action" is quite vague in itself and open to various interpretations that depend on various "explanatory perspectives." And, in general, I think that interesting attempts at solving genuinely difficult philosophical questions will often be incomplete and dependent to some extent on intuitions, rather than general principles.

Surely it would be setting the bar too high to demand that any candidate for a solution to a philosophical puzzle must have all of its components defended in a fully general way, with no vagueness, no fuzzy edges, and no appeal to intuitions. I am afraid that this would limit the candidates rather drastically! On the other hand, it is quite fair and legitimate to point out that there is an important incompleteness in the theory of moral responsibility sketched by Ravizza and me, and to press the issue of whether the vagueness of the notion of "sameness of kind of mechanism" allows the proponent of the theory to allow his intuitions, rather than the theory, to do all (or most) of the work. That is, it is a perfectly reasonable worry that we simply apply the theory in such a way to get the results that match our intuitions, exploiting the vagueness of "sameness of kind of mechanism" to come down one way in this case, another way in that one, and so forth.[50] If this were so, then the theory really would not be illuminating and systematizing our intuitions—it would simply be a front for them.

This worry raises deep and difficult methodological and substantive questions. I can only gesture at a response, in the most preliminary of ways. First, the structure of our theory of moral responsibility—in which one holds fixed the actual-sequence mechanism—is similar to the structure of "reliabilist" theories of knowledge.[51] In these theories, ascertaining whether an individual has knowledge involves holding fixed the actual-sequence belief-producing mechanism and asking whether it is "reliable"—whether, for instance, it tracks truth (in Robert

Nozick's terms).[52] Indeed, since Nozick offers no general account of mechanism individuation (of belief-producing mechanisms), he is aware of a problem for his theory of knowledge which is parallel to the problem about mechanism individuation I described above.[53]

Just as Nozick is not convinced that he is guilty of putting the cart before the horse, as it were, I am not convinced that the vagueness of our notion of mechanism individuation renders our theory of moral responsibility otiose. Various philosophers have offered penetrating and challenging criticisms of reliabilist accounts of knowledge, which press concerns about mechanism individuation. I do not know whether these critiques are decisive; I certainly think that reliabilist approaches in epistemology are illuminating and worthy of serious consideration, even if one wants to reject them ultimately (because of the worries about mechanism individuation, or for other reasons). Further, I have not seen *any* argument that contends that our actual application of our theory of moral responsibility to cases is problematic in the ways in which reliabilism in epistemology is (allegedly) problematic.

Any theory which involves *generality* appears to have problems, at some level, of the sort we have been considering. Rule-consequentialism (of which rule-utilitarianism is an example) and Kantianism (in ethics) are salient examples (along with reliabilism in epistemology) of theories that are "generalizing" theories. Rule-consequentialism asks what the consequences of a general acceptance of a certain rule would be, where the rule specifies *kinds* of acts. Kantianism asks whether it would be (say, logically) consistent for all agents to act in certain ways—motivated by certain *kinds* of maxims or intentions. Typically (although perhaps not universally), reliabilists, rule-consequentialists, and Kantians do not offer reductive, general accounts of the individuation of the relevant "kinds." At some level they rely on intuitions; they implicitly adopt approaches to individuation that help the theory yield the "right" results. Surely, generalization approaches in ethics, as well as reliabilism in epistemology, are serious, illuminating approaches, which should be taken seriously, even if they are ultimately rejected. I would hope that the theory of moral responsibility in terms of guidance control, as sketched by Ravizza and me, could be similar to the other generalizing theories at least in the respect that it may be considered to be illuminating and worthy of serious consideration. I would hope that it could be seen to throw into relief a whole host of traditional issues, restructuring some of the traditional debates in a way that makes them more tractable, or, at a minimum, makes the precise points of disagreement more perspicuous.

Finally, I want to emphasize a feature of the methodology employed by Ravizza and me that helps to provide an answer to the worries pressed by Watson and McKenna (and others) about mechanism individuation. I am afraid that we did not highlight this sufficiently, and our defect in this regard has led to some unclarity about our goals. I hope to help to clarify our position here. In *Responsibility and Control*, we write:

> We aim to give what Robert Nozick has called "philosophical explanations," not to do "coercive philosophy." That is, we will be seeking to show that it is very plausible

and appealing to say that (for example) agents can be held morally responsible for their behavior, regardless of the truth (or falsity) of causal determinism. And we will be trying to show exactly *how* this sort of view can be developed and defended. But we do not suppose that we can give a knockdown argument for this conclusion (or the other major contentions of the book). Thus, when we contend that we have argued successfully for (say) the compatibility of causal determinism with moral responsibility, we are claiming that we have offered a strong plausibility argument for this conclusions, but not an argument that any rational agent is compelled to accept.[54]

We go on to point out that we are seeking to systematize our society's shared consensus about cases in which certain factors undermine moral responsibility—and to distinguish them from cases in which no such uncontroversial responsibility-undermining factors operate.[55]

So the overall dialectical structure of our argument can be limned as follows. We offer what we take to be strong plausibility arguments for the claims that moral responsibility does not require alternative possibilities, and that causal determinism in itself does not rule out moral responsibility.[56] We then offer a general theory of moral responsibility that shows how it is *possible* to defend, in detail, these views—in particular, that moral responsibility is compatible with causal determinism. This theory gains some credibility from its *systematic and unified* treatment of moral responsibility for actions, omissions, consequences, and even traits of character. Of course, our arguments for the overall approach are not *decisive*, and various elements remain to some degree or another vague and undeveloped. The vagueness in the notion of mechanism individuation allows us to apply the account of guidance control in such a way as to match our considered judgments about the cases. In a sense, we here allow our intuitions to guide us in that they point to the way of individuating mechanisms, if our theory is to "work." This is part of the project of showing in some detail how it is *possible* to defend a kind of compatibilism about causal determinism and moral responsibility, and, as far as I can see, it does not imply any sort of problematic inconsistency or circularity.

Of course, it follows that we cannot convince a committed incompatibilist of the truth of compatibilism (by invoking the theory, as developed thus far). But this is no big surprise. We never supposed that we could *prove* compatibilism—we did not set out to do coercive philosophy. It is a big enough job, I think, to show exactly why it would be desirable if compatibilism turned out to be true, why compatibilism (about causal determinism and moral responsibility) does not involve obviously unacceptable commitments (in contrast, perhaps at least, to compatibilism about causal determinism and freedom to do otherwise), and how—in some detail—one might present a systematic compatibilist theory.

Watson's Challenge and the Different Modalities

Gary Watson has posed a particularly pointed challenge—one that goes to the very heart of our theory of moral responsibility:

> It is also somewhat curious that Fischer and Ravizza feel the need to make this modal claim [the claim that, when an agent is morally responsible, the mechanism on

which he acts has the general capacity to respond to the actual reasons]. The objection regarding fairness seems to arise from intuitions supporting a principle of alternative possibilities (holding people responsible is unfair unless they could have done otherwise). Fischer and Ravizza reject this principle because of so-called Frankfurt cases, in which some fail-safe device stands by to ensure that an individual behaves in a certain way. For example, suppose that if Goldie were to change her mind at the last moment about voting for the Green candidate, the fail-safe device would ensure that she punched the "Nader" tab anyway. So, there is no possibility that she would not punch that tab. Fischer and Ravizza reasonably conclude that this modal fact does not entail that her actual voting behavior is not reasons-responsive. This leads them to reject the idea that to be responsible, the agent must have alternatives to what she does. In Frankfurt cases, Fischer and Ravizza like to say, the agents could not have responded differently in the face of contrary incentives, but the actually operative mechanisms could have. . . .

What is curious, then, is that Fischer and Ravizza seem to feel the need to employ a notion of alternative possibilities at the level of mechanisms. They seem to be conceding that there is a sense in which the fairness of holding someone responsible depends upon the capacity of the mechanism in question to respond otherwise, a capacity that must be compatible with causal determinism, on their view. But it is hard to see how this move can answer the concern about fairness, unless we can translate talk about the capacities of mechanisms into talk about what persons can do. And if we can do that, we should endorse a compatibilistic version of the principle of alternative possibilities rather than rejecting the relevance of alternative possibilities altogether.[57]

This is a probing and difficult challenge. In seeking to respond, I begin by noting an analogy between the active power, freedom, and certain passive powers, such as (say) solubility in water. As I have pointed out in previous work, Frankfurt-type examples are just one kind of example of "Schizophrenic Situations." Objects in Schizophrenic Situations can exhibit either active or passive powers—these situations contain a kind of "swerve" in metaphysical space. One can construct the analogues of Frankfurt-type cases for passive powers.[58]

Consider, for example, Alvin Goldman's example of a grain of salt, which is an ordinary piece of salt, with an ordinary structure (in virtue of which it is soluble in water); what is unusual is that there is a magician associated with this grain of salt, and if the grain of salt were about to be placed in water, the magician would wave his magic wand and cause the salt to have an impermeable coating. So the salt actually displays a structure in virtue of which it is plausibly thought to be soluble in water; but it is not the case that it would dissolve, were it placed in water. Given the presence of the magician, and the fact (let us suppose that it is a fact) that the magician cannot be distracted or otherwise deterred, this particular grain of salt cannot dissolve in water. And yet it seems to be water-soluble. It is water-soluble in virtue of actually displaying a certain sort of structure—a structure that underwrites a general capacity.

An approach to analyzing the water solubility of such a grain of salt would be to hold fixed the actual structure of the grain of salt (i.e., the structure *sans* special impermeable coating), and to ask what would happen if the salt is put into contact with water (given that the magician does not intervene). This is an actual-sequence approach to analyzing the passive power, solubility, which is parallel to the analysis of the active power, guidance control. In both cases the general capacity which is actually displayed or exhibited is held fixed under counterfactual circumstances (in which other factors are allowed to vary). I suppose one could object that this is an untenable or analytically unstable analysis of water solubility. One could say that the grain of salt is not really soluble in water, since it cannot dissolve in water: it would not dissolve if it were placed in water. Why focus on the general capacity of salt with the actually displayed structure, if *this* grain would not display that structure if it were placed in water? And if we choose to say that this grain of salt is indeed water-soluble in virtue of actually displaying a certain structure (and thus general capacity), why not define a notion of "possibility" relative to which this grain of salt *can* dissolve in water?

I do not know how to *argue* for the contention that a grain of salt that actually has the normal chemical structure of salt is water-soluble, even if it has a weird magician of the sort described above associated with it. I do think that anything actually having the normal chemical structure of salt is soluble in water. I do not think that there is anything analytically unstable about defining water solubility in terms of this actually displayed structure (and general capacity), while noting that the particular grain of salt cannot dissolve in water. I suppose that one might define a notion of possibility that abstracts away from "obstacles" or conditions that would prevent the manifestation of a certain dispositional property, and then employ this notion of possibility to say that, yes, Goldman's grain of salt can indeed dissolve in water. Whereas I do not see exactly what is gained by this move, it is certainly available.

I have invoked the analogy between active and passive powers to suggest that at a certain level of analysis there is nothing problematic or unstable about fixing on the general capacity that is actually exhibited, while noting that the object in question lacks a certain sort of power to do (or be) otherwise. This sort of analysis is, I believe, natural and plausible for passive powers, and I would suggest that it is similarly attractive for active powers (such as freedom or guidance control).

But Watson's challenge pertains more specifically to "fairness." How is it fair to hold an agent morally responsible for acting on a general capacity that is indeed sensitive to the particular reasons that actually obtain, even where the agent cannot respond to that reason? I do not know how fully to address this worry, but I would at least sketch the following idea.

Clearly, an individual can act in a way that is not a manifestation of a particular trait of character or general capacity. A courageous person may act in a cowardly manner in a particular situation. In this situation, the cowardly act does not exhibit or display the trait of courage. Whereas the person may be commendable for his courage, we hold him responsible, in the context in which he acts in a cowardly manner, precisely for his cowardly behavior. Similarly, an agent may not act in such a way as to manifest the general capacity for moderate reasons-responsiveness—he may act from a compulsion or because of direct stimulation of the brain, and so forth. But when an agent does manifest this sort of capacity, he *links* or *connects* himself with this capacity in a distinctive way. In forging this link or connection, the agent is, as it were, inviting (or, in effect, allowing) others to treat him *as acting from this sort of mechanism*. In reacting to the agent's behavior (and thus holding him responsible), we are thus justified in replying to the agent qua agent-acting-from-the-actual-sequence-mechanism. Thus, considerations of fairness *shift* from the agent to agent qua practical-reasoner-of-a-certain-sort. If we are considering the agent-as-acting-from-a-certain-general-capacity, we want to know whether the general capacity that is actually displayed can respond to the actual incentives. (Similarly, when we are considering a piece of salt qua piece-of-salt-with-the-actually-displayed-structure [and thus general capacity], we want to know whether a piece of salt with *that* structure and capacity would indeed dissolve in water.)

On my approach to moral responsibility, I focus on the general capacity for reasons-responsiveness actually displayed by the agent. I contend that an agent can exhibit a suitable sort of reasons-responsiveness (and guidance control) even if the agent could not have done otherwise (and thus does not possess regulative control). But once one makes the move to actually displayed general capacities, why not *also* define a notion of possibility relative to which the agent *can* do otherwise? So we could say that the agent qua practical-reasoner-of-a-certain-sort could have done otherwise, even in a Frankfurt-type case, just as the piece of salt-*sans*-intervention-by-the-magician could have dissolved in water in the Goldman-type case.

As I pointed out above, I do not see that anything is gained in terms of analytical penetration by making this sort of move. But I do not have any strong objection to pointing out that the agent qua practical-reasoner-of-a-certain-sort (i.e., qua acting-on-the-actual-sequence-mechanism) can do otherwise in the Frankfurt-type case. What *would* be objectionable would be to conclude from this that the agent can, in the ordinary sense of "can in the particular circumstances," do otherwise (in the Frankfurt-type case).

There is nothing problematic, as far as I can see, in fixing on the actually displayed general capacity (and its modal characteristics) in the context of causal determinism. That is, there is nothing problematic, in my view, in contending that the relevant agent acts freely (exhibits guidance control) in such a context. In contrast, if one says that the agent could have done otherwise (possessed regulative control), then one must say that the agent could have either so acted that the past would have been different from what it actually was, or the laws would have been different from what they actually are. So there is the following important asymmetry between imputing regulative and guidance control in a causally deterministic context: attributing regulative control requires an answer to the powerful skeptical arguments flowing from the fixity of the past and natural laws, whereas attributing guidance control does *not*.

My theory of moral responsibility has a specific modal structure. I have called it an "actual-sequence" theory of moral responsibility. This means that I do not require that agents have genuine access to alternative possibilities—they need not have regulative control. On the other hand, I *do* require that morally responsible agents act from actual-sequence mechanisms that are *moderately reasons-responsive*—that is, from actual-sequence mechanisms that have certain *modal* or *dispositional* characteristics.[59] Note that this puts my approach—semicompatibilism—in the midpoint of a certain spectrum. On the one hand, the libertarian argues that moral responsibility requires regulative control—I deny this. On the other end of the spectrum, R. Jay Wallace argues that moral responsibility does not require such control, but simply requires the possession of the general capacity for reasons-sensitivity, not necessarily the actual display of this capacity. My view is in the middle: I argue that moral responsibility requires not just the possession of a certain general capacity for reasons-sensitivity, but the actual display of such a capacity: moral responsibility requires action from a mechanism that is (in addition to being the agent's own) moderately reasons-responsive.

Concluding Remarks

I (together with my coauthor, Mark Ravizza) have sought at least to provide the skeletal structure of an overall approach to moral responsibility. This approach is distinctive in that it is an actual-sequence approach; that is, we do not require the sort of control that involves genuine access to alternative possibilities at *any* point: in forming character, performing actions or omitting to act, and bringing about consequences. In developing this overall theory, we fix exclusively on features of the actual pathways to the behavior (or character traits), albeit (sometimes) modal or dispositional features of these pathways. It is an actual-sequence approach in that we do not require alternative possibilities. It may or may not be the case that the future is a garden of forking paths (depending in part on whether or not causal determinism obtains), but this does not matter for moral responsibility.

The approach is a cohesive package, consisting of various separable parts. The parts themselves contain parts (in some instances). We have offered arguments for some of the parts, but have not been able to offer explicit arguments for all components (or their elements). A basic motivating engine of semicompatibilism is that moral responsibility, and even personhood (robustly construed), should not depend on whether the formulas that physicists develop (to describe the world) are univeral generalizations or merely almost-universal generalizations. The fundamental differences between persons and nonpersons, and morally responsible agents and those individuals who are not morally responsible, should not hinge on arcane deliverances of theoretical physicists—we should not have to stop treating other human beings as deeply different from other animals (and computers) if a consortium of scientists discovers the truth of causal determinism.

Against the background of this motivation, we argue that moral responsibility (and personhood) does not require regulative control. Thus, some of the most disturbing arguments for the incompatibility of causal determinism and moral responsibility are rendered irrelevant. We go on to consider *other* arguments for this sort of incompatibilism, and find none of them compelling (or even strong). Given this dialectical niche, we present an overall, systematic compatibilist account of moral responsibility. On this approach, the freedom-relevant condition necessary and sufficient for moral responsibility is guidance control, and the conditions for responsibility for actions, omissions, consequences, and even traits of character are *tied together* in a unified way.

The account of guidance control assumes a certain intuitive way of individuat-ing the kinds of mechanisms that issue in behavior; we concede that we can offer no entirely "principled" way of individuating mechanisms. In my view, this shows that the overall approach is incomplete, but not fatally flawed. The specific ac-count of guidance control we offer shows how it is possible to develop a compati-bilist account of moral responsibility, but it clearly (in itself) does not *justify* or *establish* compatibilism.

Here I have tried to address some of the most penetrating and illuminating crit-icisms of the overall approach. In doing so, I have sought to clarify the theory. This clarification has in some instances revealed the goals of the theory to be dif-ferent from, and perhaps less lofty than, those attributed to it by its critics. For ex-ample, Ravizza and I seek to give an account of moral responsibility, but not (yet) a full account (say) of praiseworthiness and blameworthiness. Also, we do not aim to *prove* or *establish* compatibilism, but to motivate it and to show how it can be developed in a coherent, attractive way. Of course, if one's aims are sufficiently modest, this renders the views immune to critical assault—but one purchases this immunity at the cost of not saying anything of interest. I hope that we have found the right mix of humility and daring.

NOTES

1. John Martin Fischer and Mark Ravizza, "Responsibility and History," in *Midwest Studies in Philosophy 19: Philosophical Naturalism*, ed. Peter French, Theodore E. Uehling, Jr. and Howard K. Wettstein (Notre Dame, Ind. University of Notre Dame Press, 1994), pp. 430–51, and *Responsibility and Control: A Theory of Moral Responsibility* (Cambridge: Cam-bridge University Press, 1998), especially pp. 207–39.

2. Fischer and Ravizza, *Responsibility and Control.*

3. My coauthor and I develop the account of taking responsibility at greater length in Fischer and Ravizza, *Responsibility and Control*, pp. 207–39.

4. John Martin Fischer, *The Metaphysics of Free Will: An Essay on Control* (Oxford: Blackwell, 1994).

5. See, for example, Eleonore Stump, "Control and Causal Determinism," in *Contours of Agency: Essays on Themes from Harry Frankfurt*, ed. Sarah Buss and Lee Overton (Cam-bridge: MIT Press, 2002), pp. 33–60.

6. In "Control and Causal Determinism," Stump also develops a critique of the criti-cism of the direct argument for incompatibilism offered by Ravizza and me. The direct ar-gument purports to show that causal determinism rules out moral responsibility, quite apart from considerations pertaining to alternative possibilities. It employs a modal principle that alleges that nonresponsibility can be transferred in a characteristic way. Ravizza and I criti-cize this argument in *Responsibility and Control*, pp. 151–69. Stump's criticisms are on pages 38–46; she offers related criticisms in "The Direct Argument for Incompatibilism," *Philoso-phy and Phenomenological Research* 61 (2000): 459–66. Stump's paper is a contribution to a book symposium on *Responsibility and Control*. Ravizza and I reply to Stump in John Martin Fischer and Mark Ravizza, "Reply to Critics," *Philosophy and Phenomenological Research* 61 (2000): 477–80. See also chapter 8 in this volume.

7. Stump, "Control and Causal Determinism," p. 38.

8. Ibid., p. 36; the quotation from Churchland is from Patricia Churchland, "Episte-mology in the Age of Neuroscience," *Journal of Philosophy* 84 (1987): 548–49.

9. Stump, "Control and Causal Determinism," pp. 36, 38; the quotation is from Richard Rorty, "Untruth and Consequences," *New Republic* (July 31, 1995), p. 36.

10. See, for example, Daniel Dennett, "Intentional Systems," *Journal of Philosophy* 68 (1971): 87–106; and "Mechanism and Responsibility," in *Essays on Freedom of Action,* ed. T. Honderich (London: Routledge and Kegan Paul, 1973), pp. 159–84. See also Daniel Dennett, *Elbow Room: The Varieties of Free Will Worth Wanting* (Cambridge: MIT Press, 1984), and *Freedom Evolves* (New York: Viking, 2003).

11. For a similar conclusion, put in a considerably more genteel fashion, see Harry Frankfurt, "Reply to Eleonore Stump," in *Contours of Agency: Essays on Themes from Harry Frankfurt,* ed. Sarah Buss and Lee Overton (Cambridge: MIT Press, 2002), pp. 61–63.

12. Stump, "Control and Causal Determinism," pp. 47–48.

13. Stump, "Control and Causal Determinism," pp. 49–50. She goes on to consider even more complex cases, but I think the reply I shall give in the text applies to all of her cases.

14. The example comes from Fischer and Ravizza, *Responsibility and Control,* p. 231.

15. Stump, "Control and Causal Determinism," pp. 50–51.

16. Frankfurt, "Reply to Eleonore Stump," p. 61.

17. Stump, "Control and Causal Determinism," p. 48.

18. Ibid.

19. Fischer and Ravizza, *Responsibility and Control,* pp. 231–32.

20. Fischer and Ravizza, *Responsibility and Control,* p. 48.

21. Derk Pereboom, *Living without Free Will* (Cambridge: Cambridge University Press, 2001), pp. 110–26.

22. Ibid., pp. 112–13.

23. Ibid., pp. 113–14.

24. Ibid., p. 114.

25. Ibid., p. 115.

26. Pereboom discusses this point in the context of a discussion of whether the added dimension of mechanism-ownership can help the Fischer-Ravizza account handle the cases presented above in the text: Pereboom, *Living without Free Will,* pp. 120–23.

27. For a discussion, see Fischer and Ravizza, *Responsibility and Control,* pp. 62–91.

28. In *Metaphysics of Free Will,* I made a similar point in regard to God's "providential activity": "Even if God causes human action via a process analogous to causal determination, simply *qua* causal determination (and not *special* causation), then arguably the process can be [suitably reasons-responsive, and the agent morally responsible]" (p. 181).

29. Fischer and Ravizza, *Responsibility and Control,* pp. 5–8.

30. The notion of "taking responsibility," a key ingredient of moral responsibility, may (quite understandably) get a "bum rap" from what I might call the "politician's use" of the phrase, "I take responsibility for . . ." Politicians seem to use this phrase precisely as a way of *escaping* accountability or blameworthiness. It is really quite galling. To illustrate the point, consider this amusing story I recently heard told by a comedian (although one can all too easily imagine its being entirely true). A conversation between Jesse Jackson and Bill Clinton takes place after the revelation of Jesse Jackson's marital infidelity. Bill Clinton says, "Jesse, remember what you told me after the public revelation of my infidelity in the Monica Lewinsky fiasco. Recall that you told me that the best way to avoid blame is to take responsibility!"

As Ravizza and I were at pains to emphasize in Fischer and Ravizza, *Responsibility and Control,* taking responsibility (on our view) is not merely a matter of mouthing certain words; it is a matter of genuinely having the attitudes in question. One cannot easily avoid blameworthiness by failing to take responsibility. Thus moral responsibility is the gateway to blameworthiness, not a back-door escape.

31. Sam Black and Jon Tweedale, "Responsibility and Alternative Possibilities: The Use and Abuse of Examples," *Journal of Ethics* 6 (2002): 292–306.

32. Ibid., p. 294.

33. Ibid. It is not clear why exactly "shame" would be appropriate, although perhaps the authors are thinking of a shame that does not involve moral responsibility.

34. Ibid.

35. Ibid., pp. 294–95.

36. Ibid., p. 295.

37. Fischer, *Metaphysics of Free Will*; Fischer and Ravizza, "Responsibility and History," and *Responsibility and Control*, pp. 170–206.

38. For probing discussions of this set of issues, see Gary Watson, "Some Worries about Semi-Compatibilism: Remarks on John Fischer's *The Metaphysics of Free Will*," *Journal of Social Philosophy* 29 (1998): 153–43, and "Reasons and Responsibility," *Ethics* 111 (2001): 383–86; and David Zimmerman, "Reasons-Responsiveness and Ownership-of-Agency: Fischer and Ravizza's Historicist Theory of Responsibility," *Journal of Ethics* 6 (2002): 199–234, and "That Was Then This Is Now: Personal History vs. Psychological Structure in Compatibilist Theories of Autonomous Agency," *Nous* (forthcoming).

39. This sort of hierarchical account was suggested (in contemporary philosophy) by Harry Frankfurt in "Freedom of the Will and the Concept of a Person," *Journal of Philosophy* 68 (1971): 5–20; it has subsequently been developed in additional essays by Frankfurt, and discussed widely.

40. David Zimmerman suggests that in order to have a plausible, deeply historicist approach to moral responsibility one must address a certain fundamental question: "How do some children manage to develop the capacity to *make up their own minds* about what values to embrace, by virtue of having gone through a process in which they play an increasingly active role in *making their own minds*, a process which begins with their virtually *having no minds at all?*" (Zimmerman, "Reasons-Responsiveness," p. 233) Addressing this question would be perhaps crucial as part of an overall theory that encompassed both moral responsibility and also an account of the conditions of blameworthiness and praiseworthiness; but our goal in presenting the account of moral responsibility was not so lofty. In order to provide a complete theory that includes a specification of the conditions of blameworthiness, praiseworthiness, indignation, resentment, and so forth, one would need to have an account of autonomous value and preference formation; but we did not set out to give such an account. An account of the kind of control required for moral responsibility need not address the very fundamental, and dauntingly difficult, question of the difference between (say) indoctrination and education, or, at the very basic level, autonomous value formation. Whew!

41. In recent work, Harry Frankfurt has given a particularly perspicuous and nuanced account of love: Harry Frankfurt, *Necessity, Volition, and Love* (Cambridge: Cambridge University Press, 1999).

42. This thought experiment comes from Mark Bernstein, "Love, Particularity, and Selfhood," *Southern Journal of Philosophy* 23 (1985): pp. 287–93. It is discussed in Fischer and Ravizza, *Responsibility and Control*, pp. 192–94. Originally, the suggestion that love is historical was made by Robert Nozick in *Anarchy, State, and Utopia* (New York: Basic Books, 1974), pp. 67–68.

43. Zimmerman, "Reasons-Responsiveness," pp. 231–32.

44. There is a helpful and penetrating alternative account of love's particularity in Robert Adams, *Finite and Infinite Goods* (Oxford: Oxford University Press, 1999), pp. 131–76. If I may explicate Adams's view in an oversimple way, I believe that Adams holds that one loves another particular individual by first loving certain tropes—certain property

instances (her courage, her sensitivity, and so forth). Loving the tropes is prior, and one constructs love of general properties from love of the tropes. In this way love is particular.

45. For the latter notions, see Fischer and Ravizza, *Responsibility and Control*, pp. 62–91.

46. For particularly forceful and penetrating discussions, see Michael McKenna, "Review of John Martin Fischer and Mark Ravizza: *Responsibility and Control: A Theory of Moral Responsibility*," *Journal of Philosophy* 98 (2001): 93–100; and Gary Watson, "Reasons and Responsibility: Review Essay on John Martin Fischer and Mark Ravizza, *Responsibility and Control: A Theory of Moral Responsibility*," *Ethics* 111 (2001): 374–94.

47. Fischer and Ravizza, *Responsibility and Control*, p. 40.

48. McKenna, "Review," p. 100

49. Ibid., p. 97.

50. For interesting and subtle cases that press essentially this concern, see Watson, "Reasons and Responsibility: Review Essay," pp. 379–83.

51. I discuss certain aspects of this isomorphism in *Metaphysics of Free Will*.

52. Robert Nozick develops this sort of theory of knowledge, and points out the structural isomorphism with a theory of "tracking bestness" (which is not exactly an account of moral responsibility), in Robert Nozick, *Philosophical Explanations* (Cambridge: Harvard University Press, 1981), pp. 167–362.

53. Nozick, *Philosophical Explanations*, pp. 179–85.

54. Fischer and Ravizza, *Responsibility and Control*, p. 11.

55. Ibid., pp. 34ff.

56. These arguments are offered in our work as a whole, including Fischer, *Metaphysics of Free Will*, and Fischer and Ravizza, *Responsibility and Control*.

57. Watson, "Reasons and Responsibility: Review Essay," p. 382.

58. I discuss Schizophrenic Situations, and the associated swerve in metaphysical (or logical) space, in *Metaphysics of Free Will*, pp. 154–58. Alvin Goldman presented his piece of salt example in Alvin Goldman, *A Theory of Human Action* (Englewood Cliffs, N.J.: Prentice-Hall, 1970), pp. 199–200. See also chapter 2 in this volume.

59. So what happens in other possible worlds is not irrelevant to one's moral responsibility on my view; rather, what happens in other possible worlds is relevant not in virtue of pointing to regulative control, but only in virtue of specifying the modal characteristics of the actual-sequence mechanisms that potentially count as part of the agent's guidance control.

INDEX